Information Systems

A Manager's Guide to Harnessing Technology

Version 7.0.5

John Gallaugher

Adapted by Erica Wagner

Information Systems: A Manager's Guide to Harnessing Technology
Version 7.0.5

John Gallaugher

Adapted by Erica Wagner

This version of *Information Systems: A Manager's Guide to Harnessing Technology* includes customizations by Erica Wagner. It was created on January 08, 2020.

Edits to the original are shown with this marker.

Additions to the original are shown with this marker.

Published by:

FlatWorld
175 Portland Street
Boston, MA 02114

Gen: 202001082207

Brief Contents

Contents

CHAPTER 1

Setting the Stage: Technology and the Modern Enterprise

1.1 Radically Changing Business Landscapes

Learning Objective

1. Appreciate how, in recent years, technology has helped bring about radical changes across industries and throughout societies.

This book is written for a world that has changed radically in the most recent years of your lifetime. Consider just a few examples: Uber, the world's largest "taxi service," owns no vehicles for hire. Airbnb, the world's largest accommodations provider, doesn't own a single hotel or rental property. Facebook, the world's most visited media destination, creates no content. And the world's most valuable retailer, China's Alibaba, owns no product inventory of its own.[1] Change is clearly afoot, and it's wearing silicon sneakers, carrying a smartphone, and is being blown forward by cloud-fueled, AI-smart hurricane tailwinds.

Here are some more examples: At the start of the prior decade, Google barely existed and well-known strategists dismissed Internet advertising models.[2] By decade's end, Google brought in more advertising revenue than any firm, online or off, and had risen to become the most profitable media company on the planet. Today, billions in advertising dollars flee old media and are pouring into digital efforts, and this shift is reshaping industries and redefining skills needed to reach today's consumers. The firm's ambitions have grown so large that Google has rechristened itself Alphabet (http://abc.xyz), a holding company with divisions focused on markets as diverse as driverless cars and life extension.

At roughly the same time Google was being hatched, Apple was widely considered a tech industry has-been, but within ten years and powered by a succession of handheld consumer electronics hits (iPod, iPhone, iPad), Apple had grown to be the most valuable firm in the United States. The firm has since posted several of the most profitable quarters of any firm in any industry, ever.[3] If app sales through iTunes, alone, were considered a separate business, they would constitute a firm larger than *more than half* of the companies ranked in the Fortune 500.[4]

The smartphone and app store are the modern accelerant of business growth. It took telephones seventy-five years to get to 50 million users, but it took Angry Birds just thirty-five days to do the same. WhatsApp gained 700 million adherents in its six years of existence, a figure Christianity took nineteen centuries to achieve.[5]

Social media barely warranted a mention a decade ago. Today, Facebook's user base is larger than any nation in the world. Mobile is its lynchpin. Facebook made no money on mobile when it first sold stock to the public, but today Mobile represents over 90 percent of Facebook's revenue.[6] Firms are harnessing social media for new product ideas, for millions in sales, and to vet and build trust. But with promise comes peril. When mobile phones are cameras just a short hop from YouTube, Facebook, Instagram, and Twitter, every ethical lapse can be captured, every customer service flaw graffiti-tagged on the permanent record that is the Internet. The service and ethics bar for today's manager has never been higher. Social media has also emerged as a catalyst for global change, with Facebook and Twitter playing key organizing roles in uprisings worldwide. While a status update alone won't depose a dictator or expunge racism, technology can capture injustice, broadcast it to the world, disseminate ideas, and rally the far-reaching. Yet technology itself has no morality. We've seen leading social media firms struggle as their platforms are used to spread hate, pornography, and fake news in ways that enrich organized crime and enable the influence of hostile foreign governments.

Moore's Law and other factors that make technology faster and cheaper have thrust computing and telecommunications into the hands of billions in ways that are both empowering the poor and poisoning the planet.

IPO

Initial public stock offering, the first time a firm makes shares available via a public stock exchange, also known as "going public."

China started the century as a nation largely unplugged and offline. But today, China has more Internet users than any other country, and China has emerged as a clear leader in smartphone payments. As of this writing, four of the ten most downloaded apps were Chinese.[7] In the first ten months of 2017, Chinese consumers spent $12.8 trillion through mobile payments (that's trillion with a "t") vs. an only $50 billion full-year total in the US.[8] China has spectacularly launched several publicly traded Internet firms that now have market caps and profits to match their US rivals, including Baidu, Tencent, and Alibaba—the largest **IPO** of all time.[9]

13 of the Smartest Artificial Intelligence Companies According to MIT

Video listing some of the global leaders in AI, and the projects they are working on. Note the diversity of industry, as well as where these firms are located. For another take on AI, see the video in the Exercises section, and prepare for additional learning in the chapter The Data Asset and Competitive Advantage: Databases, Analytics, AI, and Machine Learning.

View the video online at: http://www.youtube.com/embed/I4qM33A2OH8?rel=0

The world's second most populous nation, India, has ridden technology to become a global IT powerhouse. In two decades, India's tech sector has grown from almost nothing to a $120 billion industry, expanding even during the recent global recession.[10] Technology has enabled the once almost exclusively agrarian nation to become a go-to destination for R&D and engineering across sectors as far-flung as aircraft engine design, medical devices, telecom equipment, and microprocessors.[11] India's TCS (Tata Consulting Services) is the world's number two technology solutions firm, second in size only to IBM.[12] India has half a billion mobile Internet users.[13] And India's consumer e-commerce sector is growing so quickly that Walmart recently won a high-stakes bidding war against Amazon, paying $16 billion for a 77 percent stake in India's FlipKart, a leader in S. Asian online shopping and payments.[14]

Think the United States holds the top ranking in Internet access speeds? Not so much. The United States didn't even make the top 25 nations in mobile download performance (but Bulgaria, Malta, Lithuania, and Macedonia are among the countries that did). The US did better in fixed broadband (landline connections like cable), but the nations ahead of the US included Hungary and Romania.[15]

Today, smartphones are used by 2 billion people worldwide. By the end of this decade that number will be 4 billion, with 80 percent of adults being smartphone equipped. The most popular brand in India, Micromax, sells entry-level smartphones priced below $40.[16]

Even in the far reaches of nations in sub-Saharan Africa, fast/cheap tech is becoming an economic lubricant. Seventy percent of the region's population lives within range of mobile phone coverage, a percentage of the population greater than those who have access to reliable and safe water or electricity. Forty percent of sub-Saharan Africans already have mobile phones.[17] Tech giants including Google, IBM, and Microsoft now run R&D centers and significant operations in several African nations, tapping into world-class tech talent that's finally gaining infrastructure for growth.[18] Many nations in sub-Saharan Africa now rank among the world's fastest-growing economies.[19] And entrepreneurs with local expertise are increasingly serving local needs and building impactful businesses. Ghanaian firm Esoko leverages mobile phones to empower the agrarian poor with farming info and commodity pricing, raising incomes and lowering the chance of exploitation by unscrupulous middlemen. The firm Sproxil uses text message verification to save lives by fighting drug counterfeiting in developing nations around the world. Kenya's M-PESA and Somaliland's Zaad use text messages to replace cash, bringing the safety and speed of electronic payment and funds transfer to the unbanked and leveraging mobile money at rates that far outstrip any nation in the West.[20] Adoption rates are astonishing: 84 percent of adults in Tanzania use mobile phones for money transactions.[21] Mobile money can cut corruption, too, an effort with broad implications as this tech spreads worldwide. When Afghan police officers adopted M-PESA and began receiving pay using mobile money, many reportedly thought they had received a big raise because the officers handing out their pay were no longer able to cheat workers by skimming cash for themselves.[22]

FIGURE 1.1
Many nations in sub-Saharan Africa are seeing significant tech-fueled growth. Throughout the continent, technologies substitute for cash, deliver insights to farmers, and help uncover counterfeit pharmaceuticals. This plant in Accra, owned by Ghanaian firm Rlg, is the first sub-Saharan PC, tablet, and cell phone assembly facility.

Source: Photograph taken by Prof. John Gallaugher with permission of the Rlg plant.

Internet of Things

A vision where low-cost sensors, processors, and communication are embedded into a wide array of products and our environment, allowing a vast network to collect data, analyze input, and automatically coordinate collective action.

Fast/cheap computing is also helping create the multibillion dollar **Internet of Things** (IoT), putting smarts in all sorts of products: lamps, watches, thermostats, and door locks. Disney has embedded smarts in a wristband it uses to replace ticketing at Disney World. GE thinks sensors and computing will save the planet trillions of dollars through a hyper-efficient, data-driven, collectively orchestrated set of devices,[23] and has embedded smarts in everything from home air conditioners to high-end aircraft parts.[24] Think the smartphone market is big? There are already more so-called Internet of Things (IoT)–connected devices than the entire world population of humans, and that number is only growing.[25]

Cheap processors and software smarts are also powering the drone revolution with far-reaching impact. Today's farmers use drones to regularly survey crops at closer distances and with greater regularity than satellite or plane flight could ever match. A combination of conventional and infrared imagery can show irrigation variation, crop success, plant damage, fungal and insect infestations, and offer other insights to improve crop yields, stave off crises, improve farmer profits, and cut consumer costs. Today's agricultural drones can be purchased for less than $1,000, as compared with agricultural plane flights that cost more than $1,000 an hour.[26] And while Amazon and rivals race to replace UPS with drone-to-doorstep delivery, Silicon Valley's Zipline is leading the charge for the humanitarian community, delivering medical supplies and blood to remote regions of the world (rural Rwanda is up first), offering lifesaving packages at pizza-delivery speed.[27]

Drones Deliver Medical Supplies in Rwanda

Tech for good: The startup Zipline is one of many organizations working to leverage cheap, accurate drones to quickly and cost-effectively deliver medical supplies to remote, underserved communities.

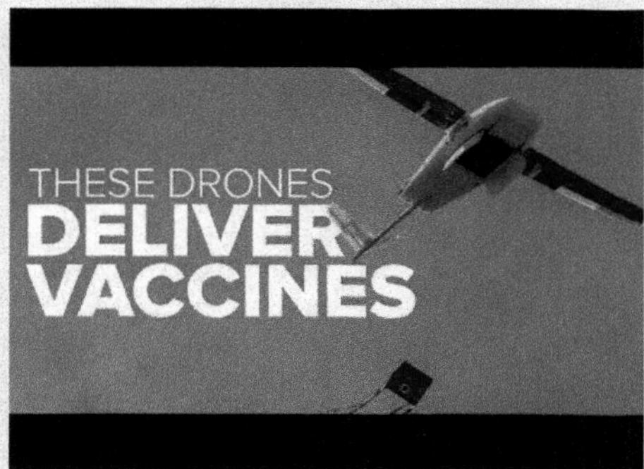

View the video online at: http://www.youtube.com/embed/nnKnMgWy_tM?rel=0

The way we conceive of software and the software industry is also changing radically. Apple, Facebook, Google, IBM, Netflix, and Oracle are among the firms that collectively pay thousands of programmers to write code that is then given away for free. Today, open source software powers most of the websites that you visit. And the rise of open source has rewritten the revenue models for the computing industry and lowered computing costs for startups to blue chips worldwide.

Cloud computing and software as a service are turning sophisticated, high-powered computing into a utility available to even the smallest businesses and nonprofits. Amazon Web Services, by far the world's biggest provider of cloud computing services, has been adding about as much server capacity each day as its entire e-commerce parent required ten years earlier.[28]

Three-dimensional printers, which allow designs for fabrication to be shared as easily as an e-mail, are poised to reshape manufacturing and transportation. Crafts marketplace Etsy is full of artist-created and custom-printed products, from jewelry to cookie cutters,[29] and this technology has also been used to print tools on-demand for the international space station.[30]

FIGURE 1.2
An astronaut shows a tool produced on-demand using a 3D printer on the International Space Station.

Source: NASA

Many organizations today collect and seek insights from massive datasets, which are often referred to as "Big Data." Data analytics, business intelligence, and so-called machine-learning are driving discovery and innovation, redefining modern marketing, and creating a shifting knife-edge of privacy concerns that can shred corporate reputations if mishandled.

And the pervasiveness of computing has created a set of security and espionage threats unimaginable to the prior generation.

As recent years have shown, tech creates both treasure and tumult. While tech creates new Giants, also know that half of the Fortune 500 companies on the list in 2000 have fallen off since then as a result of mergers, acquisitions, and bankruptcies.[31] These disruptions aren't going away and will almost certainly accelerate, impacting organizations, careers, and job functions throughout your lifetime. It's time to place tech at the center of the managerial playbook.

Key Takeaways

- In the previous decade, tech firms have created profound shifts in the way firms advertise and individuals and organizations communicate.
- New technologies have fueled globalization, redefined our concepts of software and computing, crushed costs, fueled data-driven decision-making, and raised privacy and security concerns.

Questions and Exercises

1. Search online and compare profits from Google, Apple, and other leading tech firms with those of major media firms and other nontech industry leaders. How have profits at firms such as Google and Apple changed over the past few years? What do you think is behind such trends? How do these compare with changes in the nontech firms that you chose?
2. How do recent changes in computing impact consumers? Are these changes good or bad? Explain. How do they impact businesses?

3. Serial entrepreneur and venture capitalist Marc Andreessen has written that "software is eating the world," suggesting that software and computing are transforming entire industries and creating disruptive new upstarts. Come to class with examples of firms and industries that have been completely transformed through the use of software.
4. Venture capitalist Ben Evans, who works with Andreessen, has said "mobile is eating the world." Give examples of how mobile has built billion dollar industries that wouldn't exist without handheld computing power. How should today's managers be thinking about mobile as an opportunity and threat?
5. How is social media impacting firms, individuals, and society?
6. What kinds of skills do today's managers need that weren't required a decade ago?
7. Investigate the role of technology in emerging markets. Come to class with examples to share on how technology is helping fuel economic growth and provide economic opportunity and public good to consumers outside of North America, Europe, and Asia's wealthier nations.
8. Work with your instructor to identify and implement ways in which your class can leverage social media. For example, you might create a Facebook group where you can share ideas with your classmates, join Twitter and create a hashtag for your class, leverage Google Hangouts, create a course wiki, or start a Slack channel. (See [Content Removed: #fwk-38086-ch06] for more on these and other services.)
9. Watch the video below, produced by the World Economic Forum. Is Artificial Intelligence (AI) really intelligence? What makes AI "smarter"? Which nations lead in AI and why? What advantages does each have? What sort of balance can be struck between fearing AI, regulating AI, and harnessing AI? Give examples of how AI can be used in business.

AI on Track to Achieving Super Intelligence?

This video from the World Economic Forum highlights the global AI race, what powers AI, concerns and benefits of AI, and short examples of how AI is being used today.

View the video online at: http://www.youtube.com/embed/Ls1_tqlpMww?rel=0

10. Watch this video on how 3D printing is spurring advances in manufacturing. How are technologies like this poised to influence the economy, society, and the jobs of the future? Work with classmates to brainstorm on ways in which 3D printing can benefit society.

3D Printing Spurring Revolutionary Advances in Manufacturing and Design

This video from PBS News Hour discusses how 3D printing is spurring revolutionary advances in manufacturing and design. Watch massive metal printers build rocket engines and fuel tanks.

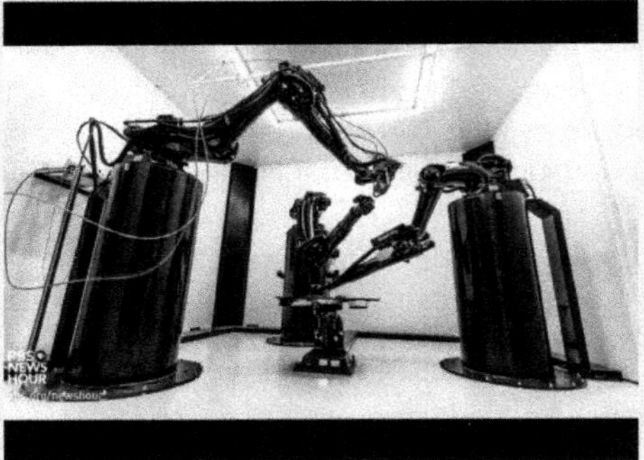

View the video online at: http://www.youtube.com/embed/AdI1Sn86ojs?rel=0

1.2 It's Your Revolution

Learning Objective

1. Name firms across hardware, software, and Internet businesses that were founded by people in their twenties (or younger).

The intersection where technology and business meet is both terrifying and exhilarating. But if you're under the age of thirty, realize that this is *your* space. While the fortunes of any individual or firm rise and fall over time, it's abundantly clear that many of the world's most successful technology firms—organizations that have had tremendous impact on consumers and businesses across industries—were created by young people. Consider just a few:

Bill Gates was an undergraduate when he left college to found Microsoft—a firm that would eventually become the world's largest software firm and catapult Gates to the top of the *Forbes* list of world's wealthiest people (enabling him to also become the most generous philanthropist of our time).

Michael Dell was just a sophomore when he began building computers in his dorm room at the University of Texas. His firm would one day claim the top spot among PC manufacturers worldwide.

Mark Zuckerberg founded Facebook as a nineteen-year-old college sophomore.

Steve Jobs was just twenty-one when he founded Apple.

Sergey Brin and Larry Page were both twenty-something doctoral students at Stanford University when they founded Google. So were Jerry Yang and David Filo of Yahoo! All would become billionaires.

Kevin Systrom was twenty-six when he founded the photo-sharing service Instagram. In just eighteen months, his thirteen-person startup garnered 35 million users worldwide, including 5 million Android users in just a single week, and was sold to Facebook for a cool $1 billion. Systrom's take was $400 million.[32] Snapchat founder Evan Spiegel dropped out of college to focus on his new firm. By age twenty-four he was running a firm valued at over $15 billion[33] with a personal net worth of over $1.5 billion.[34] Tony Hsieh proved his entrepreneurial chops when, at twenty-four, he sold LinkExchange to Microsoft for over a quarter of a billion dollars.[35] He'd later serve as CEO of Zappos, eventually selling that firm to Amazon for $900 million.[36]

FIGURE 1.3

Wealth accumulation wasn't the only fast-paced activity for young Bill Gates. The Microsoft founder appears in a mug shot for a New Mexico traffic violation. Microsoft, now headquartered in Washington state, had its roots in New Mexico when Gates and partner Paul Allen moved there to be near early PC maker Altair.

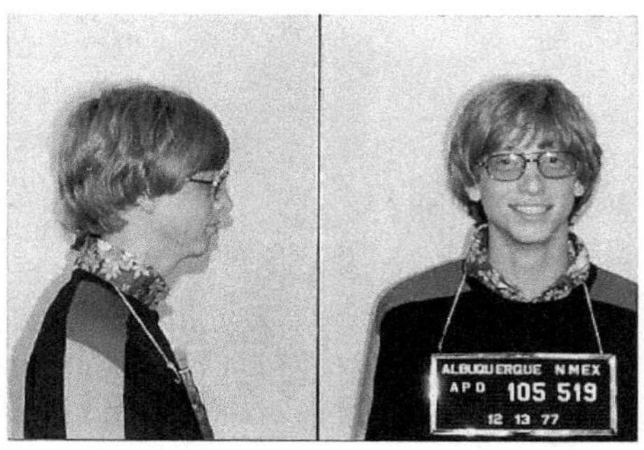

Source: Wikimedia Commons.

Steve Chen and Chad Hurley of YouTube were in their late twenties when they launched their firms. Jeff Bezos hadn't yet reached thirty when he began working on what would eventually become Amazon. The founders of Dropbox, Box, and Spotify were all under thirty when they founded businesses that would go on to be worth billions.[37] The founders of Rent the Runway, Jenn Hyman and Jenny Fleiss, were in their twenties and still in grad school when they launched the firm that is recasting how millions of consumers engage with high-end designer apparel and accessories. And just a few years out of undergrad, dancer and fitness enthusiast Payal Kadakia launched ClassPass, a service allowing customers to take fitness classes from multiple providers. Today the firm is valued at over $400 million, more than the firm behind the New York, Boston, Washington DC, and Philadelphia Sports Clubs.[38]

David Karp was another early bloomer. Karp wasn't just another college dropout; he actually quit high school for self-paced, tech-focused home schooling. It was a good move: He was taking meetings with venture capitalists at twenty, went on to found what would become one of the world's most visited websites, and sold that website, Tumblr, to Yahoo! for $1.1 billion at an age when he was younger than most MBA students.[39] Another young home-schooler, Palmer Luckey, started "modding" video game controllers at age fifteen, founded Oculus as a teenager, and sold it to Facebook for $2 billion (that's two Instagrams) by age twenty-one, and all before his company had even shipped its first consumer product.[40] In another brilliant sign of the times, Luckey jump-started his effort not by gaining investment from angel investors or venture capitalists, who would demand an ownership stake in his business, but from a Kickstarter campaign. Hoping to raise $250,000, Luckey's Oculus Rift campaign actually raised over $2.4 million without giving up a single share of equity.[41]

FIGURE 1.4

Payal Kadakia, founder of ClassPass

Source: Image courtesy of ClassPass.

This trend will almost certainly accelerate. We're in a golden age of tech entrepreneurship where ideas can be vetted and tested online, and funding crowdsourced, Kickstarter-style; "the cloud" means a startup can rent the computing resources one previously had to buy at great expense; app stores give code jockeys immediate, nearly zero-cost distribution to a potential market of hundreds of millions of people worldwide; and social media done right can virally spread awareness of a firm with nary a dime of conventional ad spending. Crafting a breakout hit is tough, but the jackpot can be immense.

But you don't have to build a successful firm to have an impact as a tech revolutionary. Shawn Fanning's Napster, widely criticized as a piracy playground, was written when he was just nineteen. Fanning's code was the first significant salvo in the tech-fueled revolution that brought about an upending of the entire music industry. Finland's Linus Torvalds wrote the first version of the Linux operating system when he was just twenty-one. Today Linux has grown to be the most influential component of the open source arsenal, powering everything from cell phones to supercomputers.

TechCrunch crows that Internet entrepreneurs are like pro athletes—"they peak around [age] 25."[42] *BusinessWeek* regularly runs a list of America's Best Young Entrepreneurs—the top twenty-five aged twenty-five and under. *Inc.* magazine's list of the Coolest Young Entrepreneurs is subtitled the "30 under 30." While not exclusively filled with the ranks of tech startups, both of these lists are nonetheless dominated with technology entrepreneurs. Whenever you see young people on the cover of a business magazine, it's almost certainly because they've done something groundbreaking with technology. The generals and foot soldiers of the technology revolution are filled with the ranks of the young, some not even old enough to legally have a beer. For the old-timers reading this, all is not lost, but you'd best get cracking with technology, quick. Junior might be on the way to either eat your lunch or be your next boss.

Key Takeaways

- Recognize that anyone reading this book has the potential to build an impactful business. Entrepreneurship has no minimum age requirement.
- The ranks of technology revolutionaries are filled with young people, with several leading firms and innovations launched by entrepreneurs who started while roughly the age of the average university student.
- Several forces are accelerating and lowering the cost of entrepreneurship. These include crowdfunding, cloud computing, app stores, 3D printing, and social media, among others.

Questions and Exercises

1. Look online for lists of young entrepreneurs. How many of these firms are tech firms or heavily rely on technology? Are there any sectors more heavily represented than tech?
2. Have you ever thought of starting your own tech-enabled business? Brainstorm with some friends. What kinds of ideas do you think might make a good business?
3. How have the costs of entrepreneurship changed over the past decade? What forces are behind these changes? What does this mean for the future of entrepreneurship?
4. Many universities and regions have competitions for entrepreneurs (e.g., business plan competitions, elevator pitch competitions). Does your school have such a program? What are the criteria for participation? If your school doesn't have one, consider forming such a program.
5. Research business accelerator programs such as Y-Combinator, TechStars, and DreamIt. Do you have a program like this in your area? What do entrepreneurs get from participating in these programs? What do they give up? Do you think these programs are worth it? Why or why not? Have you ever used a product or service from a firm that has participated in one of these programs?
6. Explore online for lists of resources for entrepreneurship. Use social media to share these resources with your class.
7. Why are we in the "golden age" of technology entrepreneurship? What factors are helping entrepreneurs more rapidly achieve their vision, and with a lower cost?
8. Have any alumni from your institution founded technology firms or risen to positions of prominence in tech-focused careers? If so, work with your professor to invite them to come speak

to your class or to student groups on campus. Your career services, university advancement (alumni giving and fundraising), alumni association, and LinkedIn searches may be able to help uncover potential speakers.

1.3 Geek Up—Tech Is Everywhere and You'll Need It to Thrive

Learning Objectives

1. Appreciate the degree to which technology has permeated every management discipline.
2. See that tech careers are varied, richly rewarding, and poised for continued growth.

Shortly after the start of the prior decade, there was a lot of concern that tech jobs would be outsourced, leading many to conclude that tech skills carried less value and that workers with tech backgrounds had little to offer. Turns out this thinking was stunningly wrong. Tech jobs boomed, and as technology pervades all other management disciplines, tech skills are becoming more important, not less. Today, tech knowledge can be a key differentiator for the job seeker. It's the worker without tech skills who needs to be concerned.

As we'll present in depth in a future chapter, there's a principle called Moore's Law that's behind fast, cheap computing. And as computing gets both faster and cheaper, it gets "baked into" all sorts of products and shows up everywhere: in your pocket, in your vacuum, and on the radio frequency identification (RFID) tags that track your luggage at the airport.

Well, there's also a sort of Moore's Law corollary that's taking place with people, too. As technology becomes faster and cheaper, and developments like open source software, cloud computing, software as a service (SaaS), and outsourcing push technology costs even lower, tech skills are being embedded inside more and more job functions. And ubiquitous tech fuels our current era of "Big Data," where bits-based insights move decision making from hunch to science. What this means is that, even if you're not expecting to become the next Tech Titan, your career will doubtless be shaped by the forces of technology. Make no mistake about it—there isn't a single modern managerial discipline that isn't being deeply and profoundly impacted by tech.

Finance

Many business school students who study finance aspire to careers in investment banking. Many i-bankers will work on IPOs (initial public stock offerings), in effect helping value companies the first time these firms wish to sell their stock on the public markets. IPO markets need new firms, and the tech industry is a fertile ground that continually sprouts new businesses like no other. Other i-bankers will be involved in valuing merger and acquisition (M&A) deals, and tech firms are active in this space, too. The technology sector has become a major driver of global M&A activity,[43] and there were 3,389 deals in the TMT (Technology, Media, Telecommunications) sector in 2017, totaling US$498.2 billion overall.[44] Leading tech firms are flush with cash and constantly on the hunt for new firms to acquire. In just five years, Google has bought a whopping 103 firms, IBM has bought sixty-four, Microsoft has bought sixty-three, Cisco has bought fifty-seven, and Intel has bought forty-eight![45] Yahoo! bought thirty-seven companies in a year and a half.[46] Apple bought twenty-seven firms in roughly the same period, spending over $14 billion, including $3 billion just for Beats (note to rappers: Want to be a billionaire? Then form a tech firm like Beats co-founder Andre Young, a.k.a. Dr. Dre).[47] And even in nontech industries, technology impacts nearly every endeavor as an opportunity catalyst or a disruptive wealth destroyer. The aspiring investment banker who doesn't understand the role of technology in firms and industries can't possibly provide an accurate guess at how much a company is worth.

TABLE 1.1 Tech Outpaces All Other Announced US M&A Deals

Sector	Deals	Value (billions)
High Tech	2,287	$240.2
Energy and Power	743	$228.6
Healthcare	1,337	$211.4
Media and Entertainment	989	$141.7
Real Estate	1,277	$139.1

Source: Mergers & Acquisitions Review, Thomson Reuters, Full Year 2017 Report.

Those in other finance careers will be lending to tech firms and evaluating the role of technology in firms in an investment portfolio. Most of you will want to consider tech's role as part of your personal investments. And modern finance simply wouldn't exist without tech. When someone arranges for a bridge to be built in Shanghai, those funds aren't carried over in a suitcase—they're digitally transferred from bank to bank. And forces of technology blasted open the 200-year-old floor trading mechanism of the New York Stock Exchange, in effect forcing the NYSE to sell shares in itself to finance the acquisition of technology-based trading platforms that were threatening to replace it. Computer-automated trading, where a human doesn't touch the deal at all, is responsible for some 60 percent of US equity trading volume.[48] As another example of the importance of tech in finance, consider that Boston-based Fidelity Investments, one of the nation's largest mutual fund firms, spends roughly $2.8 billion a year on technology. Tech isn't a commodity for finance—it's the discipline's lifeblood.

Accounting

Sarbanes-Oxley Act

Also known as Sarbox or SOX; US legislation enacted in the wake of the accounting scandals of the early 2000s. The act raises executive and board responsibility and ties criminal penalties to certain accounting and financial violations. Although often criticized, SOX is also seen as raising stakes for mismanagement and misdeeds related to a firm's accounting practices.

If you're an accountant, your career is built on a foundation of technology. The numbers used by accountants are all recorded, stored, and reported by information systems, and the reliability of any audit is inherently tied to the reliability of the underlying technology. Increased regulation, such as the heavy executive penalties tied to the **Sarbanes-Oxley Act** in the United States, have ratcheted up the importance of making sure accountants (and executives) get their numbers right. Negligence could mean jail time. This means the link between accounting and tech has never been tighter, and the stakes for ensuring systems accuracy have never been higher.

Business students might also consider that while accounting firms regularly rank near the top of *BusinessWeek*'s "Best Places to Start Your Career" list, many of the careers at these firms are highly tech-centric. Every major accounting firm has spawned a tech-focused consulting practice, and in many cases, these firms have grown to be larger than the accounting services functions from which they sprang. Today, Deloitte's tech-centric consulting division is larger than the firm's audit, tax, and risk practices. At the time of its spin-off, Accenture was larger than the accounting practice at former parent Arthur Andersen (Accenture executives are also grateful they split before Andersen's collapse in the wake of the prior decade's accounting scandals). Now, many accounting firms that had previously spun off technology practices are once again building up these functions, finding strong similarities between the skills of an auditor and skills needed in emerging disciplines such as information security and privacy.

Marketing

Technology has thrown a grenade onto the marketing landscape, and as a result, the skill set needed by today's marketers is radically different from what was leveraged by the prior generation. Online channels have provided a way to track and monitor consumer activities, and firms are leveraging this insight to understand how to get the right product to the right customer, through the right channel, with the right message, at the right price, at the right time. The success or failure of a campaign can often be immediately assessed based on online activity such as website visit patterns and whether a campaign results in an online purchase.

The ability to track customers, analyze campaign results, and modify tactics has amped up the return on investment of marketing dollars, with firms increasingly shifting spending from tough-to-track media such as print, radio, and television to the Web.[49] And new channels continue to emerge: smartphone, tablet, smart TV, smart watch and other wearables, smart auto, and more. Look to Apple to show how fast things grow: in roughly four years, iOS devices were in the hands, backpacks, purses, and pockets of over two hundred million people worldwide, delivering location-based messages and services and even allowing for cashless payment.[50] Roughly one-third of mobile phones used worldwide are smartphones, with the number expected to exceed 50 percent in four years. Billions will have a computer in their pockets, and this will become the primary channel for all sorts of customer engagement.[51]

The rise of social media is also part of this blown-apart marketing landscape. Now all customers can leverage an enduring and permanent voice, capable of broadcasting word-of-mouth influence in ways that can benefit and harm a firm. Savvy firms are using social media to generate sales, improve their reputations, better serve customers, and innovate. Those who don't understand this landscape risk being embarrassed, blindsided, and out of touch with their customers.

Search engine marketing (SEM), search engine optimization (SEO), customer relationship management (CRM), personalization systems, and a sensitivity to managing the delicate balance between gathering and leveraging data and respecting consumer privacy are all central components of the new marketing toolkit. And there's no looking back—tech's role in marketing will only grow in prominence. Analyst firm Gartner predicts that chief marketing officers are on a path to spend more on technology than any other function within the firm.[52]

Operations

A firm's operations management function is focused on producing goods and services, and operations students usually get the point that tech is the key to their future. Quality programs, process redesign, supply chain management, factory automation, and service operations are all tech-centric. These points are underscored in this book as we introduce several examples of how firms have designed fundamentally different ways of conducting business (and even entirely different industries), where value and competitive advantage are created through technology-enabled operations.

Human Resources

Technology helps firms harness the untapped power of employees. Knowledge management systems are morphing into social media technologies—social networks, wikis, and Twitter-style messaging systems that can accelerate the ability of a firm to quickly organize and leverage teams of experts. And crowdsourcing tools and question-and-answer sites like Quora and Stack Overflow allow firms to reach out for expertise beyond their organizations. Human resources (HR) directors are using technology for employee training, screening, and evaluation. The accessibility of end-user technology means that every employee can reach the public, creating an imperative for firms to set policy on issues such as firm representation and disclosure and to continually monitor and enforce policies as well as capture and push out best practices. The successful HR manager recognizes that technology continually changes an organization's required skill sets as well as employee expectations.

The hiring and retention practices of the prior generation are also in flux. Recruiting hasn't just moved online; it's now grounded in information systems that scour databases for specific skill sets, allowing recruiters to cast a wider talent net than ever before. Job seekers are writing résumés with keywords in mind, aware that the first cut is likely made by a database search program, not a human being. The rise of professional social networks also puts added pressure on employee satisfaction and retention. Prior HR managers fiercely guarded employee directories for fear that a headhunter or competitive firm might raid top talent. Now the equivalent of a corporate directory can be easily pulled up via LinkedIn, a service complete with discrete messaging capabilities that can allow competitors to rifle-scope target your firm's best and brightest. Thanks to technology, the firm that can't keep employees happy, engaged, and feeling valued has never been more vulnerable.

And while many students have been wisely warned that inappropriate social posts can ruin their job candidacy, also know that the inverse is also true. In many ways social media is "the new résumé."[53] Thoughtful blog posts, a compelling LinkedIn presence, Twitter activity reflecting an enthusiastic and engaged mind, and, for tech students, participation in collaborative coding communities like GitHub all work to set apart a candidate from the herd. If you can't be found online, some employers may wonder if you have current skills, or if you have something to hide.

The Law

And for those looking for careers in corporate law, many of the hottest areas involve technology. Intellectual property, patents, piracy, and privacy are all areas where activity has escalated dramatically in recent years. The number of US patent applications waiting approval has tripled in the past decade, while China saw a threefold increase in patent applications in just five years.[54] Firms planning to leverage new inventions and business methods need legal teams with the skills to sleuth out whether a firm can legally do what it plans to. Others will need legal expertise to help them protect proprietary methods and content, as well as to help enforce claims in the home country and abroad.

Information Systems Careers

While the job market goes through ebbs and flows, recent surveys have shown there to be no end in sight for the demand for technical skills. *Money* magazine ranked tech jobs as three of the top ten "Best Jobs in America."[55] Around 1 in every 20 open job postings in the United States relates to information systems or computer science, and tech specializations are among the top three most-demanded college majors.[56] By some estimates, there will be three times the number of new US programming jobs created than newly minted programmers graduating from US colleges.[57] In some regions demand is even more pressing. In Massachusetts, for example, there is only one qualified graduate for every seventeen tech firm job openings requiring a bachelor's degree.[58] Tech jobs make up two of the top three "Best Jobs" on the *US News* list.[59] *BusinessWeek* ranks consulting (which heavily hires tech grads) and technology as the second and third highest paying industries for recent college graduates.[60] Technology careers have actually ranked among the safest careers to have during the most recent downturn.[61] The *Harvard Business Review* has declared "Data Scientist" the "Sexiest Job of the 21st Century."[62] And *Fortune's* ranks of the "Best Companies to Work For" is full of technology firms and has been topped by a tech business for eight years straight.[63] Want to work for a particular company? Chances are they're looking for tech talent. The demand for technology skills stretches across industries. Employers with the greatest number of recent technical job openings included JP Morgan Chase (finance), UnitedHealth (health care/insurance), Northrup Grumman (defense), and General Motors (automotive). And everyone wants to hire more coders from underrepresented groups. Apple,[64] Etsy,[65] Square,[66] Facebook,[67] and Google[68] are among the firms with programs to prep and encourage more women and minorities to pursue tech careers (details in endnotes).[69]

Students studying technology can leverage skills in ways that range from the highly technical to those that emphasize a tech-centric use of other skills. And why be restricted to just the classes taught on campus? Resources like Coursera, iTunes U., Codeacademy, Udemy, edX, YouTube, and others provide a smorgasbord of learning where the smart and motivated can geek up. Carve out some time to give programming a shot—remember, the founders of Tumblr and Instagram were largely self-taught. The high demand for scarce technical talent has also led many tech firms to offer six-figure starting salaries to graduating seniors from top universities.[70] Take some advice from the *Harvard Business Review*: "Leading a digital transformation? Learn to code."[71] Opportunities for programmers abound, particularly for those versed in new technologies. But there are also nonprogramming roles for experts in areas such as user-interface design (who work to make sure systems are easy to use), process design (who leverage technology to make firms more efficient), and strategy (who specialize in technology for competitive advantage). Nearly every large organization has its own information systems department. That group not only ensures that systems get built and keep running but also increasingly takes on strategic roles targeted at proposing solutions for how technology can give the firm a competitive edge. Career paths allow for developing expertise in a particular technology (e.g., business intelligence analyst, database administrator, social media manager), while project management careers leverage skills in taking projects from idea through deployment.

Even in consulting firms, careers range from hard-core programmers who "build stuff" to analysts who do no programming but might work identifying problems and developing a solutions blueprint that is then turned over to another team to code. Careers at tech giants like Apple, Google, and Microsoft don't all involve coding end-user programs either. Each of these firms has its own client-facing staff that works with customers and partners to implement solutions. Field engineers at these firms may work as part of (often very lucratively compensated) sales teams to show how a given company's software and services can be used. These engineers often put together prototypes that are then turned over to a client's in-house staff for further development. An Apple field engineer might show how a firm can leverage iPads in its organization, while a Google field engineer can help a firm incorporate search, banner, and video ads into its online efforts. Careers that involve consulting and field engineering are often particularly attractive for those who are effective communicators who enjoy working with an ever-changing list of clients and problems across various industries and in many different geographies.

Upper-level career opportunities are also increasingly diverse. Consultants can become partners who work with the most senior executives of client firms, helping identify opportunities for those organizations to become more effective. Within a firm, technology specialists can rise to be chief information officer or chief technology officer—positions focused on overseeing a firm's information systems development and deployment. And many firms are developing so-called *C-level* specialties in emerging areas with a technology focus, such as chief information security officer (CISO), and chief privacy officer (CPO). Senior technology positions may also be a ticket to the chief executive's suite. A recent *Fortune* article pointed out how the prominence of technology provides a training ground for executives to learn the breadth and depth of a firm's operations and an understanding of the ways in which a firm is vulnerable to attack and where it can leverage opportunities for growth.[72]

Your Future

With tech at the center of so much change, realize that you may very well be preparing for careers that don't yet exist. But by studying the intersection of business and technology today, you develop a base to build upon and critical thinking skills that will help you evaluate new, emerging technologies. Think you can afford to wait on tech study, and then quickly get up to speed at a later date? Whom do you expect to have an easier time adapting and leveraging a technology like social media—today's college students who are immersed in technology or their parents who are embarrassingly dipping their toes into the waters of Facebook? Those who put off an understanding of technology risk being left in the dust.

Consider the nontechnologists who have tried to enter the technology space these past few years. News Corp. head Rupert Murdoch piloted his firm to the purchase of MySpace only to see this one-time leader lose share to rivals.[73] Former Warner executive Terry Semel presided over Yahoo!'s[74] malaise as Google blasted past it. Barry Diller, the man widely credited with creating the Fox Network, led InterActive Corp. (IAC) in the acquisition of a slew of tech firms ranging from Expedia to Ask.com, only to break the empire up as it foundered.[75] And Time Warner head Jerry Levin presided over the acquisition of AOL, executing what many consider to be one of the most disastrous mergers in US business history.[76] Contrast these guys against the technology-centric successes of Mark Zuckerberg (Facebook), Steve Jobs (Apple), and Sergey Brin and Larry Page (Google).

While we'll make it abundantly clear that a focus solely on technology is a recipe for disaster, a business perspective that lacks an appreciation for tech's role is also likely to be doomed. At this point in history, technology and business are inexorably linked, and those not trained to evaluate and make decisions in this ever-shifting space risk irrelevance, marginalization, and failure.

Key Takeaways

- As technology becomes cheaper and more powerful, it pervades more industries and is becoming increasingly baked into what were once nontech functional areas.
- Technology is impacting every major business discipline, including finance, accounting, marketing, operations, human resources, and the law.
- Tech jobs rank among the best and highest-growth positions, and tech firms rank among the best and highest-paying firms to work for.
- Information systems (IS) jobs are profoundly diverse, ranging from those that require heavy programming skills to those that are focused on design, process, project management, privacy, and strategy.

Questions and Exercises

1. Look at *Fortune*'s "Best Companies to Work For" list. How many of these firms are technology firms? Which firm would you like to work for? Are they represented on this list?
2. Look at *BusinessWeek*'s "Best Places to Start Your Career" list. Is the firm you mentioned above also on this list?
3. What are you considering studying? What are your short-term and long-term job goals? What role will technology play in that career path? What should you be doing to ensure that you have the skills needed to compete?
4. Which jobs that exist today likely won't exist at the start of the next decade? Based on your best guess on how technology will develop, can you think of jobs and skill sets that will likely emerge as critical five and ten years from now?
5. Explore online resources to learn technology on your own and search for programs that encourage college students. If you are from an underrepresented group in technology (i.e., a woman or minority), search for programs that provide learning and opportunity for those seeking tech careers. Share your resources with your professor via a class wiki or other mechanism to create a common resource everyone can use to #geekup. Then tweet what you create using that hashtag!

Endnotes

1. T. Goodwin, "The Battle Is For The Customer Interface," *TechCrunch*, March 3, 2015.
2. M. Porter, "Strategy and the Internet," *Harvard Business Review* 79, no. 3 (March 2001): 62–78.
3. G. Kumparak, "Apple Just Had The Most Profitable Quarter Of Any Company Ever," *TechCrunch*, Jan. 27, 2015.
4. Reported App stores sales in 2014 = $14 billion (source: Ulloa, "The App Store Brought in More than $14 Billion in 2014," *Digital Music News*, Jan. 8, 2015. The 250th ranked firm in the 2015 *Fortune* 500 was JCPenney, with revenues of just $12.2 billion (source: 2015 *Fortune* 500). Reported App stores sales in 2014 = $14 billion (source: Ulloa, "The App Store Brought in More than $14 Billion in 2014," *Digital Music News*, Jan. 8, 2015. The 250th ranked firm in the 2015 *Fortune* 500 was JCPenney, with revenues of just $12.2 billion (source: 2015 *Fortune* 500).
5. C. Frey and M. Osborne, *Technology at Work: The Future of Innovation and Employment*, published by Citibank, New York, NY, February 2015.
6. E. Protalinski, "Over 90% of Facebook's advertising revenue now comes from mobile," *VentureBeat*, April 25, 2018.
7. A. Hartmann's, "The most downloaded iPhone app in the world right now is one you've probably never heard of," *Business Insider*, May 3, 2018.
8. A. Shen, "China pulls further ahead of US in mobile payments with record US$12.8 trillion in transactions," *South China Morning Post*, Feb. 20, 2018.
9. R. Mac, "Alibaba Claims Title For Largest Global IPO Ever With Extra Share Sales," *Forbes*, Sept. 22, 2014.
10. Unattributed, "Facts about the IT Industry in India," *Statista*. Accessed June 27, 2016. http://www.statista.com/topics/2256/it-industry-in-india/.
11. V. Wadhwa, "Indian Technology's Fourth Wave," *BusinessWeek*, December 8, 2010.
12. N. Chandrasekaran, "Five Digital Forces That Are Changing the Tech Industry," *Knowledge@Wharton*, Aug. 11, 2015.
13. PTI, "Mobile Internet Users In India Seen At 478 Million By June, Says Report," *Bloomberg*, March 25, 2018.
14. R. Iyengar and S. Pham, "Walmart is buying India's Flipkart," *CNN Money*, May 9, 2018.
15. Speedtest Global Index, May 2018, accessed May 29, 2018 from http://www.speedtest.net/global-index
16. Unattributed, "The truly personal computer," *The Economist*, Feb. 28, 2015.
17. M. Maneker, "Benedict Evans wants you to know that Google is a tiny company," *Quartz*, Feb. 23, 2015.
18. *Economist*, "The Next Frontier," February 16, 2013.
19. J. O., "Growth and Other Good Things," *Economist*, May 1, 2013.
20. G. York, "How Mobile Phones Are Making Cash Obsolete in Africa," *The Globe and Mail*, June 21, 2013.
21. Unattributed, "Tanzania Top Country in Mobile Money," *TanzaniaInvest*, Dec. 20, 2015
22. Unattributed, "A phoneful of dollars," *The Economist*, Nov. 15, 2014.
23. S. Higginbotham, "GE's Industrial Internet Focus Means It's a Big Data Company Now," *GigaOM*, June 18, 2013.
24. T. Team, "GE Is Beginning To See Strong Returns On Its Industrial Internet Investments," *Forbes*, Nov. 12, 2014.
25. L. Tung, "IoT devices will outnumber the world's population this year for the first time," *ZDNet*, Feb. 7, 2017.
26. C. Anderson, "10 Breakthrough Technologies: Agricultural Drones," *MIT Technology Review*, 2014 (available at https://www.technologyreview.com/s/526491/agricultural-drones/).
27. A. Toor, "This Startup Is Using Drones to Deliver Medicine in Rwanda," *The Verge*, April 5, 2016.
28. Unattributed, "The truly personal computer," *The Economist*, Feb. 28, 2015.
29. E. Palermo, "How 3D Printing Is Changing Etsy," *TomsGuide*, Aug. 7, 2013.
30. J. Buck, T. McMahan, and D. Huot, "Space Station 3-D Printer Builds Ratchet Wrench To Complete First Phase Of Operations," *Nasa*, Dec. 22, 2014.
31. T. Novellino, "Don't Get Cozy *Fortune* 500. It's Do or Die Time for Digital Disruption," *Upstart*, June 4, 2015.
32. J. Guynn, "Insta-Rich: How Instagram Became a $1 Billion Company in 18 Months," *Los Angeles Times*, April 20, 2012.
33. B. Stone and S. Friar, "Evan Spiegel Reveals Plan to Turn Snapchat Into a Real Business," *BusinessWeek*, May 26, 2015.
34. M. Stone, "The fabulous life of Snapchat CEO Evan Spiegel, the youngest billionaire in the world," *Business Insider*, March 12, 2015.
35. M. Chafkin, "The Zappos Way of Managing," *Inc.*, May 1, 2009.
36. S. Lacy, "Amazon Buys Zappos; The Price Is $928m., Not $847m.," *TechCrunch*, July 22, 2009.
37. J. Bort, "Oculus Founder Palmer Luckey Dropped Out of College—And So Did All These Other Tech Superstars," *Business Insider*, March 25, 2014.
38. C. Sorvino, "Why Failing Twice Helped Payal Kadakia Build a $50 Million (and Growing) Fortune," *Forbes*, June 17, 2016
39. J. Wortham and N. Bolton, "Before Tumblr, Founder Made Mom Proud. He Quit School," *New York Times*, May 20, 2013.
40. T. Clark, "How Palmer Luckey Created Oculus Rift," *Smithsonian Magazine*, Nov. 2014.
41. D. Ewalt, "Palmer Luckey: Defying Reality," *Forbes*, January 5, 2015.
42. M. Arrington, "Internet Entrepreneurs Are Like Professional Athletes, They Peak Around 25," *TechCrunch*, April 30, 2011.
43. PR Newswire, "Technology and Digital Takeovers Drive Global M&A," *CNBC*, Sept. 26, 2017.
44. T. Trumbull, "Technology, Media, and Telecom M&A: 2017's Record Stats," *Channel e2d*, Feb. 12, 2018.
45. S. Miller, "The Trouble with Tech M&A," *The Deal*, May 7, 2012.
46. V. Ravisankar, "How to Hack Hiring," *TechCrunch*, April 26, 2014.
47. D. Dilger, "Apple's Voracious Appetite for Acquisitions Outspent Google in 2013," *AppleInsider*, March 3, 2014; P. Kafka, "Tim Cook Explains Why Apple Is Buying Beats (Q&A)," *Re/code*, May 28, 2014; and P. Kafka, "Apple Will Buy Beats for $3 Billion," *Re/code*, May 28, 2014.

48. M. Philips, "How the Robots Lost: High-Frequency Trading's Rise and Fall," *BusinessWeek*, June 6, 2013.
49. J. Pontin, "But Who's Counting?" *Technology Review*, March/April 2009.
50. D. Coldewey, "iOS Passes 200 Million Devices, 25 Million of Which Are iPads," *TechCrunch*, June 6, 2011.
51. *eMarketer*, "Smartphone Adoption Tips Past 50 Percent in Major Markets Worldwide," May 29, 2013.
52. L. Arthur, "Five Years from Now, CMOs Will Spend More on IT than CIOs Do," *Forbes*, February 8, 2012.
53. R. Silverman and L. Weber, "The New Résumé: It's 140 Characters," *Wall Street Journal*, April 9, 2013.
54. J. Schmid and B. Poston, "Patent Backlog Clogs Recovery," *Milwaukee Journal Sentinel*, August 15, 2009.
55. "Best Jobs in America 2013," *CNNMoney*.
56. S. Gallagher, "Software Is Eating The Job Market," *TechCrunch*, June 9, 2015.
57. K. McDonald, "Sorry, College Grads, I Probably Won't Hire You," *Wall Street Journal*, May 9, 2013.
58. D. Adams, "Mass. tech sector flourishing with challenges ahead," *The Boston Globe*, March 13, 2015.
59. "The 100 Best Jobs," *U.S. News & World Report*, accessed July 1, 2014.
60. L. Gerdes, "The Best Places to Launch a Career," *BusinessWeek*, September 15, 2008.
61. T. Kaneshige, "Surprise! Tech Is a Safe Career Choice Today," *InfoWorld*, February 4, 2009.
62. T. Davenport and D. Patil, "Data Scientist: The Sexiest Job of the 21st Century," *Harvard Business Review*, October 2012.
63. See "Best Companies to Work For," *Fortune*, 2007–2014.
64. M. Lev-Ram, "Apple commits more than $50 million to diversity efforts," *Fortune*, March 10, 2015.
65. A. Kamanetz, "How Etsy Attracted 500 Percent More Female Engineers," *Fast Company*, March 5, 2013.
66. L. Rao, "For Aspiring Female Engineers, a Square Meal of Code," *TechCrunch*, May 17, 2014.
67. Careers at Facebook, https://www.facebook.com/careers/university/fbu.
68. J. Jackson, "Google Boldly Did the Right Thing," June 2, 2014.
69. A. Kuchment, "Encouraging More Minority Girls to Code," *Scientific American,* July 9, 2013.
70. E. Goode, "For Newcomers in Silicon Valley, the Dream of Entrepreneurship Still Lives," *New York Times*, January 24, 2012.
71. S. Anthony, "Leading a Business Transformation? Learn to Code," *Harvard Business Review*, Sept. 22, 2015.
72. J. Fortt, "Tech Execs Get Sexy," *Fortune*, February 12, 2009.
73. O. Malik, "MySpace, R.I.P.," *GigaOM*, February 10, 2010.
74. J. Thaw, "Yahoo's Semel Resigns as Chief amid Google's Gains," *Bloomberg*, June 18, 2007.
75. G. Fabrikant and M. Helft, "Barry Diller Conquered. Now He Tries to Divide," *New York Times*, March 16, 2008.
76. J. Quinn, "Final Farewell to Worst Deal in History—AOL-Time Warner," *Telegraph* (UK), November 21, 2009.

CHAPTER 2

A Brief Introduction to Excel

This is not a course about Excel, but it does showcase some pretty amazing things that you can do with Excel. Excel is the de facto standard software used in business. There are competing products such as Apple's Numbers or Google Sheets. But no other product is as comprehensive or powerful as Excel. Furthermore, once you learn concepts in Excel, you can generalize that knowledge to the other products.

Excel is far more than a calculating machine. The best use of the product is to model a business problem or a solution to a business problem. If that sounds rather abstract then consider the Excel spreadsheet below that models how much of two different kinds of coffee (drip coffee or espresso drinks) a coffee shop needs to sell in order to generate a desired level of revenue. The beauty of the model is that only the inputs, the yellow boxes, need to change. All other aspects of the model depend on those. The numbers highlighted in green represent good outcomes—where we exceed our desired revenue. But all the numbers in the matrix will change if we change any of the three inputs. Even which numbers are highlighted in green will change!

Coffee Shop Model

	A	B	C	D	E	F	G	H	I	J	K	L
1												
2		**Price**	**Volume**	**Revenue**								
3	**Espresso Drink**	$2.25	100	$225.00		**Desired Revenue**		$100				
4	**Drip Coffee**	1.25	100	$125.00								
5				$350.00								
6												
7							**Espresso Volume**					
8		$350.00	**10**	**20**	**30**	**40**	**50**	**60**	**70**	**80**	**90**	**100**
9		**10**	35	58	80	103	125	148	170	193	215	238
10		**20**	48	70	93	115	138	160	183	205	228	250
11		**30**	60	83	105	128	150	173	195	218	240	263
12		**40**	73	95	118	140	163	185	208	230	253	275
13	**Drip Volume**	**50**	85	108	130	153	175	198	220	243	265	288
14		**60**	98	120	143	165	188	210	233	255	278	300
15		**70**	110	133	155	178	200	223	245	268	290	313
16		**80**	123	145	168	190	213	235	258	280	303	325
17		**90**	135	158	180	203	225	248	270	293	315	338
18		**100**	148	170	193	215	238	260	283	305	328	350

Before we can model with Excel, we need to learn some of the basic building blocks. These are covered below.

2.1 Formulas

The fundamental unit of work in Excel is a formula such as =B2*C2. This formula takes the values located in cells B2 and C2 and multiplies them together. It doesn't matter what those values are or how frequently we change them—Excel is always monitoring the B2 and C2 cells ready to recalculate the minute anything changes. Now, the formula itself must live in some cell within the worksheet, say D2. So most cells in Excel contain values, calculations on those values, or are just left blank.

Starting the Spreadsheet

D2 fx =B2*C2

	A	B	C	D
1	**Product**	**Quantity**	**Price**	**Total**
2	t-shirt	25	7	175

Here are some other examples of Excel formulas using the same two cells whether or not they make sense from a business standpoint:

- =B2+C2 (addition)
- =B2-C2 (subtraction)
- =B2/C2 (division)
- =B2^2+C2^2 (the sum of both values squared)

Copying Formulas

Our original formula, =B2*C2, calculates quantity * price as total price. But it is likely that we sell more than one product and these could appear on separate lines. The magic of Excel is its ability to identify and repeat a pattern when copying a formula. Repeating the pattern while adjusting to changing circumstances is called a relative copy, and it is the default behavior of Excel. Here's how it works: When the formula is copied from D2 to D3, Excel recognizes that the row has changed and that it probably makes more sense to dive into the formula and change the row numbers there as well. So the new formula in D3 becomes =B3*C3. We can even copy the pattern to multiple rows in one command. Using the little black square (fill handle) in the lower right corner of D2, we can pull and copy the formula down to as many rows as we like.

Copying the formula

D2 fx =B2*C2

	A	B	C	D
1	**Product**	**Quantity**	**Price**	**Total**
2	t-shirt	25	7	175
3	hoodie	15	23	345
4	sweatpants	40	18	720

Naming Cells

There are times that we would like one or more of referenced cells not to adjust during the copy. There are real fixed values in the world, such as a tax rate, that we would like to apply to all the totals equally. The best way to stop a fixed value from updating while copying is to give the cell containing that value a name, and then reference that cell by its name, not by its cell location. The name will not change when copied.

Copying a formula with a named cell

E2 fx =D2*(1+TaxRate)

	A	B	C	D	E
1	**Product**	**Quantity**	**Price**	**Total**	**Total plus tax**
2	t-shirt	25	7	175	186.38
3	hoodie	15	23	345	367.43
4	sweatpants	40	18	720	766.80
5					
6	Tax Rate	6.50%			

To prove that the name did not change we show the same spreadsheet below in formula view. You can toggle back and forth from spreadsheet to formula view at any time by pressing Control + ~ on your keyboard. (If you ever ask your professor for help with Excel, it is likely that Control + ~ will be the first place he/she goes to diagnose the problem).

Formula view using CTL ~

E2 fx =D2*(1+TaxRate)

	A	B	C	D	E
1	**Product**	**Quantity**	**Price**	**Total**	**Total plus tax**
2	t-shirt	25	7	=B2*C2	=D2*(1+TaxRate)
3	hoodie	15	23	=B3*C3	=D3*(1+TaxRate)
4	sweatpants	40	18	=B4*C4	=D4*(1+TaxRate)
5					
6	Tax Rate	0.065			

Naming a cell in Excel is simply a matter of making the cell active (by clicking on it) then typing a name in the name box that appears in the upper left. Finally, you must press the ENTER key to make the name stick. Whenever that cell is active (clicked on), the name will show in the name box. Note that B6, the cell that actually contains the tax rate, is the cell that we named, not the label that we placed in A6.

Naming a cell

TaxRate | fx 6.5%

	A	B	C	D	E
1	**Product**	**Quantity**	**Price**	**Total**	**Total plus tax**
2	t-shirt	25	7	175	186.38
3	hoodie	15	23	345	367.43
4	sweatpants	40	18	720	766.80
5					
6	Tax Rate	6.50%			

Unfortunately, Excel gives no other indication that the cell is named. There is no thought bubble that floats above the cell with its name. However, Excel knows all the named cells in the workbook and can show you a list of them at any time in Formulas > Define Name. (Windows: Formulas > Name Manger). This is also the only place that you can remove a name in case you make a mistake in naming—which happens more often than you might imagine.

Define Name

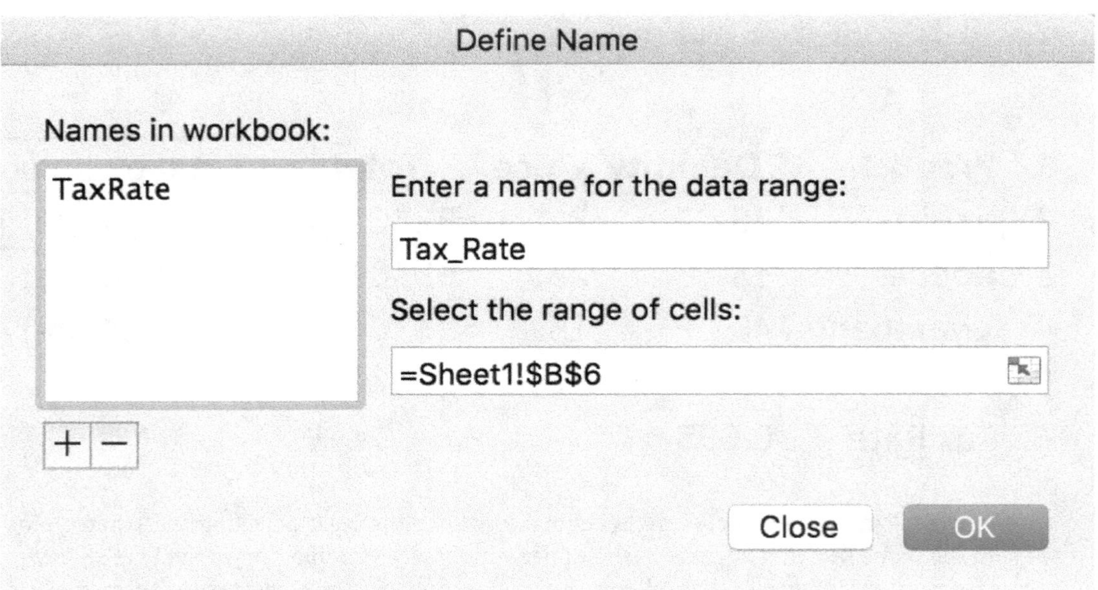

2.2 Functions

In addition to formulas that the user constructs, like =B2*C2, Excel also provides built-in functions that can perform complex calculations that we might want to avoid writing ourselves for the sake of efficiency and accuracy. The equivalent function for our formula would be =PRODUCT(B2:C2), which means multiply the numbers from B2 to C2 together. All functions begin with a keyword, in this case PRODUCT, followed by open parentheses. What goes inside the parentheses are one or more arguments separated by commas. We wrote the PRODUCT function as a single argument that is the range of cells from B2 to C2. But we could also have written it as cells separated by commas—for example, =PRODUCT(B2,C2). Excel is very helpful and will tell you exactly which arguments the function is expecting and whether any of them are optional. Optional arguments usually appear at the end of the comma list and are enclosed in square brackets. For example, the PMT function, which calculates loan payments, looks like this:

=PMT(rate, nper, pv, [fv], [type])

where

- rate is the interest rate;
- nper is the number of payment periods;
- pv is the amount of the loan today;
- fv] is the optional future value of the loan; and
- [type] is the optional indication of whether payments take place at the beginning or end of each payment period.

Function vs. Formula

When there are only a few data points and/or the calculation is simple, then a formula is easier and more intuitive. But what if the operation is to compute loan payments? Then the PMT function is clearly easier to manage than a complex calculation. Furthermore, functions are less prone to error since they have been debugged and tested by Microsoft. There are also things that a formula simply can't do. For example, looking up values in a long list can only be done with a function. But it is really not a competition. Most good spreadsheets contain a combination of formulas and functions. Use whatever the cognitive task at hand demands to model the business situation.

CHAPTER 3

Moore's Law and More: Fast, Cheap Computing, and What This Means for the Manager

3.1 Introduction

Learning Objectives

1. Define Moore's Law and understand the approximate rate of advancement for other technologies, including magnetic storage (disc drives) and telecommunications (fiber-optic transmission).
2. Understand how the price elasticity associated with faster and cheaper technologies opens new markets, creates new opportunities for firms and society, and can catalyze industry disruption.
3. Recognize and define various terms for measuring data capacity.
4. Consider the managerial implications of faster and cheaper computing on areas such as strategic planning, inventory, and accounting.

Faster and cheaper—those two words have driven the computer industry for decades, and the rest of the economy has been along for the ride. Today it's tough to imagine a single industry not impacted by more powerful, less expensive computing. Faster and cheaper puts mobile phones in the hands of peasant farmers, puts a free video game in your Happy Meal, and drives the drug discovery that may very well extend your life.

Some Definitions

This phenomenon of "faster, cheaper" computing is often referred to as **Moore's Law**, after Intel cofounder Gordon Moore. Moore didn't show up one day, stance wide, hands on hips, and declare "behold my law," but he did write a four-page paper for *Electronics* magazine in which he described how regular advances in the process of chip making enabled more powerful chips to be manufactured at cheaper prices.[1]

Moore's Law

Chip performance per dollar doubles every eighteen months.

Moore's friend, legendary chip entrepreneur and Caltech professor Carver Mead, later coined the "Moore's Law" moniker. That name sounded snappy, plus as one of the founders of Intel, Moore had enough geek cred for the name to stick. Moore's original paper offered language only a chip designer would love, so we'll rely on the more popular definition: *chip performance per dollar dou-*

bles every eighteen months (Moore's original paper stated transistors per chip, a proxy for power, would double every two years, but many sources today refer to the *eighteen*-month figure, so we'll stick with that since managers are often blindsided by unanticipated rate of technology change). Intel has recently speculated that Moore's Law may slow to a doubling every 2.5 years.[2] Even at that rate, we're still talking about ridiculously accelerating power and plummeting costs, a concept vital for managers to be aware of. And even as Intel's server, desktop, and laptop microprocessors hit their limit, others have pointed out that the calculating power of smartphones has actually outpaced the predictions of Moore's Law.[3]

Moore's Law at 50

Hear Intel co-founder Gordon Moore discuss Moore's Law at 50, and watch scenes showing the microprocessor manufacturing process.

View the video online at: http://www.youtube.com/embed/ylgk3HEyZ_g?rel=0

microprocessor

The part of the computer that executes the instructions of a computer program.

Moore's Law applies to chips—broadly speaking, to *processors* and chip-based storage: think of the stuff in your consumer electronics that's made out of silicon.[4] The **microprocessor** is the brain of a computing device. It's the part of the computer that executes the instructions of a computer program, allowing it to run a Web browser, word processor, video game, or virus. For processors, Moore's Law means that next-generation chips should be twice as fast in about *eighteen* months, but cost the same as today's models (or from another perspective, in about a year and a half, chips that are same speed as today's models should be available for half the price).

random-access memory (RAM)

The fast, chip-based volatile storage in a computing device.

volatile memory

Storage (such as RAM chips) that is wiped clean when power is cut off from a device.

nonvolatile memory

Storage that retains data even when powered down (such as flash memory, hard disk, or DVD storage).

Random-access memory (RAM) is chip-based memory. The RAM inside your personal computer is **volatile memory**, meaning that when the power goes out, all is lost that wasn't saved to **nonvolatile memory** (i.e., a more permanent storage media like a hard disc or flash memory). Think of RAM as temporary storage that provides fast access for executing computer programs and files. When you "load" or "launch" a program, it usually moves from your hard drive or flash storage to those RAM chips, where it can be more quickly executed by the processor.

Cameras, MP3 players, USB drives, mobile phones, and even many lightweight notebook computers often use **flash memory** (sometimes called *flash RAM* or *flash storage*). It's not as fast as the RAM used in most traditional PCs, but holds data even when the power is off (so flash memory is also nonvolatile memory). You can think of flash memory as the chip-based equivalent of a hard drive. Apple's MacBook Air was one of the first commercial notebook computers to offer chip-based, nonvolatile memory as an alternative to laptop hard drives, although now several manufacturers and models also use the technology. The big advantage? Chips are **solid state electronics** (meaning no moving parts), so they're less likely to fail, and they draw less power. Data can also be accessed faster from flash memory than from conventional hard drives. For RAM chips and flash memory, Moore's Law means that in *eighteen* months you'll pay the same price as today for twice as much storage.

flash memory

Nonvolatile, chip-based storage, often used in mobile phones, cameras, and MP3 players. Sometimes called flash RAM, flash memory is slower than conventional RAM, but holds its charge even when the power goes out.

solid state electronics

Semiconductor-based devices. Solid state components often suffer fewer failures and require less energy than mechanical counterparts because they have no moving parts. RAM, flash memory, and microprocessors are solid state devices. Hard drives are not.

FIGURE 3.1 Advancing Rates of Technology (Silicon, Storage, Telecom)

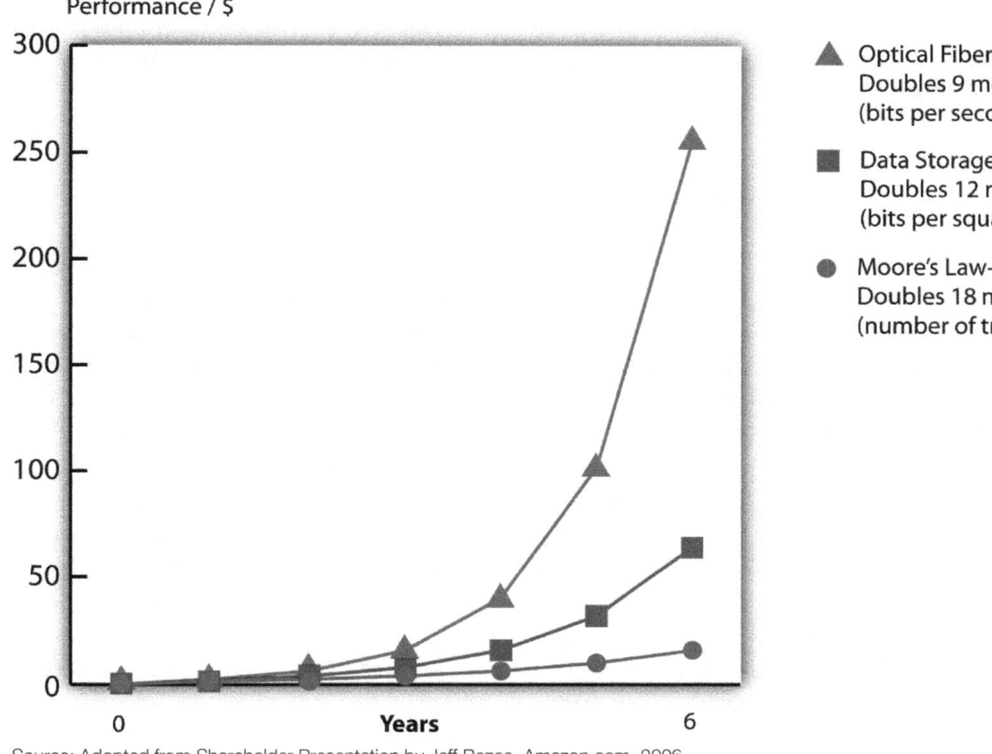

Source: Adopted from Shareholder Presentation by Jeff Bezos, Amazon.com, 2006.

Computer chips are sometimes also referred to as **semiconductors** (a substance such as silicon dioxide used inside most computer chips that is capable of enabling as well as inhibiting the flow of electricity). So if someone refers to the *semiconductor industry*, they're talking about the chip business.[5]

semiconductor

A substance such as silicon dioxide used inside most computer chips that is capable of enabling as well as inhibiting the flow of electricity. From a managerial perspective, when someone refers to semiconductors, they are talking about computer chips, and the semiconductor industry is the chip business.

optical fiber line

A high-speed glass or plastic-lined networking cable used in telecommunications.

Strictly speaking, Moore's Law does not apply to other technology components. But other computing components are also seeing their price versus performance curves skyrocket exponentially.[6] Data storage doubles every twelve months. Networking speed is on a tear, too. With an equipment change at the ends of the cables, the amount of data that can be squirted over an **optical fiber line** has, at times, doubled every nine months.[7] These numbers should be taken as rough approximations and shouldn't be expected to be strictly precise over time. And predictability precision is tough to achieve. For example, some think the advance in hard drive storage (sometimes referred to as Kryder's Law[8]) is decelerating,[9] while others think it is poised to accelerate.[10] Others have claimed that network speeds are now doubling about every twenty-one months.[11] And as mentioned earlier, some say the rate of microprocessor performance relative to Moore's predictions is either slowing or accelerating, depending on if you're looking at traditional PCs or smartphones. Despite any fluctuation, it's clear that the price/performance curve for many technologies is exponential, offering astonishing improvement over time. While the pace of change may vary over time, these graphs (or recalibrated versions, if you like) are useful to managers as rough guides regarding future computing price/performance trends. As so many examples in this text have illustrated, managers without an eye on technology's advancing capabilities are often leading candidates for professional roadkill.

Get Out Your Crystal Ball

price elasticity

The rate at which the demand for a product or service fluctuates with price change. Goods and services that are highly price elastic (e.g., most consumer electronics) see demand spike as prices drop, whereas goods and services that are less price elastic are less responsive to price change (think heart surgery).

Faster and cheaper makes possible the once impossible. As a manager, your job will be about predicting the future. First, consider how the economics of Moore's Law opens new markets. When technology gets cheap, **price elasticity** kicks in. Tech products are highly *price elastic*, meaning consumers buy more products as they become cheaper.[12] And it's not just that existing customers load up on more tech; entire *new markets* open up as firms find new uses for these new chips, technology becomes embedded in new products, and fast/cheap technology enables new services.

Just look at the *evolving waves of computing* we've seen over the previous decades.[13] In the *first wave* in the 1960s, computing was limited to large, room-sized mainframe computers that only governments and big corporations could afford. Moore's Law kicked in during the 1970s for the *second wave*, and minicomputers were a hit. These were refrigerator-sized computers that were as speedy as or speedier than the prior generation of mainframes, yet were affordable for work groups, factories, and smaller organizations. The 1980s brought *wave three* in the form of PCs, and by the end of the decade nearly every white-collar worker in America had a fast and cheap computer on their desk. In the 1990s, *wave four* came in the form of Internet computing; cheap servers and networks made it possible to scatter data around the world at the same time that fast, cheap PCs became mouse-click easy and PC ownership became common in the industrialized world. The following decade saw mobile phones drive what can be considered *computing wave five*. Cheap processors enabled billions of low-end phones, while the march of Moore's Law is driving the smartphone revolution. Today many say this *sixth wave* of computing can be considered the era of *pervasive computing*, where technology is fast and so inexpensive that it is becoming ubiquitously woven into products in ways few imagined years before. Silicon is everywhere! It's in the throwaway radio frequency identification (RFID) tags that track your luggage at the airport. It's the brains inside robot vacuum cleaners, it's built into Legos, it's in the locks that allow Starwood hotel rooms to be opened with a guest's phone, it's in the iBeacon sensors that help you find a hot dog and beer at the ballpark, it's in smart speakers like Echo and HomePod, and it's empowering wearables from smartwatches to in-shirt sensors to Snapchat Spectacles. These digital shifts can rearrange entire industries. Consider that today the firms that sell the most cameras aren't camera companies; they're phone manufacturers offering increasingly sophisticated chip-based digital cameras as a giveaway inside their main product offering. This shift has occurred with such sweeping impact that former photography giants Kodak and the now-merged Konica Minolta have exited the conventional camera business.

Tech Everywhere: From the Smart Thermostat to a Tweeting Diaper

Former Apple vice president Tony Fadell has been called the "Father of the iPod," and he guided the first three iPhones through production. But his next act after Apple, Nest Labs, was decidedly sixth wave—smartening up the lowly thermostat with high-impact results. The Nest is loaded with Moore's Law smarts: motion sensors to tell if anyone's in a room, a temperature sensor, a Wi-Fi connection to grab weather conditions outside—it even runs Linux. The goal is to pay attention to you and the world around your home and to automatically and efficiently adjust your energy use to best fit your needs—no programming needed (although you can tinker with settings via smartphone app if you'd like). Current "dumb" thermostats control about half of the energy use in a typical US home, so this is a big and important market with a potentially massive payoff for consumers and for the environment.[14] Nest users report shaving their heating and cooling bills by about 20 percent on average, saving a collective 2 billion kilowatt hours in two years.[15] Google believed in the less-than-four-year-old firm enough to buy it for $3.2 billion, at the time Google's second most expensive acquisition ever.[16] Apple apparently also believes in the power of the connected home. The firm's HomeKit iOS extensions can control all sorts of Nest-like smart devices for the home, including thermostats, lighting, locks, home security systems, and more.

Nest is just one example of fast, cheap computing showing up in all sorts of products. Cambridge, Massachusetts–based Ambient Devices manufactures a smart umbrella that regularly receives wireless weather reports and will flash when rain is likely, as if to say, "You will soon require my services!" Smart billboards in Japan peer back at passersby to guess at their demographics and instantly change advertising for on-the-spot targeting.[17] And there are experimental efforts that range from the promising Airbus Bag2Go suitcases, which with RFID, GPS, and phone smarts offer quick check-in and never-lost luggage,[18] to the chuckle-worthy Huggies TweetPee, which can send a text or social media post when a child's diaper "activity" is detected.[19] Robust, low-cost hardware hacking is made easier with products like the Raspberry Pi and Arduino, credit card-sized computers that can run a full PC operating system and cost as little as $5.[20] Hacker magazine *The MagPi* included a Raspberry Pi Zero as a freebee in a newstand issue.[21] Netflix shared plans on how to embed an Arduino in a pair of socks to automatically pause the service if motion detection suggests the viewer has fallen asleep (also shared, knitting instructions for show-themed toe-warmers. *Master of None* taco-socks, anyone?).

Internet of Things

A vision where low-cost sensors, processors, and communication are embedded into a wide array of products and our environment, allowing a vast network to collect data, analyze input, and automatically coordinate collective action.

Netflix Socks Video

Netflix shared plans for *Netflix Socks* as a holiday gift idea: Arduino-embedded toe warmers that can sense if the wearer has fallen asleep, and can pause streaming video so you won't miss out because you snoozed while you binged.

View the video online at: //www.youtube.com/embed/Fi6RLrJrjLQ?rel=0

Some refer to these devices as the "**Internet of Things**," where low-cost sensors, computing, and communication put embedded smarts in all sorts of mundane devices so that these products can communicate with one another for data collection, analysis, and collective action.[22] We've already learned that buying a product from Zara that has an RFID tag attached to it will trigger a message to restock shelves, ship more products from a warehouse, and spin up factories for a new order. And there's more to come. Imagine your Nest thermometer coordinating with the rest of your house: closing automated blinds when the sun is hot and high, turning off your water heater when you're away from home, and turning on lights to mimic activity while you're out of town. Smart tags in clothing could communicate with washing machines and dryers and warn the operator if settings could ruin a shirt.

FIGURE 3.2 The Raspberry Pi

The $10 Raspberry Pi Zero W offers impressive specs, including: a 1GHz, single-core CPU, 512MB RAM, Mini-HDMI port, Micro-USB On-The-Go port, Micro-USB power, HAT-compatible 40-pin header, Composite video and reset headers, CSI camera connector, 802.11n Wi-Fi, and Bluetooth 4.0. That's a fairly robust computing platform for less money than most spend on an iPhone cable.

Source: Adafruit Industries.

IBM (you've seen those "Smarter Planet" ads) and General Electric (GE) are among firms pushing to create technology and common languages to turn this vision into a reality. Cities are using smart devices as constant monitors that share information on traffic, available parking spaces, and water quality. GE is outfitting almost everything it builds—from medical equipment to jet engines—with sensors and software so that these devices can share data and coordinate automatically to drive efficiency.[23] GE thinks efficiency gains across multiple sectors—transportation, health care, energy—could boost global GDP by as much as $10 trillion to $15 trillion by 2030[24] (to geek out with video examples like medical imaging, logistics, and 3D printing, see GE's In The Wild series on YouTube). Research group Gartner predicts that there are already some 5 billion connected devices in use today, with an expected 25 billion to be in use by 2020.[25]

Moore's Law Inside Your Medicine Cabinet... and Your Colon

FIGURE 3.3 The GlowCap

The GlowCap from Vitality, Inc., will flash, beep, call, and text you if you've skipped your meds. It can also send reports to you, your doctor, and your loved ones and even notify your pharmacy when it's time for a refill.

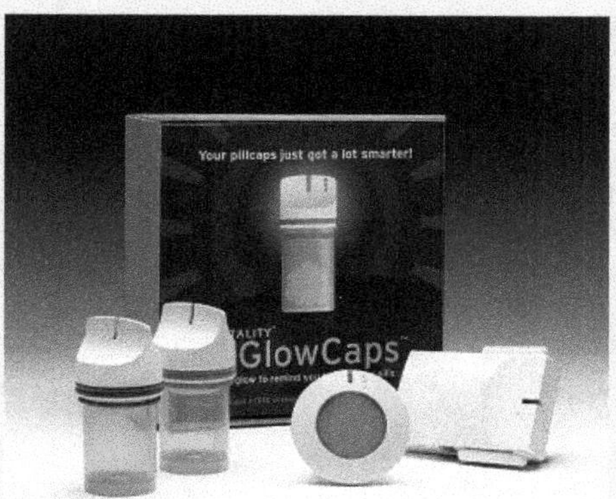

Source: Used with permission from Vitality, Inc.

Moore's Law is coming to your medicine cabinet, and several early-stage efforts show the potential for low-cost computing to improve health care quality while lowering costs. The GlowCap from Vitality, Inc. (now part of NantHealth), is a "smart" pill bottle that will flash when you're supposed to take your medicine. It will play a little tune if you're an hour late for your dose and will also squirt a signal to a nightlight that flashes as a reminder (in case you're out of view of the cap). GlowCaps can also be set to call or send a text if you haven't responded past a set period of time. And the device will send a report to you, your doc, or whomever else you approve. The GlowCap can even alert your pharmacy when it's time for refills. For other kinds of medicines such as inhalers, blister packs, and liquids, Vitality also sells a GlowPack—same concept, different form factor. The bottles sell for as little as $10 but in some cases are likely to be free. The business case for that? The World Health Organization estimates drug adherence at just 50 percent, and analysts estimate that up to $300 billion in increased medical costs and 125,000 annual deaths are due to patients missing their meds.[26] Vitality CEO David Rose (who incidentally also cofounded Ambient Devices) recently cited a test in which GlowCap users reported a 98 percent medication adherence rate.[27]

FIGURE 3.4 PillCam

Swallow the PillCam and the device's twin cameras will relay live video of your insides, helping diagnose gastrointestinal problems.

Source: Medtronic.

And there might also be a chip inside the pills, too! Proteus, a Novartis-backed venture, has developed a sensor made of food and vitamin materials that can be swallowed in medicine. While there is a lot of talk about "wearable" technology, Proteus is an ingestible tech. The sensor is activated and powered by the body's digestive acids (think of your stomach as a battery). Once inside you, the chip sends out a signal with vitals such as heart rate, body angle, temperature, sleep, and more. A waterproof skin patch worn outside the body picks up the signal and can wirelessly relay the pill's findings when the patient walks within twenty feet of their phone. Proteus will then compile a report from the data and send it to their mobile device or e-mail account. The gizmo has already received FDA approval,[28] and Proteus has conducted additional trials for heart disease, hypertension, and tuberculosis, and for monitoring psychiatric illnesses.[29] And a pill with built-in smarts can identify itself to help guard against taking counterfeit drugs, a serious worldwide concern. The CEO of Proteus Health says that soon you may be able to think of your body as "the ultimate game controller."[30]

Pills that chat with mobile phones could help promote telemedicine, bringing health care to hard-to-reach rural populations. The Medtronic PillCam comes with up to two cameras that, once swallowed, can relay images of your innards, used to diagnose intestinal and colon problems[31] (YouTube video of the device in action has been mercifully excluded from this textbook). Your textbook author has ingested a similar device, a Medtronic Bravo Reflux Capsule. No cameras in this one, but it does have sensors and communication smarts to monitor and report on stomach acid. I wore a receiver device around my neck for a weekend, while the heartburn sensor beamed messages through my body from its perch at the end of my esophagus (verdict—no ulcer, but a stomach hernia, ugh). The tweet below shows the lengths I'll go to in capturing a teachable moment for you, dear reader.

John Gallaugher @gallaugher · May 18
Internet of things, get in my belly! As of this morning, my gut has gone high tech. Wearing the oh-so-stylish accompanying data recorder around my neck like a Flavor Flav clock. Of course a teachable moment for Fall.
BRAVO™ REFLUX CAPSULE
The Bravo™ reflux capsule is a device that attaches to the esophageal tissue to assess pH levels and transmits data to the recorder.
1
2

One of the most agile surfers of new generations of computing waves is Apple, Inc.—a firm with a product line that grew so broad, it dropped the word "Computer" from its name. Apple's keen insight on where trends in computing power and performance are headed is captured in this statement by the firm's cofounder the late Steve Jobs: "There's an old Wayne Gretzky quote that I love. 'I skate to where the puck is going to be, not where it has been.' And we've always tried to do that at Apple."[32] The curves above aren't perfect, but they can point to where the puck is headed, helping the savvy manager predict the future, plan for the impossible to become possible, and act as the disruptor rather than the disrupted.

Apple's breakout resurgence owes a great deal to the iPod. At launch, the original iPod sported a 5 GB hard drive that Steve Jobs declared would "put 1,000 songs in your pocket." Cost? $399. Less than six years later, Apple's highest-capacity iPod sold for fifty dollars less than the original, yet held *forty times* the songs. By the iPod's tenth birthday, Apple was giving away 5 GB of storage (for music or other media) for free via its iCloud service. Apple's high-end iPod models have morphed into Internet browsing devices capable of showing maps, playing videos, and gulping down songs from Starbucks' Wi-Fi while waiting in line for a latte.

The original iPod has also become the jumping-off point for new business lines including the iPhone, Apple TV, Apple Watch, iPad, iTunes, the App Store, and HomePod. Surfing the ever-evolving waves of computing has turned Apple into the most valuable company in the United States and the most profitable firm on the planet.[33] Ride these waves to riches, but miss the power and promise of Moore's Law and you risk getting swept away in its riptide. Apple's rise occurred while Sony, a firm once synonymous with portable music, sat on the sidelines unwilling to get on the surfboard. Sony's stock stagnated, barely moving in six years. The firm has laid off thousands of workers while ceding leadership in digital music (and video) to Apple.

TABLE 3.1 Tech's Price/Performance Trends in Action: Amazon Kindle and Apple Music Storage

Amazon Kindle		Apple	
First Generation	Fourth Generation	iPod	iCloud
250 MB	2 GB	5 GB	5 GB
November 2007	September 2011	October 2001	October 2011
$399	$79	$399	Free

Amazon's Kindle also dramatically demonstrates Moore's Law-fueled evolution. The first Kindle sold for nearly $400. Less than four years later, Amazon was selling an updated version for one-fifth that price. Other factors influence price drops, such as being able to produce products and their components at scale, but Moore's Law and related price/performance trends are clearly behind the price decreases we see across a wide variety of tech products and services. Apple's introduction of the iPad, complete with an iBook store, shows how Moore's Law rewrites the boundaries of competition, bringing a firm that started as a computer manufacturer and a firm that started as an online bookstore in direct competition with one another.

While the change in hard drive prices isn't directly part of Moore's Law (hard drives are magnetic storage, not silicon chips), as noted earlier, the faster and cheaper phenomenon applies to storage, too. Amazon provides another example of creating a once-impossible offering courtesy of the trajectory of price/performance technology curves. The firm's "Search Inside the Book" feature required digitizing the images and text from thousands of books in Amazon's catalog. Not only did making books searchable before purchase help customers; titles supporting "Search Inside the Book" enjoyed a 7 percent sales increase over nonsearchable books. Here's where fast/cheap technology comes in. When the feature launched, the database to support this effort was twenty *times* larger than *any* database used by any commercial firm just eight years earlier. For Amazon, the impossible had not just become possible; it became good business.

Bits and Bytes

Computers express data as bits that are either one or zero. Eight bits form a byte (think of a byte as being a single character you can type from a keyboard). A kilobyte refers to roughly a thousand bytes, or a thousand characters, megabyte = 1 million, gigabyte = 1 billion, terabyte = 1 trillion, petabyte = 1 quadrillion, and exabyte = 1 quintillion bytes.

While storage is most often listed in bytes, telecommunication capacity (bandwidth) is often listed in bits per second (bps). The same prefixes apply (Kbps = kilobits, or one thousand bits, per second, Mbps = megabits per second, Gbps = gigabits per second, and Tbps = terabits per second).

These are managerial definitions, but technically, a kilobyte is 2^{10} or 1,024 bytes, mega = 2^{20}, giga = 2^{30}, tera = 2^{40}, peta = 2^{50}, and exa = 2^{60}. To get a sense for how much data we're talking about, see the following table.[34]

TABLE 3.2 Bytes Defined

	Managerial Definition	Exact Amount	To Put It in Perspective
1 Byte	One keyboard character	8 bits	1 letter or number = 1 byte
1 Kilobyte (KB)	One thousand bytes	2^{10} bytes	1 typewritten page = 2 KB
			1 digital book (Kindle) = approx. 500–800 KB
1 Megabyte (MB)	One million bytes	2^{20} bytes	1 digital photo (7 megapixels) = 1.3 MB
			1 MP3 song = approx. 3 MB
			1 CD = approx. 700 MB
1 Gigabyte (GB)	One billion bytes	2^{30} bytes	1 DVD movie = approx. 4.7 GB
			1 Blu-ray movie = approx. 25 GB
1 Terabyte (TB)	One trillion bytes	2^{40} bytes	Printed collection of the Library of Congress = 20 TB
1 Petabyte (PB)	One quadrillion bytes	2^{50} bytes	Master copies of the shows and movies available on Netflix (2013) = 3.14 PB[35]
1 Exabyte (EB)	One quintillion bytes	2^{60} bytes	Estimated total data stored in the NSA's Bluffdale, Utah, data center (includes data from hard drives, overseas data centers, cell phones, and more) = 12 EB[36]
1 Zettabyte (ZB)	One sextillion bytes	2^{70} bytes	Estimated total annual amount of data transmitted over the Internet by 2018 = 1.6 ZB[37]

Here's another key implication for the curves shown earlier: if you are producing products subject to radically improving price/performance, then these products will rapidly fall in value over time. That's great when it makes your product cheaper and opens up new markets for your firm, but it can be deadly if you overproduce and have excess inventory sitting on shelves for long periods of time. Dell claims its inventory depreciates as much as a single percentage point in value each week.[38] That's a big incentive to carry as little inventory as possible, and to unload it, fast!

While the strategic side of tech may be the most glamorous, Moore's Law impacts mundane management tasks, as well. From an accounting and budgeting perspective, as a manager you'll need to consider a number of questions: How long will your computing equipment remain useful? If you keep upgrading computing and software, what does this mean for your capital expense budget? Your training budget? Your ability to make well-reasoned predictions regarding tech's direction will be key to answering these questions.

Tech: A Helping Hand to Escape Poverty

Another tech product containing a microprocessor is transforming the lives of some of the world's most desperate poor—the cell phone. There are three billion people worldwide who don't yet have a phone, but they will, soon. In the ultimate play of Moore's Law opening up new markets, Chinese mobiles priced at $10 have been available for years,[39] while Google hopes its Android Go with its stripped-down, data-light, low-power smartphone experience, will connect a billion of the world's currently unconnected population.[40] It took roughly twenty years to sell a billion mobile phones worldwide; the second billion sold in four years; and the third billion took just two years. Today, some 80 percent of the world's population lives within cellular network range, and the vast majority of mobile subscriptions are in developing countries.[41]

Why such demand? Mobiles change lives for the better. According to economist Jeffrey Sachs, "The cell phone is the single most transformative technology for world economic development."[42] A London Business School study found that for every ten mobile phones per one hundred people, a country's GDP bumps up 0.5 percent.[43] Think about the farmer who can verify prices and locate buyers before harvesting and transporting perishable crops to market; the laborer who was mostly unemployed but with a mobile is now reachable by those who have day-to-day work; the mother who can find out if a doctor is in and has medicine before taking off work to make the costly trek to a remote clinic with her sick child; or the immigrant laborer serving as a housekeeper who was "more or less an indentured servant until she got a cell phone," enabling new customers to call and book her services.[44]

Three-quarters of the world's poorest people get their food and income by farming.[45] But isolated rural farmers often suffer from an information asymmetry problem (see [Content Removed: #fwk-38086-ch02]). These farmers traditionally don't have accurate information on what their products are worth, and in many communities, less scrupulous traders will buy up harvests at far-below-market rates, only to resell them and pocket the profits for themselves. Coming to the aid of farmers, the Ghanaian firm Esoko delivers market prices, farming tips, and other key information via text message on even the lowest-end cell phones. In one study, farmers using Esoko reported a 10 percent increase in revenue.[46] Other reports have revenue increases as high as 25 to 40 percent.[47] Esoko offers a breadth of services that range from helping farmers find transport services to helping buyers locate farmers with goods to sell.

Promotional Video of Esoko's Market Information System

View the video online at: //www.youtube.com/embed/tcGuW-Mc48k?rel=0

The Launch of Safaricom's M-PESA

This TechChange video is narrated by Michael Joseph, managing director of mobile money at Vodafone.

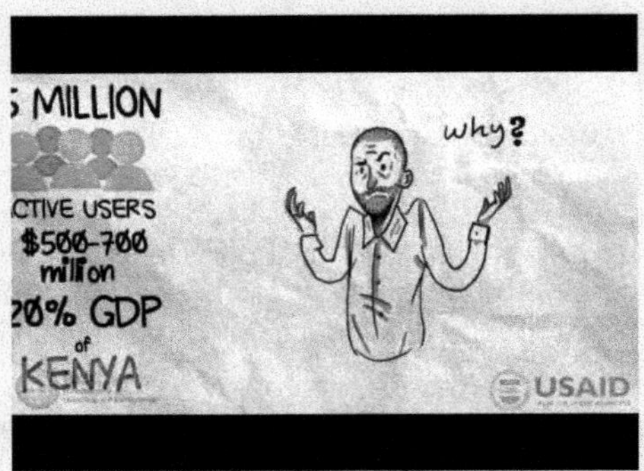

View the video online at: //www.youtube.com/embed/i0dBWaen3aQ?rel=0

When phones can be used as currency for purchases or payments, who needs Visa or, for that matter, a wallet and cash? The M-PESA mobile banking service, run by Kenya's Safaricom, allows customers to transfer cash using text messages. Nearly every Kenyan adult has an M-PESA account, paying for everything from groceries to cab rides to school tuition. The service can also allow family members to quickly and securely send cash across the country. Only 4 million Kenyans have traditional bank accounts, but 25 million use M-PESA, and upwards of 44 percent of Kenya's GDP flows through the service.[48] M-PESA is spreading to other regions and is even used in Afghanistan, while similar schemes are offered by firms such as WIZZIT in South Africa, Zaad in Somaliland, and GCash in the Philippines. The "mobile phone as bank" may bring banking to a billion unserved customers in a few years.

Key Takeaways

- Moore's Law applies to the semiconductor industry. The widely accepted managerial interpretation of Moore's Law states that for the same money, roughly eighteen months from now you should be able to purchase computer chips that are twice as fast or store twice as much information. Or over that same time period, chips with the speed or storage of today's chips should cost half as much as they do now.
- Nonchip-based technology also advances rapidly. Disk drive storage doubles roughly every twelve months, while equipment to speed transmissions over fiberoptic lines has doubled every nine months. While these numbers are rough approximations, the price/performance curve of these technologies continues to advance exponentially.
- These trends influence inventory value, depreciation accounting, employee training, and other managerial functions. They also help improve productivity and keep interest rates low.
- From a strategic perspective, these trends suggest that what is impossible from a cost or performance perspective today may be possible in the future. Fast/cheap computing also feeds a special kind of price elasticity where whole new markets are created. This fact provides an opportunity to those who recognize and can capitalize on the capabilities of new technology. As technology advances, new industries, business models, and products are created, while established firms and ways of doing business can be destroyed.

- Managers must regularly study trends and trajectory in technology to recognize opportunity and avoid disruption.
- Moore's Law (and related advances in fast/cheap technologies in things like storage and telecommunications) has driven six waves of disruptive, market-transforming computing. The sixth wave involves embedding intelligence and communications in all sorts of mundane devices. Some point to a future "Internet of Things," where objects will collect and share data and automatically coordinate collective action for radical efficiency improvements.

Questions and Exercises

1. What is Moore's Law? What does it apply to?
2. Are other aspects of computing advancing as well? At what approximate rates? What is Kryder's Law?
3. What is a microprocessor? What devices do you or your family own that contain microprocessors (and hence are impacted by Moore's Law)?
4. What is a semiconductor? What is the substance from which most semiconductors are made?
5. How does flash memory differ from the memory in a PC? Are both solid state?
6. Which of the following are solid-state devices: an iPod shuffle, an iPhone, a USB flash drive, a TiVo DVR, a typical laptop PC?
7. Why is Moore's Law important for managers? How does it influence managerial thinking?
8. What is price elasticity? How does Moore's Law relate to this concept? What's special about falling chip prices compared to price drops for products like clothing or food?
9. Give examples of firms that have effectively leveraged the advancement of processing, storage, and networking technology.
10. What are the six waves of computing? Give examples of firms and industries impacted by the sixth wave.
11. As Moore's Law advances, technology becomes increasingly accessible to the poor. Give examples of how tech has benefited those who likely would not have been able to afford the technology of a prior generation.
12. How have cheaper, faster chips impacted the camera industry? Give an example of the leadership shifts that have occurred in this industry.
13. What has been the impact of "faster, cheaper" on Apple's business lines?
14. How did Amazon utilize the steep decline in magnetic storage costs to its advantage?
15. How does Moore's Law impact production and inventory decisions?
16. Research the impact of mobile phones on poor regions of the world. Come to class prepared to discuss examples that demonstrate the potential for fast/cheap technology to improve society, even for individuals with extremely low incomes.
17. The "Internet of Things" makes for compelling commercials, but what needs to happen before a world of interconnected, coordinating devices can become a reality? What implications does this raise for business and society with respect to issues such as privacy and security? If you were GE, would you seek to keep the communication language among smart devices proprietary or open? Why or why not?

3.2 The Death of Moore's Law?

Learning Objectives

1. Describe why Moore's Law continues to advance and discuss the physical limitations of this advancement.
2. Name and describe various technologies that may extend the life of Moore's Law.
3. Discuss the limitations of each of these approaches.

fabs

Semiconductor fabrication facilities; the multibillion dollar plants used to manufacture semiconductors.

silicon wafer

A thin, circular slice of material used to create semiconductor devices. Hundreds of chips may be etched on a single wafer, where they are eventually cut out for individual packaging.

Moore's Law isn't a precise scientific truth, like Boyle's Law or relativity. Moore simply observed that we're getting better over time at squeezing more stuff into tinier spaces. Moore's Law is possible because the distance between the pathways inside silicon chips gets smaller with each successive generation. While chip factories (semiconductor fabrication facilities, or **fabs**) are incredibly expensive to build, each new generation of fabs can crank out more chips per **silicon wafer**. And since the pathways are closer together, electrons travel shorter distances. If electronics now travel half the distance to make a calculation, that means the chip is twice as fast.

While shrinking silicon pathways creates better chips, packing pathways tightly together creates problems associated with three interrelated forces—*size*, *heat*, and *power*—that together are threatening to slow down Moore's Law's advance. When you make processors smaller, the more tightly packed electrons will heat up a chip—so much so that unless today's most powerful chips are cooled down, they will melt inside their packaging. To keep the fastest computers cool, many PCs, laptops, and video game consoles need fans, and most corporate data centers have elaborate and expensive air conditioning and venting systems to prevent a meltdown. A trip through the Facebook data center during its early growth would have shown that the firm was a "hot" startup in more ways than one. The firm's servers ran at temperatures so high that the Plexiglas sides of the firm's server racks were warped and melting![49] The need to cool modern data centers draws a lot of power and that costs a lot of money.

The chief eco officer at Sun Microsystems has claimed that computers draw 4 to 5 percent of the world's power. Google's chief technology officer has said that the firm spends more to power its servers than the cost of the servers themselves.[50] Apple, Facebook, Microsoft, Yahoo! and Google have all built massive data centers in the Pacific Northwest, away from their corporate headquarters, specifically choosing these locations for access to cheap hydroelectric power. Google's location in The Dalles, Oregon, is charged a cost per kilowatt hour less than one-fifth the rate the firm pays in Silicon Valley.[51] This difference means big savings for a firm that runs more than a million servers.

And while these powerful shrinking chips are getting hotter and more costly to cool, it's also important to realize that chips can't get smaller forever. At some point Moore's Law will run into the unyielding laws of nature. While we're not certain where these limits are, chip pathways certainly can't be shorter than a single molecule, and the actual physical limit is likely larger than that. Get too small and a phenomenon known as quantum tunneling kicks in, and electrons start to slide off their paths. Yikes! While the death of Moore's Law has been predicted for years, scientists continue to squeeze advancement through new manufacturing techniques. Many think that while Moore's Law has celebrated its fiftieth birthday, it may not make it to sixty.[52]

Buying Time

One way to address the problem of densely packed, overheating chip designs is with **multicore microprocessors**, made by putting two or more lower power processor cores (think of a core as the calculating part of a microprocessor) on a single chip. Philip Emma, IBM's manager of systems technology and microarchitecture, offers an analogy. Think of the traditional fast, hot, single-core processors as a 300-pound lineman, and a dual-core processor as two 160-pound guys. Says Emma, "A 300-pound lineman can generate a lot of power, but two 160-pound guys can do the same work with less overall effort."[53] For many applications, the multicore chips will outperform a single speedy chip, while running cooler and drawing less power. Multicore processors are now mainstream.

multicore microprocessors

Microprocessors with two or more (typically lower power) calculating processor cores on the same piece of silicon.

Today, nearly all smartphones, PCs, and laptops sold have at least a two-core (dual-core) processor. The Microsoft Xbox One and PlayStation 4 both have eight core processors. Intel has even demonstrated chips with upwards of fifty cores.

Multicore processors can run older software written for single-brain chips. But they usually do this by using only one core at a time. To reuse the metaphor above, this is like having one of our 160-pound workers lift away, while the other one stands around watching. Multicore operating systems can help achieve some performance gains. Versions of Windows or the Mac OS that are aware of multicore processors can assign one program to run on one core, while a second application is assigned to the next core. But in order to take full advantage of multicore chips, applications need to be rewritten to split up tasks so that smaller portions of a problem are executed simultaneously inside each core.

Writing code for this "divide and conquer" approach is not trivial. In fact, developing software for multicore systems has been described by Shahrokh Daijavad, software lead for next-generation computing systems at IBM, as "one of the hardest things you learn in computer science."[54] Microsoft's chief research and strategy officer has called coding for these chips "the most conceptually different [change] in the history of modern computing."[55] Despite this challenge, some of the most aggressive adaptors of multicore chips have been video game console manufacturers. Video game applications are particularly well suited for multiple cores since, for example, one core might be used to render the background, another to draw objects, another for the "physics engine" that moves the objects around, and yet another to handle Internet communications for multiplayer games.

Another way of accelerating processing speed is to use chips that are designed to be really good at a subset of tasks. The graphics chip firms Nvidia (pronounced "en-VID-ee-ah") and AMD were originally designed to do lots of simultaneous calculations necessary for animation and other image work. Many graphics chips have been built with hundreds or in some cases thousands of cores to handle such tasks. And it turns out those multiple, small calculations, while not good for running end-user apps like Word or Excel, are especially well suited for so-called artificial intelligence/machine learning tasks like image and voice recognition. These tasks are usually performed "in the cloud," as opposed to on your smartphone or computer. Speak to Siri, Alexa, Cortana, or say "OK Google," and your voice is sent over the Internet to be decoded by a collection of computers at Apple, Amazon, Microsoft, or Google, which will then work to find the best result for your query, then send the answer back from the cloud to your device.

Google has even begun designing its own chips to handle its specific AI needs. Terms you might hear in this space include ASICs (pronounced "ay-sicks"), which means "application-specific integrated circuits," chips specifically designed to be really good at a specific kind of task; and field-programmable gate arrays (FPGAs), which are chips that can be programmed after purchase, rerouting logical pathways for application-specific efficiency in ways that aren't possible with a general purpose microprocessor like the Intel chip in your laptop (an approach preferred by Microsoft).[56] And while writing "divide and conquer" code to split up tasks to get single, best results is still tricky, new programming environments, such as Nvidia's CUDA, are making this easier.[57]

TABLE 3.3 Comparison Chart

Microprocessors	ASICs	FPGAs
General Purpose Microprocessors: Sometimes called CPUs for central processing units. Can handle most any tasks, so you'll find them as the "main brain" in your PC (Intel-based) and smart phone (ARM-based). **Pros**: Can do just about anything, so they are far better generalists than ASICs or FPGAs. Supported by a large base of existing software. **Cons**: Are slower for many tasks, and chips are power-hungry, requiring more energy. **Players**: Intel (leader in PCs and servers), ARM (designs are the basis of most smartphone microprocessors, including Apple, Samsung, and Qualcomm)	**ASICs**: Application-specific integrated circuits are chips designed to do a subset of tasks very quickly and efficiently. **Pros**: Very fast and power efficient. Great for graphics and AI/machine learning. **Cons**: Can be costly to design and expensive to manufacture a very custom product. **Players**: Nvidia and AMD. Google has built its own AI-specific chip (the Tensor processing unit), but only the biggest firms with a specific need for a massive amount of such chips could justify the expense of doing this.	**FPGAs**: Field programma gate arrays can have their on-chip logic re-routed to better performance for a s task. **Pros**: Faster and more energy-efficient than gene purpose microprocessors be upgraded via software field" after installation. A c alternative than designing manufacturing a custom b unchangeable ASIC. **Cons**: ASICs designed fro scratch for specific tasks faster/more efficient. **Players**: Intel-owned Alte Xilinx. Microsoft uses FPG Bing and other cloud task

Source: https://newsroom.intel.com/press-kits/intel-core-x-series-processors/ and https://www.altera.com/about/news_room.html

Another approach that's breathing more life into Moore's Law moves chips from being paper-flat devices to built-up 3-D affairs. By building up as well as out, firms are radically boosting speed and efficiency of chips. Intel has flipped upward the basic component of chips—the transistor. Transistors are the supertiny on-off switches in a chip that work collectively to calculate or store things in memory (a high-end microprocessor might include over two billion transistors). While you won't notice that chips are much thicker, Intel says that on the miniscule scale of modern chip manufacturing, the new designs are 37 percent faster and half as power hungry as conventional chips.[58]

New Materials and Quantum Leaps? Thinking Beyond Moore's Law—Constraining Silicon

Think about it—the triple threat of size, heat, and power means that Moore's Law, perhaps the greatest economic gravy train in history, will likely come to a grinding halt in your lifetime. Multicore and 3-D transistors are here today, but what else is happening to help stave off the death of Moore's Law?

Every once in a while a material breakthrough comes along that improves chip performance. A few years back researchers discovered that replacing a chip's aluminum components with copper could increase speeds up to 30 percent. Now scientists are concentrating on improving the very semiconductor material that chips are made of. While the silicon used in chips is wonderfully abundant (it has pretty much the same chemistry found in sand), researchers are investigating other materials that might allow for chips with even tighter component densities. New processors made with silicon germanium, germanium, or grapheme have all been mentioned as next-gen candidates.[59] Hyperefficient chips of the future may also be made out of carbon nanotubes, once the technology to assemble the tiny structures becomes commercially viable.

Other designs move away from electricity over silicon. Optical computing, where signals are sent via light rather than electricity, promises to be faster than conventional chips, if lasers can be mass produced in miniature (silicon laser experiments show promise). Others are experimenting by crafting computing components using biological material (think a DNA-based storage device).

One yet-to-be-proven technology that could blow the lid off what's possible today is quantum computing. Conventional computing stores data as a combination of bits, where a bit is either a one or a zero. Quantum computers, leveraging principles of quantum physics, employ qubits that can be both one *and* zero at the same time. Add a bit to a conventional computer's memory and you double its capacity. Add a bit to a quantum computer and its capacity increases exponentially. For comparison, consider that a computer model of serotonin, a molecule vital to regulating the human central nervous system, would require 10^{94} bytes of information. Unfortunately there's not enough matter in the universe to build a computer that big. But modeling a serotonin molecule using quantum computing would take just 424 qubits.[60]

Some speculate that quantum computers could one day allow pharmaceutical companies to create hyperdetailed representations of the human body that reveal drug side effects before they're even tested on humans. Quantum computing might also accurately predict the weather months in advance or offer unbreakable computer security. Opportunities abound. Of course, before quantum computing can be commercialized, researchers need to harness the freaky properties of quantum physics wherein your answer may reside in another universe, or could disappear if observed (Einstein himself referred to certain behaviors in quantum physics as "spooky action at a distance").

Pioneers in quantum computing include IBM, HP, NEC, and a Canadian startup named D-Wave, which has sold early-stage quantum computers to Google, NASA, and Lockheed Martin.[61] If or when the full promise of quantum computing will become a reality is still unknown, but scientists and engineers are hoping that by the time Moore's Law runs into Mother Nature's limits, a new way of computing may blow past anything we can do with silicon, continuing to make possible the once impossible.

Key Takeaways

- As chips get smaller and more powerful, they get hotter and present power-management challenges. And at some point, Moore's Law will stop because we will no longer be able to shrink the spaces between components on a chip.
- Multicore chips use two or more low-power calculating "cores" to work together in unison, but to take optimal advantage of multicore chips, software must be rewritten to "divide" a task among multiple cores.
- 3-D transistors are also helping extend Moore's Law by producing chips that require less power and run faster.
- New materials may extend the life of Moore's Law, allowing chips to get smaller. Entirely new methods for calculating, such as quantum computing, may also dramatically increase computing capabilities far beyond what is available today.

Questions and Exercises

1. What three interrelated forces threaten to slow the advancement of Moore's Law?
2. Which commercial solutions, described in the previous section, are currently being used to counteract the forces mentioned? How do these solutions work? What are the limitations of each?
3. Will multicore chips run software designed for single-core processors?
4. As chips grow smaller they generate increasing amounts of heat that needs to be dissipated. Why is keeping systems cool such a challenge? What are the implications for a firm like Yahoo! or Google? For a firm like Apple or Dell?
5. What are some of the materials that may replace the silicon that current chips are made of?
6. Search online to assess the current state of quantum computing. What kinds of problems might be solved if the promise of quantum computing is achieved? How might individuals and organizations leverage quantum computing? What sorts of challenges could arise from the widespread availability of such powerful computing technology?

3.3 The Power of Parallel: Supercomputing, Grids, Clusters, and Putting Smarts in the Cloud

Learning Objectives

1. Understand the differences between supercomputing, grid computing, cluster computing, and cloud computing.
2. Describe how grid computing can transform the economics of supercomputing.
3. Recognize that these technologies provide the backbone of remote computing resources used in cloud computing.
4. Understand the characteristics of problems that are and are not well suited for parallel processing found in modern supercomputing, grid computing, cluster computing, and multicore processors. Also be able to discuss how network latency places limits on offloading computing to the cloud.

supercomputers

Computers that are among the fastest of any in the world at the time of their introduction.

As Moore's Law makes possible the once impossible, businesses have begun to demand access to the world's most powerful computing technology. **Supercomputers** are computers that are among the fastest of any in the world at the time of their introduction.[62] Supercomputing was once the domain of governments and high-end research labs, performing tasks such as simulating the explosion of nuclear devices, or analyzing large-scale weather and climate phenomena. But it turns out with a bit of tweaking, the algorithms used in this work are profoundly useful to business.

Corporate use of supercomputing varies widely. United Airlines used supercomputing to increase the number of flight-path combinations for scheduling systems from 3,000 to 350,000. Estimated savings through better yield management? Over $50 million! CIBC (the Canadian Imperial Bank of Commerce), one of the largest banks in North America, uses supercomputing to run its portfolio through Monte Carlo simulations that aren't all that different from the math used to simulate nuclear explosions. The muscular mathematics CIBC performs allows the firm to lower capital on hand by hundreds of millions of dollars, a substantial percentage of the bank's capital, saving millions a year in funding costs. Also noteworthy: the supercomputer-enabled, risk-savvy CIBC was relatively unscathed by the subprime crisis.

Modern supercomputing is typically done via a technique called **massively parallel** processing (computers designed with many microprocessors that work together, simultaneously, to solve problems). The fastest of these supercomputers are built using hundreds or even thousands of microprocessors, all programmed to work in unison as one big brain. While supercomputers use special electronics and software to handle the massive load, the processors themselves are often of the off-the-shelf variety that you'd find in a computer at BestBuy. For example, the recent speed champ, China's Tianhe (or "Milky Way") 2, uses 32,000 Intel Xeon chips, 48,000 co-processing chips, and sports a total of 3.1 million cores.[63]

massively parallel

Computers designed with many microprocessors that work together, simultaneously, to solve problems.

Another technology, known as **grid computing**, is further transforming the economics of high performance. With grid computing, firms place special software on its existing PCs or servers that enables these computers to work together on a common problem. While many firms set up grids in data centers from servers they've bought specifically to work together on corporate tasks, large organizations have also created grids by harnessing excess capacity from staff PCs when these computers aren't being used or aren't used to full capacity. With grid software installed, idle devices can be marshaled to attack portions of a complex task as if they collectively were one massively parallel supercomputer. *BusinessWeek* reports that while a middle-of-the-road supercomputer could run as much as $30 million, grid computing software and services to perform comparable tasks can cost as little as $25,000, assuming an organization already has PCs and servers in place.

grid computing

A type of computing that uses special software to enable several computers to work together on a common problem, as if they were a massively parallel supercomputer.

The biotech firm Monsanto uses this technology to explore ways to manipulate genes to create crop strains that are resistant to cold, drought, bugs, and pesticides, or that are more nutritious. The fiftyfold time savings the firm achieved through grid computing lets Monsanto consider thousands of genetic combinations in a year.[64] Lower R&D time means faster time to market—critical to both the firm and its customers. Movie studios use grids for animation and special effects; Procter & Gamble used the technology to redesign manufacturing for Pringles potato chips; Pratt & Whitney tests aircraft engine designs by employing grid technology; GM and Ford use grids to simulate crash tests; and JP Morgan Chase launched a grid effort that mimics CIBC's supercomputer, but at a fraction of the latter's cost. By the second year of operation, the JP Morgan Chase grid was saving the firm $5 million per year.

Another term you might hear is **cluster computing**. Computing clusters are also built with commodity servers, but they usually take advantage of special software and networking hardware to more tightly link them together to function as one. The geeky details of how tightly or loosely coupled devices are—and whether this classifies as a grid or cluster—are less important, but as a manager you should be able to recognize these terms and think critically about their potential use and limitations.

cluster computing

Connecting server computers via software and networking so that their resources can be used to collectively solve computing tasks.

Multicore, massively parallel, grid, and cluster computing are all related in that each attempts to lash together multiple computing devices so that they can work together to solve problems. Think of multicore chips as having several processors in a single chip. Think of massively parallel supercomputers as having several chips in one computer, and think of grid and cluster computing as using existing computers to work together on a single task (essentially a computer made up of multiple computers), with clusters being more "tightly coupled" with additional software and networking hardware to facilitate their coordination. While these technologies offer great promise, they're all subject to the same limitation: software must be written to divide existing problems into smaller pieces that can be handled by each core, processor, or computer, respectively. Some problems, such as simulations, are easy to split up, but for problems that are linear (where, for example, step two can't be started until the results from step one are known), the multiple-brain approach doesn't offer much help.

software as a service (SaaS)

A form of cloud computing where a firm subscribes to a third-party software and receives a service that is delivered online.

cloud computing

Replacing computing resources—either an organization's or individual's hardware or software—with services provided over the Internet.

server farms

A massive network of computer servers running software to coordinate their collective use. Server farms provide the infrastructure backbone to SaaS and hardware cloud efforts, as well as many large-scale Internet services.

latency

A term often used in computing that refers to delay, especially when discussing networking and data transfer speeds. Low-latency systems are faster systems.

Massive collections of computers running software that allows them to operate as a unified service also enable new service-based computing models, such as **software as a service (SaaS)** and **cloud computing**. In these models, organizations replace traditional software and hardware that they would run in-house with services that are delivered online. Google, Microsoft, Salesforce.com, and Amazon are among the firms that have sunk billions into these Moore's Law-enabled **server farms**, creating entirely new businesses that promise to radically redraw the software and hardware landscape while bringing gargantuan computing power to the little guy (see [Content Removed: #fwk-38086-ch10]). Technology such as the IBM Watson cloud act like a supercomputer for hire. Researchers have leveraged the technology to, as *New Scientist* states "make discoveries scientists can't" by scanning massive databases of research and hunting for patterns humans have missed.[65] Moving "brains" to the cloud can help increase calculating performance even when we can't pack more processing brawn into our devices, but the cloud requires a long-distance connection that's a lot slower and perhaps less reliable than the quick hop from storage to processor that occurs inside most consumer electronics. In tech circles, delay is sometimes referred to as **latency**—and low latency is good. It means communications are speedy. As an example of how latency limits what the cloud can do, consider the new generation of Xbox: the Xbox One. Microsoft has designed the gaming system so that it can offload some tasks to its massive 300,000-server gaming data centers if they don't require an immediate response. Latency-sensitive tasks that can't be shipped to the cloud might include reactions to bumping collisions in a racing game, or crossfire in a shooter. But the cloud could easily handle complex calculations to load as needed, such as rendering a scene's background and lighting.[66]

Paging Doctor Watson... And Teacher Watson... And Trader Watson... And...

If there were a Supercomputer Hall of Fame, it would almost certainly include the IBM-created, Jeopardy-playing Watson. However, while initially billed as a "supercomputer," Watson today is a robust, cloud-based computing platform that allows any organization to tap into all sorts of services, including natural language processing (to easily create interactive query systems and chat bots), image recognition, data analysis, machine learning to uncover new insights and identify unseen patterns, and more.

Originally built to quickly answer questions posed in natural language, by the end of a televised three-day tournament Watson had put the hurt on prior Jeopardy champs Ken Jennings and Brad Rutter, trouncing the human rivals and winning one million dollars (donated to a children's charity). Watson's accomplishment represented a four-year project that involved some twenty-five people across eight IBM research labs, creating algorithms, in a system with ninety servers, "many, many" processors, terabytes of storage, and "tens of millions of dollars" in investment.[67] Winning Jeopardy makes for a few nights of interesting TV, but what else can it do? Well, the "Deep QA" technology behind Watson is already being used by health care professionals as a kind of "exobrain." On average, "primary care physicians spend less than twenty minutes face-to-face with each patient per visit, and average little more than an hour each week reading medical journals."[68] Now imagine a physician assistant Watson that could leverage massive diagnosis databases while scanning hundreds of pages in a person's medical history, surfacing a best guess at what docs should be paying attention to. A *JAMA* study suggested that medical errors may be the third leading cause of death in the United States,[69] so there's apparently an enormous and mighty troubling opportunity in health care alone. IBM is partnering with Massachusetts voice-recognition leader Nuance Communications (the tech that originally made Apple's Siri such a good listener) to bring Watson to the doc's office. Med schools at Columbia and the University of Maryland are helping with the research effort. Manipal Hospitals in India are using Watson to bring global insights from research and practice worldwide for use creating individual cancer treatment programs.[70] Of course, you wouldn't want to completely trust a Watson recommendation. While Watson was good enough to be tournament champ, IBM's baby missed a final Jeopardy answer of "Chicago" because it answered that Toronto was a US city.

FIGURE 3.5 Watson Competes on Jeopardy

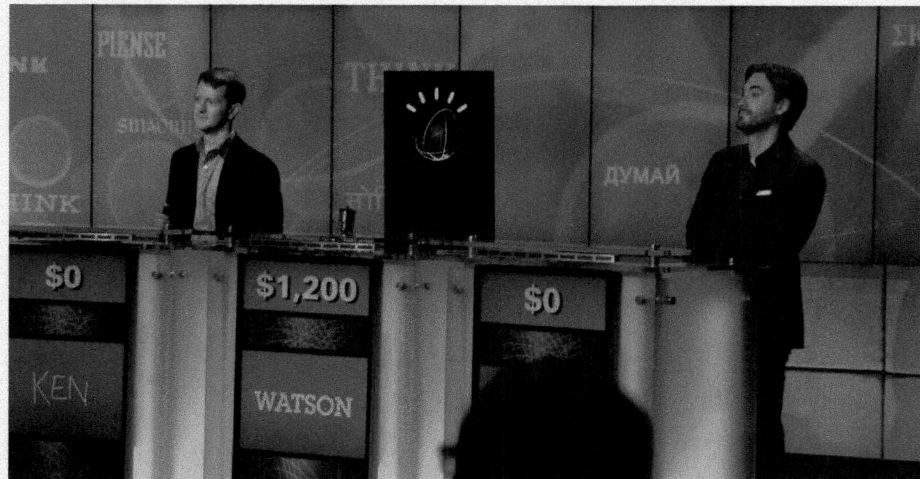

Source: http://www.ibm.com/press.

IBM is aggressively encouraging others to take advantage of Watson technology. Today, Watson tech has been applied to over 75 industries in 17 nations, with tens of thousands of people leveraging Watson-smarts to assist their own work.[71] Pfizer is using Watson to speed drug discovery research by leveraging IBM technology to dig insights from a vast library that ranges from medical publications to patent applications.[72] In finance, IBM offers Watson services to comply with banking regulation (some 20,000 new regulatory requirements were introduced in a single year, and regulatory compliance eats up more than 10 percent of operation spending at major banks).[73] A suite of Watson marketing tools helps firms from Kia Motors to The North Face analyze and mine social media, identify audiences, predict behavior, and build targeted marketing plans.[74] And Sesame Workshop (the firm behind Grover and Big Bird), have used Watson to develop software that delivers kid-specific vocabulary learning.[75] The group's swanky Manhattan digs provide a base for showcasing the tech to clients, and provide resources to third parties looking to bake Watson smarts into their own offerings using the "Watson Cloud," and other resources. The suite of tools for using Watson range from no-code platforms for any manager to highly technical products that allow programmers and data analysts to deeply customize help sought through the Watson cloud. IBM will even provide seed capital to efforts it deems most promising. A recent Watson Mobile App Challenge winner, the firm Elemental Path, is launching a dinosaur-shaped child's toy that uses Watson's Q&A smarts to answer kid questions, tell jokes and stories, and quiz kids as a learning buddy. The toy learns a child's interests and comprehension level, and tailors interaction as its understanding of its owner develops. A Kickstarter campaign for the product zoomed past its initial goal, and underscores how a few bright researchers can leverage cloud resources and plummeting costs to build something that was not just cost-prohibitive, it was impossible just a few years back.[76]

Cognitoys Dinosaur with Watson Smarts

Kickstarter video for Elemental Path's CogniToys Dinosaur, which interacts with children using Watson smarts accessed over the cloud. Moore's Law combined with savvy networking brings supercomputing-class technology into a sub-$90 child's toy.

View the video online at: //www.youtube.com/embed/o1tm5Xs5vlw?rel=0

Moore's Law will likely hit its physical limit in your lifetime, but no one really knows if this "Moore's Wall" is a decade away or more. What lies ahead is anyone's guess. Some technologies, such as still-experimental quantum computing, could make computers that are more powerful than all the world's conventional computers combined. Think strategically—new waves of innovation might soon be shouting "surf's up!"

Key Takeaways

- Most modern supercomputers use massive sets of microprocessors working in parallel.
- The microprocessors used in most modern supercomputers are often the same commodity chips that can be found in conventional PCs and servers.
- Moore's Law means that businesses as diverse as financial services firms, industrial manufacturers, consumer goods firms, and film studios can now afford access to supercomputers.
- Grid computing software uses existing computer hardware to work together and mimic a massively parallel supercomputer. Using existing hardware for a grid can save a firm the millions of dollars it might otherwise cost to buy a conventional supercomputer, further bringing massive computing capabilities to organizations that would otherwise never benefit from this kind of power.
- Cluster computing refers to collections of server computers that are linked together via software and networking hardware so that they can function as a single computing resource.
- Massively parallel computing also enables the vast server farms that power online businesses like Google and Facebook, and creates new computing models, like software as a service (SaaS) and cloud computing.
- The characteristics of problems best suited for solving via multicore systems, parallel supercomputers, grid, or cluster computing are those that can be divided up so that multiple calculating components can simultaneously work on a portion of the problem. Problems that are linear—where one part must be solved before moving to the next and the next—may have difficulty benefiting from these kinds of "divide and conquer" computing. Fortunately,

many problems such as financial risk modeling, animation, manufacturing simulation, and gene analysis are all suited for parallel systems.

- Many computer tasks can be offloaded to the cloud, but networking speeds (latency)—that is, the time needed to send results back and forth—can limit instances where collections of off-site computing hardware can replace or augment local computing.

Questions and Exercises

1. Show your familiarity with key terms: What are the differences between supercomputing, grid computing, and cluster computing? How are these phenomena empowered by Moore's Law?
2. How does grid computing using slack or excess computing resources change the economics of supercomputing?
3. Name businesses that are using supercomputing and grid computing. Describe these uses and the advantages they offer their adopting firms. Are they a source of competitive advantage? Why or why not?
4. What are the characteristics of problems that are most easily solved using the types of parallel computing found in grids, clusters, and modern-day supercomputers? What are the characteristics of the sorts of problems not well suited for this type of computing?
5. You can join a grid, too! Visit the SETI@home website (http://setiathome.ssl.berkeley.edu/). What is the purpose of the SETI@Home project? How do you participate? Is there any possible danger to your computer if you choose to participate? (Read their rules and policies.) Do some additional research on the Internet. Are there other interesting grid efforts that you can load onto your laptop or even game console?
6. Search online to identify the five fastest supercomputers currently in operation. Who sponsors these machines? What are they used for? How many processors do they have?
7. What is "Moore's Wall"?
8. What is the advantage of using computing to simulate an automobile crash test as opposed to actually staging a crash?
9. Moore's Law may limit the amount of computing done on the PC, smartphone, or gaming console in front of you. How can cloud computing make these devices seem more powerful? Give examples of when using a powerful, remote, cloud computing resource might work well to enhance computing on a local device, and mention when the cloud might be less effective. What is the main constraint in your example?

3.4 e-waste: The Dark Side of Moore's Law

Learning Objectives

1. Understand the magnitude of the environmental issues caused by rapidly obsolete, faster and cheaper computing.
2. Explain the limitations of approaches attempting to tackle e-waste.

3. Understand the risks firms are exposed to when not fully considering the life cycle of the products they sell or consume.
4. Ask questions that expose concerning ethical issues in a firm's or partner's products and processes, and that help the manager behave more responsibly.

e-waste

Discarded, often obsolete technology; also known as electronic waste.

We should celebrate the great bounty Moore's Law and the tech industry bestow on our lives. Costs fall, workers become more productive, innovations flourish, and we gorge at a buffet of digital entertainment that includes music, movies, and games. But there is a dark side to this faster and cheaper advancement. A laptop has an expected lifetime of around two to four years. A cell phone? Eighteen months or less.[77] Rapid obsolescence means the creation of ever-growing mountains of discarded tech junk, known as electronic waste or **e-waste**, and represents the fastest growing waste stream on the planet.[78] Each year the planet generates over 50 million tons tons of e-waste[79] and the results aren't pretty. Consumer electronics and computing equipment can be a toxic cocktail that includes cadmium, mercury, lead, and other hazardous materials. Once called the "effluent of the affluent," e-waste will only increase with the rise of living standards worldwide.

The quick answer would be to recycle this stuff. Not only does e-waste contain mainstream recyclable materials we're all familiar with, like plastics and aluminum, it also contains small bits of increasingly valuable metals such as silver, platinum, and copper. In fact, there's more gold in one pound of discarded tech equipment than in one pound of mined ore,[80] and it's 13x cheaper to extract precious and rare earth metals from discarded electronics than it is to mine it from the earth.[81] But as the sordid record of e-waste management shows, there's often a disconnect between consumers and managers who *want* to do good and those efforts that are *actually* doing good. The complexities of the modern value chain, the vagaries of international law, and the nefarious actions of those willing to put profits above principle show how difficult addressing this problem will be.

The process of separating out the densely packed materials inside tech products so that the value in e-waste can be effectively harvested is extremely labor intensive, more akin to reverse manufacturing than any sort of curbside recycling efforts. Sending e-waste abroad can be ten times cheaper than dealing with it at home,[82] so it's not surprising that up to 80 percent of the material dropped off for recycling is eventually exported.[83] Much of this waste ends up in China, South Asia, or sub-Saharan Africa, where it is processed in dreadful conditions.

Consider examples extensively chronicled by organizations such as the Silicon Valley Toxics Coalition, the Basel Action Network (BAN), and Greenpeace. Their research has documented workers without protective equipment, breathing clouds of toxins generated as they burn the plastic skins off of wires to get at the copper inside. Others use buckets, pots, or wok-like pans (in many cases the same implements used for cooking) to sluice components in acid baths to release precious metals—recovery processes that create even more toxins. The area around one site had lead and heavy metal contamination levels some four hundred to six hundred times greater than what international standards deem safe.[84] That area was so polluted that drinking water had to be trucked in from eighteen miles away. Pregnancies were six times more likely to end in miscarriage, and 70 percent of the kids in the region had too much lead in their blood.[85] China has recently moved to block large amounts of recycling importing, including e-waste, and is moving to change practices in its most notorious recycling regions. However much of what once went to China is now migrating to other parts of Southeast Asia or Africa.[86] The world's largest e-dump is in Accra, the capital of the West African nation of Ghana. Known as Agbogbloshie, roughly 700 people, including children as young as 12, eke out a living as electronics scavengers.

Conditions in the e-Waste Capital of the World

This video from Hong Kong's *South China Morning Post* documents the horrible conditions found at a recycling endpoint in Guiyu, China. While, as the report mentions, China has curtailed imports of goods for recycling, and is moving to migrate recyclers to higher-standard practices, much of what was once recycled here has moved to other facilities in Southeast and South Asia, and sub-Saharan Africa.

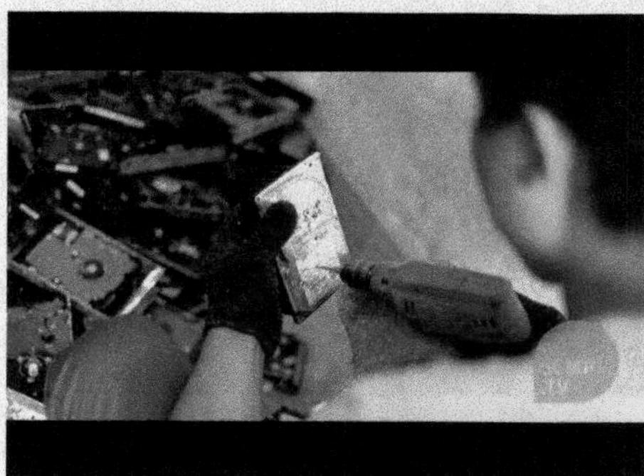

View the video online at: http://www.youtube.com/embed/RJ6VX3pC02s?rel=0

The trade is often brokered by unscrupulous middlemen who mask the eventual destination and fate of the products purchased. Each year BAN exposes the e-waste flow overseas by hiding GPS tracking devices inside equipment dropped off at various recyclers and charity drives.[87] BAN investigators in Lagos, Nigeria, documented mountains of e-waste with labels from schools, US government agencies, and even some of the world's largest corporations. And despite Europe's prohibition on exporting e-waste, many products originally labeled for repair and reuse end up in toxic recycling efforts. Even among those products that gain a second or third life by being refurbished and resold in developing nations, the inevitable is simply postponed, with e-waste almost certain to end up in landfills that lack the protective groundwater barriers and environmental engineering of their industrialized counterparts. The reality is that e-waste management is extraordinarily difficult to monitor and track, and loopholes are rampant.

Uncovering Fraudulent Recyclers

Watch the Basel Action Network track e-waste to global locations where they are processed under hazardous and environmentally damaging conditions. Organizations including Dell and Goodwill have been fleeced into thinking they were dealing with reputable providers.

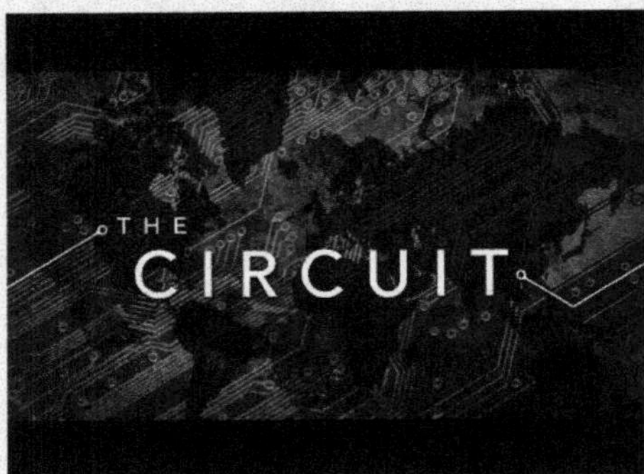

View the video online at: http://www.youtube.com/embed/n6FJJ29k8uc?rel=0

Thinking deeply about the ethical consequences of a firm's business is an imperative for the modern manager. A slipup (intentional or not) can, in seconds, be captured by someone with a cell phone, uploaded to YouTube, or offered in a blog posting for the world to see. Big firms are big targets, and environmentalists have been quick to push the best-known tech firms and retailers to take back their products for responsible recycling and to eliminate the worst toxins from their offerings. Consider that even Apple (where Al Gore sits on the firm's board of directors), has been pushed by a coalition of environmental groups on all of these fronts. Critics have shot back that singling out Apple is unfair. The firm was one of the first computer companies to eliminate lead-lined glass monitors from its product line, and has been a pioneer of reduced-sized packaging that leverages recyclable materials. And Apple eventually claimed the top in Greenpeace's "Greener Electronics" rankings.[88] Apple has even worked to automate responsible recycling by creating robots that can disassemble, repurpose, and recycle components in returned iPhones (see video below).[89] Despite the good works, if the firm that counts Al Gore among its advisors can get tripped up on green issues, all firms are vulnerable.

Apple's Daisy—The Robot That Recycles iPhones

Apple's Daisy recycling robot can disassemble any of nine models of iPhone, processing 200 iPhones in an hour.

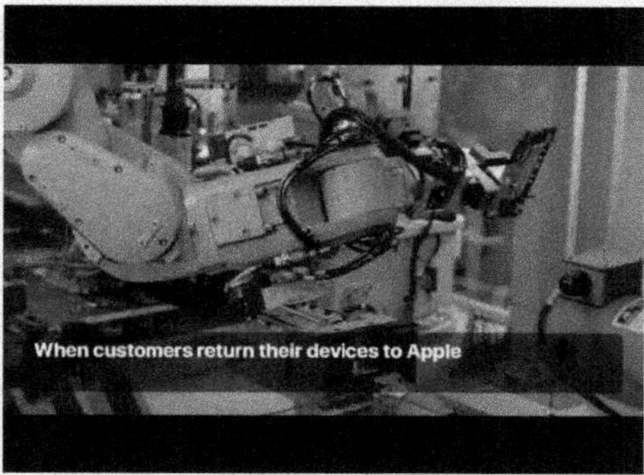

View the video online at: http://www.youtube.com/embed/2Bu-gl7v-P8?rel=0

Environmentalists see this pressure to deal with e-waste as yielding results: Most tech firms have continually moved to eliminate major toxins from their manufacturing processes. All this demonstrates that today's business leaders have to be far more attuned to the impact not only of their own actions, but also to those of their suppliers and partners. How were products manufactured? Using which materials? Under what conditions? What happens to items when they're discarded? Who provides collection and disposal? It also shows the futility of legislative efforts that don't fully consider and address the problems they are meant to target.

Finding Responsible e-Waste Disposers

A recent sting operation led by the US Government Accountability Office (US GAO) found that forty-three American recyclers were willing to sell e-waste illegally to foreign countries, without gaining EPA or foreign country approval. Appallingly, at least three of them held Earth Day electronics-recycling events.[90]

So how can firms and individuals choose proper disposal partners? Several certification mechanisms can help shed light on whether the partner you're dealing with is a responsible player. The Basel Action Network e-Stewards program certifies firms via a third-party audit, with compliant participants committing to eliminating e-waste export, land dumping, incineration, and toxic recycling via prison labor. The International Association of Electronics Recyclers (IAER) also offers audited electronics recycler certification. And firms certified as ISO 9001 and ISO 14001 compliant attest to quality management and environmental processes. Standards, techniques, and auditing practices are constantly in flux, so consult these organizations for the latest partner lists, guidelines, and audit practices.[91] http://www.e-stewards.org/certification-overview/; International Standards Organization accessed via http://www.iso.org/iso/home.htm; AER Worldwide accessed via https://www.aerworldwide.com/; and G. MacDonald, "Don't Recycle 'E-waste' with Haste, Activists Warn," *USA Today*, July 6, 2008.

FIGURE 3.6 e-Stewards

The e-Stewards program can help you find a vetted, responsible recycler.

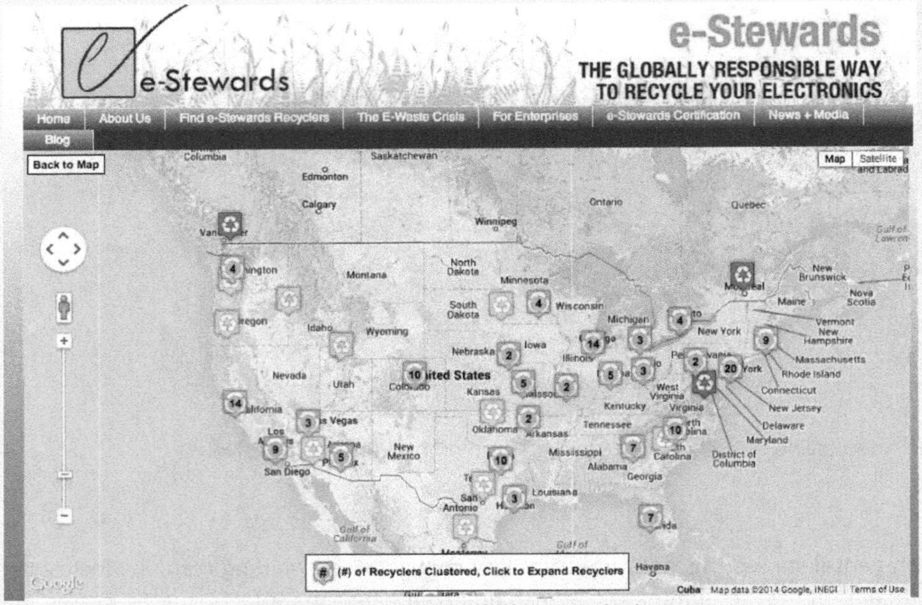

Source: e-Stewards.org; http://e-stewards.org/find-a-recycler/.

Which brings us back to Gordon Moore. To his credit, Moore is not just the founder of the world's largest microprocessor firm and first to identify the properties we've come to know as Moore's Law, he has also emerged as one of the world's leading supporters of environmental causes. The generosity of the Gordon and Betty Moore foundation includes, among other major contributions, the largest single gift to a private conservation organization. Indeed, Silicon Valley, while the birthplace of products that become e-waste, also promises to be at the forefront of finding solutions to modern environmental challenges. The Valley's leading venture capitalists, including Sequoia and Kleiner Perkins (where Al Gore is now a partner), have started multimillion-dollar green investment funds, targeted at funding the next generation of sustainable environmental initiatives.

Key Takeaways

- e-waste may be particularly toxic since many components contain harmful materials such as lead, cadmium, and mercury.
- Managers must consider and plan for the waste created by their products, services, and technology used by the organization. Consumers and governments are increasingly demanding that firms offer responsible methods for the disposal of their manufactured goods and the technology used in their operations.
- Managers must audit disposal and recycling partners with the same vigor as their suppliers and other corporate partners. If not, an organization's equipment may end up in environmentally harmful disposal operations.

Questions and Exercises

1. What is e-waste? What is so dangerous about e-waste?
2. What sorts of materials might be harvested from e-waste recycling?
3. Many well-meaning individuals thought that recycling was the answer to the e-waste problem. But why hasn't e-waste recycling yielded the results hoped for?
4. What lessons do the challenges of e-waste offer the manager? What issues will your firm need to consider as it consumes or offers products that contain computing components?
5. Why is it difficult to recycle e-waste?
6. Why is e-waste exported abroad for recycling rather than processed domestically?
7. What part does corruption play in the recycling and disposal of e-waste?
8. What part might product design and production engineering play in the reduction of the impact of technology waste on the environment?
9. What are the possible consequences should a US firm be deemed "environmentally irresponsible"?
10. Name two companies that have incurred the wrath of environmental advocates. What might these firms have done to avoid such criticism?

3.5 Mickey's Wearable: Disney's Magic Band

Learning Objectives

1. Illustrate the value that Disney accrued from embedding technology in otherwise manual experiences.
2. Recognize how the experience improved the value of the customer's Disney World experience.
3. Understand some of the issues involved in deploying large-scale information systems in a corporate environment.

Plan a trip to Disney World in Orlando, Florida, and the park is armed to leverage tech to streamline your experience, delight you at every turn, and keep you spending money. The centerpiece is the MagicBand, a stylish, rubberized, waterproof wristband mailed in advance to guests' homes. Bands can be used for park and attraction admission, for keyless entry into your Disney hotel room, to pay for rides, and to locate your group to deliver restaurant meals, personalized greetings, match you to photos taken by park photographers and attraction cameras, and more. And of course, the tech is tied to your credit card, so you can pay for everything, from an in-park Starbucks fix to gourmet restaurant meals to mouse ears and *Frozen* dolls, all with a wave of your wrist. Magic Band is now on its v. 2 iteration—a slimmer model where the tech at the center can be popped out to be mounted on a carabiner or lanyard. In roughly two years since launch, Disney has distributed over 30 million magic bands, making Disney the fourth largest provider of wearable technology.[92]

Family members choose the color of their individual band from a rainbow of options, and a band box arrives for the family with each guest's names etched inside their custom wearable. Each band is packed with low-cost, high-powered tech, courtesy of Moore's Law. Bands have both an

RFID chip and a 2.4 GHz radio, akin to what you'd find in many cordless phones. MagicBands can transmit in a radius of 40 feet. Embedded batteries last two years.[93]

Disney's MagicBand

A video by Orlando Attractions Magazine shows the MagicBand in action in a variety of settings.

View the video online at: http://www.youtube.com/embed/I3ojftUvWWU?rel=0

MagicBands are part of a broader set of technologies that Disney calls MyMagic+ that link together various systems that include the Web and mobile MyDisneyExperience to plan and share your vacation itinerary, manage your schedule, and deliver GPS-park maps and schedules to smartphone apps; the FastPass+ ride reservation system; and the Disney PhotoPass that stitches together a custom media album gathered from your visit (with an option to purchase prints, of course).[94] The mandate from Meg Crofton, previous president of Walt Disney World Resort, was to remove the friction in the Disney World experience. Says another Disney exec, "If we can get out of the way, our guests can create more memories."[95]

A band that tracks users and contains payment information can lead to privacy concerns, but Disney seems to have this covered. Any data collected is anonymized and encrypted. The band itself doesn't store any personal information; instead, it contains a code that identifies users within Disney's internal encrypted databases. Lose a band and it can be disabled and replaced. Purchases also require a PIN, and parents concerned with free-spending children can disable purchasing on their bands, or set a spending limit.[96]

Experience Examples

Band up as soon as you arrive in Orlando, then just hop a shuttle and head to your hotel or directly to the park. No need to even check in at the front desk—your band is your room key, as well as your park admission ticket, the pass to zip into any rides you've reserved in advance, and your payment method. No need to delay the fun waiting for baggage claim carousels; Disney's systems will also make sure your luggage is delivered to your room.

The MagicBand rollout in Disney World's *Be Our Guest* restaurant, inspired by the fairy-tale dining experience in *Beauty and the Beast*, launched to glowing reviews. Guests arriving at the restaurant are greeted by name by a hostess that gets a heads-up on her modified iOS device. The welcome is followed by a suggestion to sit wherever you want. The kitchen already has the order you've made online. Wireless receivers on the table and in the walls know where you are, so your food is whisked right to you, as if you were Belle herself. All in all, a seamless experience that won top innovation honors from the National Restaurant Association.[97]

MagicBand can also turn a long ride wait into a time-filling interactive experience. Photos taken by park photographers and other in-experience cameras are linked to your band's ID and will feed images to your My Disney Experience smartphone app, ready for saving or social sharing—a nice way to kill time while waiting in line.[98] The popular Epcot Test Track ride is notorious for its lines, but clever design fills the wait with a touch-screen auto-design session where users create their own car for integration into the attraction when they're ready to roll. Guests can also create a custom car commercial. Disney survey data suggests a 35-minute wait time for Test Track feels like it's only been 15 to 20 minutes.[99]

Big Data and Big Benefits

Disney World is really more of a city than a resort. It occupies twice as much land as Manhattan, contains four major theme parks, some 140 attractions, 300 dining locations, and 36 hotels. The 15-mile monorail alone hosts an average of 150,000 rides each day.[100] Driving far-reaching delight alongside efficiency at scale is the major goal of the MyMagic+ system that contains the magic band plus trip planning and operations technology.

Guests use the park's website and apps before they show up in Orlando so that they can reserve their favorite rides for priority seating. They can also select shows and parades, choose to attend fireworks displays, and set up character greetings. Information from these systems, when coupled with real-time data collected from MagicBand wearing guests, delivers more insight to tailor many more service improvements, than if guests were free-ranging around Disney World without prior planning.[101] Disney analysts saw that some guests were traversing the park upwards of 20 times a day to see all the rides they were most interested in, but with MyMagic+, park systems crunch data so the Mouse House can craft a custom guest itinerary that eliminates a frustrating zigzag across the many realms of the Magic Kingdom. MyMagic+ books ride reservations to minimize wait and spread out guests to further cut line time. With an average of 8,000 to 10,000 guests flowing through the park's main entrance every hour, big data analytics and efficient scheduling algorithms keep everyone happier.[102]

Data helps Disney know when to add more staff at rides and restaurants; how to stock restaurants, snack bars, and souvenir stands; and how many costumed cast members should be roaming in various areas of the park. If a snafu arises, such as an unexpectedly long line or a restaurant menu change, a custom-crafted alert with alternative suggestions can go out via text or e-mail.[103] At some point, systems might be able to detect when guests have waited too long or otherwise had an unexpectedly frustrating experience, offering a treat coupon or a pass to another ride. These kinds of systems have allowed casinos to turn negative experiences (losing big in slots) into positive ones.[104]

Disney says the MagicBand and supporting systems have cut turnstile transaction time by 30 percent, guests are spending more money, and systems have increased efficiency to the point where Disney World can serve 3,000 to 5,000 additional guests per day.[105] Another benefit to satisfied customers? They're less likely to decamp for nearby rival parks such as Universal Studios, Sea World, and Legoland.[106]

Magical Experiences Cost Serious Coin

These systems don't come cheap. It's estimated that Disney spent $1 billion on MyMagic+. Over 100 systems needed to be integrated to make the park function in a unified, guest-delighting way.[107]

The cost just to redesign and integrate the DisneyWorld.com website with MyMagic+ is said to have cost about $80 million.[108]

Moore's Law turns embedded technology at scale, a once impossible proposition, into a now justifiable business-enhancing expense (albeit a big one). More than 28,000 hotel doors needed replacement locks to work with MagicBand. Two dozen workers spent eight months upgrading 120 doors per day, trying to be unobtrusive in properties that boast an 80 percent average guest occupancy rate. Two hundred eighty-three park-entry points also had to be upgraded. More than 6,000 mobile devices (mostly iPod Touch and iPads with custom apps) were deployed to support new park systems. Disney World also needed to install more than 30 million square feet of Wi-Fi coverage.[109] According to a source in a *Fast Company* article, "It was a huge effort to wire a communications infrastructure that was basically the same size as San Francisco."[110] And you can't roll out a major tech initiative without making sure your staff knows how to use it. Over 70,000 "cast members" (Disney's name for its employees) received MyMagic+ training, with 15,000 skilled-up in specifics such as the FastPass+ ride reservation system and MagicBand merchandising.[111]

Putting tech on the wrist of every guest also adds a marginal cost to everyone coming through the door. The firm spent only four cents each to print paper tickets, but the early prototype for MagicBand came in at $35. Fortunately[112] Moore's Law, savvy engineering, and buying at scale kicked in, and manufacturing costs for bands are now below $5,[113] a much more tolerable price when tallied against the myriad of benefits delivered to each visiting guest.

Magical Experiences can Require Magical Coordination

A *Fast Company* article on the development of MyMagic+ also underscores political challenges when designing and deploying large-scale systems. Lots of groups had a stake in the outcome, and coordinating differing ideas, opinions, and agendas can be taxing. The systems impacted park operations, infrastructure, hotels, and marketing, among many other areas. Disney's IT group would be heavily involved in systems development and operation, and would need to lead integration with many existing systems and the replacement of others. The powerful Imagineering team, the group that designs much of the theme park wizardry that puts the magic in the Magic Kingdom, was also deep into the decision-making. Add to this additional work from third parties, including Frog Design, a renown high-end global design consultancy whose prior clients include Apple, Lufthansa, and UNICEF; and tech consulting from Accenture, HP, and Synapse among others.[114] In such a disparate group, conflict, even among the well-intended, was inevitable.

Fortunately, the project benefited from strong executive leadership—a key to many successful transformative projects. The effort had the full support and backing of Disney CEO Bob Iger, who regularly discussed the project with the firm's board of directors. Iger's involvement sent a clear message: we're doing this, and the resources will be there to support the effort. The exploratory team for the Next Generation Experience project, or NGE (the early name for what would develop into MyMagic+ and MagicBand), included some of the firm's most senior execs in theme[115] park and Disney World management. The core team for project included senior execs in technology, Imagineering, theme parks, and business development.[116] Disney's COO has stated the project actually came in a bit under budget, although delays and a staged rollout had left many of originally envisioned features to be introduced over time.[117]

Look to the Future

Additional services on deck include sharing data so that hosts and costumed cast members can issue birthday greetings, and rollout of even more interaction, such as animatronics that call you by name as you walk up to them.[118] Look for even deeper integration as new Disney World areas Pandora, World of Avatar, and Star Wars Land come online. Disney's theme park and resort destinations are, collectively, a $14.1 billion business.[119] Full rollout at other parks is less clear, but the Disney attractions empire is massive and includes theme parks in Anaheim, Paris, Shanghai, Tokyo, and Hong Kong; cruise lines; adventure travel; arcades; and ESPN properties. It's suspected that MagicBand wouldn't roll out in Disneyland in Anaheim, because the restructuring costs for a much smaller park wouldn't be efficient. Shanghai users may opt for a mobile phone experience, given the higher penetration and usage pattern of smartphones.[120] However, learning and various system components are expected to show up worldwide, with the firm stating it plans to roll out "variations on MyMagic+."[121] Disney parks have an annual admission of over 120 million guests a year. At that scale, innovations and bar-setting experiences have a massive influence on overall customer expectations.[122] Universal has already introduced its TapuTapu wearable, which will vibrate with alerts and includes a screen notifying users when it's time for their ride—no long queue needed![123] Expect players in other hospitality and entertainment markets to study Disney's magic in hopes of creating a bit of sorcery of their own.

Universal's Wristband

See the Universal Orlando TapuTapu wearable, complete with vibrating alerts and a message screen, in action at the Volcano Bay theme park.

View the video online at: http://www.youtube.com/embed/Hb0T1ZjzCPY?rel=0

Key Takeaways

- The Disney MagicBand handles many tasks, including park and attraction admission, payment, staff notification for improved service, and security such as hotel room admission.
- Deploying a project like MagicBand involves integrating over one hundred existing and new systems in a broader effort called MyMagic+. Infrastructure needed to be upgraded, and employees trained. The experience cost roughly $1 billion to deploy.
- Many internal and external groups were involved. Differing opinions and agendas often make large projects politically challenging to coordinate. Having the CEO champion the effort, and

senior executives from various groups lead development, helped reduce debilitating infighting and helped the project come in under budget.

Questions and Exercises

1. What is the MagicBand? What technology is inside it and what does it do? How do the bands benefit the customer experience? What benefits does Disney realize from the system?
2. In addition to designing and creating bands, what else did Disney need to do to pull off this effort? How many systems were involved? What infrastructure needed to be upgraded?
3. There's a lot you can do with technology, but Disney is also crafting a very special, branded experience. Do you think Disney got it right, or does the technology seem like it would interfere with the experience? Why or why not?
4. What more can and should Disney do with this technology?
5. Large technical projects can be a challenge to design and deploy. Why? How did Disney cut through some of these challenges and eventually deliver a project within goals and within budget?
6. How does Disney deal with security and privacy concerns? Do you think these precautions are enough? Why or why not?

Endnotes

1. G. Moore, "Cramming More Components onto Integrated Circuits," *Electronics*, April 19, 1965.
2. K. Krewell, "The Slowing of Moore's Law and Its Impact," *Forbes*, July 30, 2015.
3. M. Assay, "Moore's Law is Dead (But Not in Mobile)," *ReadWrite*, April 20, 2015.
4. Although other materials besides silicon are increasingly being used.
5. Semiconductor materials, like the silicon dioxide used inside most computer chips, are capable of enabling as well as inhibiting the flow of electricity. These properties enable chips to perform math or store data.
6. Some argue it may be more accurate to refer to Moore's law as "geometric" rather than "exponential"; however, we'll stay true to the nomenclature of referring to "really fast acceleration" as exponential. For more on this you can explore: D. Stewart, "Moore's Curse: not everything is exponential," *dunstewart.com*, April 2015.
7. Fiber-optic lines are glass or plastic data transmission cables that carry light. These cables offer higher transmission speeds over longer distances than copper cables that transmit electricity.
8. C. Walter, "Kryder's Law," *Scientific American*, July 25, 2005.
9. D. Rosenthal, "Storage Will be a Lot Less Free than It Used to be," *DSHR Blog*, October 1, 2012; Gwern Branwen, "Slowing Moore's Law: How It Could Happen," *Gwern.net*, last modified June 03, 2014.
10. K. Fisher, "All or Nothing in 2014," *Forbes*, February 10, 2014.
11. G. Satell, "What We Can Expect from the Next Decade of Technology," *Business Insider*, July 7, 2013.
12. As opposed to goods and services that are *price inelastic* (like health care and housing), which consumers will try their best to buy even if prices go up.
13. M. Copeland, "How to Ride the Fifth Wave," *Business 2.0*, July 1, 2005.
14. N. Patel, "Inside the Nest: iPod Creator Tony Fadell Wants to Reinvent the Thermostat," *The Verge*, November 14, 2011.
15. M. Meeker, "Internet Trends 2014," *KPCB*, May 28, 2014.
16. J. Salter, "Tony Fadell, Father of the iPod, iPhone and Nest, on Why He Is Worth $3.2bn to Google," *Telegraph*, June 14, 2014.
17. M. Chui, M. Loffler, and R. Roberts, "The Internet of Things," *McKinsey Quarterly*, March 2010.
18. M. Brian, "Airbus Smart Luggage Prototype Offers iPhone Tracking, Faster Check-in," *The Verge*, June 7, 2013.
19. T. Nudd, "Huggies App Sends You a Tweet Whenever Your Kid Pees in His Diaper," *AdWeek*, May 8, 2013.
20. K. Komando, "Should You Buy a $25 Computer? Meet the Raspberry Pi," *USA Today*, June 14, 2013.
21. https://www.raspberrypi.org/blog/raspberry-pi-zero-w-joins-family/.
22. J. Manyika, M. Chui, J. Bughin, R. Dobbs, P. Bisson, and A. Marrs, "Disruptive Technologies: Advances That Will Transform Life, Business, and the Global Economy," *McKinsey Quarterly*, May 2013.
23. C. Boulton, "GE Launches Industrial Internet Analytics Platform," *Wall Street Journal*, June 18, 2013.
24. S. Higginbotham, "GE's Industrial Internet Focus Means It's a Big Data Company Now," *GigaOM*, June 18, 2013.
25. B. Cha, "A Beginner's Guide to Understanding the Internet of Things," *Re/code*, Jan. 15, 2015.
26. E. Gray, "CVS Wants to Be Your Doctor's Office," *Time*, Feb. 12, 2015.
27. D. Rose, presentation as part of "From Disruption to Innovation" at the MIT Enterprise Forum, Cambridge, MA, June 23, 2010.
28. S. Baum, "Digital medicine Take 2: Proteus Digital Health, Otsuka resubmit FDA application," *MedCityNews*, May 23, 2017.
29. E. Landau, "Tattletale Pills, Bottles Remind You to Take Your Meds," *CNN*, February 2, 2010.
30. K. Rozendal, "The Democratic, Digital Future of Healthcare," *Scope*, May 13, 2011.
31. J. Whalen, ""Tiny Cameras to See in the Intestines," *The Wall Street Journal*, Feb. 29, 2016.
32. H. Mitchell, "Steve Jobs Used Wayne Gretzky as Inspiration," *Los Angeles Times*, October 6, 2011.
33. G. Kumparak, "Apple Just Had The Most Profitable Quarter of Any Company Ever," *TechCrunch*, Jan. 27, 2015.
34. E. Schuman, "At Walmart, World's Largest Retail Data Warehouse Gets Even Larger," *eWeek*, October 13, 2004; and J. Huggins, "How Much Data Is That?" *Refrigerator Door*, August 19, 2008.
35. A. Vance, "Netflix, Reed Hastings Survive Missteps to Join Silicon Valley's Elite," May 9, 2013.
36. M. Riley and D. Gambrell, "The NSA Spying Machine," *BusinessWeek*, April 3, 2014.
37. N. Myslewski, "Cisco: You Think the Internet Is Clogged with Video Now? Just Wait until 2018," *The Register*, June 13, 2014.
38. B. Breen, "Living in Dell Time," *Fast Company*, November 24, 2004.
39. C. Mims, "The world's cheapest cell phones are now just $10 each," *Quartz*, March 14, 2013.
40. A. Cuthbertson, "How Google Plans to Reach Its 'Next Billion' Users with Android Go," *Newsweek*, May 18, 2017.
41. S. Corbett, "Can the Cellphone Help End Global Poverty?" *New York Times Magazine*, April 13, 2008.
42. J. Ewing, "Upwardly Mobile in Africa," *BusinessWeek*, September 24, 2007, 64–71.
43. J. Ewing, "Upwardly Mobile in Africa," *BusinessWeek*, September 24, 2007, 64–71.
44. S. Corbett, "Can the Cellphone Help End Global Poverty?" *New York Times Magazine*, April 13, 2008.

45. Bill and Melinda Gates Foundation, *What We Do: Agricultural Development Strategy Overview*, accessed via http://www.gatesfoundation.org/What-We-Do/Global-Development/Agricultural-Development (accessed June 11, 2013).
46. Esoko Press Release, *Groundbreaking Study Confirms That Farmers Using Esoko Receive More for Their Crops*, December 15, 2011.
47. K. A. Domfeh, "Esoko Impact on Farmers Assessed for Expansion," *AfricaNews.com*, March 1, 2012.
48. J. Masinde, "Kenya's M-Pesa platform is so successful regulators worry it could disrupt the economy," *Quartz*, Dec. 28, 2016.
49. E. McGirt, "Hacker, Dropout, C.E.O.," *Fast Company*, May 2007.
50. D. Kirkpatrick, "The Greenest Computer Company under the Sun," *CNN*, April 13, 2007.
51. S. Mehta, "Behold the Server Farm," *Fortune*, August 1, 2006. Also see [Content Removed: #fwk-38086-ch10] in this book.
52. A. Hesseldahl, "Moore's Law Hits 50, but It May Not See 60," *Re/code*, April 15, 2015.
53. A. Ashton, "More Life for Moore's Law," *BusinessWeek*, June 20, 2005.
54. A. Ashton, "More Life for Moore's Law," *BusinessWeek*, June 20, 2005.
55. M. Copeland, "A Chip Too Far?" *Fortune*, September 1, 2008.
56. V. Savov, "The demand for AI is helping Nvidia and AMD leapfrog Intel," *The Verge*, Jan. 11, 2017.
57. Unattributed, "The rise of artificial intelligence is creating new variety in the chip market, and trouble for Intel," *The Economist*, Feb. 25, 2017.
58. K. Bourzac, "How Three-Dimensional Transistors Went from Lab to Fab," *Technology Review*, May 6, 2011.
59. A. Hesseldahl, "Moore's Law Hits 50, but It May Not See 60," *Re/code,* April 15, 2015.
60. P. Kaihla, "Quantum Leap," *Business 2.0*, August 1, 2004.
61. D. Love, "Quantum Computing Could Lead to a Gigantic Leap Forward," *Business Insider*, June 11, 2013.
62. A list of the current supercomputer performance champs can be found at http://www.top500.org.
63. T. Valich, "100 PFLOPS: China's Supercomputer Circumvents U.S. Sales Ban," *VR World*, April 13, 2016.
64. P. Schwartz, C. Taylor, and R. Koselka, "The Future of Computing: Quantum Leap," *Fortune*, August 2, 2006.
65. H. Hodson, "Supercomputers make discoveries that scientists can't," *NewScientist*, Aug. 27, 2014.
66. K. Orland, "How the Xbox One Draws More Processing Power from the Cloud," *Ars Technica*, May 23, 2013.
67. L. Sumagaysay, "After Man vs. Machine on 'Jeopardy,' What's Next for IBM's Watson?" *Good Morning Silicon Valley*, February 17, 2011.
68. C. Nickisch, "IBM to Roll Out Watson, M.D.," *WBUR*, February 18, 2011.
69. B. Starfield, "Is U.S. Health Really the Best in the World?" *Journal of the American Medical Association*, July 26, 2000.
70. IBM Watson for Oncology at Manipal Hospitals, YouTube Video published July. 26, 2016. https://www.youtube.com/watch?v=cEiixVHqs6Q.
71. B. Wallace-Wells, "Boyhood," *New York Magazine*, May 20, 2015.
72. B. Japsen, "Pfizer Partners With IBM Watson To Advance Cancer Drug Discovery," *Forbes*, Dec. 1, 2016.
73. T. Green, "IBM Aims Watson at the Financial Services Industry," *The Motley Fool*, Oct. 10, 2016.
74. M. Greenwald, "Way Beyond Jeopardy: 5 Marketing Uses of IBM Watson," *Forbes*, Sept. 20, 2016.
75. K. Johnson, "Sesame Workshop and IBM Watson partner on platform to help kids learn," *Venture Beat*, June 6, 2017. You can find video on this effort at: https://venturebeat.com/2017/06/06/sesame-workshop-and-ibm-watson-to-launch-platform-to-help-kids-learn/.
76. S. Perez, "Elemental Path Debuts The First Toys Powered By IBM Watson," *TechCrunch, Feb.* 16, 2015.
77. L. Gilpin, "The Depressing Truth about e-Waste: 10 Things to Know," *TechRepublic*, June 11, 2014.
78. J. Shegerian, "The E-Waste Stream is Growing. What Can We Do?" *TriplePundit*, Aug. 21, 2015.
79. M. Hardy, "The Hellish E-Waste Graveyards Where Computers are Mined for Metal," *Wired*, Jan. 8, 2018.
80. P. Kovessy, "How to Trash Toxic Tech," *Ottawa Business Journal*, May 12, 2008.
81. M. Griggs, "Your old computer could be a better source of metals than a mine," *Popular Science*, April 4, 2018.
82. C. Bodeen, "In 'E-waste' Heartland, a Toxic China," *International Herald Tribune*, November 18, 2007.
83. E. Royte, "E-waste@Large," *New York Times*, January 27, 2006.
84. E. Grossman, "Where Computers Go to Die—and Kill," *Salon.com*, April 10, 2006, http://www.salon.com/news/feature/2006/04/10/ewaste.
85. *60 Minutes*, "Following the Trail of Toxic E-waste," November 9, 2008.
86. Y. Lee, "The world is scrambling now that China is refusing to be a trash dumping ground," *CNBC*, April 16, 2018.
87. M. Hardy, "The Hellish E-Waste Graveyards Where Computers are Mined for Metal," *Wired*, Jan. 8, 2018.
88. J. Dalrymple, "Apple Ranks Highest among Greenpeace's Top Tech Companies," *The Loop*, January 7, 2010.
89. S. Kelley, "Inside Liam, Apple's Super-Secret 29 Armed Robot That Tears Down Your iPhone," *Mashable*, March 21, 2016.
90. U.S. Government Accountability Office (U.S. GAO), *Report to the Chairman: Committee on Foreign Affairs, House of Representatives: Electronic Waste*, August 2008.
91. Basal Action Network e-Stewards program accessed via http://www.ban.org/e-stewardship/.
92. C. Smith, "A Day Out With Disney's Magic Band 2," *Wareable*, April 11, 2017.
93. C. Kuang, "Disney's $1 Billion Bet on a Magical Wristband," *Wired*, March 10, 2015.
94. A. Carr, "The Messy Business of Reinventing Happiness," *Fast Company*, May 2015.
95. C. Kuang, "Disney's $1 Billion Bet on a Magical Wristband," *Wired*, March 10, 2015.
96. B. Cha, "Tomorrowland Today: Disney MagicBand Unlocks New Guest Experience for Park Goers," *AllThingsD*, May 29, 2013.
97. A. Carr, "The Messy Business of Reinventing Happiness," *Fast Company*, May 2015.
98. C. Smith, "A Day Out With Disney's Magic Band 2," *Wareable*, April 11, 2017.
99. A. Carr, "The Messy Business of Reinventing Happiness," *Fast Company*, May 2015.
100. A. Carr, "The Messy Business of Reinventing Happiness," *Fast Company*, May 2015.
101. C. Kuang, "Disney's $1 Billion Bet on a Magical Wristband," *Wired*, March 10, 2015.
102. A. Carr, "The Messy Business of Reinventing Happiness," *Fast Company*, May 2015.
103. C. Palmeri, "Disney Bets $1 Billion on Technology to Track Theme Park Visitors," *BusinessWeek*, March 7, 2014.
104. C. Kuang, "Disney's $1 Billion Bet on a Magical Wristband," *Wired*, March 10, 2015.
105. A. Carr, "The Messy Business of Reinventing Happiness," *Fast Company*, May 2015. And C. Palmeri, "Disney Bets $1 Billion on Technology to Track Theme Park Visitors," *BusinessWeek*, March 7, 2014.
106. C. Palmeri, "Disney Bets $1 Billion on Technology to Track Theme Park Visitors," *BusinessWeek*, March 7, 2014.
107. C. Kuang, "Disney's $1 Billion Bet on a Magical Wristband," *Wired*, March 10, 2015.
108. A. Carr, "The Messy Business of Reinventing Happiness," *Fast Company*, May 2015.
109. A. Carr, "The Messy Business of Reinventing Happiness," *Fast Company*, May 2015.
110. A. Carr, "The Messy Business of Reinventing Happiness," *Fast Company*, May 2015.
111. A. Carr, "The Messy Business of Reinventing Happiness," *Fast Company*, May 2015.
112. A. Carr, "The Messy Business of Reinventing Happiness," *Fast Company*, May 2015.
113. A. Carr, "The Messy Business of Reinventing Happiness," *Fast Company*, May 2015.
114. A. Carr, "The Messy Business of Reinventing Happiness," *Fast Company*, May 2015.
115. C. Kuang, "Disney's $1 Billion Bet on a Magical Wristband," *Wired*, March 10, 2015.
116. C. Kuang, "Disney's $1 Billion Bet on a Magical Wristband," *Wired*, March 10, 2015.
117. A. Carr, "The Messy Business of Reinventing Happiness," *Fast Company*, May 2015.
118. A. Carr, "The Messy Business of Reinventing Happiness," *Fast Company*, May 2015.
119. C. Palmeri, "Disney Bets $1 Billion on Technology to Track Theme Park Visitors," *BusinessWeek*, March 7, 2014.
120. A. Carr, "The Messy Business of Reinventing Happiness," *Fast Company*, May 2015.
121. A. Carr, "The Messy Business of Reinventing Happiness," *Fast Company*, May 2015.
122. C. Kuang, "Disney's $1 Billion Bet on a Magical Wristband," *Wired*, March 10, 2015.
123. M. Schneider, "Universal Orlando Resort's new wristband lets you skip lines, pays for food at new water park," *The Associated Press*, May 17, 2017.

CHAPTER 4

Data Integration

Learning Objectives

1. Determine what information can or can not be found when integrating datasets
2. Answer business questions by integrating datasets and analyzing the integrated data

VLOOKUP is a useful function but it has some limitations. The greatest limitation is that VLOOKUP requires that the lookup value be searched for in the leftmost column of the lookup table. It is not realistic to expect that the lookup column will always appear in the leftmost column of a table.

Therefore, in this chapter we introduce Index (Match), which does not have this limitation. Index(Match) is actually a combination of two functions. Match finds the row that you want and Index returns the value that lives in that row. For example, if the data you are looking for is in the seventh row, the Match function will return the number 7. Index uses the number 7 to retrieve any field that you would like in the seventh row. Using Index and Match functions together actually retrieves the value, whether it is a word or number, in the row that the Match function finds. The Index (Match) function allows data to be integrated from one table into another, which enables us to better answer business questions.

We also introduce structured table references help to make the Index (Match) function, and other functions, easier to interpret and debug. These references name columns and areas of tables that can be used to refer to specific data among tables in a workbook.

4.1 Structured Table References and the Index(Match) Function

Math Class Needs a Makeover

In real life, problems usually involve either an insufficient amount of information, or too much information that you need to sort through to find the solution. Math classes in the United States are taught so that students only search for the simplest answer where they can apply a clear formula to the problem. Math classes should teach students patient problem solving and how to sort through data to find the relevant information. Just like the Index (Match) function, students need to sort through and integrate the right information into their problems.

Math Class Needs a Makeover by Dan Meyer

View the video online at: http://www.youtube.com/embed/qocAoN4jNwc?rel=0

Data Integration

Very often the information that you need is stored in separate tables. Your job might be to combine that information by matching data. Examples may include

1. finding the city and state for customers if all you are given is ZIP codes;
2. looking up the names of participants if all you are given are their IDs; or
3. tracking whether a new employee has completed each step of an onboarding process.

There is a rich database theory behind how the tables should be constructed to allow for these matches to take place. Each table must have a field or combination of fields that serve as a unique identifier. Why unique? Because otherwise we might match the wrong record. The unique identifier is called a primary key and is underlined in the following tables:

ZIP (<u>Zipcode</u>, city, state)

CUSTOMER (<u>ID</u>, last, first, phone, zipcode)

Zipcode is the primary key of the ZIP table. It uniquely identifies each record. But notice that zipcode is also found at the end of the CUSTOMER table. When primary key values are repeated in another table, they are called foreign keys (like a foreigner visiting that table). Foreign keys repeat the values of primary keys and serve as the matching link between the tables. The common zipcode field is what allows us to match records in the two tables. In database terms we say that there is a one-to-many relationship between the tables—one zipcode contains many customers.

Another way to think of the relationship is that the ZIP table is the parent table and CUSTOMER is the child table. One parent may have multiple children—a one-to-many relationship. The way that the relationship is established is by having the primary key of the parent table match the foreign key of the child table.

In this unit we are going to copy or integrate data from the parent table into the child table. For example, we will populate the Custmer table with the city and state that we pull in from the ZIP table.

If this were a database course we would use a language called SQL to join data from the parent and child tables. However, in Excel we use a combination of functions called INDEX(MATCH). Before delving into Index(Match), we need to prepare both the parent and child tables so that we can easily refer to the columns that we need. To prepare the tables we first format them as tables, and then refer to individual columns using structured table references.

Structured Table References

Whenever you have lots of data in Excel, you should ask Excel to define that data as a table. Simply place the cursor anywhere in the data and format as table. Excel will automatically give the table a name such as Table1, Table2, and so forth. It is a good idea to rename each table to something more explanatory. To name a table, simply overwrite the default name in the Table Name box, then press the enter (return) key to confirm the name.

Home Insert Page Layout Formulas Data Review

Table Name: Student | Summarize with PivotTable | Remove Duplicates | Convert to Range | Refresh | Header Row | Total Row | Banded Rows

A17 fx P828

	A	B	C	D	E	F	G	H
1	Student					Grades		
2	ID	First	Last	Phone		ID	Course	Grade
3	P345	Mana	Gorley	555-2345		P118	BA 2000	B-
4	P497	Fe	Grandberry	375-3979		P118	ACCT 1020	A-
5	P801	Elaina	Gryder	335-9987		P211	FIN 2400	B
6	P384	Kaitlin	Keane	442-5583		P270	BA 1000	B
7	P907	Debra	Keebler	423-8849		P270	MIS 2020	A
8	P270	Yasuko	Kimbrell	993-3395		P270	MIS 2800	B+
9	P118	Kyra	Kirkbride	283-9975		P345	MIS 2010	A
10	P337	Cami	Lamotte	228-5742		P345	QBA 2010	B-
11	P229	Chana	Leishman	245-9488		P345	MKT 4500	A-
12	P881	Jane	Lyttle	443-0357		P445	ACCT 1010	A
13	P902	Genie	Markus	452-9947		P828	QBA 3710	B-
14	P994	Josephine	Martell	542-5584		P828	MGT 2100	B+
15	P046	Shaunna	Mcglothin	442-9957		P828	MGT 1300	C+
16	P211	Shirly	Milliron	593-9947		P881	BA 1000	A-
17	P828	Nickolas	Milner	442-9957		P881	ACCT 1010	B
18	P445	Lavenia	Mumaw	442-2224		P902	FIN 2500	B+
19	P991	Hannah	Ogata	442-2211		P902	FIN 2100	B
20						P902	MIS 2800	A
21						P991	MIS 2800	C
22						P991	MKT 2300	A-

For example, a table containing student data could be named Student; the table with the grades data could be named Grades, as you see in the image above. Table names allow us to reference every column in the table by name. For example, the ID column in the Student table is Student[ID]. (The column name is enclosed in square brackets.) Similarly, Student[First], Student[Last], and Student[Phone] are all column names. So, too, are Grades[ID], Grades[Course], and Grades[Grade].

In addition, if you want to reference an individual cell rather than the whole column, then use the @ symbol. Student[@First] references the first name in the current row, whereas Student[First] references the entire column. When you reference a cell in a table, Excel may assume that you want just that cell, and you may have to remove the @ symbol to indicate the whole column.

The goal in data integration is to combine data from parent and child tables together. More specifically, we transfer matching data from the parent table into the child table. The match is made possible because the parent and child tables share a common key field. In the parent table that field is the primary key or unique identifier, and in the child table that field is called a foreign key. In Excel we use the INDEX(MATCH) functions together to establish the link across the common key fields. Next we will look at both the index and match functions in isolation before combining them to retrieve and integrate data.

The MATCH Function

Below you can see that we have two tables, a Student table (the parent table) and a Grades table (the child table). Both share the student ID field. ID is the primary key of the student table and is a foreign key in the Grades table. (What is the primary key of the Grades table?) But notice that the data in the Grades table isn't in the same order as the Student table. You want to match data from the Student table and place it into the Grades table. Begin by finding the row number of each ID in the Student table. To find these numbers, you use the match function. The match function returns the row number of a lookup value. The function looks like this:

=MATCH (lookup value, lookup column, match type)

In our scenario the function typed in the first row of the Match column in the Grades table would look like this:

=MATCH(F3, Student[ID],0), which tells Excel to lookup "P118" from the ID column of the Student table (cells A3 through A19). (Note that the "0" at the end of the function ensures that Excel looks for an exact match to the lookup value of P118.) In this case, P118 is found in the seventh row down.

When we copy the Match formula down, we reveal all of the matching row numbers in the Student table. The highlighted value, P828 is in the fifteenth row.

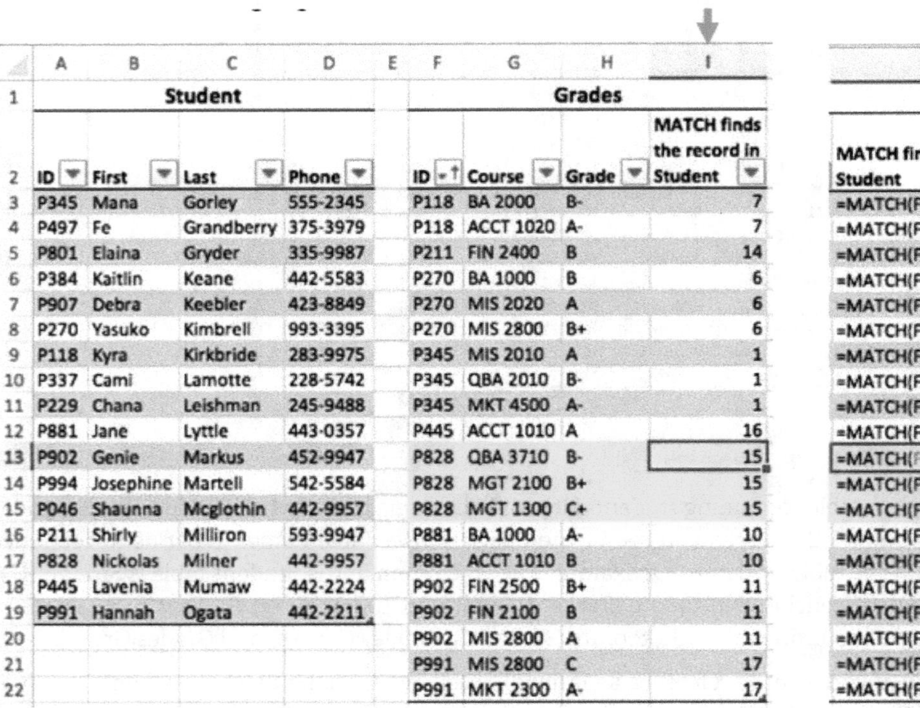

	A	B	C	D	E	F	G	H	I	I
1	Student					Grades				
2	ID	First	Last	Phone		ID	Course	Grade	MATCH finds the record in Student	MATCH finds the record in Student
3	P345	Mana	Gorley	555-2345		P118	BA 2000	B-	7	=MATCH(F3,Student[ID],0)
4	P497	Fe	Grandberry	375-3979		P118	ACCT 1020	A-	7	=MATCH(F4,Student[ID],0)
5	P801	Elaina	Gryder	335-9987		P211	FIN 2400	B	14	=MATCH(F5,Student[ID],0)
6	P384	Kaitlin	Keane	442-5583		P270	BA 1000	B	6	=MATCH(F6,Student[ID],0)
7	P907	Debra	Keebler	423-8849		P270	MIS 2020	A	6	=MATCH(F7,Student[ID],0)
8	P270	Yasuko	Kimbrell	993-3395		P270	MIS 2800	B+	6	=MATCH(F8,Student[ID],0)
9	P118	Kyra	Kirkbride	283-9975		P345	MIS 2010	A	1	=MATCH(F9,Student[ID],0)
10	P337	Cami	Lamotte	228-5742		P345	QBA 2010	B-	1	=MATCH(F10,Student[ID],0)
11	P229	Chana	Leishman	245-9488		P345	MKT 4500	A-	1	=MATCH(F11,Student[ID],0)
12	P881	Jane	Lyttle	443-0357		P445	ACCT 1010	A	16	=MATCH(F12,Student[ID],0)
13	P902	Genie	Markus	452-9947		P828	QBA 3710	B-	15	=MATCH(F13,Student[ID],0)
14	P994	Josephine	Martell	542-5584		P828	MGT 2100	B+	15	=MATCH(F14,Student[ID],0)
15	P046	Shaunna	Mcglothin	442-9957		P828	MGT 1300	C+	15	=MATCH(F15,Student[ID],0)
16	P211	Shirly	Milliron	593-9947		P881	BA 1000	A-	10	=MATCH(F16,Student[ID],0)
17	P828	Nickolas	Milner	442-9957		P881	ACCT 1010	B	10	=MATCH(F17,Student[ID],0)
18	P445	Lavenia	Mumaw	442-2224		P902	FIN 2500	B+	11	=MATCH(F18,Student[ID],0)
19	P991	Hannah	Ogata	442-2211		P902	FIN 2100	B	11	=MATCH(F19,Student[ID],0)
20						P902	MIS 2800	A	11	=MATCH(F20,Student[ID],0)
21						P991	MIS 2800	C	17	=MATCH(F21,Student[ID],0)
22						P991	MKT 2300	A-	17	=MATCH(F22,Student[ID],0)

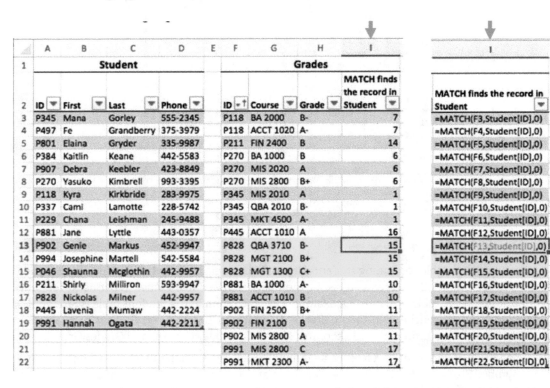

You may be wondering why you need to find the row numbers of the matching values. The reason is the Index function needs the row number to retrieve other data in that record.

The Index Function

The function that retrieves values for a specific row is called the index function. Index allows you to retrieve one cell from that row at a time. So if we want student first name, we run an Index function, and a separate index function for last name and phone. The syntax is INDEX(column, row number), which, roughly translated, means "get me the value of that column in the row that I give you."

Let's go back to our Student/Grades example. IDs are helpful, but you want to know the first and last names of the students in the table. We've already found the row position number using the match function, so we can use those numbers in our index functions. In the first cell in column J we tell Excel to retrieve the first name of the seventh record in the Student table. That function looks like this: =INDEX(Student[First], I3), which is Kyra. Moving down to J13, we can see that the index function is looking for the first name in the fifteenth row of Student, which is Nickolas.

	A	B	C	D	E	F	G	H	I	J	K
1	Student					Grades					
2	ID	First	Last	Phone		ID	Course	Grade	MATCH finds the record in Student	INDEX retrieves First name	INDEX retrieves Last name
3	P345	Mana	Gorley	555-2345		P118	BA 2000	B-	7	Kyra	Kirkbride
4	P497	Fe	Grandberry	375-3979		P118	ACCT 1020	A-	7	Kyra	Kirkbride
5	P801	Elaina	Gryder	335-9987		P211	FIN 2400	B	14	Shirly	Milliron
6	P384	Kaitlin	Keane	442-5583		P270	BA 1000	B	6	Yasuko	Kimbrell
7	P907	Debra	Keebler	423-8849		P270	MIS 2020	A	6	Yasuko	Kimbrell
8	P270	Yasuko	Kimbrell	993-3395		P270	MIS 2800	B+	6	Yasuko	Kimbrell
9	P118	Kyra	Kirkbride	283-9975		P345	MIS 2010	A	1	Mana	Gorley
10	P337	Cami	Lamotte	228-5742		P345	QBA 2010	B-	1	Mana	Gorley
11	P229	Chana	Leishman	245-9488		P345	MKT 4500	A-	1	Mana	Gorley
12	P881	Jane	Lyttle	443-0357		P445	ACCT 1010	A	16	Lavenia	Mumaw
13	P902	Genie	Markus	452-9947		P828	QBA 3710	B-	15	Nickolas	Milner
14	P994	Josephine	Martell	542-5584		P828	MGT 2100	B+	15	Nickolas	Milner
15	P046	Shaunna	Mcglothin	442-9957		P828	MGT 1300	C+	15	Nickolas	Milner
16	P211	Shirly	Milliron	593-9947		P881	BA 1000	A-	10	Jane	Lyttle
17	P828	Nickolas	Milner	442-9957		P881	ACCT 1010	B	10	Jane	Lyttle
18	P445	Lavenia	Mumaw	442-2224		P902	FIN 2500	B+	11	Genie	Markus
19	P991	Hannah	Ogata	442-2211		P902	FIN 2100	B	11	Genie	Markus
20						P902	MIS 2800	A	11	Genie	Markus
21						P991	MIS 2800	C	17	Hannah	Ogata
22						P991	MKT 2300	A-	17	Hannah	Ogata

J	K
INDEX retrieves First name	INDEX retrieves Last name
=INDEX(Student[First],I3)	=INDEX(Student[Last],I3)
=INDEX(Student[First],I4)	=INDEX(Student[Last],I4)
=INDEX(Student[First],I5)	=INDEX(Student[Last],I5)
=INDEX(Student[First],I6)	=INDEX(Student[Last],I6)
=INDEX(Student[First],I7)	=INDEX(Student[Last],I7)
=INDEX(Student[First],I8)	=INDEX(Student[Last],I8)
=INDEX(Student[First],I9)	=INDEX(Student[Last],I9)
=INDEX(Student[First],I10)	=INDEX(Student[Last],I10)
=INDEX(Student[First],I11)	=INDEX(Student[Last],I11)
=INDEX(Student[First],I12)	=INDEX(Student[Last],I12)
=INDEX(Student[First],I13)	=INDEX(Student[Last],I13)
=INDEX(Student[First],I14)	=INDEX(Student[Last],I14)
=INDEX(Student[First],I15)	=INDEX(Student[Last],I15)
=INDEX(Student[First],I16)	=INDEX(Student[Last],I16)
=INDEX(Student[First],I17)	=INDEX(Student[Last],I17)
=INDEX(Student[First],I18)	=INDEX(Student[Last],I18)
=INDEX(Student[First],I19)	=INDEX(Student[Last],I19)
=INDEX(Student[First],I20)	=INDEX(Student[Last],I20)
=INDEX(Student[First],I21)	=INDEX(Student[Last],I21)
=INDEX(Student[First],I22)	=INDEX(Student[Last],I22)

The index function assumes you already know the row position of the records. In the example above we found those row positions with the match function and stored them in column I. But who wants to create an extra column when you don't have to? Instead, you can nest the index and match functions together and get your values in one step.

INDEX(MATCH)

You can use the index and match functions together to look for a value you want based on data you already know without knowing the position of that data. When the index and match functions are combined, the number that the match formula finds is used as the row number in the index formula. It looks like this: =INDEX (Column, MATCH formula)

Referring to our Student/Grades scenario, we now want to find the phone numbers associated with each student ID. The function for the first record in the Grades would look like this:

=INDEX (Student[Phone], MATCH(ID,Student[ID],0)).

Because functions inside parenthesis are completed first, the match function first determines the row position number of P118 to be 7. The index function uses that 7 to display the phone number for the seventh record in the table, which is 283-9975. The real power of Index(Match) comes when looking up values for an entire column. We simply repeat the formula down the column to retrieve every corresponding value from the parent table. Looking further down, you can see that the function works similarly for P828, but it looks for the fifteenth record based on the results of the match function used in conjunction with the index function.

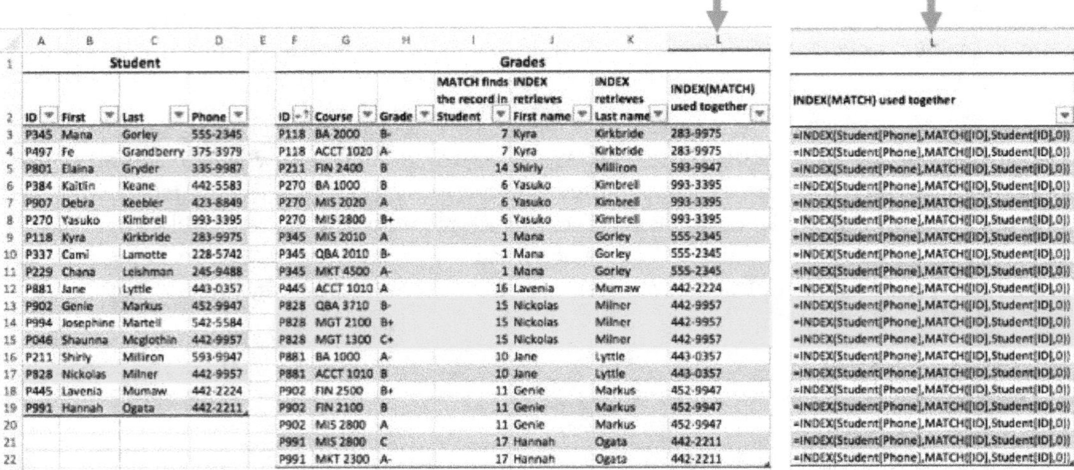

	A	B	C	D
1	**Student**			
2	ID	First	Last	Phone
3	P345	Mana	Gorley	555-2345
4	P497	Fe	Grandberry	375-3979
5	P801	Elaina	Gryder	335-9987
6	P384	Kaitlin	Keane	442-5583
7	P907	Debra	Keebler	423-8849
8	P270	Yasuko	Kimbrell	993-3395
9	P118	Kyra	Kirkbride	283-9975
10	P337	Cami	Lamotte	228-5742
11	P229	Chana	Leishman	245-9488
12	P881	Jane	Lyttle	443-0357
13	P902	Genie	Markus	452-9947
14	P994	Josephine	Martell	542-5584
15	P046	Shaunna	Mcglothin	442-9957
16	P211	Shirly	Milliron	593-9947
17	P828	Nickolas	Milner	442-9957
18	P445	Lavenia	Mumaw	442-2224
19	P991	Hannah	Ogata	442-2211
20				
21				
22				

	F	G	H	I	J	K	L	L
1	**Grades**							
2	ID	Course	Grade	MATCH finds the record in Student	INDEX retrieves First name	INDEX retrieves Last name	INDEX(MATCH) used together	INDEX(MATCH) used together
3	P118	BA 2000	B-	7	Kyra	Kirkbride	283-9975	=INDEX(Student[Phone],MATCH([@ID],Student[ID],0))
4	P118	ACCT 1020	A-	7	Kyra	Kirkbride	283-9975	=INDEX(Student[Phone],MATCH([@ID],Student[ID],0))
5	P211	FIN 2400	B	14	Shirly	Milliron	593-9947	=INDEX(Student[Phone],MATCH([@ID],Student[ID],0))
6	P270	BA 1000	B	6	Yasuko	Kimbrell	993-3395	=INDEX(Student[Phone],MATCH([@ID],Student[ID],0))
7	P270	MIS 2020	A	6	Yasuko	Kimbrell	993-3395	=INDEX(Student[Phone],MATCH([@ID],Student[ID],0))
8	P270	MIS 2800	B+	6	Yasuko	Kimbrell	993-3395	=INDEX(Student[Phone],MATCH([@ID],Student[ID],0))
9	P345	MIS 2010	A	1	Mana	Gorley	555-2345	=INDEX(Student[Phone],MATCH([@ID],Student[ID],0))
10	P345	QBA 2010	B-	1	Mana	Gorley	555-2345	=INDEX(Student[Phone],MATCH([@ID],Student[ID],0))
11	P345	MKT 4500	A-	1	Mana	Gorley	555-2345	=INDEX(Student[Phone],MATCH([@ID],Student[ID],0))
12	P445	ACCT 1010	A	16	Lavenia	Mumaw	442-2224	=INDEX(Student[Phone],MATCH([@ID],Student[ID],0))
13	P828	QBA 3710	B-	15	Nickolas	Milner	442-9957	=INDEX(Student[Phone],MATCH([@ID],Student[ID],0))
14	P828	MGT 2100	B+	15	Nickolas	Milner	442-9957	=INDEX(Student[Phone],MATCH([@ID],Student[ID],0))
15	P828	MGT 1300	C+	15	Nickolas	Milner	442-9957	=INDEX(Student[Phone],MATCH([@ID],Student[ID],0))
16	P881	BA 1000	A-	10	Jane	Lyttle	443-0357	=INDEX(Student[Phone],MATCH([@ID],Student[ID],0))
17	P881	ACCT 1010	B	10	Jane	Lyttle	443-0357	=INDEX(Student[Phone],MATCH([@ID],Student[ID],0))
18	P902	FIN 2500	B+	11	Genie	Markus	452-9947	=INDEX(Student[Phone],MATCH([@ID],Student[ID],0))
19	P902	FIN 2100	B	11	Genie	Markus	452-9947	=INDEX(Student[Phone],MATCH([@ID],Student[ID],0))
20	P902	MIS 2800	A	11	Genie	Markus	452-9947	=INDEX(Student[Phone],MATCH([@ID],Student[ID],0))
21	P991	MIS 2800	C	17	Hannah	Ogata	442-2211	=INDEX(Student[Phone],MATCH([@ID],Student[ID],0))
22	P991	MKT 2300	A-	17	Hannah	Ogata	442-2211	=INDEX(Student[Phone],MATCH([@ID],Student[ID],0))

Ways To Remember

Here are some equivalent ways to remember INDEX(MATCH):

=INDEX (column that has the field you want, MATCH (field you know, column that has the field you know, 0))

Or, more simply:

=INDEX (result column, MATCH (lookup Value, lookup Column, 0))

To look up the phone number for student P828 it would look like this:

=INDEX (student[phone], MATCH (P828, student[id], 0))

Since the match function is inside of the index function, match runs first and gives its value to index. That being said, it is always true that with nested functions, the interior function runs first. We already mentioned that student id P828 is in record 15, so what the computer sees is:

=INDEX (student[phone],15))

And so it returns the phone number corresponding to record 15, which of course is the phone number for student P828. That phone number is 442-9957.

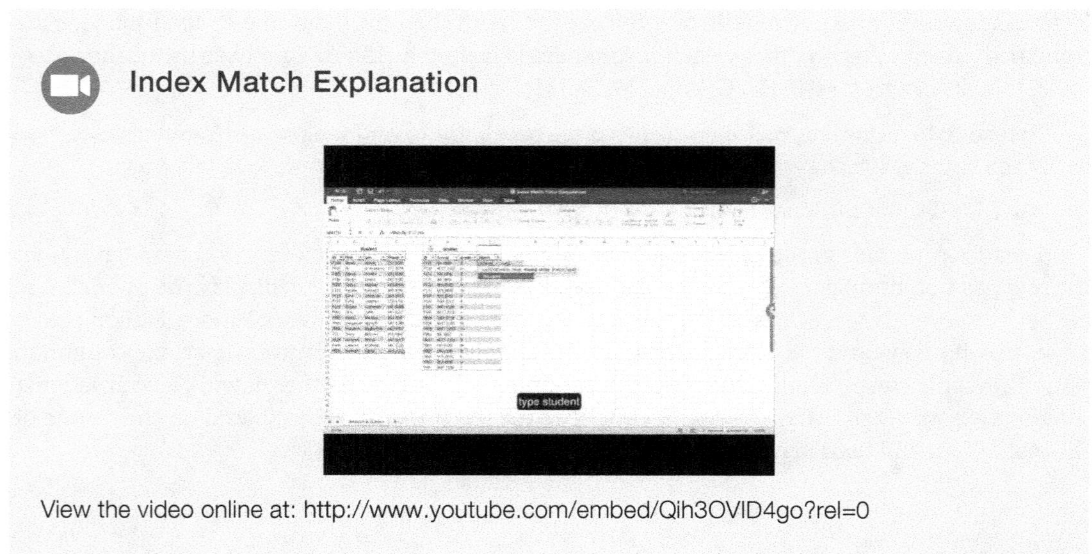

Index Match Explanation

View the video online at: http://www.youtube.com/embed/Qih3OVID4go?rel=0

Group Application 4.1: Dating Database

A. Who has been on the most dates? (From Dating Database)

- Develop the most efficient procedure to answer the question above. Be prepared to explain the procedure step by step.

Digital Downloads

GA 4.1a Date Matching by Hand.xlsx
http://scholar1.flatworldknowledge.com/uploads/GA_4_1a_Date_Matching_by_Hand-d9ff.xlsx

A. Date Matching using Database concepts and Index(Match)

1. Identify parent and child tables.
2. Identify primary and foreign keys
3. Identify one-to-many relationships
4. The primary purpose of Index(Match) is to…
   A. Integrate data that lives in separate tables
   B. Lookup values in a table
5. How does naming tables help with Index(Match)?
   A. Using table and column names is more intutive than cell ranges
   B. Index(Match) only works if the table is named
6. Which of the following statements is true?
   A. Index finds rows, Match retrieves values
   B. Match finds rows, Index retrieves values
7. You would like to retrieve both the GuyFirst name and GuyLast name for a particular record. How many Index(Match) commands will you need to run?
   A. 1
   B. 2

	A	B	C	D	E	F	G	H	I	J	K	L	M	N
1							**Dating Database**							
2														
3		**GUYS**				**GALS**						**DATES**		
4														
5	**GuyID**	**GuyFirst**	**GuyLast**		**GalID**	**GalFirst**	**GalLast**		**DateID**	**GuyID**	**GalID**	**DateTime**	**Location**	**Rating**
6	12	Archie	Abner		27	Sheryll	Albin		1	43	40	1/1/15	Philadelphia	Good
7	8	Britt	Ali		45	Iluminada	Bakos		2	29	3	1/1/15	Washington	Good
8	28	Charlie	Alls		41	Julianne	Bean		3	3	49	1/1/15	Cincinatti	Fair
9	7	Duncan	Armistead		20	Su	Berkey		4	31	42	1/1/15	Cleveland	Fair
10	33	Allen	Arsenault		6	Jeraldine	Burell		5	39	29	1/1/15	Dayton	Good
11	44	Jamison	Baade		16	Susann	Canada		6	6	9	1/1/15	Cincinatti	Good
12	43	Ray	Baylis		26	Shirlee	Cermak		7	7	24	1/2/15	Miami	Good
13	10	Roderick	Benge		31	Bernardine	Cerny		8	2	13	1/2/15	San Francisco	Poor
14	49	Alejandro	Bibbins		9	Talisha	Christon		9	50	34	1/2/15	Washington	Poor
15	18	Cyrus	Caminiti		17	Anglea	Claggett		10	18	18	1/2/15	Dayton	Fair
16	27	Branden	Coonrod		46	Keli	Cuneo		11	44	23	1/2/15	Cleveland	Good
17	4	Ralph	Cope		34	Maryln	Dean		12	31	18	1/2/15	Columbus	Good
18	42	Elwood	Damiano		36	Joeann	Decaro		13	9	24	1/2/15	Philadelphia	Good
19	21	Jere	Dedmon		7	Loyce	Delamater		14	34	29	1/2/15	Phoenix	Fair
20	38	Dee	Deramus		25	Tamar	Delorme		15	7	14	1/2/15	San Francisco	Fair
21	20	Johnie	Ebert		13	Therese	Dibenedetto		16	35	30	1/3/15	Seattle	Good

Exercise 4.1: Dating Database

Basic data analysis is relatively easy when all the data is stored in a single database table, but what if you need to analyze data that is stored in separate tables? Is there a way to find data from a table if you have related data in another table?

If you read the Index(Match) explanation document you already know that the answer is yes. The Index(Match) function enables you to use data that you already know to retrieve related, unknown values. The ability to analyze data from multiple tables really explains data analysis capabilities, which is good, because out in the real world you will often find that the data you need isn't usually neatly packaged into a single table or database. The process of analyzing data among related tables isn't difficult, but it will take some practice. In this exercise, you will get practice doing just that.

The first part of the exercise analyzes the dating data, which you see grouped in the blue colored tabs. The second part of the exercise involves addresses and zip codes; the tabs related to that part are shown in red. When both portions of the exercise are complete, please submit your Excel file online.

In the Guys-Gals-Dates tab you will find three tables of data from a dating website. Your job is to answer the questions below, which will require you to use data from multiple tables. Analyze the data from the tables using pivot tables to answer the questions and graph the results. Please add your name to the first pivot table tab.

1. Convert GUYS, GALS, and DATES to tables with those exact names.
2. Use Index(Match) to complete each record to include the first and last names of the guy and gal involved in the date. Insert columns to put those names right after their respective IDs.
3. **% City**: What percent of dates occur in each city? Show in descending order of popularity and graph.
4. **% Rating**: What percent of dates received each rating? Show in descending order of popularity and graph.
5. **Popular Guys:** Which guy(s) have been on the most dates? Produce a list of all guys on dates in descending order.
6. **Popular Gals:** Which gal(s) have been on the most dates? Produce a list of all gals on dates in descending order.
7. Which guys were never on a date? Add a column to the GUYS table and use the match function to see if there is a corresponding match in the Dates table. If there is a match, it will return the GUYID; if no match then you will get #N/A.
8. Which gals were never on a date? Similar to above.

In this portion of the exercise you will convert both the address data and ZIP code data into tables, naming them appropriately. Then you will complete the address records using the ZIP codes to look up the correct cities and states.

Although the Address and ZIP Code tables are in separate worksheets, the Index(Match) function still works the same way. Note how much easier it is to understand the functions when you have structured cell references and can refer to "Address[Zip]" instead of "D2:D53" on the Addresses tab.

Follow this link to the Excel file and video tutorial: http://tinyurl.com/zm59sa9

Exercise 4.2: Accounting and Onboarding

Data analysis is part of nearly all jobs, from entry-level positions to high-level managers in every industry. You'll often find that the data you need isn't stored nicely together where you want it so you can find the answers you need to make better decisions. In this two-part exercise, you'll again be using the Index(Match) function to insert the data you want where you need it, and analyze that data where necessary.

There are two separate scenarios in this exercise, the accounting scenario, grouped in the yellow tabs and the onboarding scenario tabs shown in blue. Please complete the worksheets associated with both scenarios and submit your completed Excel file online.

In accounting, cost and profit centers are important because they ensure that revenues and expenses are applied to the correct group within a firm. For instance, a firm's southeast region budgets $2,000 per month for mileage reimbursement. Each time a representative in the region incurs a mileage reimbursement expense, the expense will be allocated to the southeast region's cost center to ensure that the region's performance can be compared to its budget. These types of scenarios are very important to all businesses, as they are part of basic business transactions.

In the accounting portion of this exercise you will be looking up data from the Lookup tables to complete the highlighted columns in the Payroll, Sales, Mileage, Products, and Employees tabs from the Lookup Tables.

Background/Definitions

- **Cost center:** budgeting tool used to allocate expenses based on the group within the firm to which they should be applied
- **Profit center**: budgeting tool used to allocate profits based on the group within the firm to which they should be applied

Onboarding is the process of getting newly hired employees up to speed on the new job. This usually includes human resources paperwork, job responsibilities and expectations, and other day-to-day information. Successful and smooth onboarding of new hires makes those new hires feel welcomed and ensures that they can be productive as soon as possible. It's important to track the onboarding process. Large companies may have a special information system that tracks the onboarding process, but most smaller companies use a spreadsheet or database to track the progress.

In this portion of the exercise you will track the onboarding process of new hires by looking up the needed information for the New Hires table. You will determine the completion status of each item, count the number of missing items and sort the data accordingly.

Follow this link to the Excel file and video tutorial: http://tinyurl.com/zm59sa9

CHAPTER 5

Platforms, Network Effects, and Competing in a Winner-Take-All World

5.1 Introduction

Learning Objectives

1. Define network effects.
2. Recognize products and services that are subject to network effects.
3. Understand the factors that add value to products and services that are subject to network effects.

network effects

Also known as Metcalfe's Law, or network externalities. When the value of a product or service increases as its number of users expands.

Network effects are sometimes referred to as "Metcalfe's Law" or "network externalities." But don't let the dull names fool you—this concept is rocket fuel for technology firms. Bill Gates leveraged network effects to turn Windows and Office into virtual monopolies and, in the process, became the wealthiest man in America. Mark Zuckerberg of Facebook; Sergey Brin and Larry Page of Google; Pierre Omidyar of eBay; Kevin Systrom of Instagram; Jack Dorsey, Evan Williams and Biz Stone of Twitter; Nik Zennström and Janus Friis of Skype; Steve Chen and Chad Hurley of YouTube; Jan Koum and Brian Acton of WhatsApp; Jeff Bezos's Kindle; Travis Kalanick of Uber; and the Airbnb triumvirate of Brian Chesky, Joe Gebbia, and Nathan Blecharczyk—all these entrepreneurs have built massive user bases by leveraging the concept. And while US firms dominate in creating gargantuan firms fueled by network effects, the phenomenon isn't limited to the United States. China's Alibaba, Tencent (with WeChat, QQ, and Qzone), and Didi are all firms that have built multibillion dollar firms leveraging the concept. When network effects are present, *the value of a product or service increases as the number of users grows.* Simply, more users = more value. Of course, most products aren't subject to network effects; you probably don't care if someone wears the same socks, uses the same pancake syrup, or buys the same trash bags as you. But when network effects are present, they're among *the most important* reasons you'll pick one product or service over another. You may care very much, for example, if others are part of your social network, if your video game console is popular, if the VR (virtual reality) platform you're considering is likely to be a market leader, and if the Wikipedia article you're referencing has had previous readers. And all those folks who bought HD DVD players sure were bummed when the rest of the world declared Blu-ray the winner. In each of these examples, network effects are at work.

platforms

Products and services that allow for the development and integration of software products and other complementary goods, effectively creating an ecosystem of value-added offerings. Windows, iOS, the Kindle, and the standards that allow users to create Facebook apps are all platforms.

Building a network of users is powerful, building a network of firms that enhance the network's value, even more so, and that's the promise of platforms. **Platforms** create an ecosystem, rather than a singular product or service offering. Think of the number of products and services available for iOS (Apps, hardware, cars, gym equipment, medical records). Still need convincing? As of this writing, ten of the world's most valuable firms by market capitalization not only benefit from network effects, they are platform firms (Apple, Alphabet, Microsoft, Amazon, Tencent, Alibaba, and Facebook).[1]

Not *That* Kind of Network

The term "network" sometimes stumps people when first learning about network effects. In this context, a network doesn't refer to the physical wires or wireless systems that connect pieces of electronics. It just refers to a common user base that is able to communicate and share with one another. So Facebook users make up a network. So do owners of Blu-ray players, traders who buy and sell stock over the NASDAQ, or the sum total of hardware and outlets that support the BS 1363 electrical standard.

Key Takeaway

- Network effects are among the most powerful strategic resources that can be created by technology-based innovation. Many category-dominating organizations and technologies, including Microsoft, Apple, NASDAQ, eBay, Facebook, and Visa, owe their success to network effects. Network effects are also behind the establishment of most standards, including Blu-ray, Wi-Fi, and Bluetooth.

Questions and Exercises

1. What are network effects? What are the other names for this concept?
2. List several products or services subject to network effects. What factors do you believe helped each of these efforts achieve dominance?
3. Which firm do you suspect has stronger end-user network effects: Google's online search tool or Microsoft's Windows operating system? Why?
4. Network effects are often associated with technology, but tech isn't a prerequisite for the existence of network effects. Name a product, service, or phenomenon that is not related to information technology that still dominates due to network effects.

5.2 Platforms Are Powerful, But Where Does All That Value Come From?

Learning Objectives

1. Identify the three primary sources of value for network effects.
2. Recognize factors that contribute to the staying power and complementary benefits of a product or service subject to network effects.
3. Understand how firms like Microsoft and Apple each benefit from strong network effects.

The value derived from network effects comes from three sources: exchange, staying power, and complementary benefits.

Exchange

Facebook for one person isn't much fun, and the first guy in the world with a fax machine didn't have much more than a paperweight. But as each new Facebook friend or fax user comes online, a network becomes more valuable because its users can potentially communicate with more people. These examples show the importance of *exchange* in creating value. Every product or service subject to network effects fosters some kind of exchange. For firms leveraging technology, this might include anything you can represent in the ones and zeros of digital storage, such as messaging, movies, music, money, video games, and computer programs. And just about any standard that allows things to plug into one another, interconnect, or otherwise communicate will live or die based on its ability to snare network effects.

Exercise: Graph It

Some people refer to network effects by the name Metcalfe's Law. It got this name when, toward the start of the dot-com boom, Bob Metcalfe (the inventor of the Ethernet networking standard) wrote a column in *InfoWorld* magazine stating that the value of a network equals its number of users squared. What do you think of this formula? Graph the law with the vertical axis labeled "value" and the horizontal axis labeled "users." Do you think the graph is an accurate representation of what's happening in network effects? If so, why? If not, what do you think the graph really looks like?

Staying Power

Users don't want to buy a product or sign up for a service that's likely to go away, and a number of factors can halt the availability of an effort: a firm could go bankrupt or fail to attract a critical mass of user support, or a rival may successfully invade its market and draw away current customers. Networks with greater numbers of users suggest a stronger **staying power**. The staying power, or

staying power

The long-term viability of a product or service.

long-term viability, of a product or service is particularly important for consumers of technology products. Consider that when someone buys a personal computer and makes a choice of Windows, Mac OS, or Linux, their investment over time usually greatly exceeds the initial price paid for the operating system. A user invests in learning how to use a system, buying and installing software, entering preferences or other data, creating files—all of which means that if a product isn't supported anymore, much of this investment is lost.

switching costs

The cost a consumer incurs when moving from one product to another. It can involve actual money spent (e.g., buying a new product) as well as investments in time, any data loss, and so forth.

The concept of staying power (and the fear of being stranded in an unsupported product or service) is directly related to **switching costs** (the cost a consumer incurs when moving from one product to another), and switching costs can strengthen the value of network effects as a strategic asset. The higher the value of the user's overall investment, the more they're likely to consider the staying power of any offering before choosing to adopt it. Similarly, the more a user has invested in a product, the less likely he or she is to leave. Considering e-book readers? A user aware of Barnes & Noble's struggles might think twice about choosing the Nook over Amazon's thriving and dominant Kindle.

Switching costs also go by other names. You might hear the business press refer to products (particularly websites) as being "sticky" or creating "friction." Others may refer to the concept of "lock-in." And the elite Boston Consulting Group is really talking about a firm's switching costs when it refers to how well a company can create customers who are "barnacles" (that are tightly anchored to the firm) and not "butterflies" (that flutter away to rivals). The more friction available to prevent users from migrating to a rival, the greater the switching costs. And in a competitive market where rivals with new innovations show up all the time, that can be a very good thing!

total cost of ownership

An economic measure of the full cost of owning a product (typically computing hardware and/or software). TCO includes direct costs such as purchase price, plus indirect costs such as training, support, and maintenance.

How Important are Switching Costs to Microsoft?

*"It is this switching cost that has given our customers the patience to stick with Windows through all our mistakes, our buggy drivers, our high TCO [**total cost of ownership**], our lack of a sexy vision at times, and many other difficulties [...] Customers constantly evaluate other desktop platforms, [but] it would be so much work to move over that they hope we just improve Windows rather than force them to move. [...] In short, without this exclusive franchise [meaning Windows] we would have been dead a long time ago."*

—Comments from a Microsoft General Manager in a memo to Bill Gates[2]

Complementary Benefits

complementary benefits

Products or services that add additional value to the primary product or service that makes up a network.

Complementary benefits are those products or services that add additional value to the network. These products might include "how-to" books, software, and feature add-ons, even labor. You'll find more books about auctioning that focus on eBay, more cameras that upload video to YouTube, and more accountants who know Excel than other rival software. Why? Book authors, camera manufacturers, and accountants invest their time and resources where they're likely to reach the biggest market and get the greatest benefit. In auctions, video, and spreadsheet software, eBay, YouTube, and Excel each dwarf their respective competition.

Products and services that encourage others to offer complementary goods are sometimes called **platforms**.[3] Many firms do this by providing **APIs** or application programming interfaces that allow third parties to integrate with their products and services. Allowing other firms to contribute to your platform can be a brilliant strategy because those firms will spend *their* time and money to enhance *your* offerings. Consider the billion-dollar hardware ecosystem that Apple has cultivated around iOS products. There are over ninety brands selling some 280 models of speaker systems.[4] Apple has begun to extend iOS into all sorts of products. CarPlay puts Siri on your steering wheel and allows auto manufacturers to integrate phone, maps, messaging, music, and other apps into automobile dashboards. Eighteen auto manufacturers, from Ford to Ferrari, committed to CarPlay at launch, and many more have been added since then. HealthKit allows Apple to use iOS as a platform for exercise and personal health measurement (products and services that measure fitness and health are sometimes referred to by the term "quantified self"). HomeKit and the Home app allow iOS to control home products including locks, lighting, security cameras, and thermostats. Today, every major maker of home accessories supports the HomeKit platform. Apple Message has also become a platform, allowing developers to build apps to share cash via a text or jointly order food with friends. Apple's CloudKit allows developers to plug into Apple's storage, hopefully creating greater bonds with iOS at the center instead of choosing rival storage platforms from Dropbox, Google, Microsoft, or others. AirPlay links Macs, iOS devices, and AppleTV. Apple Watch is designed as a tool that integrates and extends the iPhone. And Apple Pay and Siri make iOS platforms all the more valuable by allowing developers to integrate payments and voice into their apps. Each add-on enhances the value of choosing iOS over rival platforms. Software-based ecosystems can grow very quickly. Less than one year after its introduction, the iTunes App Store boasted over fifty thousand applications, collectively downloaded over one billion times. Today, well over two million iOS apps have been downloaded over 130 billion times, collectively.[5]

platforms

Products and services that allow for the development and integration of software products and other complementary goods, effectively creating an ecosystem of value-added offerings. Windows, iOS, the Kindle, and the standards that allow users to create Facebook apps are all platforms.

APIs

Programming hooks, or guidelines, published by firms that tell other programs how to get a service to perform a task such as send or receive data. For example, Amazon provides application programming interfaces (APIs) to let developers write their own applications and websites that can send the firm orders.

Overview of Apple's HomeKit

A video overview of Apple's HomeKit, including partner products and capabilities.

View the video online at: http://www.youtube.com/embed/JdazaciENGk?rel=0

These three value-adding sources—*exchange, staying power,* and *complementary benefits*—often work together to reinforce one another in a way that makes the network effect even stronger. When users *exchanging* information attract more users, they can also attract firms offering *complementary* products. When developers of complementary products invest time writing software—and users install, learn, and customize these products—switching costs are created that enhance the *staying power* of a given network. From a strategist's perspective this can be great news for dominant firms in markets where network effects exist. The larger your network, the more difficult it becomes for rivals to challenge your leadership position.[6]

Key Takeaways

- Products and services subject to network effects get their value from exchange, perceived staying power, and complementary products and services. Tech firms and services that gain the lead in these categories often dominate all rivals.
- Many firms attempt to enhance their network effects by creating a platform for the development of third-party products and services that enhance the primary offering.

Questions and Exercises

1. What are the factors that contribute to the value created by network effects?
2. Why is staying power particularly important to many technology products and services?
3. Think about the kinds of technology products that you own that are subject to network effects. What sorts of exchange do these products leverage (e.g., information, money, software, or other media)?
4. Think about the kinds of technology projects you own. What sorts of switching costs are inherent in each of these? Are these strong switching costs or weak switching costs? What would it take for you to leave one of these services and use a rival? How might a competitor try to lessen these switching costs to persuade you to adopt their product?
5. Which other terms are sometimes used to describe the phenomenon of switching costs?
6. Think about the kinds of technology products that you own that are subject to network effects. What sorts of complementary benefits are available for these products? Are complementary benefits strong or weak (meaning, do people choose the product primarily based on these benefits, or for some other reason)?
7. Identify firms that you believe have built a strong platform. Can you think of firms that have tried to develop a platform, but have been less successful? Why do you suppose they have struggled?

5.3 One-Sided or Two-Sided Markets?

Learning Objectives

1. Recognize and distinguish between one-sided and two-sided markets.
2. Understand same-side and cross-side exchange benefits.

Understanding Network Structure

To understand the key sources of network value, it's important to recognize the structure of the network. Some networks derive most of their value from a single class of users. An example of this kind of network is messaging. While you might have different messaging apps for different purposes (Snapchat for disposable posts, Instagram for photos), you pretty much choose a tool based on how many of your contacts you can reach. Economists would call messaging a **one-sided market** (a market that derives most of its value from a single class of users), and the network effects derived from users attracting more users as being **same-side exchange benefits** (benefits derived by interaction among members of a single class of participant).

But some markets comprise two distinct categories of network participants. Consider video games. People buy a video game console largely based on the number of really great games available for the system. Software developers write games based on their ability to reach the greatest number of paying customers, so they're most likely to write for the most popular consoles first. Economists would call this kind of network a **two-sided market** (network markets that comprise two distinct categories of participant, both of which are needed to deliver value for the network to work). When an increase in the number of users on one side of the market (console owners, for example) creates a rise in the other side (software developers), that's called a **cross-side exchange benefit**.

one-sided market

A market that derives most of its value from a single class of users (e.g., instant messaging).

same-side exchange benefits

Benefits derived by interaction among members of a single class of participant (e.g., the exchange value when increasing numbers of IM users gain the ability to message each other).

two-sided market

Network market that comprises two distinct categories of participant, both of which are needed to deliver value for the network to work (e.g., video game console owners and developers of video games).

cross-side exchange benefit

When an increase in the number of users on one side of the market (console owners, for example) creates a rise in the other side (software developers).

The Positive Feedback Loop of Network Effects: One-Sided, Two-Sided, and Sometimes a Bit of Both

Messaging is considered a one-sided market (or one-sided network), where the value-creating, positive-feedback loop of network effects comes mostly from same-side benefits from a single group (messaging members who attract other members who want to communicate with them). Mobile payment efforts like Square, Apple Pay, and Android Pay, however, are considered to be two-sided markets, where significant benefits come from two distinct classes of users that add value by attracting each other. In the case of mobile payments, the more people who use a given payment platform, the more attractive that platform will be to storefronts and other businesses, and if more businesses accept these forms of mobile payment, then this in turn should attract more end consumers (and so on). Jump-starting a two-sided network can be tricky. Google and Apple use their mobile operating systems to embed their payment apps in millions of hardware products. Google hopes that its presence on Android and its ad relationship with many retailers will help it jump-start Android Pay–accepting merchant adoption. iTunes and the App Store helped Apple have over 800 million credit cards on file at the launch of Apple Pay for iOS.[7] Firms need a strong incentive for users to download and set up payments. Starbucks built a wildly successful payments app by offering rewards for frequent customer purchases. However, Square's payment app struggled when customers saw little incentive to install an app when cash and credit worked fine and using the app offered no incentive over alternatives.

It's also possible that a network may have both same-side and cross-side benefits. Microsoft's Xbox benefits from cross-side benefits in that more users of that console attract more developers writing more software titles and vice versa. However, the Xbox Live network that allows users to play against each other has same-side benefits. If your buddies use Xbox Live and you want to play against them, you're more likely to buy an Xbox. Apple also created a two-sided game in messaging when it turned iOS messaging into a platform, allowing app developers to add all sorts of new capabilities, from custom emojis and animations to collaborative apps shared via what used to be simple text messaging.

Key Takeaways

- In one-sided markets, users gain benefits from interacting with a similar category of users (think messaging apps, where everyone can send and receive messages to and from one another).
- In two-sided markets, users gain benefits from interacting with a separate, complementary class of users (e.g., in the mobile payment business, payment app–wielding consumers are attracted to a platform because there are more merchants offering convenient payment, while merchants are attracted to a payment system that others will actually use and that yields clear benefits over cash).

Questions and Exercises

1. What is the difference between same-side exchange benefits and cross-side exchange benefits?
2. What is the difference between a one-sided market and a two-sided market?
3. Give examples of one-sided and two-sided markets.
4. Identify examples of two-sided markets where both sides pay for a product or service. Identify examples where only one side pays. What factors determine who should pay? Does paying have implications for the establishment and growth of a network effect? What might a firm do to encourage early network growth?
5. The Apple iOS Developer Program provides developers access to the App Store, where they can distribute their free or commercial applications to millions of iPad, iPhone, and iPod touch customers. Would the iPhone market be considered a one- or two-sided market? Why?

5.4 How Are These Markets Different?

Learning Objectives

1. Understand how competition in markets where network effects are present differ from competition in traditional markets.
2. Understand the reasons why it is so difficult for late-moving, incompatible rivals to compete in markets where a dominant, proprietary standard is present.

When network effects play a starring role, competition in an industry can be fundamentally different than in conventional, non-network industries.

First, network markets experience *early, fierce competition*. The positive-feedback loop inherent in network effects—where the biggest networks become even bigger—causes this. Firms are very aggressive in the early stages of these industries because once a leader becomes clear, *bandwagons* form, and new adopters begin to overwhelmingly favor the leading product over rivals, tipping the market in favor of one dominant firm or standard. This tipping can be remarkably swift. Once the majority of major studios and retailers began to back Blu-ray over HD DVD, the latter effort folded within weeks.

These markets are also often winner-take-all or winner-take-most, *exhibiting monopolistic tendencies* where one firm dominates all rivals. Look at all of the examples listed so far—in nearly every case the dominant player has a market share well ahead of all competitors. When, during the US Microsoft antitrust trial, Judge Thomas Penfield Jackson declared Microsoft to be a **monopoly** (a market where there are many buyers but only one dominant seller), the collective response should have been "of course." Why? The *natural state* of markets where strong network effects are present (and this includes operating systems and Office software) is for there to be one major player. Since bigger networks offer more value, they can charge customers more. Firms with a commanding network effects advantage may also enjoy substantial bargaining power over partners. For example, Apple, which controls over 75 percent of digital music sales, for years was able to dictate song pricing despite the tremendous protests of the record labels.[8] In fact, Apple's stranglehold was so strong that it leveraged bargaining power even though the "Big Four" record labels (Universal, Sony, EMI, and Warner) were themselves an **oligopoly** (a market dominated by a small number of powerful sellers) that together provide over 85 percent of music sold in the United States.

monopoly

A market where there are many buyers but only one dominant seller.

oligopoly

A market dominated by a small number of powerful sellers.

Finally, it's important to note that the best product or service doesn't always win. PlayStation 2 dominated the original Xbox in a prior generation's game console war, despite the fact that nearly every review claimed the Xbox was hands-down a technically superior machine. Why were users willing to choose an inferior product (PS2) over a superior one (Xbox)? The power of network effects! PS2 had more users, which attracted more developers offering more games.

FIGURE 5.1 Battling a Leader with Network Effects

A new rival facing a strong, incompatible incumbent can't just offer a superior product—the upstart must have an overwhelming additional value that exceeds the benefit of exchange, switching costs, and complementary products, as well.[9]

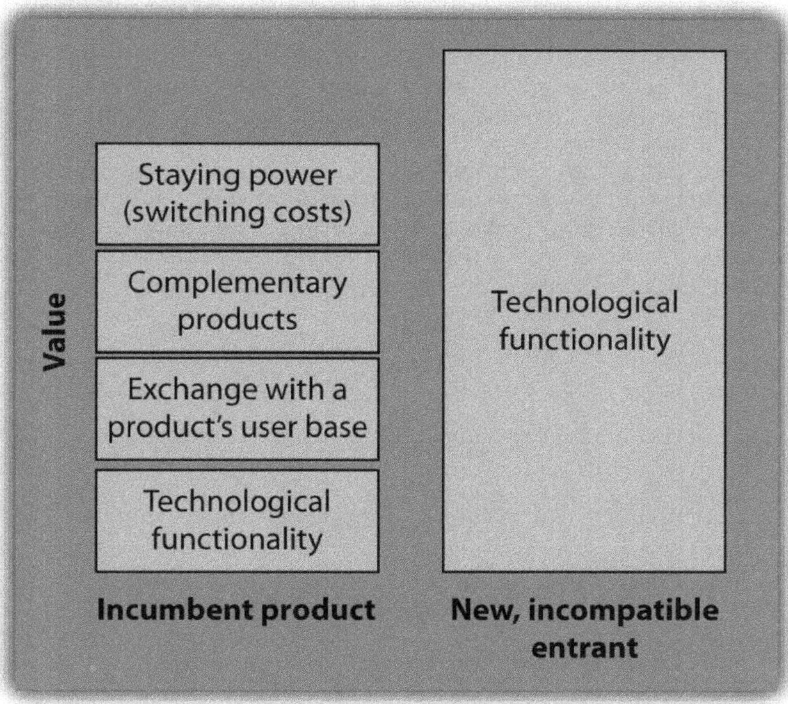

technological leapfrogging

Competing by offering a new technology that is so superior to existing offerings that the value overcomes the total resistance that older technologies might enjoy via exchange, switching cost, and complementary benefits.

This last note is a critical point to any newcomer wishing to attack an established rival. Winning customers away from a dominant player in a network industry isn't as easy as offering a product or service that is better. Any product that is incompatible with the dominant network has to exceed the value of the technical features of the leading player, plus (since the newcomer likely starts without any users or third-party product complements) the value of the incumbent's exchange, switching cost, and complementary product benefit (see Figure 5.1). And the incumbent must not be able to easily copy any of the newcomer's valuable new innovations; otherwise the dominant firm will quickly match any valuable improvements made by rivals. As such, **technological leapfrogging**, or competing by offering a superior generation of technology, can be really tough.[10]

Is This Good for Innovation?

Critics of firms that leverage proprietary standards for market dominance often complain that network effects are bad for innovation. But this statement isn't entirely true. While network effects limit competition *against* the dominant standard, innovation *within* a standard may actually blossom. Consider Windows. Microsoft has a huge advantage in the desktop operating system market, so few rivals try to compete with it. Apple's Mac OS and the open source Linux operating system are the firm's only credible rivals, and both have tiny market shares. But the dominance of Windows is a magnet for developers to innovate within the standard. Programmers with novel ideas are willing to make the investment in learning to write software for Windows because they're sure that a Windows version can be used by the overwhelming majority of computer users.

By contrast, look at the mess we initially had in the mobile phone market. With so many different handsets containing differing computing hardware, offering different screen sizes, running different software, having different key layouts, and working on different carrier networks, writing a game that's accessible by the majority of users is nearly impossible. Glu Mobile, a maker of online games, launched fifty-six reengineered builds of Monopoly to satisfy the diverse requirements of just one telecom carrier.[11] As a result, entrepreneurs with great software ideas for the mobile market were deterred because writing, marketing, and maintaining multiple product versions is both costly and risky. It wasn't until Apple's iPhone arrived, offering developers both a huge market and a consistent set of development standards, that third-party software development for mobile phones really took off. The fact that there are many different Android devices with different hardware specs running different versions of Google's mobile operating system also creates a challenge for developers. Hong Kong mobile app developer Animoca does quality assurance testing with about four hundred Android devices on every app the firm offers.[12]

FIGURE 5.2 Innovation in Fractured Standards

Because Android runs on so many different devices using various versions of the OS, game developers like Hong Kong-based Animoca test each product released on as many as four hundred devices.

Source: TechCrunch, http://techcrunch.com/2012/05/11/this-is-what-developing-for-android-looks-like/; https://creativecommons.org/licenses/by-nd/3.0/.

Key Takeaways

- Unseating a firm that dominates with network effects can be extremely difficult, especially if the newcomer is not compatible with the established leader. Newcomers will find their technology will need to be so good that it must leapfrog not only the value of the established firm's tech, but also the perceived stability of the dominant firm, the exchange benefits provided by the existing user base, and the benefits from any product complements. For evidence, just look at how difficult it's been for rivals to unseat the dominance of Windows.
- Because of this, network effects might limit the number of rivals that challenge a dominant firm. But the establishment of a dominant standard may actually encourage innovation within the standard, since firms producing complements for the leader have faith the leader will have staying power in the market.

Questions and Exercises

1. How is competition in markets where network effects are present different from competition in traditional markets?
2. What are the reasons why it is so difficult for late-moving, incompatible rivals to compete in markets where a dominant, proprietary standard is present? What is technological leapfrogging and why is it so difficult to accomplish?
3. Does it make sense to try to prevent monopolies in markets where network effects exist?
4. Are network effects good or bad for innovation? Explain.
5. What is the relationship between network effects and the bargaining power of participants in a network effects "ecosystem"?
6. Cite examples where the best technology did not dominate a network effects–driven market.

5.5 Competing When Network Effects Matter

Learning Objectives

1. Plot strategies for competing in markets where network effects are present, both from the perspective of the incumbent firm and the new market entrant.
2. Give examples of how firms have leveraged these strategies to compete effectively.

Why do you care whether networks are one-sided, two-sided, or some sort of hybrid? Well, when crafting your plan for market dominance, it's critical to know if network effects exist, how strong they might be, where they come from, and how they might be harnessed to your benefit. Here's a quick rundown of the tools at your disposal when competing in the presence of network effects.

Strategies for Competing in Markets with Network Effects (Examples in Parentheses)

- Move early (Yahoo! auctions in Japan).
- Subsidize product adoption (PayPal).
- Leverage viral promotion (Skype, WhatsApp, Uber, Airbnb, Blue Apron).
- Expand by redefining the market to bring in new categories of users (Nintendo Wii) or through convergence (iPhone).
- Form alliances and partnerships (NYCE vs. Citibank, Didi/Ola/GrabTaxi/Lyft global ride-sharing alliance vs. Uber).
- Establish distribution channels (Java with Netscape; Microsoft bundling Media Player with Windows; Apple embedding Apple Music in all Macs and iOS devices).
- Seed the market with complements (Blu-ray, Nintendo, thredUP).
- Encourage the development of complementary goods—this can include offering resources, subsidies, reduced fees, market research, development kits, and training (Oculus and Amazon Echo developer funds, Apple Swift Playgrounds).
- Maintain backward compatibility (Apple's Mac OS X Rosetta translation software for PowerPC to Intel, Samsung Pay using existing mag-stripe standards).
- For rivals, be compatible with larger networks (Apple's move to Intel; Samsung Pay's compatibility with magstripe credit card standards).
- For incumbents, constantly innovate to create a moving target and block rival efforts to access your network (Apple's efforts to block access to its own systems).
- For large firms with well-known followers, make preannouncements (Microsoft, Apple).

Move Early

In the world of network effects, this is a biggie. Being first allows your firm to start the network effects snowball rolling in your direction. In Japan, worldwide auction leader eBay showed up just five months after Yahoo! launched its Japanese auction service. But eBay was never able to mount a credible threat and ended up pulling out of the market. Being just five months late cost eBay billions in lost sales, and the firm eventually retreated, acknowledging it could never unseat Yahoo!'s network effects lead.

Another key lesson from the loss of eBay Japan? Exchange depends on the ability to communicate! eBay's huge network effects in the United States and elsewhere didn't translate to Japan because most Japanese aren't comfortable with English, and most English speakers don't know Japanese. The language barrier made Japan a "greenfield" market with no dominant player, and Yahoo!'s early move provided the catalyst for victory.

Timing is often critical in the video game console wars, too. Sony's PlayStation 2 enjoyed an eighteen-month lead over the technically superior Xbox (as well as Nintendo's GameCube). That time lead helped to create what for years was the single most profitable division at Sony. By contrast, the technically superior PS3 showed up months after Xbox 360 and at roughly the same time as the Nintendo Wii, and has struggled in its early years, racking up multibillion-dollar losses for Sony.[13]

What If Microsoft Threw a Party and No One Showed Up?

Microsoft launched the Zune media player with features that should be subject to network effects—the ability to share photos and music by wirelessly "squirting" content to other Zune users. The firm even promoted Zune with the tagline "Welcome to the Social." The problem was the Zune Social was a party no one wanted to attend. The late-arriving Zune garnered a market share of just 3 percent, and users remained hard-pressed to find buddies to leverage these neat social features.[14] A cool idea does not automatically make a network effect happen.

Subsidize Adoption

Starting a network effect can be tough—there's little incentive to join a network if there's no one in the system to communicate with. In one admittedly risky strategy, firms may offer to subsidize initial adoption in hopes that network effects might kick in shortly after. Subsidies to adopters might include a price reduction, rebate, or other giveaways. PayPal, a service that allows users to pay one another using credit cards, gave users a modest rebate as a sign-up incentive to encourage adoption of its new effort (in one early promotion, users got back $15 when spending their first $30). This brief subsidy paid to early adopters paid off handsomely. eBay later tried to enter the market with a rival effort, but as a late mover its effort was never able to overcome PayPal's momentum. PayPal was eventually purchased by eBay for $1.5 billion, and spun out of eBay at a $45 billion valuation.

FIGURE 5.3 Gilt Groupe iPad App

Gilt's ten-dollar iPad subsidy and instant membership offer helped fuel adoption of the iPad app. Mobile apps now account for 15 percent of the high-end fashion site's sales.

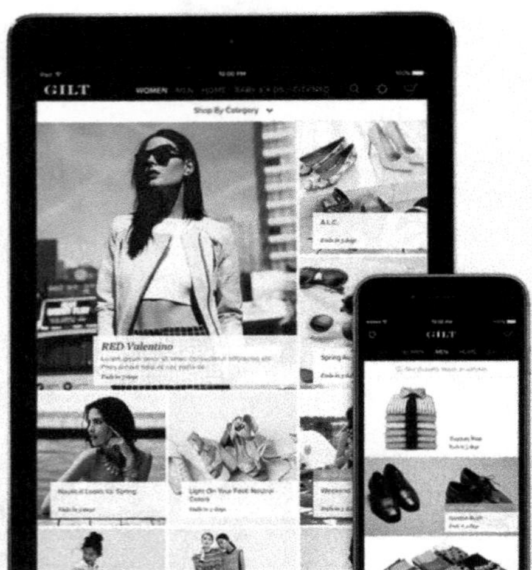

Source: "Tap into the Gilt App," Gilt, https://www.gilt.com/apps/iphone.

Gilt Groupe, a high-end fashion flash deals site, used subsidies to increase adoption of the firm's mobile app "Gilt on the Go"—fueling the growth of a new and vital distribution channel. Gilt knew that getting its app into the purses and pockets of more of its users would increase the chance that a customer would view more deals and act on them. To encourage mobile owners to download the Gilt app, the company offered instant membership (as opposed to its normal invitation-only model) and a ten-dollar credit to the first ten thousand new subscribers. Awareness of Gilt on the Go spread virally, and apps grew in a flash, accounting for 15 percent of the firm's revenue within months.[15] Some of the best approaches to competing in network markets will simultaneously leverage several of the strategies we're outlining here, and in the case of Gilt, the *subsidy* helped create *viral* promotion that in turn helped establish a new *distribution channel*. Mobile is especially important for Gilt, since the firm offers flash sales. Making sure the firm can message users on their nondesktop screens increases the chances for the firm to reach and engage consumers, and rack up more sales.

When Even Free Isn't Good Enough

Subsidizing adoption after a rival has achieved dominance can be an uphill battle, and sometimes even offering a service for free isn't enough to combat the dominant firm. When Yahoo! introduced a US auction service to compete with eBay, it initially didn't charge sellers at all (sellers typically pay eBay a small percentage of each completed auction). The hope was that with the elimination of seller fees, enough sellers would jump from eBay to Yahoo! and help the late-mover catch up in the network effect game.

But eBay sellers were reluctant to leave for two reasons. First, there weren't enough buyers on Yahoo! to match the high bids they earned on much-larger eBay. Some savvy sellers played an arbitrage game where they'd buy items on Yahoo!'s auction service at lower prices and resell them on eBay, where more users bid prices higher.

Second, any established seller leaving eBay would give up their valuable "seller ratings," and would need to build their Yahoo! reputation from scratch. Seller ratings represent a critical switching cost, as many users view a high rating as a method for reducing the risk of getting scammed or receiving lower-quality goods.

Auctions work best for differentiated goods. While Amazon has had some success in peeling away eBay sellers who provide commodity products (a real danger as eBay increasingly relies on fixed-price sales), eBay's dominant share of the online auction market still towers over all rivals.[16] While there's no magic in the servers used to create eBay, the early use of technology allowed the firm to create both network effects and switching costs—a dual strategic advantage that has given it a hammerlock on auctions even as others have attempted to mimic its service and undercut its pricing model.

Leverage Viral Promotion

Since all products and services foster some sort of exchange, it's often possible to leverage a firm's customers to promote the product or service. Internet calling service Skype (now owned by Microsoft) has over 600 million registered users yet has spent almost nothing on advertising. Neither has WhatsApp (now part of Facebook) with over a billion monthly active users.[17] Most Skype and WhatsApp users were recruited by others who shared the word on free and low-cost Internet calls and text messaging. And rise of social media has made viral promotion a tool that many firms can exploit. Facebook, Twitter, and mobile app integration with a phone's address book all act as a catalyst for friends to share deals, spread a good word, sign up for services, and load applications.

Viral promotions are also often linked to subsidies (e.g., recruit a new customer and you both get money to spend), but they can also provide the additional benefit of leveraging a trusted friend to overcome adoption inertia. Sharing economy firms Uber and Airbnb have both used these kinds of incentives as trust proxies, or what is sometimes referred to as **social proof**. When a friend sends an invite to a service where users may otherwise have trust concerns (e.g., Uber and stepping into a car driven by a stranger, staying in someone's home through Airbnb), an endorsement by a friend can ease concerns. Airbnb saw bookings increase as much as 25 percent in markets after offering friend referral incentives, and the firm says patrons referred by friends are more likely to revisit the site and book future trips, and they are much more likely to send referrals themselves.[18]

social proof

The positive influence created when someone finds out that others are doing something.

Meal kit service Blue Apron leveraged social proof as a key to building a $3 billion firm with $600 million in annual sales in just three years.[19] Users love photographing food they've prepared, so Facebook and Instagram posts raise awareness. Members are also rewarded with meals they can "gift" to friends who haven't yet tried the service. And leveraging the subsidy method mentioned above, Blue Apron also gives new subscribers free meals as an incentive to try the service. These strategies have helped the firm grow to profitability and become the undisputed market leader in a crowded market.[20]

Expand by Redefining the Market

If a big market attracts more users (and in two-sided markets, more complements), why not redefine the space to bring in more users? Nintendo did this when launching the Wii. While Sony and Microsoft focused on the graphics and raw processing power favored by hard-core male gamers, Nintendo chose to develop a machine to appeal to families, women, and age groups that normally shunned alien shoot-'em-ups. By going after a bigger, redefined market, Nintendo was able to rack up sales that exceeded the Xbox 360, even though it followed the system by twelve months.[21]

blue ocean strategy

An approach where firms seek to create and compete in uncontested "blue ocean" market spaces, rather than competing in spaces and ways that have attracted many, similar rivals.

Seeking the Blue Ocean? Better Think Strategically

Reggie Fils-Aimé, the president of Nintendo of America, has described the Wii Strategy as a blue ocean effort.[22] The concept of **blue ocean strategy** was popularized by European Institute of Business Administration (INSEAD) professors W. Chan Kim and Renée Mauborgne (authors of a book with the same title).[23] The idea—instead of competing in *blood-red* waters where the sharks of highly competitive firms vie for every available market scrap, firms should seek the *blue waters* of uncontested, new market spaces.

For Nintendo, the granny gamers, moms, and party-goers who flocked to the Wii represented an undiscovered feast in the blue ocean. Talk about new markets! Consider that the best-selling video game following the Wii's breakout launch was Wii Fit—a genre-busting title that comes with a scale so you can weigh yourself each time you play. That's a far cry from Grand Theft Auto IV, the title ranking fifth in 2008 sales, and trailing four Wii-only exclusives.

Blue ocean strategy often works best when combined with strategic positioning described in [Content Removed: #fwk-38086-ch02]. If an early mover into a blue ocean can use this lead to create defensible assets for sustainable advantage, late moving rivals may find markets unresponsive to their presence. Of course, if your firm's claim in the blue ocean is based on easily imitated resources (like technology features), then holding off rivals will be tougher. For holiday season 2010, Microsoft showed up with its own motion-gaming controller, the Kinect video camera system. Kinect was such a hit with generation Wii that it became the fastest-selling consumer electronics product in history, pumping up Xbox 360 console sales and goosing Microsoft's entertainment division from zero to a billion dollars in profits in just two years.[24]

convergence

When two or more markets, once considered distinctly separate, begin to offer features and capabilities. As an example: the markets for mobile phones and media players are converging.

envelopment

When one market attempts to conquer a new market by making it a subset, component, or feature of its primary offering.

Market expansion sometimes puts rivals who previously did not compete on a collision course as markets undergo **convergence** (when two or more markets, once considered distinctly separate, begin to offer similar features and capabilities). Consider the market for portable electronic devices. Separate product categories for media players, cameras, gaming devices, phones, and global positioning systems (GPS) are all starting to merge. Rather than cede its dominance as a media player, Apple leveraged a strategy known as **envelopment**, where a firm seeks to make an existing market a subset of its product offering. Apple deftly morphed the iPod into the iPhone, a device that captures all of these product categories in one device. But the firm went further; the iPhone is Wi-Fi capable and offers browsing, e-mail, and an application platform in iOS that was initially based on a scaled-down version of the same OS X operating system used in Macintosh computers. As a "Pocket Mac," the appeal of the device broadened beyond just the phone or music player markets, and within two quarters of launch, iPhone became the second-leading smartphone in North America—outpacing Palm, Microsoft, Motorola and every other rival, except RIM's BlackBerry,[25] and it was only a matter of time before that rival was vanquished, as well.

Alliances and Partnerships

Firms can also use partnerships to grow market share for a network. Sometimes these efforts bring rivals together to take out a leader. In a classic example, consider ATM networks. Citibank was the first major bank in New York City to offer a large ATM network. But the Citi network was initially proprietary, meaning customers of other banks couldn't take advantage of Citi ATMs. Citi's innovation was wildly popular, and being a pioneer in rolling out cash machines helped the firm grow deposits fourfold in just a few years. Competitors responded with a partnership. Instead of each rival bank offering another incompatible network destined to trail Citi's lead, competing banks agreed to share their ATM operations through NYCE (New York Cash Exchange). While Citi's network was initially the biggest, after the NYCE launch a Chase bank customer could use ATMs at a host of other banks that covered a geography far greater than Citi offered alone. Network effects in ATMs shifted to the rival bank alliance, Citi eventually joined NYCE and today, nearly every ATM in the United States carries a NYCE sticker.

While Uber continues its relentless march toward world domination, four of its biggest global competitors have formed an alliance to reduce costs, preserve their strength in markets where they lead, and build a global rival to Uber-everywhere. The firms Lyft, Ola, Didi Chuxing, and GrabTaxi, now known as Grab, share technology, local market knowledge, and business resources, with the leading firm in each nation handling mapping, routing, and payments. The firms, which operate regionally and don't really compete with one another, will allow users to book cabs from each other's apps in all the regions where they operate. Didi dominates China and enjoys deep integration in the wildly popular WeChat app (it is so dominant there that Uber sold its China business to Didi). Ola is India's local leader. GrabTaxi is big in Malaysia, Singapore, Indonesia, Philippines, Vietnam, and Thailand. Firms hope that cost savings, tech sharing, and global appeal will keep Uber at bay,[26] although it is unclear how the deal between Uber and Didi will impact the future of this alliance.[27]

Share or Stay Proprietary?

Defensive moves like the ones above are often meant to diffuse the threat of a proprietary rival. Sometimes firms decide from the start to band together to create a new, more open standard, realizing that collective support is more likely to jump-start a network than if one firm tried to act with a closed, proprietary offering. Examples of this include the coalitions of firms that have worked together to advance standards like Bluetooth and Wi-Fi. While no single member firm gains a direct profit from the sale of devices using these standards, the standard's backers benefit when the market for devices expands as products become more useful because they are more interoperable.

Leverage Distribution Channels

Firms can also think about novel ways to distribute a product or service to consumers. Sun faced a challenge when launching the Java programming language—no computers could run it. In order for Java to work, computers need a little interpreter program called the Java Virtual Machine (JVM). Most users weren't willing to download the JVM if there were no applications written in Java, and no developers were willing to write in Java if no one could run their code. Sun broke the logjam when it *bundled* the JVM with Netscape's browser. When millions of users downloaded Netscape, Sun's software snuck in, almost instantly creating a platform of millions for would-be Java developers. Today, even though Netscape has failed, Sun's Java remains one of the world's most popular programming languages. Indeed, Java was cited as one of the main reasons for Oracle's 2009 acquisition of Sun, with Oracle's CEO saying the language represented "the single most important software asset we have ever acquired."[28]

FIGURE 5.4 Apple's Retail Stores

Most pundits expected Apple retail to fail. Instead the stores provided a wildly successful channel to reach customers, explain products, and make sales.

Source: View Apart / Shutterstock.com

And when you don't have distribution channels, create them. That's what Apple did when it launched the Apple retail stores a little over a decade ago. At the time of launch, nearly every pundit expected the effort to fail. But it turns out, the attractive, high-service storefronts were the perfect platform to promote the uniqueness of Apple products. Apple's more than four hundred stores worldwide now bring in over $21 billion in revenue[29] and are among the world's most successful retail outlets on a sales-per-square-foot basis.[30]

As mentioned in [Content Removed: #fwk-38086-ch02], Microsoft is in a particularly strong position to leverage its products as distribution channels. The firm often bundles its new products into its operating systems, Office suite, Internet Explorer browser, and other offerings. The firm used this tactic to transform once market-leader Real Networks into an also-ran in streaming audio. Within a few years of bundling Windows Media Player (WMP) with its other products, WMP grabbed the majority of the market, while Real's share had fallen to below 10 percent.[31]

Caution is advised, however. Regional antitrust authorities may consider product bundling by dominant firms to be anticompetitive. European regulators have forced Microsoft to unbundle Windows Media Player from its operating system and to provide a choice of browsers alongside Internet Explorer. Over the past decade the EU has slapped Microsoft with penalties that have amounted to over 2 billion euros in total.[32]

Seed the Market

When Sony launched the PS3, it subsidized each console by selling at a price estimated at three hundred dollars below unit cost.[33] Subsidizing consoles is a common practice in the video game industry—game player manufacturers usually make most of their money through royalties paid by game developers. But Sony's subsidy had an additional benefit for the firm—it helped sneak a Blu-ray player into every home buying a PS3 (Sony was backing the Blu-ray standard over the rival HD DVD effort). PS3 has struggled with fierce competition, but initially seeding the market with low-cost Blu-ray players at a time when that hardware sold at a very high price gave eventual winner Blu-ray some extra momentum. Since Sony is also a movie studio and manufacturer of DVD players and other consumer electronics, it had a particularly strong set of assets to leverage to encourage the adoption of Blu-ray over rival HD DVD.

Giving away products for half of a two-sided market is an extreme example of this kind of behavior, but it's often used. In two-sided markets, you charge the one who will pay. Adobe gives away the Acrobat reader to build a market for the sale of software that creates Acrobat files. Firms with Yellow Page directories give away countless copies of their products, delivered straight to your home, in order to create a market for selling advertising. And Google does much the same by providing free, ad-supported search.

Consignment firm thredUP buys clothing from one group of customers, then photographs and warehouses them for resale to others. Sending high-quality used clothes to thredUP can be a quick way to earn cash, but it can also lead to a lopsided market, where supply exceeds demand. In order to seed the "buy" side for its duds by encouraging sellers to become buyers, too, thredUP will give clothes sellers immediate purchase credit for any resale items that thredUP accepts for sale. Want cash instead? You'll get it, but you'll have to wait two weeks.

Encourage the Development of Complementary Goods

There are several ways to motivate others to create complementary goods for your network. These efforts often involve some form of developer subsidy or other free or discounted service. A firm may charge lower royalties or offer a period of royalty-free licensing. It can also offer free software development kits (SDKs), training programs, co-marketing dollars, or even startup capital to potential suppliers. Microsoft and Apple both allow developers to sell their products online through Xbox LIVE Marketplace and iTunes, respectively. This channel lowers developer expenses by eliminating costs associated with selling physical inventory in brick-and-mortar stores and can provide a free way to reach millions of potential consumers without significant promotional spending.

Firms are also leveraging several techniques to encourage the creation of complementary goods for their platforms. Oculus has a $10 million fund to encourage indie game developers to build for the platform; Slack has announced an $80 million investment fund intended to boost companies that are building products that enhance the firm's business productivity platform[34]; and Amazon has a $100 million fund to developers enhancing technologies and providing new apps (called "skills" by Amazon) for its voice-activated Echo products.[35] Apple has taken encouraging developers a step further by offering Swift Playgrounds in the iPad, a kid-focused learn-to-program environment featuring the created-by-Apple Swift programming language. Apple has since open sourced Swift so it can be used on development efforts outside its own products, and its broad efforts to encourage Swift adoption have made Swift one of the world's most popular and in-demand programming languages.[36]

Leverage Backward Compatibility

Those firms that control a standard would also be wise to ensure that new products have **backward compatibility** with earlier offerings. If not, they reenter a market at installed-base zero and give up a major source of advantage—the switching costs built up by prior customers. For example, when Nintendo introduced its 16-bit Super Nintendo system, it was incompatible with the firm's highly successful prior generation 8-bit model. Rival Sega, which had entered the 16-bit market two years prior to Nintendo, had already built up a large library of 16-bit games for its system. Nintendo entered with only its debut titles, and no ability to play games owned by customers of its previous system, so there was little incentive for existing Nintendo fans to stick with the firm.[37] iTunes users also found migration to Spotify made particularly easy since the latter offered the option of importing iTunes playlists.

backward compatibility

The ability to take advantage of complementary products developed for a prior generation of technology.

adaptor

A product that allows a firm to tap into the complementary products, data, or user base of another product or service.

Backward compatibility was the centerpiece of Apple's strategy to revitalize the Macintosh through its move to the Intel microprocessor. Intel chips aren't compatible with the instruction set used by the PowerPC processor used in earlier Mac models. Think of this as two entirely different languages—Intel speaks French, PowerPC speaks Urdu. To ease the transition, Apple included a free software-based **adaptor**, called Rosetta, that automatically emulated the functionality of the old chip on all new Macs (a sort of Urdu to French translator). By doing so, all new Intel Macs could use the base of existing software written for the old chip; owners of PowerPC Macs were able to upgrade while preserving their investment in old software; and software firms could still sell older programs while they rewrote applications for new Intel-based Macs. Even more significant, since Intel is the same standard used by Windows, Apple developed a free software adaptor called Boot Camp that allowed Windows to be installed on Macs. Boot Camp (and similar solutions by other vendors) dramatically lowered the cost for Windows users to switch to Macs. Within two years of making the switch, Mac sales skyrocketed to record levels. Apple now boasts a commanding lead in notebook sales to the education market,[38] and a survey by Yankee Group found that 87 percent of corporations were using at least some Macintosh computers, up from 48 percent at the end of the PowerPC era two years earlier.[39]

Samsung also leveraged backward compatibility to make Samsung Pay accepted at more retailers than either Apple Pay or Android Pay. Samsung Pay uses a technology called magnetic secure transmission (MST), which emits a magnetic signal that simulates the magnetic strip found on the back of a credit or debit card. Since vendor point-of-sale (POS) systems see Samsung Pay as if it were a regular credit card, merchants don't even need to agree to accept Samsung, it just works like plastic. A small subset of POS systems, like gas station pumps and ATMs, still require physically inserting a card, but the vast majority of merchant terminals accept the Samsung MST signal. Samsung Pay is still limited because it only works with certain phones, bank cards, and carriers, but its broad acceptance removes a major barrier to customer acceptance.[40]

Rivals: Be Compatible with the Leading Network

Companies will want to consider making new products compatible with the leading standard. Microsoft's Live Maps and Virtual Earth 3D arrived late to the Internet mapping game. Users had already put in countless hours building resources that meshed with Google Maps and Google Earth. But by adopting the same keyhole markup language (KML) standard used by Google, Microsoft could, as *TechCrunch* put it, "drink from Google's milkshake." Any work done by users for Google in KML could be used by Microsoft. Voilà, an instant base of add-on content!

Incumbents: Close Off Rival Access and Constantly Innovate

Oftentimes, firms that control dominant networks will make compatibility difficult for rivals who try to connect with their systems. For example, while many firms offer video conferencing and Internet calling, the clear leader is Skype, a product that for years had been closed to unauthorized Skype clients.

Firms that constantly innovate make it particularly difficult for competitors to become compatible. Again, we can look to Apple as an example of these concepts in action. While Macs run Windows, Windows computers can't run Mac programs. Apple has embedded key software in Mac hardware, making it difficult for rivals to write a software emulator like Boot Camp that would let

Windows PCs drink from the Mac milkshake. And if any firm gets close to cloning Mac hardware, Apple sues. The firm also modifies software on other products like the iPhone and iTunes each time wily hackers tap into closed aspects of its systems. And Apple has regularly moved to block competing third-party hardware products from plugging into iTunes.[41] Even if firms create adaptors that emulate a standard, a firm that constantly innovates creates a moving target that's tough for others to keep up with.

Apple has been far more aggressive than Microsoft in introducing new versions of its software. Since the firm never stays still, would-be cloners never get enough time to create a reliable emulator that runs the latest Apple software.

Large, Well-Known Followers: Preannouncements

Large firms that find new markets attractive but don't yet have products ready for delivery might *preannounce* efforts in order to cause potential adaptors to sit on the fence, delaying a purchasing decision until the new effort rolls out. Preannouncements only work if a firm is large enough to pose a credible threat to current market participants. While Apple rarely preannounces products, it previewed Apple Watch roughly eight months before it was ready to ship. Rivals from the Kickstarter darling, Pebble, to Google's Android Wear were courting developers, but Apple's early product demonstration caused many customers considering wearables to hold off until Apple Watch was out. Developers also knew that, unlike fragmented Android Wear offerings with varying watch face shapes and capabilities, Apple Watch would provide a uniform standard offered by the industry's biggest player. While large, respected firms may be able to influence markets through preannouncements, startups often lack credibility to delay user purchases. The tech industry acronym for the impact firms try to impart on markets through preannouncements is *FUD*, for fear, uncertainty, and doubt.

The Osborne Effect

Preannouncers, beware. Announce an effort too early and a firm may fall victim to what's known as "**The Osborne Effect**." It's been suggested that portable computer manufacturer Osborne Computer announced new models too early. Customers opted to wait for the new models, so sales of the firm's current offerings plummeted. While evidence suggests that Osborne's decline had more to do with rivals offering better products, the negative impact of preannouncements has hurt a host of other firms.[42] Among these, Sega, which exited the video game console market entirely after preannouncements of a next-generation system killed enthusiasm for its Saturn console.[43]

The Osborne Effect

When a firm preannounces a forthcoming product or service and experiences a sharp and detrimental drop in sales of current offerings as users wait for the new item.

Too Much of a Good Thing?

When network effects are present, more users attract more users. That's a good thing as long as a firm can earn money from this virtuous cycle. But sometimes a network effect attracts too many users, and a service can be so overwhelmed that it becomes unusable. These so-called **congestion effects** occur when increasing numbers of users lower the value of a product or service. This most often happens when a key resource becomes increasingly scarce. *Fortune* reported how the launch of a new version of the hit EA game SimCity fell victim to congestion effects, stating that "thanks to what the company called 'overwhelming demand,' players experienced a myriad of problems like failures to load the game entirely and wait times of twenty minutes to log in. Gameplay became so problematic that Amazon temporarily halted sales of the

congestion effects

When increasing numbers of users lower the value of a product or service.

game, and EA offered users the option of downloading a free game from its online store."[44] Twitter's early infrastructure was often unable to handle the demands of a service in hypergrowth (leading to the frequent appearance of a not-in-service graphic known in the Twitter community as the "fail whale"). Facebook users with a large number of friends may also find their attention is a limited resource, as feeds push so much content that it becomes difficult to separate interesting information from the noise of friend actions.

And while network effects can attract positive complementary products, a dominant standard may also be the first place where virus writers and malicious hackers choose to strike.

FIGURE 5.5 The Twitter Fail Whale

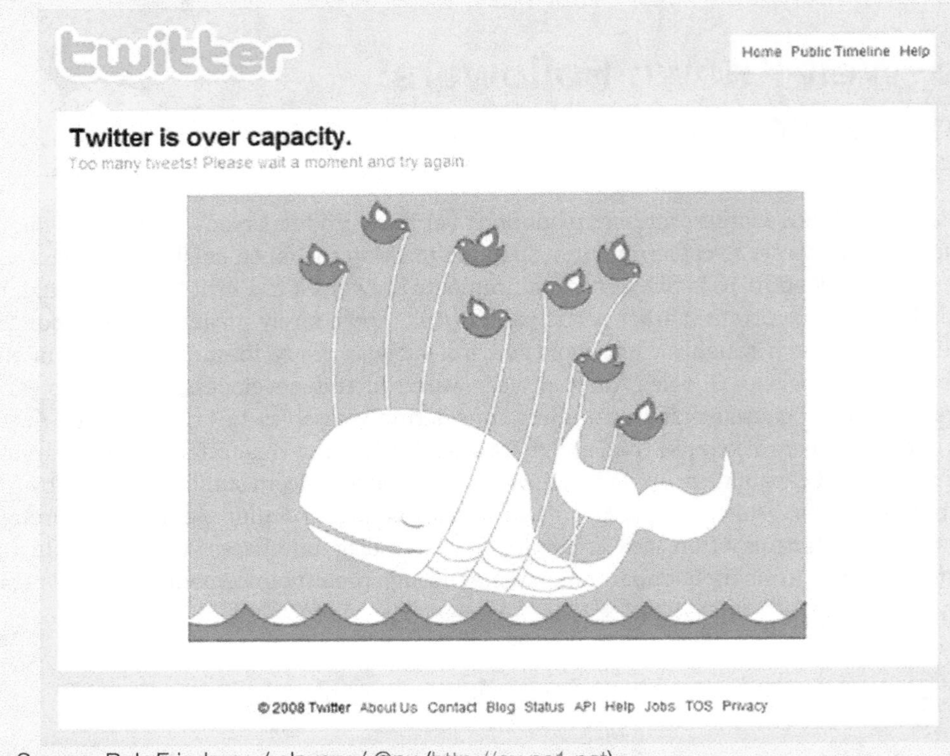

Source: Rob Friedman / playerx / @px (http://px.ns1.net).

Feel confident! Now you've got a solid grounding in network effects, the key resource leveraged by some of the most dominant firms in technology. And these concepts apply beyond the realm of tech, too. Network effects can explain phenomena ranging from why some stock markets are more popular than others to why English is so widely spoken, even among groups of nonnative speakers. On top of that, the strategies explored in the last half of the chapter show how to use these principles to sniff out, create, and protect this key strategic asset. Go forth, tech pioneer—opportunity awaits!

Key Takeaways

- Moving early matters in network markets—firms that move early can often use that time to establish a lead in users, switching costs, and complementary products that can be difficult for rivals to match.
- Additional factors that can help a firm establish a network effects lead include subsidizing adoption; leveraging viral marketing, creating alliances to promote a product or to increase a service's user base; redefining the market to appeal to more users; leveraging unique distrib-

ution channels to reach new customers; seeding the market with complements; encouraging the development of complements; and maintaining backward compatibility.

- Established firms may try to make it difficult for rivals to gain compatibility with their users, standards, or product complements. Large firms may also create uncertainty among those considering adoption of a rival by preannouncing competing products.

Questions and Exercises

1. Is market entry timing important for network effects markets? Explain and offer an example to back up your point.
2. How might a firm subsidize adoption? Give an example.
3. Give an example of a partnership or alliance targeted at increasing network effects.
4. Is it ever advantageous for firms to give up control of a network and share it with others? Why or why not? Give examples to back up your point.
5. Do firms that dominate their markets with network effects risk government intervention? Why or why not? Explain through an example.
6. How did Sony seed the market for Blu-ray players?
7. What does backward compatibility mean and why is this important? What happens if a firm is not backward compatible?
8. What tactic did Apple use to increase the acceptability of the Mac platform to a broader population of potential users?
9. How has Apple kept clones at bay?
10. What are preannouncements? What is the danger in announcing a product too early? What is the term for negative impacts from premature product announcements?
11. How did PayPal subsidize adoption?
12. Why is viral adoption especially important to PayPal and Uber?
13. Name two companies that leveraged viral promotion to compete.
14. Name a product that is the result of the *convergence* of media players, cameras, and phones.
15. What is bundling? What are the upsides and downsides of bundling?
16. Why does Adobe allow the *free* download of Acrobat Reader?
17. How does thredUP leverage its seller payout policy to balance sell-side supply with buy-side demand?
18. What tactic might an established firm employ to make it impossible, or at least difficult, for a competitor to gain access to, or become compatible with, their product or service?
19. How do Apple, Microsoft, and Facebook encourage the development of complementary products?
20. What is the "congestion effect"? Give an example.
21. Do network effects apply in nontech areas? Give examples.

5.6 From Bitcoin to Blockchain and Beyond: A Disruptive Innovation for Money and More?

Learning Objectives

1. Understand what bitcoin is, to whom it appeals and why, its strengths, and its limitations.
2. Understand Blockchain technologies—their potential benefit, current weaknesses, and areas of promising and impactful use.
3. Gain additional insights into evaluating the trajectory of technology and its disruptive capacity.

bitcoin

An open source, decentralized payment system (sometimes controversially referred to as a digital, virtual, or cryptocurrency) that operates in a peer-to-peer environment, without bank or central authority.

Bitcoin is the transaction method favored by cybercriminals and illegal trade networks like the now shuttered Silk Road drugs bazaar.[45] It's not backed by gold or government and appeared seemingly out of thin air as the result of mathematics performed by so-called "miners." It's been a wildly volatile currency, where an amount that could purchase a couple of pizzas would, in three years, appreciate to be worth over $6 million.[46] Its one-time largest exchange handled hundreds of millions in digital value, yet it was originally conceived as the "Magic: The Gathering Online card eXchange" (Mt. Gox), and that service suffered a massive breach where the digital equivalent of roughly $450 million disappeared.[47] Many don't even know what to call bitcoin. Is it a cryptocurrency, a digital currency, digital money, or a virtual currency?[48] The US government has ruled that bitcoin is property (US marshals have auctioned off bitcoins seized from crooks).[49]

FIGURE 5.6
The B symbol with two bars is used to refer to bitcoin.

Source: https://en.bitcoin.it/wiki/Promotional_graphics

Despite this checkered start, many think bitcoin and similar schemes (often referred to as **cryptocurrencies**) could upend money as we know it. And bitcoin isn't the only player in town. Other cryptocurrencies, such as Ethereum, Ripple, and Litecoin, have all grown to the point where the value of tokens in circulation is well into the billions of dollars for each. Deloitte has written that the negative hype surrounding bitcoin and related technologies has underestimated its potential to revolutionize not just payments but all sorts of asset transactions.[50] The Bank of England has issued a report describing bitcoin as a "significant innovation" that could have "far-reaching implications."[51]

cryptocurrencies

A digital asset where a secure form of mathematics (cryptography) is used to handle transactions, control the creation of additional units, and verify the transfer of assets. Cryptocurrencies usually take advantage of a technology known as a blockchain.

Others look beyond crypto as a money substitute, instead focusing on an enabling technologies known as the **blockchain**, a highly secure, decentralized, distributed transaction recording and verification mechanism that has been adapted for all sorts of uses, including stock sales and digital document signing.[52] The government of Singapore has worked with several large banks in a test of its own digital currency, used in a trial of a blockchain-driven system for interbank payments.[53] The National Bank of Australia and the Canadian Imperial Bank of Commerce have tested international currency transfer using the Ripple.[54] The Central Bank of Kazakhstan has developed a blockchain system to sell short-term bonds directly to retail customers without commissions or transaction fees.[55] These technologies have demonstrated enough promise that venture capitalists have poured over $1.3 billion into crypto and blockchain startups in the fourteen months from January 2017 through February 2018 and this does not include ICOs (initial coin offerings) described later.[56]

blockchain

A distributed and decentralized ledger that records and verifies transactions and ownership, making it difficult to tamper with or shut down.

How It Works

Although you might see news reports that include a graphic of a bitcoin token, that's all just the graphic arts department. In reality there is no such physical representation of bitcoin—it exists only and entirely online. Bitcoins and other cryptocurrencies are transferred from person to person like cash. Instead of using a bank as a middleman, transactions are recorded in a distributed, decentralized public ledger (known as a *blockchain*). Verification and time-stamping of transactions in the blockchain is performed across the network by a pool of users known as *miners*. The miners get an incentive for being involved: they can donate their computer power in exchange for the opportunity to earn additional tokens in the cryptocurrency—for example, fractions of bitcoin—and sometimes miners earn modest transaction fees. This means bitcoin and other crypto is a *peer-produced* financial instrument (for more on peer production, see [Content Removed: #fwk-gallaugher-ch07]). While the ledger records transactions, no one can transfer the asset without a special password (called a *private key*, which is often stored in what is referred to as a cryptocurrency *wallet*, which is really just an encrypted holding place). The technology behind most crypto and blockchain technologies is open source and considered rock solid. Passwords are virtually impossible to guess, and verification makes sure no one spends the same currency in two places at once. And the decentralized nature of the system makes it extremely unlikely that the system can be directly tampered with or altered.

Introduction to Blockchain Technology

A video introduction to blockchain technology offered by IBM, a firm with a thriving practice offering blockchain technology and consulting to organizational clients.

View the video online at: http://www.youtube.com/embed/lD9KAnkZUjU?rel=0

Also note that there is no single blockchain software used by all efforts. While bitcoin has its own blockchain, other cryptocurrencies have their own versions, often involving different software. Many firms have also developed their own technologies or created solutions built on existing open source efforts.

Benefits

Much of the blockchain's appeal comes from the fact that asset ownership records are transferred from person to person like cash, rather than using an intermediary like banks or credit card companies if a cryptocurrency is used as a cash replacement. Getting rid of card companies *cuts out transaction fees*, which can top 3 percent. Overstock.com was one of the first large online retailers to accept bitcoin. Its profit margins? Just 2 percent. Needless to say, Overstock's CEO is a bitcoin enthusiast.[57] Crypto also opens up the possibility of *micropayments* (or small digital payments) that are now impractical because of fees (think of everything from gum to bus fare to small donations).

It's often thought that cryptocurrencies could be a boon for *international commerce*, especially for *cross-border remittance* and in *expanding e-commerce in emerging markets*. Family members working abroad often send funds home via services like Western Union or MoneyGram, but these can cost \$10 to \$17 for a \$200 transfer and take up to five days to clear in some countries.[58] A blockchain-based transfer would be immediate and could theoretically eliminate all transaction fees, although several firms are charging small fees to ease transactions and quickly get money moved from national currency to a cryptocurrency and back. In such a case, the bitcoin or other cryptocurrencies used are less about the currency itself and more about transfer of ownership. For example, if someone in the US wishes to send dollars to Nigeria, a service could buy bitcoin in the US for dollars, then immediately sell these bitcoin in Nigeria in the local naira currency. Firms looking at cross-border funds transfer are going after a big market: global remittances total over half a trillion dollars.[59] Cryptocurrencies might also lubricate the wheels of commerce between nations where credit card companies and firms like PayPal don't operate, and where internationally accepted cards are tough to obtain. Less than one-third of the population in emerging markets has any sort of credit card, but bitcoin could provide a vehicle to open this market up to online purchases. Remember, credit cards aren't just about cash, they're also about credit, and currently credit works for most people in highly industrialized economies. But unique, albeit limited use, cases are often the first step in the march taken by eventually disruptive technologies.

Civil libertarians like the idea of transactions happening without the prying eyes of data miners inside card companies, having their transaction history shared by others, or the government. As *Wired* points out, blockchain technologies *straddle the line between transparency and privacy*. All transactions are recorded in the open, via the blockchain, but individuals can be anonymous. You can create your anonymous private key and have someone transfer funds to you, or earn cryptocurrency via mining, and no one can see who you are. This also means that these distributed, decentralized blockchains have *no single controlling entity where fraud, corruption, damage, hacking, or government shutdown could occur*. While governments can try to shut down or legislate blockchain activity within their borders, there's no single "bitcoin" company, no "blockchain" organization to take to court and force their servers to be unplugged. It's been noted that following the revelations in WikiLeaks, Visa, Mastercard, and PayPal refused donations to WikiLeaks. In that aftermath, bitcoin became the go-to vehicle for those supporting WikiLeaks' efforts.[60] If a bitcoin transaction is not permitted in your country, go abroad and you've got full access to everything in your wallet.

A paper by Deloitte University sees the blockchain as far more than a replacement for money—it could make all sorts of financial transactions better by (potentially) making them cheaper, faster, and more secure. At its core, blockchains are *a standard for securely exchanging value and recording ownership over a network without an intermediary*. Most new blockchain technologies use software that exists outside of bitcoin (network effects are at work here—success will depend on the widespread adoption of any new blockchain standard). Blockchain technology has the potential to disrupt all sorts of systems that rely on intermediaries, including the transfer of property, execution of contracts, and identity management. The paper's authors envision using the blockchain as a sort of ownership stamp that is attached to things like vehicles, where repair history and accidents can be referenced to an ownership-representing bitcoin fragment in the way registry paperwork happens now, and where vehicle titles can be transferred by passing the ownership token from one person to another—no lawyers, no notaries, no vehicle registration required—and hence the predictions of *less expensive, faster, and more secure transactions*.[61] As the *Wall Street Journal* points out, "almost any document can be digitized, codified, and inserted into the blockchain, a record that is indelible, cannot be tampered with, and whose authenticity is verified by the consensus of a community of computer users rather than by the discretionary order of a centralized authority."[62] It's important to recognize that while bitcoin uses a blockchain ledger, not all blockchain technologies use the bitcoin blockchain. If blockchain transactions are to emerge as mainstream, governments would likely want to link to such systems when ownership needs to be verified, but all this is technically possible to build, and if it works, the disruption across industries would be massive.[63]

Examples of Blockchains in Action

Real world examples of blockchain technology can be found across industries—from banking to entertainment—practical examples and experiments that point to disruptive possibilities.

- The Nasdaq stock exchange has tested blockchain technology for transactions in its private market subsidiary, stating the exchange could eventually use the technology for Nasdaq trades in the public market.[64] Nasdaq is also using the technology to allow private companies to issue stock and stockholders of public companies to vote their shares.[65]
- A collection of over forty-five of the world's leading financial institutions, including Bank of America, Citigroup, HSBC, and ING have formed R3CEV to build infrastructure based on blockchain technology, and have engaged several national central banks, including the government of Singapore and the Bank of Canada in participation.[66]

- IBM has a growing blockchain practice, including efforts focused on managing products in the firm's supply chain, tracking items location and ownership from sourced raw materials through distribution to customers. IBM is also creating a whole new firm with shipping giant Maersk (look for their name along the side of container ships) to commercialize blockchain use in shipping.[67]
- Insurer Nationwide wants to put the blockchain on your side with a solution to help verify insurance coverage in real time, benefiting the insured, insurers, and even law enforcement.[68]
- Overstock.com has used blockchain to issue corporate bonds, and was one of the first well-known Internet retailers to accept bitcoin as payment. The firm has since created its own subsidiary tZero, to work on blockchain innovations.[69]
- De Beers, a firm that mines, trades, and markets about one-third of the world's diamonds, is developing blockchain technology for tracing diamonds from the mine to the customer purchase, a practice that should reduce fraud and help ensure that gems in the age of "Blood Diamonds" are indeed conflict free.[70]
- Spotify acquired the blockchain startup Mediachain Labs to help the firm build attribution systems, so that music rights holders are tracked and paid.[71]
- Kodak, the poster child for the disrupted market leader, is developing blockchain system for tracking rights and payments for photographers.[72]
- Facebook has a blockchain division run by the former head of PayPal.[73]

The availability of tools and services from mainstream suppliers are likely to spread blockchain use. Blockchain services, which might include do-it-yourself software and cloud services or consulting and setup for creating a functioning market using blockchain, are now offered by mainstream tech firms like Amazon, Google, IBM, and Microsoft.

Tastes Like Blockchain

Food-borne illness and a tainted food supply can be a terrifying problem with serious financial and societal implications. The US romaine lettuce e-coli epidemic sickened people across 25 states and estimates of impact run into the hundreds of millions of dollars.[74] In China, a compound used in plastics production had tainted milk, sickening some 300,000 dairy customers and killing at least six infants. Other recent examples of food foul play include wood pulp blended with Parmesan cheese, horse meat passed off as beef, and plastic found in chicken nuggets.[75] While RFID tags are being used throughout the agricultural industry to track items, another method of following food from farm to fork is the blockchain.

One firm experimenting with the technology is French department store giant Carrefour. The retailer sells over a million chickens under its house brand,[76] and now the life story of those birds is available by scanning a QR code on the package. Carrefour's supply chain is set up so that each step along the way, from hatchery to producer to store, is tracked via a blockchain entry. And the blockchain isn't just for the birds. The World Wildlife Fund is using an RFID plus blockchain solution to track tuna from boat to processing plant, potentially keeping your sushi ocean friendly and healthy. IBM is bringing together major players worldwide, including food suppliers Dole, Nestlé, Unilever, and Tyson Foods, plus retailers Walmart, Kroger, and China's JD.com, in a similar scheme to track items through the food supply.[77]

Of course, blockchain is just software, so procedures and auditing need to be put in place to ensure that the data that goes into the system is, in fact, valid, but the societal impact may be massive. Insurance lowered, supplier and restaurant bankruptcy avoided, jobs saved, illness avoided, and of course, lives saved. One study estimates that for every 1 percent reduction in food-borne diseases in the US, would prevent half a million people from getting sick,[78] resulting in a net $700 million benefit from reduced sick days and work interruptions.[79]

Concerns

Blockchain technology's future could be bright, or it could fizzle as another overhyped, underperforming technology. There are several challenges faced by cryptocurrencies, blockchain technologies, or both, that need to be overcome before it makes it in the mainstream.

For cryptocurrencies, *consumer benefit needs to be stronger*. While international remittance customers and those otherwise left out of the banking and credit card system can see immediate benefit from crypto cash replacements, most of the population isn't impacted by this market. For most, cryptocurrency is a *difficult to understand* and often *difficult to use* technology that offers little benefit. Slick apps and firms offering streamlining support services that allow, for example, the easy and quick conversion from dollars (or other currencies) to cryptocurrencies and back will help, but unless this offers consumer value beyond the credit card, few will bother to switch from plastic.

Cryptocurrencies have a *reputation problem*. Being embraced by drug dealers, extortion hackers, tax evaders, and fringe libertarians doesn't instill a lot of confidence. And it doesn't help that bitcoin was created by a mysterious, unknown entity referred to as Satoshi Nakamoto.[80]

Security concerns also pose a problem. While bitcoin software is considered to be solid, it's not a guarantee that other entities are as secure. The multimillion-dollar theft from Mt. Gox is a prime example.[81] The wallets that hold your private key are also potentially vulnerable. If your computer is wiped out by a virus and you haven't written down your password or saved a backup copy in another secure and accessible location, you're hosed; it's like money burned up in a fire. Hackers that steal passwords—whether they're on your computer or the cloud—effectively have access to anything in your crypto wallet; they can walk away with all your cash and it's unlikely that there'll be a way to recover the loot. And for all of the security and anonymity promised by the blockchain, if the sender or receiver of any data is compromised, information could escape into the wild or be captured by the nefarious.

Many firms that hope to strengthen cryptocurrency and blockchain technologies (including rival currencies, wallet builders, exchanges, and payment processors) have struggled under an *ambiguous cloud of not knowing how they will be regulated* and what legal issues apply to them.[82] China has banned bitcoin,[83] but California has moved forward to legalize the use of alternative currencies.[84] New York has announced bitcoin-friendly initiatives.[85] The government of Japan now recognizes bitcoin as a legal payment method, Russia has reversed its initial anti-bitcoin stance, and Australia has eliminated a double-taxation penalty impacting bitcoin.[86] The US government has also created regulations around bitcoin that make it less amorphous and safer for investors, while the IRS ruled that bitcoins are property.[87] Trends seem to be moving in the right direction, but financial institutions don't work well in environments of uncertainty, and clear operating guidelines and legal protections will be vital for bitcoin to thrive.

Volatility is also an issue. The chart below shows bitcoin's wild ride, over a less than 18-month period, swinging from a low of $368 to nearly $20,000. The world's second largest cryptocurrency, Ethereum, saw its value increase fifty-fold during the first half of 2017, but lost 20 percent of its value shortly after an erroneous report that its founder had died in a car crash.[88] This kind of volatility makes bitcoin and other cryptocurrencies less useful as dollar-like currencies, limiting its appeal to speculators, who often seem like get-rich-quick schemers, or the much smaller legitimate market that is looking for in-and-out transactions such as cross-border payments. Some also worry about a crypto valuation bubble.[89]

FIGURE 5.7 Bitcoin Price Fluctuation from January 1, 2016 through May 25, 2018

From 2016 through mid-2018, the price of one bitcoin fluctuated wildly, from a low of $368 to a high of nearly $20,000.

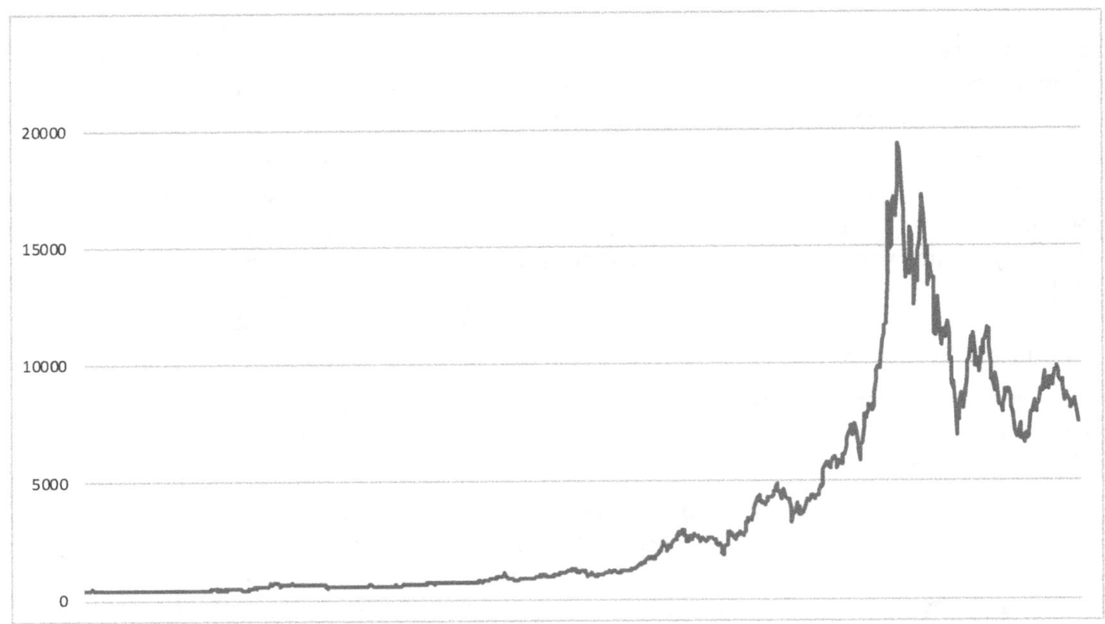

Source: Data from "Bitcoin USD (BTC-USD)." Yahoo Finance website, https://finance.yahoo.com/quote/BTC-USD/history?p=BTC-USD.

Increased *transaction volume* should help stabilize the market, increase liquidity, and bring some stability to the currency. Substantial volume means a network effect is present—the technology becomes valuable and useful because so many others are using it. But while volume will be vital for any cryptocurrency or blockchain standard, bitcoin has a long way to go. As of mid-2018, bitcoin's highest daily transaction volume was about 440,000[90] compared with the 150 million daily transactions that Visa processes.[91] And to get to that kind of volume, bitcoin will need more infrastructure support. Visa currently has the capability to handle 56,000 transactions a second, while the entire bitcoin miner network could only handle seven. That's not seven thousand, that's one hand plus two fingers.[92]

Perhaps most troubling, early bitcoin technology couldn't handle increasing transaction volume. A limitation in the structure of underlying bitcoin software limits transaction processing, and processing times ballooned to the point where several firms that once accepted bitcoin have stopped doing so. Fixes for the *scalability problem* (which has also hampered other cryptocurrencies like Ethereum) are possible, and several have been proposed, but issuing a fix involves a massive upgrade of software, and certain factions of the community (including many in the large network of small-time bitcoin miners) are wary of the impact of any change.[93] A controversial 2017 proposal to improve scalability and reduce steadily increasing bitcoin transaction costs resulted in a "hard fork" of bitcoin into an adjacent currency known as bitcoin cash.[94] Your old bitcoin could work on the new network, but there were effectively two ledgers at that point. Confused? It gets worse. Less than a year after bitcoin cash appeared, there were no less than 44 additional "forks" of bitcoin, new software ledgers that TNW referred to as "useless."[95] Blockchain technology is hurt by a *lack of standards*, and while there may be successes if a single standard emerges around, say, food safety or music licensing, we're not there yet. As crypto continues to get repeatedly "forked up," bitcoin *balkanization* and other software schisms will reinforce a perception that these technologies are not yet ready for widespread use.

ICOs: Initial Coin Offerings as a New Way for Startups to Raise Cash

Some firms are engaging in a new type of fundraising, widely referred to as an ICO or initial coin offering. Firms raising money via an ICO issue a coin or other token that represents some form of value. While some ICO tokens represent an ownership stake in the firm that can even be matched to voting rights and future dividend distributions like a stock, others simply issue an amount of a new cryptocurrency (e.g., a bitcoin rival), or offer usage credits or loyalty points for a given service—usually something they plan on building.[96] In this respect, ICOs can be a sort of crowd sale and share something in common with crowdfunding sites like Kickstarter.[97] The advantage of an ICO for issuing firms is that they can *raise capital with limited to no regulation*. The advantage for consumers is that *a token can be instantly traded with anyone*, provided the coin or token received is linked to some publicly available blockchain used by both buyer and seller. An investor that owns shares in a public company can trade those shares in the stock market for cash. But an investor that makes a private investment in a pre-IPO company has private shares that are less **liquid** (i.e., harder to turn into cash). In theory, the owner of ICO tokens (even those that aren't tied to any sort of equity or ownership stake in a firm) can trade them at any time, if they can find a buyer; no need to own publicly traded shares or even a stock market.

ICOs got a lot of press in early 2017. The startup Golem, described as a sort of Airbnb where organizations can sell excess computing power, raised $8.6M in twenty-nine minutes. Brave, a browser startup from a former Mozilla CEO, raised $35M in thirty seconds. Another firm, Gnosis, a decentralized predictive market platform, raised $12.5M in twelve minutes. These firms needed to create awareness so that there were buyers for the tokens offered in the ICO, but buyer beware—neither firm had a product that had passed its beta-testing phase at the time of the offering.[98] TechCrunch reports that according to its own data, over the fourteen months from the start of 2017 through the first two months of 2018, blockchain and related startups raised nearly $1.3 billion in traditional venture capital rounds worldwide, but nearly $4.5 billion was raised via ICOs.[99] That's about 3.5x more money from the crowd than from the VC! ICOs have downsides for firms raising capital, too. Startups raising money via an ICO token sale might hit their fundraising goals, but professional investors such as venture capitalists and angel investors that are the traditional source of capital for startups, typically come with professional networks that can offer advice, mentorship, and important contacts for recruiting, sales, legal advice, and more (some describe ICOs as "dumb money" as opposed to "smart money"). Right now, ICOs are pretty much an unregulated dice roll. In the early days of this model of fundraising, 35 percent of ICOs failed completely but 45 percent showed returns in excess of 500 percent.[100] And there's no guarantee that government entities won't try to step in—a good thing if that helps curtail the possibility of sham ICOs used by scammers. Efforts including Ethereum and Storj (an online marketplace for cloud storage) were careful to call their fundraising "token crowdsales," both to helps investors understand that they aren't purchasing equity or a security, and to try to make it clear to the SEC that they aren't offering something akin to stock.[101]

liquid

An asset which is liquid can be easily turned into cash. Stocks of public companies traded on major exchanges are highly liquid. Private shares in a company that has not yet gone public are illiquid since there is not a readily available public market.

A Look Inside an Initial Coin Offering

Bloomberg offers a look inside an initial coin offering. The ICO of Brooklyn-bsaed AirSwap shows fundraising through phishing attempts, eventually raising $50 million.

View the video online at: //www.youtube.com/embed/T2uJ6cCwqh0?rel=0

What Do You Think?

If all this sounds sketchy to you, consider how currencies have evolved. We've moved from precious materials (gold, silver, etc.) to a currency backed by precious materials (the gold standard), to one based largely on laws and governmental trust, to one allowing physical cash to be replaced by hand-signed paper receipts (checks), and then to bits—that is, credit cards and money transfers. Now, many of us use smartphone apps to snap photos of checks and have them electronically deposited into banks. Rip up the check when you're done, because the transaction was completed by sending its digital image. With this evolution as context, does cryptocurrency seem like such an unlikely next step?

Bitcoin used its early mover status to jumpstart network effects value from a larger number of buyers and sellers. However, there are quite a few alternatives to bitcoin. *The Guardian* says nearly 800 cryptocurrencies are in existence, with some of the larger efforts being Ethereum, Ripple, and Litecoin.[102] You might even have seen a NASCAR sponsored by Dogecoin (the fact that this bitcoin rival was named after an Internet meme dog doesn't help credibility among the financially conservative). As of this writing, Ethereum is getting the most traction. Its market cap had, at one point, come within 80 percent of the total value of all bitcoin. Larger firms, including Microsoft and JP Morgan Chase, are working together on Ethereum-based technologies, which from the start have been designed to be a transaction-recording platform as well as a cryptocurrency.[103] To get a look at the current value of leading cryptocurrencies, check out https://coinmarketcap.com/.

And remember that cryptocurrencies are just an element of what the blockchain can do. This revolution may be less about monetary exchange and more about using technologies to redefine processes. What's your take? Do you see credible opportunity here? Disruptive threat? Or flash-in-the-pan hype that'll fizzle and go nowhere?

Key Takeaways

- Bitcoin is an open source, decentralized payment system (sometimes controversially referred to as a digital, virtual, or cryptocurrency) that operates in a peer-to-peer environment without bank or central authority.
- Cryptocurrencies are entirely digital—there are no physical "coins". Cryptocurrencies are created and can be earned by miners who participate in verifying and permanently recording transactions in a secure, distributed public ledger (the blockchain).
- While bitcoin was the first cryptocurrency to gain transaction, hundreds of rivals have emerged. Some, such as Ethereum and Ripple, have currencies that are, in total, valued in multibillions of dollars.
- Various exchanges have been developed to make it easier for consumers to trade conventional currency for bitcoin or other cryptocurrencies, and vice versa. An increasingly long list of retailers and other providers have begun accepting bitcoin as cash.
- Since blockchain technologies provide a mechanism to instantly exchange value over the Internet without an intermediary, techniques are being developed that use the concept of a blockchain to move beyond cash-substitute uses, facilitating the exchange and ownership record of other types of assets (autos, real estate, diamonds and hard assets, and intellectual property), providing digital signatures, and more. If widely adopted, this technology has the potential to disrupt and improve operations among not only financial institutions but also aspects of the legal system, government regulation, health care, and other sectors.
- Many governments, financial institutions, and startups have launched blockchain initiatives targeted at bond issues, capital raising, and financial settlement.
- Lower or no transaction costs appeal to retailers, and those wishing to exchange currency across borders. Bitcoin could lower retailer transaction costs, create an opportunity for the digital purchase of goods with small value (micropayments), and open up markets where credit card access is limited.
- Civil libertarians also like the fact that bitcoin transactions can happen without revealing the sorts of personal data that credit card companies and other financial institutions are gathering. Since it's a peer-to-peer transaction, there is no central authority that can freeze accounts or impose other policies on users.
- Limited consumer benefit, difficulty of use, reputation problems, security concerns, ambiguous regulation, volatility, transaction volume, and the scalability of current infrastructure are all concerns that may limit bitcoin's mainstream appeal.

Questions and Exercises

1. Bitcoin's technology is in flux. Investigate how to get dollars into bitcoin, where you can pay for things using bitcoin, and how to get money out. Did you try this out? Why or why not?
2. Based on your experience in number 1, what will need to happen with bitcoin for it to gain mainstream consumer acceptance?
3. What's the status of bitcoin vs. the bitcoin cash fork? Who favored the fork and who opposed it? Why?
4. To whom do cryptocurrencies appeal? Why? Do some exploring online. Where are bitcoin or other cryptocurrencies accepted? Have any of these firms commented on results (positive or negative) of accepting crypto? Share your findings with your class and discuss likely resulting market trends.
5. What can retailers do to encourage more customers to use cryptocurrencies?
6. Members of the MIT bitcoin club each received $100 to experiment with the technology. Perform some additional research. What have they done? Come to class prepared to discuss their results and the value of this initiative.

7. Conduct a search online and investigate the total currency value (market capitalization or market cap) for current leading cryptocurrencies. Which firms are the most widely used and most valuable? Why?
8. Investigate current uses of blockchain technology. Which seem successful? Have any failed? Build a list of industries that you think have a high likelihood of disruption by blockchain. If you were a manager in this industry, what would you do to deal with the potential for a blockchain revolution? Report your results to the class and share what you, as a manager, can take away from these experiments.

Endnotes

1. Market capitalization retrieved from *Google Finance*, May 1, 2018.
2. M. Parsons, "Microsoft: 'We'd Have Been Dead a Long Time Ago without Windows APIs,'" *ZDNet UK*, April 22, 2004, http://news.zdnet.co.uk/software/0,1000000121,39152686,00.htm.
3. T. Eisenmann, G. Parker, and M. Van Alstyne, "Strategies for Two-Sided Markets," *Harvard Business Review*, October 2006.
4. S. Hansell, "The iPod Economy and C.E.S.," *New York Times*, January 7, 2008.
5. T. Cook, keynote address at Apple World Wide Developer Conference, San Francisco, California, June 13, 2016.
6. Content in this section sourced to: M. Parsons, "Microsoft: 'We'd Have Been Dead a Long Time Ago without Windows APIs,'" *ZDNet UK*, April 22, 2004, http://news.zdnet.co.uk/software/0,1000000121,39152686,00.htm.
7. A. Jeffries, "Apple Pay allows you to pay at the counter with your iPhone 6," *The Verge*, Sept. 9, 2014.
8. B. Barnes, "NBC Will Not Renew iTunes Contract," *New York Times*, August 31, 2007.
9. Adapted from J. Gallaugher and Y. Wang, "Linux vs. Windows in the Middle Kingdom: A Strategic Valuation Model for Platform Competition" (paper, Proceedings of the 2008 Meeting of Americas Conference on Information Systems, Toronto, CA, August 2008), extending M. Schilling, "Technological Leapfrogging: Lessons from the U.S. Video Game Console Industry," *California Management Review*, Spring 2003.
10. M. Schilling, "Technological Leapfrogging: Lessons from the U.S. Video Game Console Industry," *California Management Review*, Spring 2003.
11. N. Hutheesing, "Answer Your Phone, a Videogame Is Calling," *Forbes*, August 8, 2006.
12. K. Cutler, "This Is What Developing for Android Looks Like," *TechCrunch*, May 11, 2012.
13. C. Null, "Sony's Losses on PS3: $3 Billion and Counting," *Yahoo! Today in Tech*, June 27, 2008, http://tech.yahoo.com/blogs/null/96355.
14. R. Walker, "AntiPod," *New York Times*, August 8, 2008.
15. B. Gutman, "Gilt Groupe Reveals Its Success with Mobile and Social," *Forbes*, May 17, 2011.
16. B. Stone, "Amid the Gloom, an E-commerce War," *New York Times*, October 12, 2008.
17. K. Yeung, "WhatsApp Passes 1 Billion Monthly Active Users," *VentureBeat*, Feb. 1, 2016.
18. M. Brown, "Airbnb: The Growth Story You Didn't Know," *GrowthHackers.com* [no publication date. accessed on June 13, 2016 at https://growthhackers.com/growth-studies/airbnb.
19. A. Shontell, "How Blue Apron Became a $2 billion Startup in 3 Years," *Inc.*, Oct. 20, 2015.
20. S. Alpher, "Blue Apron Mulling IPO," *SeekingAlpha*, June 6, 2016.
21. M. Sanchanta, "Nintendo's Wii Takes Console Lead," *Financial Times*, September 12, 2007.
22. R. Fils-Aimé (presentation and discussion, Carroll School of Management, Boston College, Chestnut Hill, MA, April 6, 2009).
23. W. C. Kim and R. Mauborgne, *Blue Ocean Strategy: How to Create Uncontested Market Space and Make Competition Irrelevant* (Cambridge, MA: Harvard Business Press, 2005). See http://www.blueoceanstrategy.com.
24. S. Kessler, "Microsoft Kinect Sales Top 10 Million, Set New Guinness World Record," *Mashable*, March 9, 2011; D. Goldman, "Microsoft Profit Soars 31% on Strong Office and Kinect Sales," *CNNMoney*, April 28, 2011.
25. R. Kim, "iPhone No. 2 Smartphone Platform in North America," *The Tech Chronicles—The San Francisco Chronicle*, December 17, 2007.
26. I. Sharma Punit, "The new global anti-Uber alliance: Ola, Lyft, Didi Kuaidi and GrabTaxi agree to ride together," *Quartz*, Dec. 3, 2015.
27. A. Hawkins,"Where does Uber's $35 Billion Deal with Didi Leave Lyft?" *The Verge*, Aug. 1, 2016.
28. A. Ricadela, "Oracle's Bold Java Plans," *BusinessWeek*, June 2, 2009.
29. Data from *Statista.com*: "Apple's revenue from company-owned retail stores from 2005 to 2014 (in billion U.S. dollars)" and "Number of Apple stores worldwide from 2005 to 2014."
30. P. Wahba, "Apple extends lead in U.S. top 10 retailers by sales per square foot," *Fortune*, March 13, 2015.
31. *BusinessWire*, "Media Player Format Share for 2006 Confirms Windows Media Remains Dominant with a 50.8% Share of Video Streams Served, Followed by Flash at 21.9%—'CDN Growth and Market Share Shifts: 2002–2006,'" December 18, 2006; and T. Eisenmann, G. Parker, and M. Van Alstyne, "Strategies for Two-Sided Markets," *Harvard Business Review*, October 2006.
32. L. Sumagaysay, "A $733M 'Error' Message: EU Fines Microsoft over Browser-Choice Deal," *SiliconBeat*, March 6, 2013.
33. C. Null, "Sony's Losses on PS3: $3 Billion and Counting," *Yahoo! Today in Tech*, June 27, 2008, http://tech.yahoo.com/blogs/null/96355.
34. H. Clancy, "Slack's $80 Million App Development Fund," *Fortune*, Dec. 15, 2015.
35. J. Wallen, "Amazon's Free Alexa API is a Boon to Developers," *TechRepublic*, Aug. 6, 2015.
36. K. Finley, "New Programming Langauges Keep Chipping Away At The Old," *Wired*, Feb. 19, 2016. And N. Garigarn, "10 Programming Languages in Highest Demand," *ImprovWorker*, April 27, 2016.
37. M. Schilling, "Technological Leapfrogging: Lessons from the U.S. Video Game Console Industry," *California Management Review*, Spring 2003.
38. P. Seitz, "An Apple for Teacher, Students: Mac Maker Surges in Education," *Investor's Business Daily*, August 8, 2008.
39. P. Burrows, "The Mac in the Gray Flannel Suit," *BusinessWeek*, May 1, 2008.
40. L. Savvides, "Samsung Pay: What You Need to Know," *CNet*, March 23, 2016.
41. Notably, Apple repeatedly blocked smartphone maker Palm from accessing music in iTunes. Apple appealed to the consortium behind the USB standard to get Palm to stop unauthorized access. C. Metz, "USB supreme court backs Apple in Palm Pre kerfuffle," *The Register*, Sept. 24, 2009.
42. A. Orlowski, "Taking Osborne out of the Osborne Effect," *The Register*, June 20, 2005.
43. M. Schilling, "Technological Leapfrogging: Lessons from the U.S. Video Game Console Industry," *California Management Review*, Spring 2003.
44. J. Mangalindan, "4 Moves Electronic Arts Must Make Now," *Fortune*, March 20, 2013.
45. P. Vigna and M. Casey, "BitBeat: Who Won the FBI's Bitcoin Auction?" *Wall Street Journal*, June 30, 2014.
46. John Biggs, "May 22 Is Bitcoin Pizza Day," *TechCrunch*, May 21, 2014.
47. R. McMillan, "The Inside Story of Mt. Gox, Bitcoin's $460 Million Disaster," *Wired*, May 3, 2014.
48. T. Wan and M. Hoblitzell, "Bitcoin: Fact. Fiction. Future," *Deloitte University Press*, June 26, 2014.
49. P. Vigna and M. Casey, "BitBeat: Who Won the FBI's Bitcoin Auction?" *The Wall Street Journal*, June 30, 2014.
50. T. Wan and M. Hoblitzell, "Bitcoin: Fact. Fiction. Future," *Deloitte University Press*, June 26, 2014.
51. A. Irrera, "UBS CIO: Blockchain Technology Can Massively Simplify Banking," *The Wall Street Journal*, Oct. 27, 2014.
52. M. Iansiti and K. Lakhani, "The Truth About Blockchain," *Harvard Business Review*, Jan-Feb, 2017.
53. C. Chanjaroen and D. Roman, "Singapore to Test Digital Currency in Latest Fintech Initiative," *Bloomberg*, Nov. 15, 2016.
54. C. Chanjaroen, "Here's What Asian Lenders Are Doing With Blockchain Technology," *Bloomberg*, Oct. 23, 2016.
55. Unattributed, "Kazakhstan central bank to sell securities through blockchain app," *Reuters*, June 13, 2017.
56. J. Rowley, "ICOs delivered at least 3.5x more capital to blockchain startups than VC since 2017," *TechCrunch*, March 4, 2017.
57. M. Carney, "For Retailers, Accepting Bitcoin Is all about the Margin," *PandoDaily*, January 13, 2014.

58. E. Ombok, "Bitcoin Service Targets Kenya Remittances with Cut-Rate Fees," *Bloomberg*, November 28, 2013.
59. T. Wan and M. Hoblitzell, "Bitcoin: Fact. Fiction. Future," *Deloitte University Press*, June 26, 2014.
60. R. Salam, "The Vice Podcast—Professor Bitcoin," *Vice*, January 8, 2014.
61. T. Wan and M. Hoblitzell, "Bitcoin: Fact. Fiction. Future," *Deloitte University Press*, June 26, 2014.
62. A. Irrera, "UBS CIO: Blockchain Technology Can Massively Simplify Banking," *The Wall Street Journal*, Oct. 27, 2014.
63. T. Wan and M. Hoblitzell, "Bitcoin: Fact. Fiction. Future," *Deloitte University Press*, June 26, 2014.
64. M. Orcutt, "Leaderless Bitcoin Struggles to Make Its Most Crucial Decision," *Technology Review*, May 19, 2015.
65. P. Coy and O. Kharif, "This Is Your Company on Blockchain," *Business-Week*, Oct. 25, 2016.
66. A. Irrera, "Bank-backed R3 launches new version of its blockchain," *Reuters*, Oct. 3, 2017.
67. R. Hacket, "IBM and Maersk Are Creating a New Blockchain Company," *Fortune*, Jan. 16, 2018.
68. S. Gordon, "Nationwide Insurance Rolls Out Proof of Insurance on the RiskBlock Blockchain," *Nasdaq*, Jan. 15, 2018.
69. A. Antonovici, "Overstock's tZero Partners with BOX Digital for Security Token Exchange," *CryptoVest*, May 24, 2018.
70. B. Marr, "30+ Real Examples of Blockchain Technology in Practice," *Forbes*, May 14, 2018.
71. S. Perez, "Spotify acquires blockchain startup Mediachain to solve music's attribution problem," *TechCrunch*, April 26, 2017.
72. S. Liao, "Kodak announces its own cryptocurrency and watches stock price skyrocket," *The Verge*, Jan. 9, 2018.
73. K. Wagner, "Facebook is launching a new team dedicated to the blockchain. Messenger's David Marcus is going to run it," *Recode*, May 8, 2018.
74. S. Rossman, "E. coli outbreak tied to romaine lettuce kills 1 in California, expands to 25 states," *USA Today*, May 2, 2018.
75. L. Javier, "Yes, These Chickens Are on the Blockchain," *Bloomberg*, April 9, 2018.
76. T. McDougal, "Carrefour launches Europe's first food blockchain," *Poultry-World*, Mar. 16, 2018.
77. L. Javier, "Yes, These Chickens Are on the Blockchain," Bloomberg, April 9, 2018.
78. H. Bottemiller, "New Estimates Lower Incidence of Food Poisoning," *Food Safety News*, Dec. 16, 2010.
79. L. Javier, "Yes, These Chickens Are on the Blockchain," *Bloomberg*, April 9, 2018.
80. P. Schimidt, "Bitcoin: Understanding What It Is," *Guardian Liberty Voice*, June 15, 2014.
81. R. McMillan, "The Inside Story of Mt. Gox, Bitcoin's $460 Million Disaster," *Wired*, May 3, 2014.
82. R. McMillan, "The Fierce Battle for the Soul of Bitcoin," *Wired*, March 26, 2014.
83. S. Yang and S. Lee, "China Bans Financial Companies from Bitcoin Transactions," *Bloomberg*, December 5, 2013.
84. J. Kirk, "California Removes Ban on Alternative Currencies," *Computer-world*, June 30, 2014.
85. E. Sherman, "New York State to Welcome Regulated Bitcoin Exchanges," *CBS Market Watch*, March 12, 2014.
86. J. Chester, "A New Way To Raise Money: The Initial Coin Offering," *Forbes*, June 12, 2017.
87. P. Rosenblum, "Bitcoin Draws Attention of Institutional Bidders and MasterCard," *Forbes*, June 30, 2014.
88. E. Helmore, "Are cryptocurrencies about to go mainstream?" *The Guardian*, July 1, 2017.
89. Unattributed, "Cryptocurrency Wealth Dropped $52 Billion During Blockchain Week. Not Even a Snoop Dogg Performance Could Save It," *Bloomberg*, May 18, 2018.
90. Unattributed, "Bitcoin Transaction Volume Is Puzzling Investors," *Bloomberg*, Marc 2, 2018.
91. T. Wan and M. Hoblitzell, "Bitcoin: Fact. Fiction. Future," *Deloitte University Press*, June 26, 2014.
92. R. McMillan, "The Fierce Battle for the Soul of Bitcoin," *Wired*, March 26, 2014. and M. Li, "Bitcoin Faces Urgent Scalability Problems," *Seeking Alpha*, June 15, 2017.
93. B. Popper, "Bitcoin's Nightmare Scenario Has Come to Pass," *The Verge*, March 2, 2016.
94. A. Cuthbertson, "The Battle Over Bitcoin: Scandal and Infighting as 'Bitcoin Cash' Threatens to Overthrow the Most Famous Cryptocurrency," *The Independent*, May 21, 2018.
95. N. Varshney, "Bitcoin has seen 44 forks since Bitcoin Cash and they are all useless," *The Next Web*, May 22, 2018.
96. J. Chester, "A New Way To Raise Money: The Initial Coin Offering," Forbes, June 12, 2017.
97. E. Ou, "Rise of the Initial Coin Offering," *Bloomberg TV*, June 2, 2017.
98. J. Young, "ICO Tokens: Ethereum's Killer App?" *CryptoCoin* News, June 7, 2017.
99. J. Rowley, "ICOs delivered at least 3.5x more capital to blockchain startups than VC since 2017," *TechCrunch*, March 4, 2018.
100. M. Adham, "Backing A New Digital Currency: Initial Coin Offerings," *Forbes*, May 23, 2017.
101. J. Chester, "A New Way To Raise Money: The Initial Coin Offering," *Forbes*, June 12, 2017.
102. E. Helmore, "Are cryptocurrencies about to go mainstream?" *The Guardian*, July 1, 2017.
103. F. Chaparro, "Something called Ethereum is Suddenly All Over the News—Here's What the Bitcoin Rival is All About," *Business Insider*, June 27, 2017.

CHAPTER 6

Search, Algorithms, Profiling, Privacy

EDITED

6.1 Understanding Search

Learning Objectives

1. Understand the mechanics of search, including how Google indexes the Web and ranks its organic search results.
2. Examine the infrastructure that powers Google and how its scale and complexity offer key sources of competitive advantages.

Before diving into how the firm makes money, let's first understand how Google's core service, search, works.

Perform a search (or **query**) on Google or another search engine, and the results you'll see are referred to by industry professionals as **organic or natural search**. Search engines use different algorithms for determining the order of organic search results, but at Google the method is called **PageRank** (a bit of a play on words, it ranks Web pages, and was initially developed by Google cofounder Larry Page). Google does not accept money for placement of links in organic search results. Instead, PageRank results are a kind of popularity contest. Web pages that have more pages *linking to them* are ranked higher (while organic search results can't be bought, firms do pay for preferred placement in some Google products, including Google Shopping, Hotels, and Flight Search).[1]

query

Search.

organic or natural search

Search engine results returned and ranked according to relevance.

PageRank

Algorithm developed by Google cofounder Larry Page to rank websites.

FIGURE 6.1 Google Query

The query for "Toyota Prius" triggers organic search results, flanked top and right by advertisements.

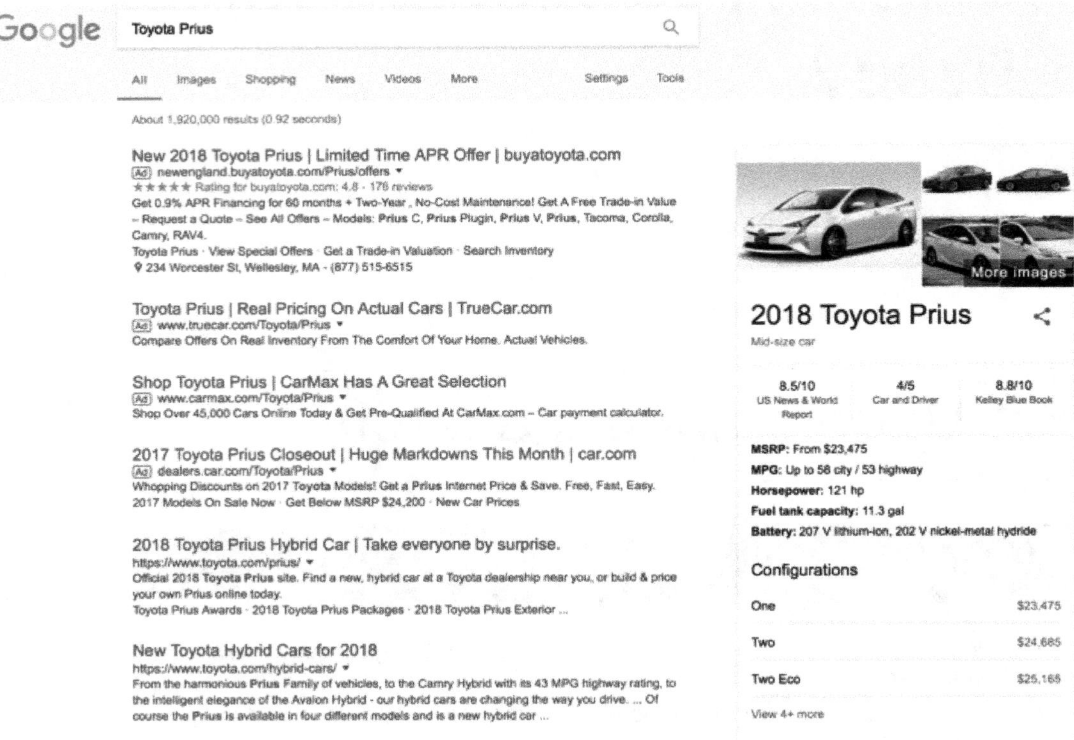

Source: Google.

search engine optimization (SEO)

The process of improving a page's organic search rankings.

link fraud

Also called "spamdexing" or "link farming." The process of creating a series of bogus websites, all linking back to the pages one is trying to promote.

The process of improving a page's organic search results is often referred to as **search engine optimization (SEO)**. SEO has become a critical function for many marketing organizations, since if a firm's pages aren't near the top of search results, customers may never discover its site.

Google is a bit vague about the specifics of precisely how PageRank has been refined, in part because many have tried to game the system. In addition to in-bound links, Google's organic search results also consider some two hundred other signals, and the firm's search quality team is relentlessly analyzing user behavior for clues on how to tweak the system to improve accuracy.[2] The less scrupulous have tried creating a series of bogus websites, all linking back to the pages they're trying to promote (this is called **link fraud**, and Google actively works to uncover and shut down such efforts—see the "Link Fraudsters" sidebar).

Link Fraudsters, Be Prepared to Experience Google's "Death Penalty"

JCPenney is a big retailer, for sure, but not necessarily the first firm to come to mind when you think of most retail categories. So the *New York Times* suspected that something fishy was up when the retailer's site came out tops for dozens of Google searches, including the phrases "skinny jeans," "dresses," "bedding," "area rugs," "home decor," "comforter sets," "furniture," and "tablecloths." The phrase "Samsonite carry-on luggage" even placed JCPenney ahead of Samsonite's own site!

The *Times* reported that "someone paid to have thousands of links placed on hundreds of sites scattered around the Web, all of which lead directly to JCPenney.com." And there was little question it was blatant link fraud. Phrases related to dresses and linking back to the retailer were coming from such nondress sites as nuclear.engineeringaddict.com, casino-focus.com, and bulgariapropertyportal.com. One SEO expert called the effort the most ambitious link farming attempt he'd ever seen.

Link fraud undercuts the credibility of Google's core search product, so when the search giant discovers a firm engaged in link farming, they drop the hammer. In this case Google both manually demoted JCPenney rankings and launched tweaks to its ranking algorithm. Within two hours JCPenney organic results plummeted, in some cases from first to seventy-first (the *Times* calls this the organic search equivalent of the "death penalty"). Getting a top spot in Google search results is a big deal. On average, 34 percent of clicks go to the top result, about twice the percentage that goes to number two. Google's punishment was administered despite the fact that JCPenney was also a large online ad customer, at times paying Google some $2.5 million a month for ads.[3]

JCPenney isn't the first firm busted. When Google discovered so-called black-hat SEO was being used to push BMW up in organic search rankings, Google made certain BMW sites virtually unfindable in its organic search results. JCPenney claims that they were the victim of rogue behavior by an SEO consultant (who was promptly fired) and that the retailer was otherwise unaware of the unethical behavior. But it is surprising that the retailer's internal team didn't see their unbelievably successful organic search results as a red flag that something was amiss, and this case highlights the types of things managers need to watch for in the digital age. JCPenney outsourced SEO, and the fraud uncovered in this story underscores the critical importance of vetting and regularly auditing the performance of partners throughout a firm's supply chain.[4]

While Google doesn't divulge specifics on the weighting of inbound links from a given website, we do know that links from some websites carry more weight than others. For example, links from websites that Google deems "influential" have greater weight in PageRank calculations than links from run-of-the-mill sites. For searches performed on mobile devices, Web pages that meet Google's criteria for being "mobile friendly" will be ranked higher than those that don't have an option for mobile devices (Google does offer testing tools to see if your pages are compliant).[5] Additionally, different users may not see identical organic search results. Google defaults to a mix of rankings that includes individual user behavior and, for those users searching while logged into Google accounts, social connections (although displaying generic results remains an option).[6]

Spiders and Bots and Crawlers—Oh My!

Google handles an average of 40 million searches *per second*, resulting in 3.5 billion searches each day, or about 1.2 trillion searches a year.[7] When performing a search via Google or another search engine, you're not actually searching the Web. What really happens is that you're searching something that amounts to a *copy* of the Web that major search engines make by storing and indexing the text of online documents on their own computers. Google's index considers over 130 trillion URLs.[8] Google starts to retrieve results as soon as you begin to type, and a line above each Google query shows you just how fast a search takes, and how many pages were considered.

To create these massive indexes, search firms use software to crawl the Web and uncover as much information as they can find. This software is referred to by several different names—**spiders, Web crawlers, software robots**—but they all pretty much work the same way. The spiders ask each public computer network for a list of its public websites (for more on this see DNS in [Content Removed: #fwk-38086-ch14]). Then the spiders go through this list ("crawling" a site), following every available link until all pages are uncovered.

Google will crawl frequently updated sites, like those run by news organizations, as often as several times an hour. Rarely updated, less popular sites might only be reindexed every few days. The method used to crawl the Web also means that if a website isn't the first page on a public server, or isn't linked to from another public page, then it'll never be found.[9] In addition, each search engine also offers a page where you can submit your website for indexing.

While search engines show you what they've found on their *copy* of the Web's contents that Google has **cached** on its own servers, clicking a search result will direct you to the actual website, not the copy. Sometimes you'll click a result only to find that the website doesn't match what the search engine found. This is rare, but it happens if a website was updated before your search engine had a chance to reindex the changes.

spiders, Web crawlers, software robots

Software that traverses available websites in an attempt to perform a given task. Search engines use spiders to discover documents for indexing and retrieval.

cached

Refers to a temporary storage space used to speed computing tasks.

deep Web

Internet content that can't be indexed by Google and other search engines.

But what if you want the content on your website to remain off limits to search engine indexing and caching? Organizations have created a set of standards to stop the spider crawl, and all commercial search engines have agreed to respect these standards. One way is to put a line of *HTML code* invisibly embedded in a Web page that tells all software robots to stop indexing a page, stop following links on the page, or stop offering old page archives in a cache. Users don't see this code, but commercial Web crawlers do. For those familiar with HTML code (the language used to describe a website), the command to stop Web crawlers from indexing a page, following links, and listing archives of cached pages looks like this:

⟨META NAME="ROBOTS" CONTENT="NOINDEX, NOFOLLOW, NOARCHIVE"⟩

There are other techniques to keep the spiders out, too. Website administrators can add a special file (called robots.txt) that provides similar instructions on how indexing software should treat the website. And a lot of content lies inside the "**deep Web**," either behind corporate firewalls or inaccessible to those without a user account—think of private Facebook updates no one can see unless they're your friend—all of that is out of Google's reach.

How Google Search Works

How Search Works—a short Google video illustrating how search works and how it decides which results to show to you, and in what order.

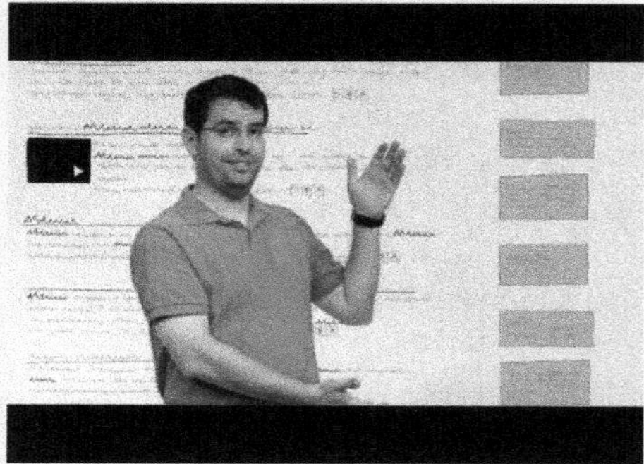

View the video online at: http://www.youtube.com/embed/BNHR6IQJGZs?rel=0

What's It Take to Run This Thing?

Sergey Brin and Larry Page started Google with just four scavenged computers.[10] But in a decade, the infrastructure used to power the search sovereign has ballooned to the point where it is now the largest of its kind in the world.[11] Google doesn't disclose the number of servers it uses, but by some estimates, it runs over 1.4 million servers in over a dozen so-called **server farms** worldwide.[12] In the first three months of 2018, Google spent $7.3 billion—that's 3x what it spent a year earlier—most of it thought to have gone to building new server farms and laying the cabling connecting them to the rest of the Internet.[13] Building massive server farms to index the ever-growing Web is now the cost of admission for any firm wanting to compete in the search market. This is clearly no longer a game for two graduate students working out of a garage.

server farm

A massive network of computer servers running software to coordinate their collective use. Server farms provide the infrastructure backbone to SaaS and hardware cloud efforts, as well as many large-scale Internet services.

fault-tolerant

Capable of continuing operation even if a component fails.

colocation facilities

Sometimes called a "colo," or carrier hotel; provides a place where the gear from multiple firms can come together and where the peering of Internet traffic can take place. Equipment connecting in colos could be high-speed lines from ISPs, telecom lines from large private data centers, or even servers hosted in a colo to be closer to high-speed Internet connections.

Tour a Google Data Center

At this video link, watch a tour of a Google data center. Or visit http://www.google.com/about/datacenters/inside/streetview to explore one of Google's data centers using the firm's Street View technology.

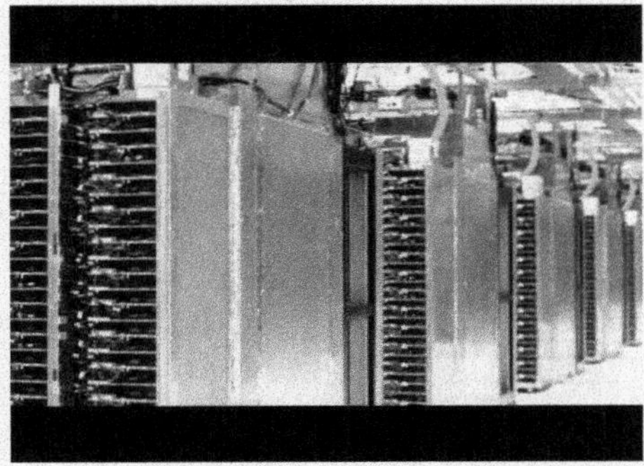

View the video online at: //www.youtube.com/embed/avP5d16wEp0?rel=0

The size of this investment not only creates a barrier to entry, it influences industry profitability, with market-leader Google enjoying huge economies of scale. Firms may spend the same amount to build server farms, but if Google has roughly two-thirds of this market while Microsoft's search draws just a fraction of this traffic, which do you think enjoys the better return on investment?

Google's server farms contain hardware that is custom built to contain just what Google needs and eliminate everything it doesn't (e.g., no graphic cards, since servers aren't attached to monitors, or enclosures, since all servers are rack-mounted). In most cases the firm uses the kind of Intel or AMD processors, low-end hard drives, and RAM chips that you'd find in a commercial PC. These components are housed in racks, slotted like very tight shelving. Each server is about 3.5 inches thick yet contains processors, RAM memory, and hard drives.[14] Google buys so many components for its custom-built servers that it, not a PC manufacturer, is Intel's fifth largest customer.[15]

In some cases, Google mounts racks of these servers inside standard-sized shipping containers, each with as many as 1,160 servers per box.[16] A given data center may have dozens of these server-filled containers all linked together. Redundancy is the name of the game. Google assumes individual components will regularly fail, but no single failure should interrupt the firm's operations (making the setup what geeks call **fault-tolerant**). If something breaks, a technician can easily swap it out with a replacement.

Google does make some custom components. Since it's such a big target for hackers, the firm designs its own custom hardware security chips that are inside its servers and peripherals. These chips allow Google to identify and authenticate its own infrastructure at the hardware level.[17] Google has also designed several versions of its own custom silicon for machine learning, something it calls the TPU for tensor processing unit (TensorFlow is a type of Google-nurtured machine learning tool). These chips are akin to the GPUs that were mentioned in the Moore's Law chapter, and the firm will gladly sell cloud access to other firms that want to use Google smarts at scale.[18] The first TPU outperformed standard processors by a factor of 30 to 80 times when measuring the calculating speed while taking into account energy cost—so much so that Google credits the TPU with saving it from having to open "dozens [more] data centers."[19]

Each server farm layout has also been carefully designed with an emphasis on lowering power consumption and cooling requirements. Instead of using big uninterrupted power supply (UPS) systems common in most data centers, Google put smaller battery backups next to each server. These cost less; are more efficient, because they leak about 15 percent less energy than big units; and don't have heavy cooling costs. Employees usually wear shorts inside the data center since the "cool aisle" in the front of machines is around 80°F. The hot aisles venting out the back and cooled via constantly circulating, heat-absorbing water coils can get up to 120°F. That's hotter than most corporate data centers, but Google learned that its systems could take the heat. These practices allow Google to set the bar high for energy efficiency. The standard used to measure data center efficiency is PUE—power usage effectiveness. 1.0 is a perfect score—it means all the power a facility draws is put to use. Everyone loses power; 2.0 (meaning half the power drawn is wasted) is considered a "reasonable number." Google regularly runs PUEs below 1.1—astonishingly efficient.[20] Saving energy helps the firm meet its green goals—the firm is formally committed to being carbon neutral and offsetting its fossil fuel energy needs—but the data centers also help meet other "green" goals: massive cash savings. The firm's infrastructure chief claims that the savings through the firm's ultraefficient data center designs are vital to keeping costs low enough to keep services like Gmail free.[21] Google also uses artificial intelligence to monitor data center performance. If it finds that one of its predicted outcomes doesn't match a current finding (e.g., the temperature is higher than what formulas suggest), this acts as a sort of data center equivalent of a car's "check engine light." AI will then suggest a course of action, like clean an air-filtering heat exchanger or check other systems.[22]

The firm's custom software (much of it built upon open source products) allows all this equipment to operate as the world's largest grid computer. Web search is a task particularly well suited for the massively parallel architecture used by Google and its rivals. For an analogy of how this works, imagine that working alone (the human equivalent of a single-server effort), you need to try to find a particular phrase in a hundred-page document. That'd take a while. Next, imagine that you can distribute the task across five thousand people, giving each of them a separate sentence to scan (that's the human equivalent of a multiserver grid). The speed difference between a single searching entity and a search involving many entities simultaneously focused on a subset of the same task gives you a sense of how search firms use massive numbers of servers and the divide-and-conquer approach of grid computing to quickly find the needles you're searching for within the Web's haystack. (For more on grid computing, see Chapter 3 and for more on the server farms employed by cloud computing providers, see [Content Removed: #fwk-38086-ch10]).

Google's got a lot of data centers, but not all Google-served data comes to you straight from Google's own server farms. The firm also scatters racks of servers in scores of spots all over the world so that it can quickly get you copies of high-value rich media content, like trending YouTube videos, or fast services for businesses using Google's cloud computing services. These racks of Google content and code are tucked away, sometimes within data centers run by big telecom firms like Comcast or AT&T, or kept inside **colocation facilities** (colos), big warehouse-like facilities where several telecom companies come together to exchange traffic.[23]

Google will even sell you a bit of its technology so that you can run your own little Google in-house without sharing documents with the rest of the world. Google's line of search appliances are rack-mounted servers that can index documents within the servers on a corporation's own network, even managing user password and security access on a per-document basis. Selling hardware isn't a large business for Google, and other vendors offer similar solutions, but search appliances can be vital tools for law firms, investment banks, and other document-rich organizations.

Key Takeaways

- Ranked search results are often referred to as organic or natural search results. PageRank is Google's algorithm for ranking search results. PageRank orders organic search results based largely on the number of websites linking to them, and the "weight" of each page as measured by its "influence."
- Search engine optimization (SEO) is the process of improving a website's organic search ranking. The scope and influence of search has made SEO an increasingly vital marketing function.
- Users don't really search the Web; they search an archived copy stored on a search firm's computers. A firm creates these copies by crawling and indexing discoverable documents.
- Google operates from a massive network of server farms containing hundreds of thousands of servers built from standard, off-the-shelf parts. The cost of the operation is a significant barrier to entry for competitors. Google's share of search suggests the firm realizes economies of scale over rivals required to make similar investments while delivering fewer results (and hence ads).
- Website owners can hide pages from popular search engine Web crawlers using a number of methods, including HTML tags, a no-index file, or ensuring that websites aren't linked to other pages and haven't been submitted to websites for indexing.

Questions and Exercises

1. How do search engines discover pages on the Internet? What kind of capital commitment is necessary to go about doing this? How does this impact competitive dynamics in the industry?
2. How does Google rank search results? Investigate and list some methods that an organization might use to improve its rank in Google's organic search results. Are there techniques Google might not approve of? What risk does a firm run if Google or another search firm determines that it has used unscrupulous SEO techniques to try to unfairly influence ranking algorithms?
3. Sometimes websites returned by major search engines don't contain the words or phrases that initially brought you to the site. Why might this happen?
4. What's a cache? What other products or services have a cache?
5. What can be done if you want the content on your website to remain off limits to search engine indexing and caching?
6. What is a "search appliance"? Why might an organization choose such a product?
7. Become a better searcher: Look at the advanced options for your favorite search engine. Are there options you hadn't used previously? Be prepared to share what you learn during class discussion.
8. Google offers several tools useful to managers trying to gain insight on the public use of search. One of these is Google Trends. Visit Google Trends. Explore the tool as if you were comparing a firm with its competitors. What sorts of useful insights can you uncover? How might businesses use these tools?

9. Some websites are accused of being "content farms," offering low-quality content designed to attract searchers that include popular query terms and using this content to generate ad revenue. Demand Media, which went public at $1.5 billion, and Associated Content, which Yahoo! purchased for $100 million, have been accused of being content farms. Investigate the claims and visit these sites. Do you find the content useful? Do you think these sites are or are not content farms? Research how Google changed its ranking algorithm to penalize content farms. What has been the impact on these sites? Would you put a site like BuzzFeed in the same category as content farms? Why or why not? Make a list of categories of firms and individuals that would likely be impacted by such moves. What does this tell you about Google's influence?
10. Consider Google's influence on society, understanding, education, and perception. When Google delivers the majority of search results and most users default first to Google's products, do you feel that gives a single firm too much power? Do you think governments have a role in regulating a firm with this amount of influence? Why or why not?

6.2 Search Advertising

Learning Objectives

1. Understand Google's search advertising revenue model.
2. Know the factors that determine the display and ranking of advertisements appearing on Google's search results pages.
3. Be able to describe the uses and technologies behind geotargeting.

search engine marketing (SEM)

The practice of designing, running, and optimizing search engine ad campaigns.

The practice of running and optimizing search engine ad campaigns is referred to as **search engine marketing (SEM).**[24] SEM is a hot topic in an increasingly influential field, so it's worth spending some time learning how search advertising works on the Internet's largest search engine.

Over two-thirds of Google's revenues come from ads served on its own sites, and the vast majority of this revenue comes from search engine ads.[25] During Google's early years, the firm actually resisted making money through ads. In fact, while at Stanford, Brin and Page even coauthored a paper titled "The Evils of Advertising."[26] But when Yahoo! and others balked at buying Google's search technology (offered for as little as $500,000), Google needed to explore additional revenue streams. It wasn't until two years after incorporation that Google ran ads alongside organic search results. That first ad, one for "Live Mail Order Lobsters," appeared just minutes after the firm posted a link reading "See Your Ad Here."[27]

keyword advertising

Advertisements that are targeted based on a user's query.

Google regularly experiments with incorporating video and image ads into search (you'll see images, for example, in paid-product search results), but for the most part, the ads you'll see to the right (and sometimes top) of Google's organic search results are text ads. These ads are **keyword advertising**, meaning they're targeted based on the words in a user's search query. Advertisers bid on the keywords and phrases that they'd like to use to trigger the display of their ad. Linking ads to search was a brilliant move, since the user's search term indicates an overt interest in a given topic. Want to sell hotel stays in Tahiti? Link your ads to the search term "Tahiti Vacation." Google ads show up when many users have some sort of *purchasing intent*. This makes Google search ads far more effective than standard display ads like those on Facebook (see [Content Removed: #fwk-38086-ch07]). Google's ability to tie advertising to purchasing intent (or to some other action that advertisers are willing to pay for) is the main reason the firm's ads are so valuable.

Not only are search ads highly targeted, advertisers only pay for results. Text ads appearing on Google search pages are billed on a **pay-per-click (PPC)** basis, meaning that advertisers don't spend a penny unless someone actually clicks on their ad. Note that the term pay-per-click is sometimes used interchangeably with the term cost-per-click (CPC).

pay-per-click (PPC)

A concept where advertisers don't pay unless someone clicks on their ad.

If an advertiser wants to display an ad on Google search, they can set up a Google AdWords advertising account in minutes, specifying just a single ad, or multiple ad campaigns that trigger different ads for different keywords. Advertisers also specify what they're willing to pay each time an ad is clicked and how much their overall ad budget is, and they can control additional parameters, such as the timing and duration of an ad campaign.

If no one clicks on an ad, Google doesn't make money, advertisers don't attract customers, and searchers aren't seeing ads they're interested in. So in order to create a winning scenario for everyone, Google has developed a precise ad ranking formula that rewards top performing ads by considering three metrics: the maximum CPC that an advertiser is willing to pay (sometimes referred to as an ad's *bid value*), the advertisement's **quality score**—(a broad measure of ad performance) and the expected impact of extensions (e.g., added info like a phone number, address, store rating) and ad formats (in some cases images or video may be expected to perform higher). Create high-quality ads and your advertisements might appear ahead of competition, even if your competitors bid more than you. But if ads perform poorly they'll fall in rankings or even drop from display consideration.

quality score

A measurement of ad performance (CTR) and ad relevance, and landing page experience. Ads that are seen as relevant and that consumers respond to have higher quality scores. The firm uses quality score multiplied by the maximum CPC to determine an ad's display ranking.

Below is the rough formula used by Google to determine the rank order of sponsored links appearing on search results pages.

Ad Rank = f (Maximum CPC, Quality Score, expected impact of extensions and formats)

Google is deliberately vague about precisely how quality score is calculated, and the firm's metrics are regularly tweaked, but factors that determine an ad's quality score have included an ad's **click-through rate (CTR)**, or the number of users who clicked an ad divided by the number of times the ad was delivered (the impressions). The CTR measures the percentage of people who clicked on an ad to arrive at a destination-site. Factors that have also appeared in the quality score weighting include things like the overall history of click performance for the keywords linked to the ad, the relevance of an ad's text to the user's query, and Google's automated assessment of the user experience on the **landing page**—the Web page displayed when a user clicks on the ad. Ads that don't get many clicks, ad descriptions that have nothing to do with query terms, and ads that direct users to generic pages that load slowly or aren't strongly related to the keywords and descriptions used in an ad will all lower an ad's chance of being displayed. In general, the more relevant your ad, and the better the experience of the consumer who clicks that ad, the higher your quality score, and the higher your quality score, the better your ad's position and the less you'll have to pay per click.[28]

click-through rate (CTR)

The number of users who clicked an ad divided by the number of times the ad was delivered (the impressions). The CTR measures the percentage of people who clicked on an ad to arrive at a destination-site.

landing page

The Web page displayed when a user clicks on an advertisement.

Google provides tools that firms can use to identify popular words and phrases for selecting keywords to associate with an ad, and for assessing ad quality score. And Google also offers **dynamic search ads**, where the firm will automatically generate ads based on your website. This is useful if you have a constantly changing and updating inventory or are having difficulty tracking the ever-evolving search terms that may be relevant to users looking for products and services that your site offers.

dynamic search ads

Ads generated automatically based on the content of a website. Dynamic ads are particularly useful for firms with rapidly updating inventory or firms struggling to keep up with new search terms that may be relevant to their product lines.

When an ad is clicked, advertisers don't actually pay their maximum CPC; Google discounts ads to the minimum necessary to maintain an ad's position on the page. So if you bid one dollar per click, but your overall ad rank is so good that you could have beat the ad ranked below yours even if you bid just ninety cents, then you'll pay just ninety cents if the ad is clicked. Discounting was a brilliant move. No one wants to get caught excessively overbidding rivals, so discounting helps reduce the possibility of this so-called bidder's remorse. And with this risk minimized, the system actually encouraged higher bids![29]

Ad ranking and cost-per-click calculations take place as part of an automated auction that occurs *every time* a user conducts a search. Advertisers get a running total of ad performance statistics so that they can monitor the return on their investment and tweak promotional efforts for better results. And this whole system is automated for self-service—all it takes is a credit card, an ad idea, and you're ready to go.

How Much Do Advertisers Pay per Click?

Google rakes in billions on what amounts to pocket change earned one click at a time. Most clicks bring in between thirty cents and one dollar. However, costs can vary widely depending on industry and current competition. Since rates are based on auctions, top rates reflect what the market is willing to bear. As an example, law firms, which bring in big bucks from legal fees, decisions, and settlement payments, often justify higher customer acquisition costs. Bids for certain legal phrases, such as those referring to structured settlements (a term often referring to payment terms of a legal settlement), or mesothelioma (a type of asbestos-associated cancer and the subject of several big money lawsuits) have been known to go for hundreds of dollars.[30] And firms that see results will keep spending. Los Angeles–based Chase Law Group has said that it brings in roughly 60 percent of its clients through Internet advertising.[31] Top Google advertisers among larger, consumer firms include Amazon, Quicken Loans, State Farm, Home Depot, Apple, Sears, Expedia, Capital One, Walmart, JCPenney, BestBuy, and eBay.[32]

IP Addresses and Geotargeting

geotargeting

Identifying a user's physical location (sometimes called geolocation) for the purpose of delivering tailored ads or other content.

IP address

A value used to identify a device that is connected to the Internet. IP addresses are usually expressed as four numbers (from 0 to 255), separated by periods.

Geotargeting occurs when computer systems identify a user's physical location (sometimes called the *geolocation*) for the purpose of delivering tailored ads or other content. On Google AdWords, for example, advertisers can specify that their ads only appear for Web surfers located in a particular country, state, metropolitan region, or a given distance around a precise locale. They can even draw a custom ad-targeting region on a map and tell Google to only show ads to users detected inside that space.

Ads in Google Search (as well as in Maps and many other offerings) can be geotargeted based on **IP address**. Every device connected to the Internet has a unique IP address assigned by the organization connecting the device to the network. Normally you don't see your IP address. It's likely a set of four numbers, from 0 to 255, separated by periods (e.g., 136.167.2.220), but this standard (known as IPv4) is gradually being replaced by the IPv6 standard, which offers far more potential addresses. IP addresses are used in targeting because the range of IP addresses "owned" by major organizations and Internet service providers (ISPs) is public knowledge. In many cases it's possible to make an accurate guess as to where a computer, laptop, or mobile phone is located simply by cross-referencing a device's current IP address with this public list.

For example, it's known that all devices connected to the Boston College network contain IP addresses starting with the numbers 136.167. If a search engine detects a query coming from an IP address that begins with those two numbers, it can be fairly certain that the person using that device is in the greater Boston area.

FIGURE 6.2 An Example of Geotargeting

In this geotargeting example, the same search term is used at roughly the same time on separate computers located in Silicon Valley area (Figure 18.5) and Boston (Figure 18.6). Note how geotargeting impacts the search results and that the Boston-based search includes a geotargeted ad that does not show up in the Palo Alto search.

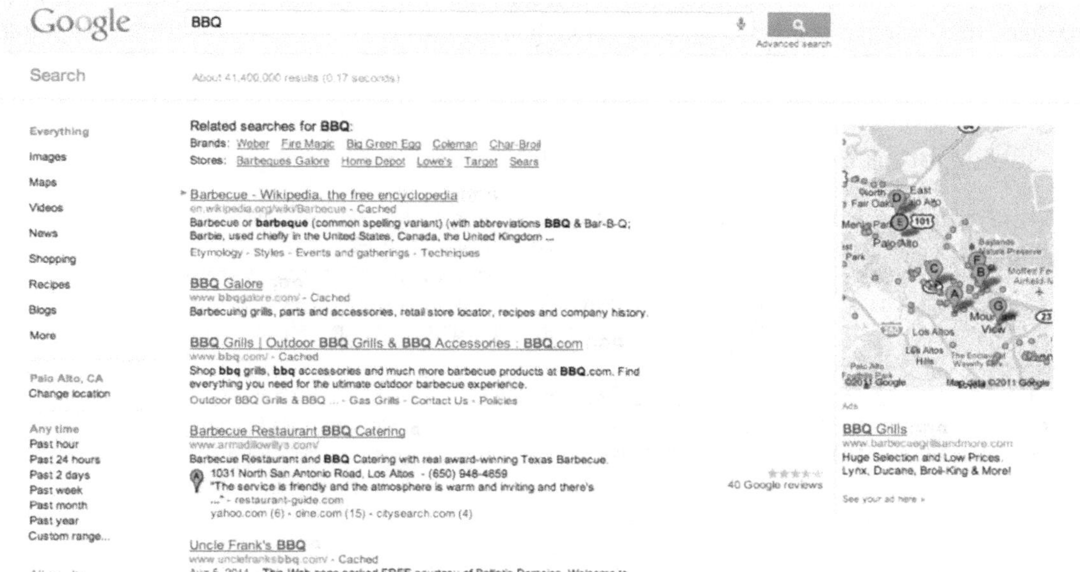

Source: Google and the Google logo are registered trademarks of Google Inc., used with permission.

FIGURE 6.3 An Example of Geotargeting

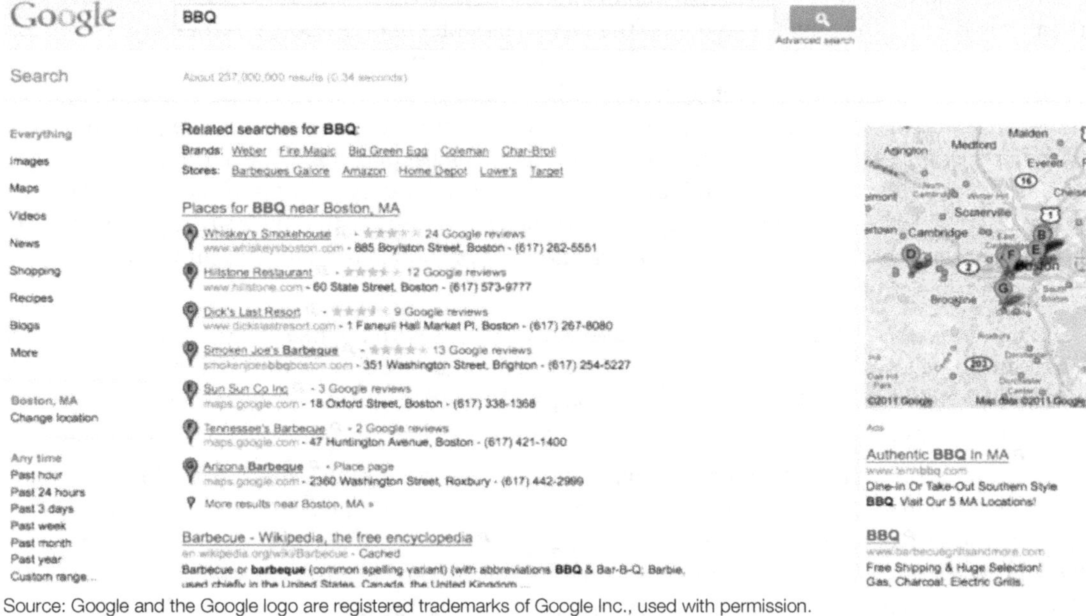

Source: Google and the Google logo are registered trademarks of Google Inc., used with permission.

IP addresses will change depending on how and where you connect to the Internet. Connect your laptop to a hotel's Wi-Fi when visiting a new city, and you're likely to see ads specific to that location. That's because your Internet service provider has changed, and the firm serving your ads has detected that you are using an IP address known to be associated with your new location.

proxy servers

A third-party computer that passes traffic to and from a specific address without revealing the address of the connected user.

Wi-Fi

A term used to brand wireless local-area networking devices. Devices typically connect to an antenna-equipped base station or hotspot, which is then connected to the Internet. Wi-Fi devices use standards known as IEEE 802.11, and various versions of this standard (e.g., b, g, n) may operate in different frequency bands and have access ranges.

global positioning system (GPS)

A network of satellites and supporting technologies used to identify a device's physical location.

Geotargeting via IP address is fairly accurate, but it's not perfect. For example, some Internet service providers may provide imprecise or inaccurate information on the location of their networks. Others might be so vague that it's difficult to make a best guess at the geography behind a set of numbers (values assigned by a multinational corporation with many locations, for example). And there are other ways locations are hidden, such as when Internet users connect to **proxy servers**, third-party computers that pass traffic to and from a specific address without revealing the address of the connected users.

Geotargeting Evolves Beyond the IP Address

There are several other methods of geotargeting. Firms like Skyhook Wireless/TruePosition, Apple, and Google can identify a location based on mapping **Wi-Fi** hotspots and nearby cell towers. Many mobile devices come equipped with **global positioning system (GPS)** chips (identifying location via the GPS satellite network). And if a user provides location values such as a home address or zip code to a website, then that value might be stored and used again to make a future guess at a user's location.

Many firms build and maintain accurate location databases by regularly collecting location information from smartphones and using this data to refine maps. Phones submit data anonymously; however, this process can be controversial.

Mobile Apps and the Challenge for Google Search

US mobile users spend roughly three hours each day on smartphones and tablets. While most online desktop time happens via the Web browser, mobile users spend an estimated 86 percent of their time in apps and only 14 percent on the Web. This shift concerns Google. When you search for restaurant reviews in Google's search engine, it can serve you ads and continue to build your user profile. But if you search via Yelp's app on an iPhone, Google can't see you at all. Yelp is thought to have earned about $550 million in ad revenue 2015, up over by 45 percent from the prior year and with the vast majority coming from mobile.[33] The growing list of context-specific apps that siphon users away from Google's Web search include Kayak and TripAdvisor for travel, Shazam for music, and even Amazon for shopping. And Apple's Siri is delivering results directly from its partners, making it the search broker, not Google. This fragmenting of mobile is having an impact on Google's share of mobile advertising.[34]

deep linking

A link that takes a user to a specific webpage (rather than the home page), or which launches an app and brings up a unique location rather than just launching the app. As an example, a deep link from Pinterest might take a user directly to the Etsy web page or app listing featuring the vendor of that item, rather than generically opening Etsy.com or the Etsy app.

App owners are becoming even more useful advertisers with the rise of so-called **deep linking**. Deep linking allows an advertisement to launch an app and call up requested information, say, clicking a Pinterest link for a vintage handbag and jumping immediately to bag vendor's page within the Etsy app. And, of course, this app-to-app advertising cuts out Google even further.

In 2012, Google had an 82.8 percent share of mobile searches, but research firm eMarketer estimates that when you consider the long tail of app-based searches that are occurring, Google's share was around 65.7 percent in 2014. The app-based niche searches like those mentioned previously have grown from 5.4 percent of mobile search to 22.9 percent in just two years.[35] Even though Google's percentage of mobile search ad revenue is declining, the firm's mobile search ad revenue is still going up. That's because the search ad pie is getting bigger as more users conduct more searches online. But the trends underscore how mobile is different (for more on the challenges of mobile, see [Content Removed: #fwk-38086-ch07]). Google has offered additional features to give users a reason to stick with its search and map products. For example, a new hotel format offers the ability to see high-quality photos, hotel ratings and book a hotel right from within a Google listing. A new car format allows a panoramic scroll through the car, the ability to "build and price" a car, and find a dealer. A mortgage format allows for side-by-side comparisons.[36] And a new restaurant format can directly summon a food delivery service via deep link.[37]

Making Google more relevant, especially on mobile, makes sense, but the new functionality comes with risks. Google's move into travel booking is upsetting some of the firm's biggest customers. Priceline spends over $1.5 billion advertising with Google each year. Expedia spends over $1 billion. Just these two firms account for about a 5 percent chunk of Google revenue. If Google can create increased ad revenue directly from hotels, airlines, and other travel providers, this might help make up the difference, but that's a serious bit of channel pressure and market shift that would need to happen. More troubling are potential legal issues. Priceline and Expedia are also members of FairSearch.org, a group that accuses Google of using its dominance in search and other products to favor its own services above those of rivals.[38]

Key Takeaways

- More than two-thirds of Google's revenues come from ads served on its own sites, and the vast majority of this revenue comes from search engine ads.
- Search ads on Google are both more effective (in terms of click-through rate) and more sought after by advertisers, because they are often associated with a user's purchasing intent.
- Advertisers choose and bid on the keywords and phrases that they'd like to use to trigger the display of their ads.
- Advertisers pay for cost-per-click advertising only if an ad is clicked on. Google makes no money on CPC ads that are displayed but not clicked.
- Google determines ad rank by multiplying CPC by quality score. Ads with low ranks might not display at all.
- Advertisers usually don't pay their maximum CPC. Instead, Google discounts ads to just one cent more than the minimum necessary to maintain an ad's position on the page—a practice that encourages higher bids.
- Geotargeting occurs when computer systems identify a user's physical location (sometimes called geolocation) for the purpose of delivering tailored ads or other content.
- Google uses IP addresses to target ads.
- Geotargeting can also be enabled by the satellite-based global positioning system (GPS) or based on estimating location from cell phone towers or Wi-Fi hotspots.
- The rise of apps as an alternative to search is a threat to Google and has shrunk the firm's percentage of mobile search. Deep linking allows websites and apps to link directly with content in other sites and apps, bypassing Google altogether. However, Google's revenues continue to rise as more users conduct more searches online.
- Google offers Web and app deep-linking, and new ad formats give the ability to do more in search and maps (e.g., compare and book hotel rooms, car shop). However, offering these services may alienate advertisers, some of whom spend $1 billion or more with Google. It also adds to concerns that Google uses its dominance in search and other categories to favor its products and services over those of rivals.

Questions and Exercises

1. Which firm invented pay-per-click advertising? Why does Google dominate today and not this firm?
2. How are ads sold via Google search superior to conventional advertising media such as TV, radio, billboard, print, and yellow pages? Consider factors like the available inventory of space to run ads, the cost to run ads, the cost to acquire new advertisers, and the appeal among advertisers.
3. Are there certain kinds of advertising campaigns and goals where search advertising wouldn't be a good fit? Give examples and explain why.
4. Can a firm buy a top ad ranking? Why or why not?

5. List the four factors that determine an ad's quality score.
6. How much do firms typically pay for a single click?
7. Sites like SpyFu.com and KeywordSpy.com provide a list of the keywords with the highest cost per click. Visit the Top Lists page at SpyFu, KeywordSpy, or a comparable site, to find estimates of the current highest paying cost per click. Which keywords pay the most? Why do you think firms are willing to spend so much?
8. What is bidder's remorse? How does Google's ad discounting impact this phenomenon?
9. Visit WhatIsMyIPaddress.com (or a similar website that displays a device's IP address) using a desktop, laptop, and mobile phone (work with a classmate or friend if you don't have access to one of these devices). How do results differ? Why? Are they accurate? What factors go into determining the accuracy of IP-based geolocation?
10. List and briefly describe other methods of geotargeting besides IP address, and indicate the situations and devices where these methods would be more and less effective.
11. The field of search engine marketing (SEM) is relatively new and rising in importance. And since the field is so new and constantly changing, there are plenty of opportunities for young, knowledgeable professionals. Which organizations, professional certification, and other resources are available to SEM professionals? Spend some time searching for these resources online and be prepared to share your findings with your class.
12. How do you, your friends, or your family members search on mobile devices? How has search changed over time? Are there certain product categories that you used to go to Google for, but where you'll now rely on an app? How do you suppose this impacts Google's revenue? If you were Google, how might you combat challenges as search shifts from a single search engine to niche apps?
13. What is Google doing to combat users migrating to other apps and services for their search? What are the risks in this approach?

6.3 Customer Profiling and Behavioral Targeting

Learning Objectives

1. Be familiar with various tracking technologies and how they are used for customer profiling and ad targeting.
2. Understand why customer profiling is both valuable and controversial.
3. Recognize steps that organizations can take to help ease consumer and governmental concerns.

cookies

A line of identifying text, assigned and retrieved by a given Web server and stored by your browser.

Advertisers are willing to pay more for ads that have a greater chance of reaching their target audience, and online firms have a number of targeting tools at their disposal. Much of this targeting occurs whenever you visit a website, where a behind-the-scenes software dialogue takes place between Web browser and Web server that can reveal a number of pieces of information, including IP address, the type of browser used, the computer type, its operating system, and unique identifiers, called **cookies**.

And remember, *any* server that serves you content can leverage these profiling technologies. You might be profiled not just by the website that you're visiting (e.g., nytimes.com), but also by any ad networks that serve ads on that site (e.g., Google, AOL, Yahoo!/Bing).

IP addresses are leveraged extensively in customer profiling. An IP address not only helps with geolocation, it can also indicate a browser's employer or university, which can be further matched with information such as firm size or industry. IBM has used IP targeting to tailor its college recruiting banner ads to specific schools, for example, "There Is Life After Boston College, Click Here to See Why." That campaign garnered click-through rates ranging from 5 to 30 percent[39] compared to average rates that are currently well below 1 percent for untargeted banner ads. DoubleClick once even served a banner that included a personal message for an executive at then-client Modem Media. The ad, reading "Congratulations on the twins, John Nardone," was served across hundreds of sites, but was only visible from computers that accessed the Internet from the Modem Media corporate network.[40]

The ability to identify a surfer's computer, browser, or operating system can also be used to target tech ads. For example, Google might pitch its Chrome browser to users detected running Internet Explorer, Firefox, or Safari; while Apple could target Mac ads just to Windows users.

But perhaps the greatest degree of personalization and targeting comes from cookies. Visit a website for the first time, and in most cases, a dialogue between server and browser takes place that goes something like this:

Server: *Have I seen you before?*

Browser: *No.*

Server: *Then take this unique string of numbers and letters (called a cookie). I'll use it to recognize you from now on.*

The cookie is just a line of identifying text assigned and retrieved by a given Web server and stored on your computer by your browser. Upon accepting this cookie your browser has been tagged, like an animal. As you surf around the firm's website, that cookie can be used to build a profile associated with your activities. If you're on a portal like Yahoo! you might type in your zip code, enter stocks that you'd like to track, and identify the sports teams you'd like to see scores for. The next time you return to the website, your browser responds to the server's "*Have I seen you before?*" question with the equivalent of "*Yes, you know me,*" and it presents the cookie that the site gave you earlier. The site can then match this cookie against your browsing profile, showing you the weather, stock quotes, sports scores, and other info that it thinks you're interested in.

Google and others provide a service called **remarketing** (also called **retargeting**), where site operators can tag users according to which page they visit on their site. They can then use this info to serve up tailored ads and special offers to that user as they browse the Web. Visited a scuba suit page on an e-commerce site? That same website can target you with special promotions, custom ads, or even dynamically generated ads when searching Google or visiting any site in the Google Display Network.[41]

Cookies are used for lots of purposes. Retail websites like Amazon use cookies to pay attention to what you've shopped for and bought, tailoring websites to display products that the firm suspects you'll be most interested in. Sites also use cookies to keep track of what you put in an online "shopping cart," so if you quit browsing before making a purchase, these items will reappear the next time you visit. And many websites also use cookies as part of a "remember me" feature, storing user IDs and passwords. Beware this last one! If you check the "remember me" box on a public Web browser, the next person who uses that browser is potentially using *your* cookie, and can log in as you!

remarketing

Lets a website show custom, targeted ads to a user when visiting other sites if that user has already visited a given page on the advertiser's site. This technique allows firms to "reintroduce" products to users or target them with special messages or promotions.

retargeting

Also known as *remarketing*, a form of online targeted advertising where ads are personalized for consumers based on previous Internet activity that did not result in a sale or conversion. Surf the Web and see ads for products you've looked at on other sties? This is likely a result of retargeting.

third-party cookies

Sometimes called "tracking cookies" and are served by ad networks or other customer-profiling firms. Tracking cookies are used to identify users and record behavior across multiple websites.

An organization can't read cookies that it did not give you. So businessweek.com can't tell if you've also got cookies from forbes.com. But you can see all of the cookies in your browser. Take a look and you'll almost certainly see cookies from dozens of websites that you've never visited before. These are **third-party cookies** (sometimes called *tracking cookies*), and they are usually served by ad networks or other customer-profiling firms.

By serving and tracking cookies in ads shown across partner sites, ad networks can build detailed browsing profiles that include sites visited, specific pages viewed, duration of visit, and the types of ads you've seen and responded to. And that surfing might give an advertising network a better guess at demographics like gender, age, marital status, and more. Visit a new parent site and expect to see diaper ads in the future, even when you're surfing for news or sports scores!

FIGURE 6.4 Web Browser Preference Settings

The Preferences setting in most Web browsers allows you to see its cookies. This browser has received cookies from several ad networks, media sites, and the University of Minnesota Carlson School of Management.

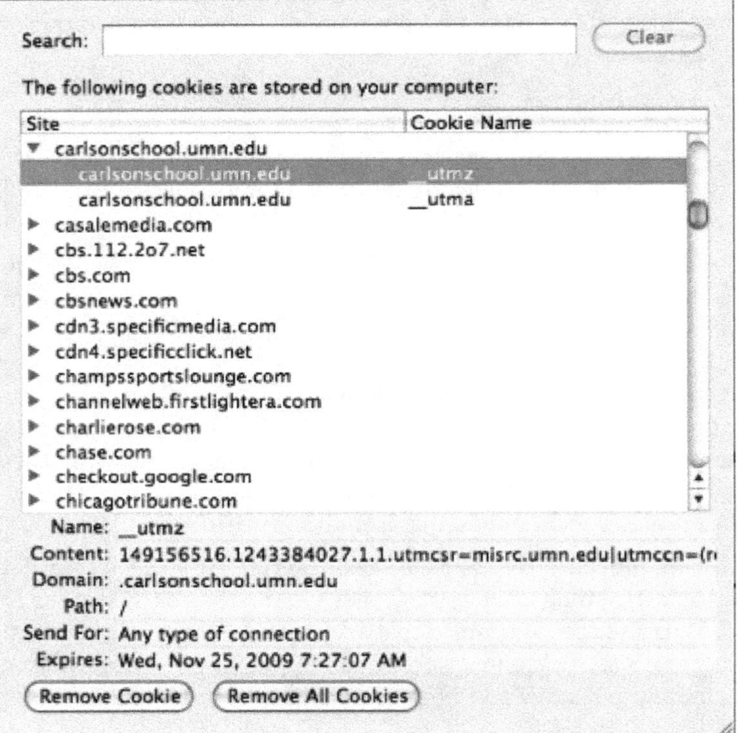

But What If I Don't Want a Cookie!

If all of this creeps you out, remember that you're in control. The most popular Web browsers allow you to block all cookies, block just third-party cookies, purge your cookie file, or even ask for your approval before accepting a cookie. Of course, if you block cookies, you block any benefits that come along with them, and some website features may require cookies to work properly. Also note that while deleting a cookie breaks a link between your browser and that website, if you supply identifying information in the future (say by logging into an old profile), the site might be able to assign your old profile data to the new cookie.

While the Internet offers targeting technologies that go way beyond traditional television, print, and radio offerings, none of these techniques is perfect. Since users are regularly assigned different IP addresses as they connect and disconnect from various physical and Wi-Fi networks, IP targeting can't reliably identify individual users. Cookies also have their weaknesses. They're assigned by browsers and associated with a given user's account on that computer. That means that if several people use the same browser on the same computer without logging on to that machine as separate users, then all their Web surfing activity may be mixed into the same cookie profile. (One solution is to create different log-in accounts on that computer. Your PC will then keep separate cookies for each account.) Some users might also use different browsers on the same machine or use different computers. Unless a firm has a way to match up these different cookies assigned across browsers (say by linking cookies on separate machines to a single log-in used at multiple locations), then a site may be working with multiple, incomplete profiles.

Big Data Analytics: Even for the Little Guy

In order to help arm firms with the insight needed for SEO, SEM, improved website design, and effective online marketing and promotion, Google offers a suite of tracking and analysis tools via a service it calls Google Analytics. The base service is offered free to websites of all sizes, with premium offerings and support available for a fee.

Using analytics, a content provider can collect statistics on its website or app's traffic, traffic sources (search engine, website, app, geographic origin, or even e-mail or .pdf link), user behavior on site (new/returning visitor stats, pages visited, etc.), sales and advertising success, social media analysis, and more. Analytics typically involve harvesting data that browsers and servers produce on their own, along with data from pages and apps that a firm will tag in advance and data from tracking cookies used to identify users. Google Analytics has more than an 80 percent market share.[42]

FIGURE 6.5 Google Analytics Sample Screens

Source: Google.

Apps, Mobile Browsing, and Default Settings: The Shifting Landscape of Profiling Technology

Mobile apps don't use cookies, as cookies are a Web-based technology. The technologies for providing a cookie-like feature in mobile apps continue to be developed. Google offers an in-app tracking scheme called Advertising ID; Apple's is called IDFA (Identifier for Advertisers). These technologies are critical for tracking things like ad impression views and click-throughs, but the two schemes behave differently and standards for both schemes have changed in just the past year.

Apple's Safari browser also disables third-party cookies by default. This is a big deal because while Android holds a much larger market share than iOS, Apple users browse way more than anyone else, and Safari holds more than 50 percent share of mobile browser usage.[43] Microsoft has also disabled cookies as the default option for Internet Explorer.[44] When these settings are in effect, traditional cookie-based user profiling by ad networks simply isn't possible.

Apple has also shut down another way mobile users were being tracked using the MAC (media access control) address. The MAC address is a permanent and unique identifier baked into every network-connected device (think of it as an unchanging IP address). All desktop, laptop, tablets, and smartphones have a MAC address. Many retailers were using MAC addresses on Wi-Fi–enabled phones to surreptitiously track store foot traffic.[45] In iOS8, Apple began randomizing the MAC number when these sorts of "Wi-Fi probe" requests were made, making it impossible to rely on any reported MAC number as a unique identifier for a repeat visitor. Apple is promoting a new location-based tracking system called iBeacon, which uses Bluetooth and (unlike MAC address snooping) can be turned off by users who wish to stay anonymous.

Taken collectively, these developments show that tracking technologies remain in flux, what works on the desktop doesn't necessarily work on mobile, and that default settings may be changed over time in ways that make life difficult for Google and other firms that rely on digital ad revenue. One analyst suggests that about half of all digital advertising spending leverages third-party cookies, and the shifts previously mentioned put these dollars in jeopardy.[46] Anyone with a stake in the digital advertising world—that is, advertisers, content operators, ad networks, even employees, investors, and regulators—will need to continually monitor the shifting landscape. It's not an understatement to say that billions in revenues are at stake.

Key Takeaways

- The communication between Web browser and Web server can identify IP address, the type of browser used, the computer type, its operating system, time and date of access, and duration of Web page visit, and can read and assign unique identifiers, called cookies—all of which can be used in customer profiling and ad targeting.
- An IP address not only helps with geolocation; it can also be matched against other databases to identify the organization providing the user with Internet access (such as a firm or university), and that organization's industry, size, and related statistics.
- A cookie is a unique line of identifying text, assigned and retrieved by a given Web server and stored on a computer by the browser, that can be used to build a profile associated with your Web activities.
- The most popular Web browsers allow you to block all cookies, block just third-party cookies, purge your cookie file, or even ask for your approval before accepting a cookie.
- Retargeting, or remarketing, allows advertisers to serve targeted ads to consumers who may have viewed a product page but did not buy that product. Google and other ad networks support retargeting.
- Cookies are a web-based technology, so they don't work in apps. Firms like Google and Apple have app-based tracking technology to help monetize ads (tracking clicks and impressions), but these technologies differ across platforms.
- Apple and Microsoft have also limited the use of cookies in their browser and mobile products. Apple has also shut off the ability of third parties to reach the MAC address, a unique number that many used to track mobile users. All these developments suggest that the future of profiling and ad technology is in flux, and managers who have a stake in this game will need to pay attention to future developments.

Questions and Exercises

1. Give examples of how the ability to identify a surfer's computer, browser, or operating system can be used to target tech ads.
2. Describe how IBM targeted ad delivery for its college recruiting efforts. What technologies were used? What was the impact on click-through rates?
3. What is a cookie? How are cookies used? Is a cookie a computer program? Which firms can read the cookies in your Web browser?
4. Does a cookie accurately identify a user? Why or why not?
5. What is the danger of checking the "remember me" box when logging in to a website using a public computer?
6. What's a third-party cookie? What kinds of firms might use these? How are they used?
7. How can users restrict cookie use on their Web browsers? What is the downside of blocking cookies? Check your desktop and mobile devices. What is your current setting for cookie tracking?
8. As firms like Microsoft and Apple block tracking technologies or set defaults for higher levels of user privacy, how might this impact the future of the ad-based Internet?
9. What is remarketing? Have you ever seen an ad that you suspect was part of a remarketing effort? If so, describe what you experienced. Do you think remarketing is effective? Why or why not?
10. Work with a faculty member and join the Google Online Marketing Challenge (held in the spring of every year—see http://www.google.com/onlinechallenge). Google offers ad credits for student teams to develop and run online ad campaigns for real clients and offers prizes for winning teams. Some of the experiences earned in the Google Challenge can translate to other ad networks as well, and firsthand client experience has helped many students secure jobs, internships, and even start their own businesses.

6.4 Profiling and Privacy

Learning Objectives

1. Understand the privacy concerns that arise as a result of using third-party or tracking cookies to build user profiles.
2. Be aware of the negative consequences that could result from the misuse of third-party or tracking cookies.
3. Know the steps Google has taken to demonstrate its sensitivity to privacy issues.
4. Know the kinds of user information that Google stores, and the steps Google takes to protect the privacy of that information.

While AdSense has been wildly successful, contextual advertising has its limits. For example, what kind of useful targeting can firms really do based on the text of a news item on North Korean nuclear testing?[47] For more accurate targeting, Google offers what it calls "interest-based ads," which is based on a third-party cookie that tracks browsing activity across Google properties and AdSense partner sites. AdSense builds a profile, identifying users within dozens of broad categories and over six hundred subcategories.[48] Of course, there's a financial incentive to do this too. Ads deemed more interesting should garner more clicks, meaning more potential customer leads for advertisers, more revenue for websites that run AdSense, and more money for Google.

Click-throughs and online purchases are great, but online ads influence offline sales, too. A study by Forrester found mobile devices were used in over one-third of all US retail sales at some point in the buying process—including research, price comparisons, and purchases. That's involvement in about $1 trillion in sales.[49] If Google can prove its ads drive in-store sales, it can make the case for greater online ad spending. In a scheme similar to Facebook's, Google is partnering with Axciom, a firm that collects information on customer e-mail addresses. If the Google cookie can be matched to a user's e-mail address, then we can identify that a user has seen an ad. If that user walks into a store, buys something, and the vendor can match their e-mail address to that purchase (perhaps they gave it to receive e-mail coupons or a loyalty card, or they've previously bought online), then a trail from "Saw the ad" to "bought the product" can be drawn. To avoid a total user creep-out, the user tracking is collected and reported in aggregate and anonymously, and that in this system, no identifying information on users is stored or reported. It's also far from a completely representative system. On Android phones Google's partners can connect just 15 to 20 percent of mobile ads to a customer account, and far fewer for harder-to-track iPhones, but for some retailers, that's enough of a sample to demonstrate ROI on ad spending. Home Depot's VP of online marketing says the data "confirmed our commitment" to search ads on smartphones.[50] Target execs claim that one-third of Target's mobile-search ads led to a user visiting one of its stores during the 2014 holiday season.[51]

opt-in

Program (typically a marketing effort) that requires customer consent. This program is contrasted with opt-out programs, which enroll all customers by default.

While targeting can benefit Web surfers, users will resist if they feel that they are being mistreated, exploited, or put at risk. Negative backlash might also result in a change in legislation. The US Federal Trade Commission has already called for more transparency and user control in online advertising and for requesting user consent (**opt-in**) when collecting sensitive data.[52] Mishandled user privacy could curtail targeting opportunities, limiting growth across the online advertising field. And with less ad support, many of the Internet's free services could suffer.

FIGURE 6.6 Example of User Interests Tracked by Google

Here’s an example of one user’s interests, as tracked by Google’s “Interest-based Ads” and displayed in the firm’s “Ad Preferences Manager.”

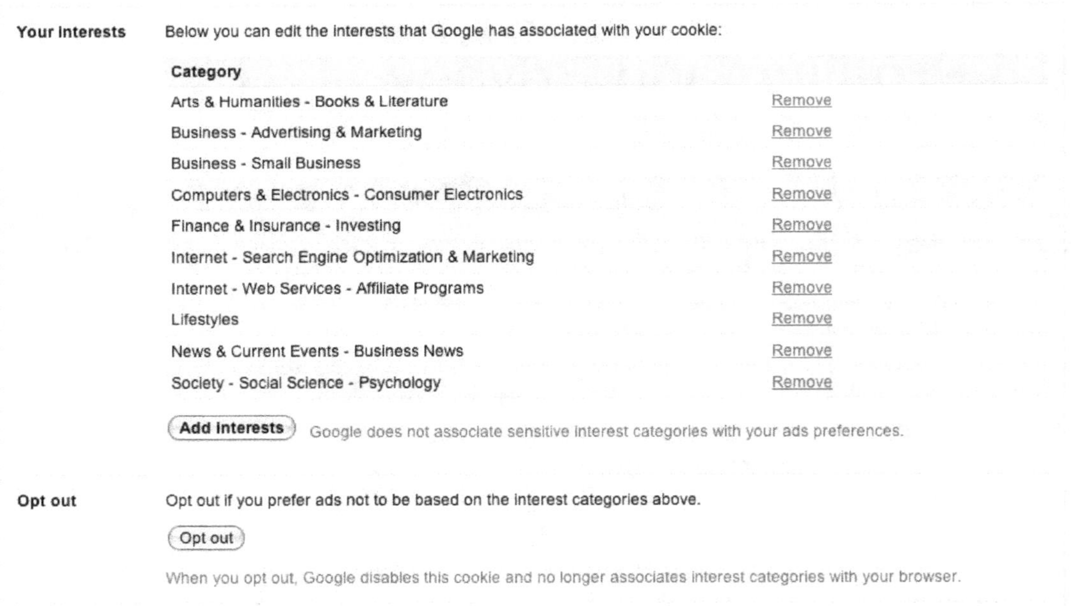

Your Interests Below you can edit the interests that Google has associated with your cookie:

Category	
Arts & Humanities - Books & Literature	Remove
Business - Advertising & Marketing	Remove
Business - Small Business	Remove
Computers & Electronics - Consumer Electronics	Remove
Finance & Insurance - Investing	Remove
Internet - Search Engine Optimization & Marketing	Remove
Internet - Web Services - Affiliate Programs	Remove
Lifestyles	Remove
News & Current Events - Business News	Remove
Society - Social Science - Psychology	Remove

Add interests Google does not associate sensitive interest categories with your ads preferences.

Opt out Opt out if you prefer ads not to be based on the interest categories above.

Opt out

When you opt out, Google disables this cookie and no longer associates interest categories with your browser.

Google's roll-out of interest-based ads shows the firm's sensitivity to these issues. The firm has also placed significant control in the hands of users, with options at program launch that were notably more robust than those of its competitors.[53] Each interest-based ad is accompanied by an "Ads by Google" link that will bring users to a page describing Google advertising and which provides access to the company's "Ads Preferences Manager." This tool allows surfers to see any of the hundreds of potential categorizations that Google has assigned to that browser's tracking cookie. Users can remove categorizations, and even add interests if they want to improve ad targeting. Some topics are too sensitive to track, and the technology avoids profiling race, religion, sexual orientation, health, political or trade union affiliation, and certain financial categories.[54]

Google also allows users to install a cookie that opts them out of interest-based tracking. And since browser cookies can expire or be deleted, the firm has gone a step further, offering a browser **plug-in** that will remain permanent, even if a user's **opt-out** cookie is purged.

plug-in

A small computer program that extends the feature set or capabilities of another application.

opt-out

Programs that enroll all customers by default, but that allow consumers to discontinue participation if they want to.

Google, Privacy Advocates, and the Law

Google's moves are meant to demonstrate transparency in its ad targeting technology, and the firm's policies may help raise the collective privacy bar for the industry. While privacy advocates have praised Google's efforts to put more control in the hands of users, many continue to voice concern over what they see as the increasing amount of information that the firm houses.[55] For an avid user, Google could conceivably be holding e-mail (Gmail), photos (Picasa), social media activity (Google+), a Web-surfing profile (AdSense and DoubleClick), location (Google Maps), appointments (Google Calendar), music and other media (Google Play), files stored in the cloud (Google Drive), transcripts of phone messages (Google Voice), work files (Google Docs), and more.

Google insists that reports portraying it as a data-hoarding Big Brother are inaccurate. Data is not sold to third parties. Any targeting is fully disclosed, with users empowered to opt out at all levels.[56] Google has introduced several tools, including Google Dashboard and Google Ad Preferences Manager, that allow users to see information Google stores about them, clear their browsing history, and selectively delete collected data.[57] But critics counter that corporate intentions and data use policies (articulated in a website's Terms of Service) can change over time, and that a firm's good behavior today is no guarantee of good behavior in the future.[58] Google has modified its policy several times in the past, including changes that now allow the firm to link search history to ad targeting. It has also unified its privacy policy in a way that allows for greater profiling, sharing, and tailored services across Google offerings.[59]

Google does enjoy a lot of user goodwill, and it is widely recognized for its unofficial motto "Don't Be Evil." However, some worry that even though Google might not be evil, it could still make a mistake, and that despite its best intentions, a security breach or employee error could leave data dangerously or embarrassingly exposed.

Gaffes have repeatedly occurred. A system flaw inadvertently shared some Google Docs with contacts who were never granted access to them.[60] When the firm introduced its now-scuttled Google Buzz social networking service, many users were horrified that their most frequently used Gmail contacts were automatically added to Buzz, allowing others to see who you're communicating with. As one report explained, "Suddenly, journalists' clandestine contacts were exposed, secret affairs became dramatically less secret, and stalkers obtained a new tool to harass their victims. Oops."[61] Google admitted that some of its "Street View" cars, while driving through neighborhoods and taking photos for Google maps, had inadvertently collected personal data, including e-mails and passwords.[62] Google scrambled to plug a hole that could potentially allow hackers to access the contacts, calendars, and photos on Android phones connecting to the Internet over open Wi-Fi networks.[63] A rogue employee was fired for violating the firm's strict guidelines and procedures on information access.[64] In addition, the firm has been accused of bypassing privacy settings in Apple's Safari Web browser in order to better track users.[65]

Privacy advocates also worry that the amount of data stored by Google serves as one-stop shopping for litigators and government investigators—a concern that gained even more attention following the disclosure of the US government's Prism surveillance program.[66] The counterargument points to the fact that Google has continually reflected an aggressive defense of data privacy in court cases. Following Prism disclosures, Google asked the US Foreign Intelligence Surveillance Court to rescind a gag order barring the firm from revealing government information requests.[67] When Viacom sued Google over copyright violations in YouTube, the search giant successfully fought the original subpoena, which had requested user-identifying information.[68] Google has also resisted Justice Department subpoenas for search queries, while rivals have complied.[69] Google has also claimed that it has been targeted by some foreign governments that are deliberately hacking or interfering with the firm's services in order to quash some information sharing and to uncover dissident activity.[70]

Google is increasingly finding itself in precedent-setting cases where the law is vague. Google's Street View, for example, has been the target of legal action in the United States, Canada, Japan, Greece, and the United Kingdom. Varying legal environments create a challenge to the global rollout of any data-driven initiative.[71] European courts have ruled that EU citizens have the so-called right to be forgotten and can demand that search engines remove links to information deemed "inadequate, irrelevant or no longer relevant, or excessive in relation to the purposes for which they were processed."[72] Does this sound vague? Enforcement of this ruling may be challenging for Google.[73] And rivals are ready to cast Google as a voracious data tracker. Apple has begun to play up the firm's contrast with Google, claiming "You are not our product."[74]

Ad targeting brings to a head issues of opportunity, privacy, security, risk, and legislation. Google is now taking a more active public relations and lobbying role to prevent misperceptions and to be sure its positions are understood. While the field continues to evolve, Google's experience will lay the groundwork for the future of personalized technology and provide a case study for other firms that need to strike the right balance between utility and privacy. Despite differences, it seems clear to Google, its advocates, and its detractors that with great power comes great responsibility.

Key Takeaways

- Possible consequences resulting from the misuse of customer tracking and profiling technologies include user resistance and legislation. Mishandled user privacy could curtail targeting opportunities and limit growth in online advertising. With less ad support, many of the Internet's free services could suffer.
- Google has taken several steps to protect user privacy. The firm offers several tools that enable users not only to see information that Google collects but also to delete, pause, or modify data collection and profiling terms.
- Google's "Ads Preferences Manager" allows surfers to see, remove, and add to any of the categorizations that Google has assigned to that browser's tracking cookie. The technology also avoids targeting certain sensitive topics. The firm's Privacy Dashboard provides additional access to and user control over Google's profiling and data collection.
- Google allows users to install a cookie or plug-in that opts them out of interest-based tracking.
- Google has begun to partner with third-party firms to tie together its data on consumer ad viewership to in-store visits. While not perfect, the data has shown that many users who view online ads go on to make in-store purchases. Google's data is reported in aggregate, and not on any individual user.
- Some privacy advocates have voiced concern over what they see as the increasing amount of information that Google and other firms collect. Apple is among the firms that have contrasted their approach to products, privacy, and business models with Google's ad-driven, profiling methods.
- Even the best-intentioned and most competent firms can have a security breach that compromises stored information. Google has suffered privacy breaches from product flaws and poorly planned feature rollouts, as well as deliberate hacks and attacks. The firm has also changed policies regarding data collection and privacy as its services have evolved. Such issues may lead to further investigation, legislation, and regulation.

Questions and Exercises

1. Gmail uses contextual advertising. The service will scan the contents of e-mail messages and display ads off to the side. Test the "creep-out" factor in Gmail—create an account (if you don't already have one), and send messages to yourself with controversial terms in them. Which ones showed ads? Which ones didn't?
2. Google has never built user profiles based on Gmail messages. Ads are served based on a real-time scanning of keywords. Is this enough to make you comfortable with Google's protection of your own privacy? Why or why not?
3. List the negative consequences that could result from the misuse of tracking cookies.
4. What steps does Google take to protect the privacy of user information? What steps has Google taken to give users control over the user data that the firm collects and the ads the users wish to see?
5. Which topics does "Ads Preferences Manager" avoid in its targeting system?
6. Visit Google's Ad Preferences page. Is Google tracking your interests? Do you think the list of interests is accurate? Browse the categories under the "Ad Interest" button. Would you add any of these categories to your profile? Why or why not? What do you gain or lose by taking advantage of Google's "Opt Out" option? Visit rival ad networks. Do you have a similar degree of control? More or less?
7. Visit Google Dashboard. What information is Google collecting about you? Does any of this surprise you? How do you suppose the firm uses this to benefit you? After seeing this information, did you make any changes to the settings in the privacy center? Why or why not?
8. List the types of information that Google might store for an individual. Do you feel that Google is a fair and reliable steward for this information? Are there Google services or other online efforts that you won't use due to privacy concerns? Why?
9. What do you think of the Google-Acxiom partnership to show online ad influence for offline purchasing. Does this concern you? Why or why not?
10. Google's "interest-based advertising" was launched as an opt-out effort. What are the pros and cons for Google, users, advertisers, and AdSense partner sites if Google were to switch to an opt-in system? How would these various constituencies be impacted if the government mandated that users explicitly opt in to third-party cookies and other behavior-tracking techniques?
11. What is Google's unofficial motto?
12. What is "Street View"? Where and on what grounds is it being challenged?
13. Cite two court cases where Google has mounted a vigorous defense of data privacy.
14. *Wired News* quoted a representative of privacy watchdog group. the Center for Digital Democracy, who offered a criticism of online advertising. The representative suggested that online firms were trying to learn "everything about individuals and manipulate their weaknesses" and that the federal government should "investigate the role [that online ads] played in convincing people to take out mortgages they should not have."[75] Do you think online advertising played a significant role in the mortgage crisis? What role do advertisers, ad networks, and content providers have in online advertising oversight? Should this responsibility be any different from oversight in traditional media (television, print, radio)? What guidelines would you suggest?
15. Even well-intentioned firms can compromise user privacy. How have Google's missteps compromised user privacy? As a manager, what steps would you take in developing and deploying information systems that might prevent these kinds of problems from occurring?
16. Research the EU's "right to be forgotten" ruling and the current status as it pertains to Google. Why is the ruling so challenging to Google? How does it burden Google? Does this harm other civil liberties like free speech? Why or why not? Advocate in favor of or against the ruling.
17. Research how Apple has contrasted its approach to privacy against those of Google and other rivals that rely on ad-driven business models. Does this contrast influence your decision to choose Apple or Google products? Why or why not?
18. The issue of civil liberties versus national security may be one of the most defining tensions of modern times. Research the US government's Foreign Intelligence Surveillance Act (FISA)

and related legislation or programs. What role do tech companies play in this effort? What are the arguments made for and against these programs? Are US firms put at risk by perceived or actual government efforts in this area? How so? If you were leading Google or another well-known US Internet firm, how would you address the tension? Be prepared to discuss and debate issues in class.

Endnotes

1. G. Duncan, "Pay Your Way to the Top of Search Results with Google Shopping," *Digital Trends*, June 1, 2012.
2. S. Levy, "Inside the Box," *Wired*, March 2010.
3. D. Segal, "The Dirty Little Secrets of Search," *New York Times*, February 12, 2011.
4. D. Segal, "The Dirty Little Secrets of Search," *New York Times*, February 12, 2011.
5. M. Bergen, "Google to Investors: Don't Worry, We've Got Mobile Figured Out," *Re/code*, April 23, 2015.
6. D. Sullivan, "Google's Results Get More Personal with 'Search Plus Your World,'" *Search Engine Land*, January 10, 2012.
7. Unattributed, "Google Data Center FAQ," *Data Center Knowledge*, May 16, 2017.
8. B. Schwartz, "Google: You Can't Judge Index Size By One Or Two Sites," *Search Engine Roundtable*, Jan. 16, 2018.
9. Most websites do have a link where you can submit a website for indexing, and doing so can help promote the discovery of your content.
10. M. Liedtke, "Google Reigns as World's Most Powerful 10-Year-Old," *Associated Press*, September 5, 2008.
11. David F. Carr, "How Google Works," *Baseline*, July 6, 2006.
12. Unattributed, "Google Data Center FAQ," *Data Center Knowledge*, May 16, 2017.
13. C. Dulaney, "The Capital Spending Boom is Mostly About Tech," *The Wall Street Journal*, May 7, 2018.
14. S. Levy, "Google Throws Open Doors to Its Top-Secret Data Center," *Wired*, October 2012.
15. C. Metz, "Google's Top Five Data Center Secrets (That Are Still Secret)," *Wired*, October 18, 2012.
16. S. Shankland, "Google Unlocks Once-Secret Server," *CNET*, April 1, 2009.
17. S. Sharwood "Google reveals its servers all contain custom security silicon," *The Register*, Jan. 16, 2017.
18. C. Metz, "Google Makes Its Special A.I. Chips Available to Others," *The New York Times*, Feb. 12, 2018.
19. C. Metz, "Building an AI Chip Saved Google From Having to Build a Dozen New Data Centers," *Wired*, April 5, 2017.
20. Unattributed, "Efficiency: How we do it," Google Data Centers, accessed May 28, 2018—https://www.google.com/about/datacenters/efficiency/internal/.
21. S. Levy, "Google Throws Open Doors to Its Top-Secret Data Center," *Wired*, October 2012.
22. C. Metz, "Google Uses Artificial Brains to Teach Its Data Centers How to Behave," *Wired*, May 28, 2014.
23. J. Lima, "Equinix, Google Deepen Global Cloud Partnership With New Interconnect Service," *Data Economy*, April 18, 2018.
24. S. Elliott, "More Agencies Investing in Marketing with a Click," *New York Times*, March 14, 2006.
25. Google, "Google Announces Fourth Quarter and Fiscal Year 2008 Results," press release, January 22, 2009.
26. D. Vise, "Google's Decade," *Technology Review*, September 12, 2008.
27. S. Levy, "The Secrets of Googlenomics," *Wired*, June 2009.
28. "Check and Understand Quality Score," Google, accessed June 30, 2014, https://support.google.com/adwords/answer/2454010?hl=en.
29. S. Levy, "The Secrets of Googlenomics," *Wired*, June 2009.
30. *SpyFu*, "Keywords with the Highest Cost-Per-Click (CPC)," accessed June 30, 2014.
31. C. Mann, "How Click Fraud Could Swallow the Internet," *Wired*, January 2006.
32. SpyFu, "Domains that Spend the Most on Adwords," accessed June 30, 2014.
33. Yelp 2015 Annual Results—accessed June 24, 2016 via: http://www.yelp-ir.com/phoenix.zhtml?c=250809&p=irol-irhome.
34. M. Bergen, "Google's Mobile Search Strategy: Bake In and Take Out," Re/code, May 9, 2015.
35. Unattributed, "US Mobile Ad Dollars Shift to Search Apps," *eMarketer*, June 5, 2014.
36. G. Marvin, "Google AdWords Announces New Tools & Formats As Mobile Search Surpasses Desktop," *SearchEngineLand*, May 5, 2015.
37. M. Bergen, "Google's Mobile Search Strategy: Bake In and Take Out," *Re/code*, May 9, 2015.
38. R. Winkler and C. Karmin, "Google Checks In to the Hotel Business," *The Wall Street Journal*, April 8, 2014.
39. M. Moss, "These Web Sites Know Who You Are," *ZDNet UK*, October 13, 1999.
40. M. Moss, "These Web Sites Know Who You Are," *ZDNet UK*, October 13, 1999.
41. J. Slegg, "Google AdWords Dynamic Remarketing Launches for Merchants," *Search Engine Watch*, June 25, 2013.
42. R. Emerson, "Google Biz Chief: Over 10M Websites Now Using Google Analytics," *TechCrunch*, April 12, 2012.
43. S. Kovach, "Apple's Safari Is Crushing Google in Mobile Browser Market Share," *Business Insider*, November 8, 2013.
44. E. Griffith, "What Will Ad-Tech Look Like without Cookies?" *PandoDaily*, December 15, 2012.
45. E. Griffith, "Apple's Privacy Moves Underscore Its Distaste for the Advertising World," *Fortune*, June 12, 2014.
46. J. Greene, "Kicking Third-Party Cookies to the Curb: The Fallout for the Digital Ad Industry," *MarketingLand*, April 15, 2013.
47. R. Singel, "Online Behavioral Targeting Targeted by Feds, Critics," *Wired News*, June 3, 2009.
48. R. Hof, "Behavioral Targeting: Google Pulls Out the Stops," *BusinessWeek*, March 11, 2009.
49. L. Lucy, "Mobile Shopping Is on the Rise, But Remains Split Between the Mobile Web and Apps," *AdWeek*, Feb. 23, 2018.
50. A. Barr, "Google Says New Store Data Help Mobile Ads," *The Wall Street Journal*, May 21, 2015.
51. G. Sterling, "Store Visits And Offline Spending Data Will Drive Massive Mobile Ad Growth," *Marketing Land*, May 22, 2015.
52. R. Singel, "Online Behavioral Targeting Targeted by Feds, Critics," *Wired News*, June 3, 2009.
53. S. Hansell, "A Guide to Google's New Privacy Controls," *New York Times*, March 12, 2009.
54. R. Mitchell, "What Google Knows about You," *Computerworld*, May 11, 2009.
55. M. Helft, "BITS; Google Lets Users See a Bit of Selves," *New York Times*, November 9, 2009.
56. R. Mitchell, "What Google Knows about You," *Computerworld*, May 11, 2009.
57. "Policies and Principles," Google, http://www.google.com/policies/privacy (accessed June 11, 2012).
58. R. Mitchell, "What Google Knows about You," *Computerworld*, May 11, 2009.
59. C. Boulton, "Google Privacy Policy Changes are Live: Here Are Your Options," *eWeek*, March 1, 2012.
60. J. Kincaid, "Google Privacy Blunder Shares Your Docs without Permission," *TechCrunch*, March 7, 2009.
61. A. Gold, "Keep Your Buzz to Yourself: Google Misjudged Its Users' Right to Privacy," *The Harvard Crimson*, February 22, 2010.
62. A. Oreskovic, "Google Admits to Broader Collection of Personal Data," *Washington Post*, October 23, 2010.
63. D. Goldman, "Major Security Flaw Found in Android Phones," *CNN*, May 18, 2011.
64. T. Kranzit, "Google Fired Engineer for Privacy Breach," *CNET*, September 14, 2010.
65. D. Basulto, "Google, Safari, and Our Final Privacy Wake-Up Call," *Washington Post*, February 22, 2012.
66. D. Rushe, "Facebook and Google Insist They Did Not Know of Prism Surveillance Program," *Guardian*, June 7, 2013.
67. C. Timberg and C. Kang, "Google Challenges U.S. Gag Order, Citing First Amendment," *Washington Post*, June 18, 2013.
68. R. Mitchell, "What Google Knows about You," *Computerworld*, May 11, 2009.
69. A. Broache, "Judge: Google Must Give Feds Limited Access to Records," *CNET*, March 17, 2006.
70. D. Rushe, "Google Accuses China of Interfering with Gmail E-mail System," *Guardian*, March 20, 2011.
71. L. Sumagaysay, "Not Everyone Likes the (Google Street) View," *Good Morning Silicon Valley*, May 20, 2009.
72. E. Weise, "Europeans Flock to be Forgotten," *USA Today*, June 30, 2014.

73. J. Polonetsky and O. Tene, "The Right Response to the 'Right to Delete,'" *Re/code*, May 21, 2014.
74. D. Smith, "Tim Cook explains why Apple Pay doesn't collect your data: 'You are not our product'" *Business Insider*, Feb. 11, 2015.
75. R. Singel, "Online Behavioral Targeting Targeted by Feds, Critics," *Wired News*, June 3, 2009.

CHAPTER 7

Pivot Tables

7.1 Pivot Table Quick Facts

Pivot tables rapidly summarize data from different points of view. There are other ways to summarize data in Excel, but none are nearly as powerful as pivot tables. Consider the following table:

5	id	member_id	funded_amn	term	int_rate
6	1077501	1296599	5000	36 months	10.65%
7	1077430	1314167	2500	60 months	15.27%
8	1077175	1313524	2400	36 months	15.96%
9	1076863	1277178	10000	36 months	13.49%
10	1075358	1311748	3000	60 months	12.69%
11	1075269	1311441	5000	36 months	7.90%
12	1069639	1304742	7000	60 months	15.96%
13	1072053	1288686	3000	36 months	18.64%
14	1071795	1306957	5600	60 months	21.28%
15	1071570	1306721	5375	60 months	12.69%
16	1070078	1305201	6500	60 months	14.65%
17	1069908	1305008	12000	36 months	12.69%
18	1064687	1298717	9000	36 months	13.49%
19	1069866	1304956	3000	36 months	9.91%

What if you wanted to find the average interest rate for 36-month loans? For 60-month loans? We would like our output to look like this:

- 36 months = xx.xx%
- 60 months = xx.xx%

When you first begin a pivot table Excel will create a new worksheet. On the left of that worksheet will appear your pivot table results. On the right of the worksheet you will see a two-by-two table called a pivot table builder with the following sections:

Report Filter	Column Labels
Row Labels	Σ Values

Your job is to drag fields from your data to the appropriate boxes in order to demonstrate by example what you want the pivot table to do. As you drag fields into the pivot table builder, the results will appear in the left-hand portion of the worksheet. For example, if you want the term of the loan in months to appear in the rows of your pivot table, then drag term to Row Labels in the pivot table builder. If you want the average interest rate to appear opposite each term then drag the interest rate to Σ Values.

Row Labels

When in doubt, put the main field you are trying to summarize (with sort and group on) here. It is very unusual to have a pivot table without an entry in Row Labels. For example, you might think that term of loan determines interest rate (**Term -> Rate**), so **Term** goes here. **Power Tip:** If the field you want to put here is numeric or a date, then make it a range or bucket by further "grouping" it. This is the equivalent of making a histogram—remember those? A histogram shows the frequency of values that appear in a particular range.

Column Labels

Only use column labels if you are summarizing by a second field as well. For example, you might think that both term of loan AND grade determine the interest rate (**Term & Grade**) **-> Rate**, so **Grade** goes here.

Report Filter

Only use the report filter if you are filtering out some of the subtotals from your report. For example, you might want to see subtotals from only a few states, so **State** goes in the report filter box.

Σ Values

Use this field to subtotal. For example, you might want the average interest rate, so **Rate** goes here. Here you sum or average numeric fields, but count other types of fields. For example, you average interest rates, but count borrower IDs. **Power Tip:** If you also have a column label, and you used "count," then you should standardize values as a percent of row total so that the values in each row can be fairly compared with the rows above and below. **Power Tip:** You can bring the same field down here twice. For example, you could count IDs and then show the same numbers as a percent of row total.

7.2 What is a Pivot Table?

What is a Pivot Table by ExcelJet

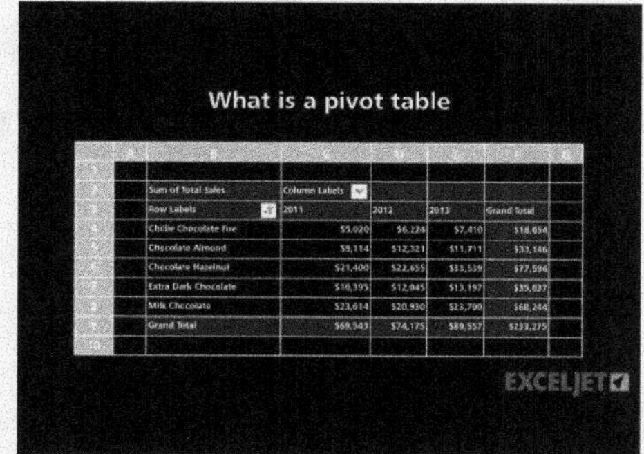

View the video online at: //www.youtube.com/embed/GCeYCGzmqN4?rel=0

"A pivot table is a special Excel tool that allows you to summarize and explore data interactively. It's a lot harder to explain a pivot table than to show you how one works, so let's take a look.

"Here we have a worksheet that contains a large set of sales data for a business that sells specialty chocolate to retailers. This data contains columns for date, customer, city, state, region, product, category, quantity, and total sales.

"You can see that there are a lot of rows, almost 3,000 rows total, each representing an order for one kind of chocolate to one customer.

"In its current form, this data is hard to understand because there is too much detail. To make sense of the information, we need to summarize it, and a pivot table is the perfect tool.

"Before we look at the pivot table, let's quickly check the total of all sales. If we select column I, and check the Status Bar, we can see the total is over $278 thousand.

"On the pivot table sheet, we see a simple pivot table that currently shows only the total of all sales. Notice the total matches the number we just checked manually.

"Building a pivot table is the process of answering questions you have about the data.

"For example, what are total sales by customer?

"With just one click, we can instantly subtotal by customer.

"What are total sales by City?

"What are total sales by Product? Or, product sales by state? Or product sales by year?

"Or, perhaps we only want to see sales for the five best-selling products?

"A pivot table makes answering these questions easy.

"A pivot table is a tool that allows you to explore large sets of data interactively. Once you create a pivot table, you can quickly transform huge numbers of rows and columns into a meaningful, nicely formatted report."

7.3 How to Manage Big Data with Pivot Tables

1. Read How to Manage Big Data with Pivot Tables (by Annie Cushing) (link)

7.4 Tables vs. Pivot Tables vs. Pivot Table Builder

Be careful not to confuse tables and pivot tables. We used the format as table feature in previous chapters to name large data sets and produce column headings that could be used to filter that data. By contrast, pivot tables take a named table as their input and then produce a separate table on a completely different worksheet that summarizes the data in the main table.

Group Application 3.1: Loan Data

Select the best answer for each question.

1. Does the term of a loan determine its interest rate?

A

Report Filter	Column Labels
Row Labels TERM	**Σ Values** INT_RATE (sum)

B

Report Filter	Column Labels
Row Labels TERM	**Σ Values** INT_RATE (average)

C

Report Filter	Column Labels
	GRADE
Row Labels	**Σ Values**
TERM	INT_RATE (average)

D

Report Filter	Column Labels
STATE	GRADE
Row Labels	**Σ Values**
TERM	INT_RATE (average)

2. Does the term and grade of a loan determine its interest rate? Show results only for Arizona.

A

Report Filter	Column Labels
STATE (AZ)	
Row Labels	**Σ Values**
TERM	INT_RATE (sum)

B

Report Filter	Column Labels
Row Labels	**Σ Values**
TERM	INT_RATE (average)

C

Report Filter	Column Labels
	GRADE
Row Labels	**Σ Values**
TERM	INT_RATE (average)

D

Report Filter	Column Labels
STATE (AZ)	GRADE
Row Labels	**Σ Values**
TERM	INT_RATE (average)

Group Application 3.2: Can You Answer This? Dining Hall Data

The file below contains card swipe data from students arriving at dining halls.

Which questions could/could not be answered given the data below?

1. Which days are the most popular?
2. Which days are the most popular in each location?
3. How many students are enrolled in each plan?
4. Which hours are the most popular on each day?
5. Which hours are the most popular on each day in Boyd?
6. Which dining hours are the most popular in each location regardless of day of the week?
7. Which plans are the most popular by location as gauged by usage?

Date and Time	Plan	Location
8/31/14 10:59 AM	Traditional 14	Boyd Court
8/31/14 11:00 AM	Traditional 14	Boyd Court
8/31/14 11:00 AM	Flex 14	Nelson Court
8/31/14 11:00 AM	Traditional 14	Boyd Court
8/31/14 11:00 AM	Flex 14	Nelson Court
8/31/14 11:00 AM	Traditional 14	Nelson Court
8/31/14 11:00 AM	Flex 14	Boyd Court
8/31/14 11:00 AM	Flex 14	Nelson Court
8/31/14 11:00 AM	Flex 14	Boyd Court
8/31/14 11:00 AM	Traditional 14	Nelson Court
8/31/14 11:00 AM	Flex 14	Nelson Court
8/31/14 11:00 AM	Traditional 20	Nelson Court
8/31/14 11:00 AM	Traditional 10	Nelson Court
8/31/14 11:00 AM	Flex 14	Shively Court
8/31/14 11:00 AM	Flex 14	Boyd Court
8/31/14 11:00 AM	Flex 14	Nelson Court
8/31/14 11:00 AM	Traditional 14	Shively Court
8/31/14 11:00 AM	Block 30	Nelson Court
8/31/14 11:00 AM	Flex 14	Nelson Court
8/31/14 11:00 AM	Traditional 14	Shively Court
8/31/14 11:00 AM	Traditional 20	Nelson Court

Exercise 3.1: Loan Data Pivot Table Configuration

You are now more familiar with Excel including how to use formulas, functions, and filtering data. These methods can give you a lot of information, but sometimes, especially with larger data sets, you can learn more about the data by sorting and grouping data using pivot tables. Pivot tables are a powerful data analysis tool that will allow us to quickly sort and summarize thousands of records to find information about specific scenarios.

For this exercise, answer questions 1-5 below by converting the data to a table, creating a pivot table and graphing the results of each question. Adjust the pivot table headings to clearly identify what each shows, and remember to title each graph and name each sheet. Be sure to comment on what you find as the results for each question. For questions 6-8, use formulas/functions to add columns of data, as asked, to the current Enrollment table. When you are finished add your name to the Day by Hour sheet, and submit your completed Excel file online.

Answer Each with a Pivot Table

1. **Plan Swipes**: How many swipes were recorded for each plan during this time period?
2. **Popular Hours**: Which hours are the most popular on each day? Group the days by hour.
3. **Meal Types**: What percentage of each flex plan swipes were used for a standard meal and as cash equivalent? Filter the pivot table to show only standard and equivalent types.

4. **Day by Hour by Location**: Which hours are the most popular on each day in each sit-down location? Group day by hour, and filter the pivot table to show only the Nelson Court, Shively Court & West Green Market District data.
5. **Make up a question** using a pivot table and chart to answer.

Answer by Adding Columns to the Enrollment Tab and Using Formulas

6. **Expected swipes**: The enrollment tab tells how many students were enrolled in each plan. If each of these students used all of their swipes, how many swipes would you expect to see for each plan in a given week?
7. **Actual swipes:** How many swipes were actually recorded in the data for each plan?
8. **Swipe difference**: What is the difference between actual and recorded swipes?

Meal types are one of the ways to control which meal plans have access to which services in which locations. The primary meal type is standard–that is, a "normal" meal at any of the dining halls. The other meal types are explained below:

- **Cash Equiv (Cash Equivalency)** – This is a meal from a flex meal plan that was used for a credit of $6.25 toward the purchase of goods at a campus market/store.
- **Smoothie** – This is a new meal plan type this year. It is used to allow any meal from any meal plan to be used to purchase a "smoothie combo" at the new West Green Market District (Boyd Dining).
- **Adj Diff Day (Adjustment – Different Day)** – This means that something occurred where the dining hall had to charge a student for a meal they had already eaten on a different day. For example, there was an issue with the customer's card that prevented a meal from being properly used, and then the manager manually ran that transaction the next day.

Exercise 3.2: Loan Data Pivot Tables

You've had some practice creating pivot tables and graphing the results. We're going to more of that, but this time with loan data. In business you might guess that there are certain relationships in data, but it's best to be sure before you use that hunch to make a decision. For example, you might guess that people who borrow the smallest amount for a home loan are the least likely to default (not finish paying back) their loan because the amount is so small. Or you might think that people who borrow the highest amounts for a home loan are the least likely to default because they need to have great credit to get approved in the first place. But which is true? Or are those somewhere in the middle the least likely to default on a loan?

In this exercise you will use pivot tables to test a series of hypothesis to find out more information about the loan data. Read through the items in the list below. You will create pivot tables and graph the results to reveal whether there is support for each hypothesis.

Please create each pivot table to appear in a separate worksheet. Adjust the pivot table headings to clearly identify the data. Graph the resulting data from the pivot table. Rename each worksheet to match the bold titles of the items in the list. Add a title to each worksheet and repeat the hypothesis offering your own evaluation as to whether it is supported in a text box. Professionally format the results. When all of the items are completed, please add your name to the Grade v Rate sheet, and submit your Excel file online.

1. **Grade v Rate:** Does the grade of the borrower determine interest rate? Hypothesis: Higher-grade borrowers receive lower interest rates.
2. **Purpose v Rate:** Does the purpose of the loan determine interest rate? Hypothesis: Home loans receive lowest interest rates; credit cards have the highest. Group interest rates in 5-percent increments.
3. **Funded Amt v Term v Rate:** Do the funded amount and length of the loan determine interest rate? Hypothesis: Lower and shorter loans will have higher rates. Group the funded amount by increments of 5,000.
4. **Grade v Status:** Does the grade of the borrower determine loan status? Hypothesis: Lower-grade borrowers are more likely to miss payments or default.

5. **Home v Grade:** Does home ownership determine borrower grade? Hypothesis: Homehome owners will be considered more stable and have a higher grade.
6. Your own hypothesis number 1

Follow this link to the Excel file and video tutorial: http://tinyurl.com/zm59sa9

CHAPTER 8

Data and Competitive Advantage: Databases, Analytics, AI and Machine Learning

8.1 Introduction

Learning Objectives

1. Understand how increasingly standardized data, access to third-party data sets, cheap/fast computing, and easier-to-use software are collectively enabling a new age of decision-making.
2. Be familiar with some of the enterprises that have benefited from data-driven, fact-based decision making.

The planet is awash in data. Cash registers ring up transactions worldwide. Web browsers leave a trail of cookie crumbs nearly everywhere they go. Fitness trackers, health monitors, and smartphone apps are collecting data on the behavior of millions. And with radio frequency identification (RFID), inventory can literally announce its presence so that firms can precisely journal every hop their products make along the value chain: "I'm arriving in the warehouse," "I'm on the store shelf," "I'm leaving out the front door."

Data collected within our "digital universe" is expected to grow fifty-fold from 2010 to 2020,[1] while research firm IDC states that the collective number of those bits already exceeds the number of stars in the universe.[2] You'll hear managers today broadly refer to this torrent of bits as "**big data**." Each hour, Walmart alone gathers data on over a million transactions and crunches over 2.5 petabytes of data for continued insights.[3] To put that amount in perspective, two petabytes is a data amount greater than the combined contents of all of the academic research libraries in the United States. Walmart claims it has built "the world's biggest private cloud," with over 40 petabytes of total data, and growing. The world's largest retailer isn't content with just its own data stash—the firm amplifies insights by combining its data with over 200 additional sources, including "meteorological data, economic data, Nielsen data, telecom data, social media data, gas prices, and local events."[4]

big data

A general term used to describe the massive amount of data available to today's managers. Big data are often unstructured and are too big and costly to easily work through use of conventional databases, but new tools are making these massive datasets available for analysis and insight.

business intelligence (BI)

A term combining aspects of reporting, data exploration and ad hoc queries, and sophisticated data modeling and analysis.

analytics

A term describing the extensive use of data, statistical and quantitative analysis, explanatory and predictive models, and fact-based management to drive decisions and actions.

machine learning

A type of artificial intelligence that leverages massive amounts of data so that computers can improve the accuracy of actions and predictions on their own without additional programming.

And with this flood of data comes a tidal wave of opportunity. Research has found that companies ranked in the top third of their industry in the use of data-driven decision making were on average 5 percent more productive and 6 percent more profitable than competitors.[5] Increasingly standardized corporate data, and access to rich, third-party datasets—all leveraged by cheap/fast computing and easier-to-use software—are collectively enabling a new age of data-driven, fact-based decision-making. You're less likely to hear old-school terms like "decision support systems" used to describe what's going on here. The phrase of the day is **business intelligence (BI)**, a catchall term combining aspects of reporting, data exploration and ad hoc queries, and sophisticated data modeling and analysis. Alongside business intelligence in the new managerial lexicon is the phrase **analytics**, a term describing the extensive use of data, statistical and quantitative analysis, explanatory and predictive models, and fact-based management to drive decisions and actions (and in our ever-imprecise world of business buzzwords, you'll often hear business intelligence and analytics used interchangeably to mean the same thing—using data for better decision making).[6] Another trend, **machine learning**, refers to a sophisticated category of software applications known as artificial intelligence that leverage massive amounts of data so that computers can "learn" and improve the accuracy of actions and predictions on their own without additional programming.[7] The implications are wide ranging, with machine learning insights making voice assistants and image recognition more accurate and fraud-fighting more comprehensive, and improving the reliability of self-driving cars.

The benefits of all this data and number crunching are very real, indeed. Data leverage lies at the center of competitive advantage in many of the firms that we've studied, including Amazon, Netflix and Zara. Data mastery has helped vault Walmart to the top of the *Fortune* 500 list. It helps Spotify craft you a killer playlist for your run. And it helps make Google's voice recognition a better listener and Google Search a better detective, so that the service can accurately show you what you've asked it to look up. There's even something here for poli sci majors, since data-driven insights are increasingly being credited with helping politicians win elections.[8] To quote from a *BusinessWeek* cover story on analytics, "Math Will Rock Your World!"[9]

Sounds great, but it can be a tough slog getting an organization to the point where it has a leveragable data asset. In many organizations data lies dormant, spread across inconsistent formats and incompatible systems, unable to be turned into anything of value. Many firms have been shocked at the amount of work and complexity required to pull together an infrastructure that empowers its managers. But not only can this be done, it must be done. Firms that are basing decisions on hunches aren't managing, they're gambling. And today's markets have no tolerance for uninformed managerial dice rolling.

While we'll study technology in this chapter, our focus isn't as much on the technology itself as it is on what you can do with that technology. Consumer products giant P&G believes in this distinction so thoroughly that the firm renamed its IT function as "Information and Decision Solutions."[10] Solutions drive technology decisions, not the other way around.

In this chapter we'll study the data asset, how it's created, how it's stored, and how it's accessed and leveraged. We'll also study many of the firms mentioned above, and more, providing a context for understanding how managers are leveraging data to create winning models, and how those that have failed to realize the power of data have been left in the dust.

Data, Analytics, and Competitive Advantage

Anyone can acquire technology—but data is oftentimes considered a defensible source of competitive advantage. The data a firm can leverage is a true strategic asset when it's rare, valuable, imperfectly imitable, and lacking in substitutes (see [Content Removed: #fwk-38086-ch02]).

If more data brings more accurate modeling, moving early to capture this rare asset can be the difference between a dominating firm and an also-ran. But be forewarned, there's no monopoly on math. Advantages based on formulas, algorithms, and data that others can also acquire will be short-lived. Moneyball advances in sports analytics originally pioneered by the Oakland A's and are now used by nearly every team in the major leagues.

This doesn't mean that firms can ignore the importance data can play in lowering costs, increasing customer service, and other ways that boost performance. But differentiation will be key in distinguishing operationally effective data use from those efforts that can yield true strategic positioning.

That Seat Will Cost You $8–Wait, Make That $45.50

For some games it's tough to fill the stands. A Wednesday night game against a mediocre rival will prompt thousands to stay home unless they get a really compelling deal. But many fans are ready to pay big bucks for a rivalry game on a weekend. To optimize demand, over thirty teams in Major League Baseball (MLB), the National Basketball Association (NBA), National Hockey League (NHL), and Major League Soccer (MLS) are using data analytics from Austin-based Qcue to fill seats and maximize revenue.[11]

Take the San Francisco Giants as an example. The baseball standout draws big crowds when playing crosstown, interleague rivals the Oakland As. A seat in the left field, upper deck of AT&T Park will cost above $45 for a Saturday afternoon game. But when the Diamondbacks are in town on a work or school night, that very same seat can be had for $8. Changing pricing based on demand conditions is known as dynamic pricing, and the Giants credits analytics-driven demand pricing with helping bump ticket revenues by at least 6 percent in a single year[12] and fuel a 250-plus sellout streak.[13] And getting fans in the stands is critical since once there, those fans usually rack up even more revenue in the form of concessions and merchandise sales. Dynamic pricing can be tricky. In some cases, it can leave consumers feeling taken advantage of (it is especially tricky in situations where consumers make repeated purchases and are more likely to remember past prices, and when they have alternative choices, like grocery or department store shopping). But dynamic pricing often works in markets where supply is constrained and subject to demand spikes. Firms from old-school airlines to app-savvy Uber regularly let data analytics set a supply-demand equilibrium through dynamic pricing, while also helping boost their bottom line. Sports teams are even leveraging weather insights and other data to drive the pricing of concession specials and to set the cost of a beer. New technologies, such as iBeacon (a tech that sends messages to iPhones using a low-energy Bluetooth signal) are being rolled out throughout MLB, making it easier to let consumers know a deal is in effect and guiding them to the quickest counter for quenching thirst and satisfying cravings.[14]

FIGURE 8.1 At the Ballpark App

Major League Baseball's At the Ballpark app will use iBeacon technology to distribute deals and guide you to concessions.

Source: Alex Colon, "MLB Completes iBeacon Installations at Dodger Stadium and Petco Park," *GigaOM*, February 14, 2014, https://gigaom.com/2014/02/14/mlb-completes-ibeacon-installations-at-dodger-stadium-and-petco-park.

Key Takeaways

- The amount of data being created doubles every two years.
- In many organizations, available data is not exploited to advantage. However new tools supporting *big data*, business intelligence, analytics, and machine learning are helping managers make sense of this data torrent.
- Data is oftentimes considered a defensible source of competitive advantage; however, advantages based on capabilities and data that others can acquire will be short-lived.

Questions and Exercises

1. Name and define the terms that are supplanting discussions of decision support systems in the modern IS lexicon.
2. Is data a source of competitive advantage? Describe situations in which data might be a source for sustainable competitive advantage. When might data not yield sustainable advantage?
3. Are advantages based on analytics and modeling potentially sustainable? Why or why not?
4. Think about the amount of data that is collected about you every day. Make a list of various technologies and information systems you engage with and the organizations that use these technologies, systems, and services to learn more about you. Does this information serve you better as a consumer? What, if any, concerns does broad data collection leave you with?
5. What role do technology and timing play in realizing advantages from the data asset?
6. What do you think about dynamic pricing? Is it good or bad for consumers? Is it good or bad for businesses? Explain your answer.
7. Have you visited a retailer or other venue using iBeacons? If so, describe your experience. If not, research the technology and come to class prepared to discuss its implications for collecting data and for driving consumer actions.
8. Research firms that are effectively using analytics, "big data," or machine learning for competitive advantage. Share interesting examples with your class and tweet links to the #BizTechBook hashtag. Do you think such tools are only available to large firms, or can smaller firms benefit, too?

8.2 Data, Information, and Knowledge

Learning Objectives

1. Understand the difference between data and information.
2. Know the key terms and technologies associated with data organization and management.

Data refers simply to raw facts and figures. Alone, it tells you nothing. The real goal is to turn data into **information**. Data becomes information when it's presented in a context so that it can answer a question or support decision-making. And it's when this information can be combined with a manager's **knowledge**—their insight from experience and expertise—that stronger decisions can be made.

data

Raw facts and figures.

information

Data presented in a context so that it can answer a question or support decision making.

knowledge

Insight derived from experience and expertise.

Trusting Your Data

The ability to look critically at data and assess its validity is a vital managerial skill. When decision makers are presented with wrong data, the results can be disastrous. And these problems can get amplified if bad data is fed to automated systems. As an example, look at the series of man-made and computer-triggered events that brought about a billion-dollar collapse in United Airlines stock.

In the wee hours one Sunday morning, a single reader browsing several years of old back stories on the *Orlando Sentinel*'s website viewed a 2002 article on the bankruptcy of United Airlines (UAL went bankrupt in 2002, but emerged from bankruptcy four years later). That lone Web surfer's access of this story during such a low-traffic time was enough for the *Sentinel*'s Web server to briefly list the article as one of the paper's "most popular." Google crawled the site and picked up this "popular" news item, feeding it into Google News.

Early that morning, a worker in a Florida investment firm came across the Google-fed story, assumed United had yet again filed for bankruptcy, then posted a summary on Bloomberg. Investors scanning Bloomberg jumped on what looked like a reputable early warning of another United bankruptcy, dumping UAL stock. Blame the computers again—the rapid plunge from these early trades caused automatic sell systems to kick in (event-triggered, computer-automated trading is responsible for about 30 percent of all stock trades). Once the machines took over, UAL dropped like a rock, falling from twelve to three dollars. That drop represented the vanishing of $1 billion in wealth, and all this because no one checked the date on a news story. Welcome to the new world of paying attention![15]

Understanding How Data Is Organized: Key Terms and Technologies

A **database** is simply a list (or more likely, several related lists) of data. Most organizations have several databases—perhaps even hundreds or thousands. And these various databases might be focused on any combination of functional areas (sales, product returns, inventory, payroll), geographical regions, or business units. Firms often create specialized databases for recording transactions, as well as databases that aggregate data from multiple sources in order to support reporting and analysis.

database

A single table or a collection of related tables.

Databases are created, maintained, and manipulated using programs called **database management systems** (DBMS), sometimes referred to as *database software*. DBMS products vary widely in scale and capabilities. They include the single-user, desktop versions of Microsoft Access or Filemaker Pro, Web-based offerings like Intuit QuickBase, and industrial strength products from Oracle, IBM (DB2), Microsoft (SQL Server), the popular open-source product MySQL (also stewarded by Oracle), and others. Oracle is the world's largest database software vendor, and database software has meant big bucks for Oracle co-founder and CEO Larry Ellison. Ellison perennially ranks in the Top 10 of the *Forbes* 400 list of wealthiest Americans.

database management system

Sometimes referred to as database software; software for creating, maintaining, and manipulating data.

The acronym SQL (often pronounced *sequel*) also shows up a lot when talking about databases. **Structured query language (SQL)** is by far the most common language for creating and manipulating databases. You'll find variants of SQL inhabiting everything from lowly desktop software, to high-powered enterprise products. Given this popularity, if you're going to learn one language for database use, SQL's a pretty good choice. And for a little inspiration, visit LinkedIn, Monster.com, or

structured query language (SQL)

A language used to create and manipulate databases.

another job site and search for openings that mention SQL. You'll find page after page of listings, suggesting that while database systems have been good for Ellison, learning more about them might be pretty good for you, too.

database administrator (DBA)

Job title focused on directing, performing, or overseeing activities associated with a database or set of databases. These may include (but not necessarily be limited to): database design, creation, implementation, maintenance, backup and recovery, policy setting and enforcement, and security.

Even if you don't become a database programmer or **database administrator (DBA)**, you're almost surely going to be called upon to dive in and use a database. You may even be asked to help identify your firm's data requirements. It's quite common for nontech employees to work on development teams with technical staff, defining business problems, outlining processes, setting requirements, and determining the kinds of data the firm will need to leverage. Database systems are powerful stuff, and can't be avoided, so a bit of understanding will serve you well.

FIGURE 8.2 A Simplified Relational Database for a University Course Registration System

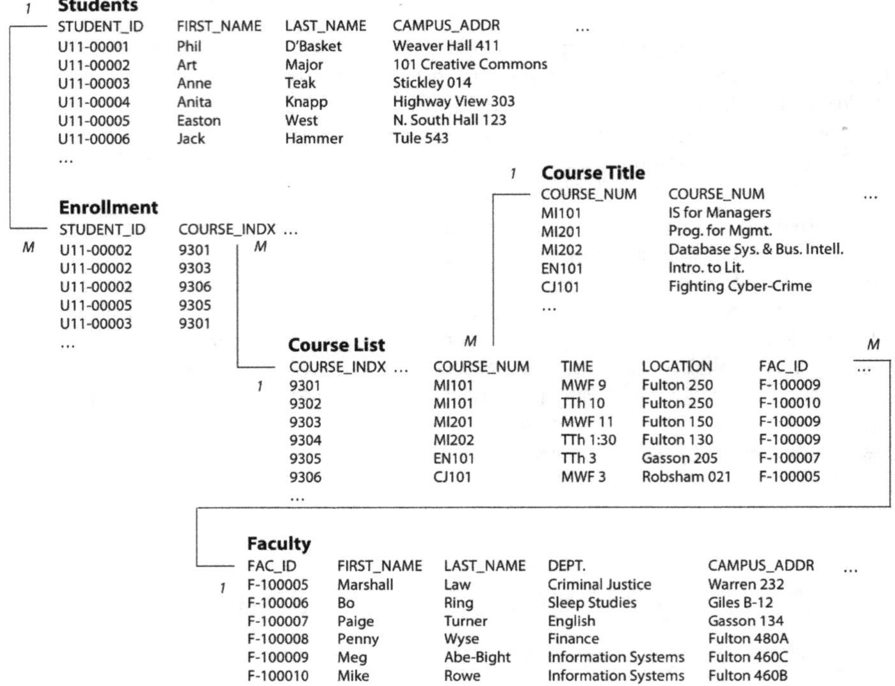

Students

STUDENT_ID	FIRST_NAME	LAST_NAME	CAMPUS_ADDR	...
U11-00001	Phil	D'Basket	Weaver Hall 411	
U11-00002	Art	Major	101 Creative Commons	
U11-00003	Anne	Teak	Stickley 014	
U11-00004	Anita	Knapp	Highway View 303	
U11-00005	Easton	West	N. South Hall 123	
U11-00006	Jack	Hammer	Tule 543	
...				

Enrollment

STUDENT_ID	COURSE_INDX	...
U11-00002	9301	
U11-00002	9303	
U11-00002	9306	
U11-00005	9305	
U11-00003	9301	
...		

Course Title

COURSE_NUM	COURSE_NUM	...
MI101	IS for Managers	
MI201	Prog. for Mgmt.	
MI202	Database Sys. & Bus. Intell.	
EN101	Intro. to Lit.	
CJ101	Fighting Cyber-Crime	
...		

Course List

COURSE_INDX ...	COURSE_NUM	TIME	LOCATION	FAC_ID	...
9301	MI101	MWF 9	Fulton 250	F-100009	
9302	MI101	TTh 10	Fulton 250	F-100010	
9303	MI201	MWF 11	Fulton 150	F-100009	
9304	MI202	TTh 1:30	Fulton 130	F-100009	
9305	EN101	TTh 3	Gasson 205	F-100007	
9306	CJ101	MWF 3	Robsham 021	F-100005	
...					

Faculty

FAC_ID	FIRST_NAME	LAST_NAME	DEPT.	CAMPUS_ADDR	...
F-100005	Marshall	Law	Criminal Justice	Warren 232	
F-100006	Bo	Ring	Sleep Studies	Giles B-12	
F-100007	Paige	Turner	English	Gasson 134	
F-100008	Penny	Wyse	Finance	Fulton 480A	
F-100009	Meg	Abe-Bight	Information Systems	Fulton 460C	
F-100010	Mike	Rowe	Information Systems	Fulton 460B	
...					

A complete discourse on technical concepts associated with database systems is beyond the scope of our managerial introduction, but here are some key concepts to help get you oriented, and that all managers should know.

- A **table or file** refers to a list of data.
- A *database* is either a single table or a collection of related tables. The course registration database above depicts five tables.
- A **column or field** defines the data that a table can hold. The "Students" table above shows columns for STUDENT_ID, FIRST_NAME, LAST_NAME, CAMPUS_ADDR (the "..." symbols above are meant to indicate that, in practice, there may be more columns or rows than are shown in this simplified diagram).
- A **row or record** represents a single instance of whatever the table keeps track of. In the example above, each row of the "Students" table represents a student, each row of the "Enrollment" table represents the enrollment of a student in a particular course, and each row of the "Course List" represents a given section of each course offered by the university.
- A key is the field or fields used to relate tables in a database. Look at how the STUDENT_ID key is used above. There is *one* unique STUDENT_ID for each student, but the STUDENT_ID may appear *many* times in the "Enrollment" table, indicating that each student may be enrolled in many classes. The "1" and "M" in the diagram above indicate the one-to-many relationships among the keys in these tables.
- These one-to-many relationships are sometimes referred to as a *primary key* and *foreign key*. There's only one unique STUDENT_ID value for each record (row) in the "Student" table, so STUDENT_ID is a *primary key* in the student table. But in the "Enrollment" table, STUDENT_ID is the *foreign key*. It appears several times and relates back to the primary key in the "Student" table, so we can find out more information about each unique student that is enrolled in a particular course.

table or file

A list of data, arranged in columns (fields) and rows (records).

column or field

A column in a database table. Columns represent each category of data contained in a record (e.g., first name, last name, ID number, date of birth).

row or record

A row in a database table. Records represent a single instance of whatever the table keeps track of (e.g., student, faculty, course title).

Databases organized like the one above, where multiple tables are related based on common keys, are referred to as **relational databases**. There are many other database formats (sporting names like *hierarchical*, and *object-oriented*), but relational databases are far and away the most popular. And all SQL databases are relational databases.

relational database

The most common standard for expressing databases, whereby tables (files) are related based on common keys.

Even though SQL and the relational model are hugely popular and dominate many corporate environments, other systems exist. An increasingly popular set of technologies known as *NoSQL* avoid SQL and the rigid structure of relational databases. NoSQL technologies are especially popular with Internet firms that rely on massive, unwieldy, and disparately structured data; and this technology is often at the heart of what are often characterized as "big data" efforts. Unlike SQL, there is not one clear standard or set of technologies for NoSQL configuration, use, and query—it's more of a catchall phrase, and you'll find incompatible products labeled "NoSQL" from a variety of vendors. Those students learning to build apps through my "Learn to Program Using Swift for iOS Development" offering use a NoSQL database from Google called Cloud Firestore.

We've just scratched the surface for a very basic introduction. Expect that a formal class in database systems will offer you far more detail and better design principles than are conveyed in the elementary example above. But you're already well on your way!

Key Takeaways

- Data includes raw facts that must be turned into information in order to be useful and valuable.
- Databases are created, maintained, and manipulated using programs called database management systems (DBMS), sometimes referred to as database software.
- Relational database management systems (RDBMS) are the most common database standard by far, and SQL (or structured query language) is the most popular standard for relational database systems.
- In relational database systems, several data fields make up a data record, multiple data records make up a table or data file, and one or more tables or data files make up a database. Files that are related to one another are linked based on a common field (or fields)

known as a key. If the value of a key is unique to a record in a table, and that value can never occur in that field while referring to another record in that table, then it is a primary key. If a key can occur many times over multiple records in a table but relates back to a primary key in another table, then it is a foreign key.

Questions and Exercises

1. Define the following terms: table, record, and field. Provide another name for each term along with your definition.
2. Answer the following questions using the course registration database system, diagramed earlier:
   a. Imagine you also want to keep track of student majors. How would you do this? Would you modify an existing table? Would you add new tables? Why or why not?
   b. Why do you suppose the system needs a "Course Title" table?
   c. This database is simplified for our brief introduction. What additional data would you need to keep track of if this were a real course registration system? What changes would you make in the database above to account for these needs?
   d. Why do you need a STUDENT_ID? Why don't you just use a student's last name?
   e. Could you use Social Security number as a STUDENT_ID? Why or why not? (Hint: feel free to search on the Internet for additional insights.)
3. Research to find additional examples of organizations that made bad decisions based on bad data. Report your examples to your class, and tweet links to the most interesting examples to #BizTechBook. What was the end result of the examples you're citing (e.g., loss, damage, or other outcome)? What could managers have done to prevent problems in the cases that you cited? What role did technology play in the examples that you cite? What role did people or procedural issues play?
4. Why is an understanding of database terms and technologies important, even for nontechnical managers and staff? Consider factors associated with both system use and system development. What other skills, beyond technology, may be important when engaged in data-driven decision-making?
5. SQL is considered one of the most valuable skills to empower managers as data analysts. Search the web for free resources that teach SQL. Try a free introductory lesson (you might find these in sites like Khan Academy, and Code Academy, among others). Is this something you might continue to explore on your own? Does your university offer classes where you can learn SQL and other methods and technologies used in data analytics?

8.3 Where Does Data Come From?

Learning Objectives

1. Understand various internal and external sources for enterprise data.
2. Recognize the function and role of data aggregators, the potential for leveraging third-party data, the strategic implications of relying on externally purchased data, and key issues associated with aggregators and firms that leverage externally sourced data.

Organizations can pull together data from a variety of sources. While the examples that follow aren't meant to be an encyclopedic listing of possibilities, they will give you a sense of the diversity of options available for data gathering.

Transaction Processing Systems

For most organizations that sell directly to their customers, **transaction processing systems (TPS)** represent a fountain of potentially insightful data. Every time a consumer uses a point-of-sale system, an ATM, or a service desk, there's a **transaction** (some kind of business exchange) occurring, representing an event that's likely worth tracking.

The cash register is the data generation workhorse of most physical retailers, and the primary source that feeds data to the TPS. But while TPS can generate a lot of bits, it's sometimes tough to match this data with a specific customer. For example, if you pay a retailer in cash, you're likely to remain a mystery to your merchant because your name isn't attached to your money. Grocers and retailers can tie you to cash transactions if they can convince you to use a **loyalty card**. Use one of these cards and you're in effect giving up information about yourself in exchange for some kind of financial incentive. The explosion in retailer cards is directly related to each firm's desire to learn more about you and to turn you into a more loyal and satisfied customer.

Some cards provide an instant discount (e.g., the CVS Pharmacy ExtraCare card), while others allow you to build up points over time (Best Buy's Reward Zone). The latter has the additional benefit of acting as a switching cost. A customer may think "I could get the same thing at Target, but at Best Buy, it'll increase my existing points balance and soon I'll get a cash back coupon."

transaction processing systems (TPS)

Systems that record a transaction (some form of business-related exchange), such as a cash register sale, ATM withdrawal, or product return.

transaction

Some kind of business exchange.

loyalty card

Systems that provide rewards and usage incentives, typically in exchange for a method that provides a more detailed tracking and recording of customer activity. In addition to enhancing data collection, loyalty cards can represent a significant switching cost.

Enterprise Software (CRM, SCM, and ERP)

Firms increasingly set up systems to gather additional data beyond conventional purchase transactions or website monitoring. CRM, or customer relationship management systems, are often used to empower employees to track and record data at nearly every point of customer contact. Someone calls for a quote? Brings a return back to a store? Writes a complaint e-mail? A well-designed CRM system can capture all these events for subsequent analysis or for triggering follow-up events.

Enterprise software includes not just CRM systems but also categories that touch every aspect of the value chain, including supply chain management (SCM) and enterprise resource planning (ERP) systems. More importantly, enterprise software tends to be more integrated and standardized than the prior era of proprietary systems that many firms developed themselves. This integration helps in combining data across business units and functions, and in getting that data into a form where it can be turned into information (for more on enterprise systems, see Chapter 10).

Surveys

Sometimes firms supplement operational data with additional input from surveys and focus groups. Oftentimes, direct surveys can tell you what your cash register can't. Zara store managers informally survey customers in order to help shape designs and product mix. Online grocer FreshDirect (see [Content Removed: #fwk-38086-ch02]) surveys customers weekly and has used this feedback to drive initiatives from reducing packaging size to including star ratings on produce.[16] Many CRM products also have survey capabilities that allow for additional data gathering at all points of customer contact.

artificial intelligence

Computer software that seeks to reproduce or mimic (perhaps with improvements) human thought, decision-making, or brain functions.

Can Technology "Cure" US Health Care?

The US health care system is broken. It's costly and inefficient, and problems seem to be getting worse. Estimates suggest that health care spending makes up a whopping 18 percent of US gross domestic product.[17] US automakers spend more on health care than they do on steel.[18] Even more disturbing, it's believed that medical errors are the third leading cause of death in the United States and are responsible for as many as 250,000 unnecessary deaths in the United States each year, more than motor vehicle accidents, breast cancer, or AIDS.[19]

For years it's been claimed that technology has the potential to reduce errors, improve health care quality, and save costs. Now pioneering hospital networks and technology companies are partnering to help tackle cost and quality issues. For a look at possibilities for leveraging data throughout the doctor-patient value chain, consider the "event-driven medicine" system built by Dr. John Halamka and his team at Boston's Beth Israel Deaconess Medical Center (part of the Harvard Medical School network).

When docs using Halamka's system encounter a patient with a chronic disease, they generate a decision support "screening sheet." Each event in the system—an office visit, a lab results report (think the medical equivalent of transactions and customer interactions)—updates the patient database. Combine that electronic medical record information with **artificial intelligence** on best practice, and the system can offer recommendations for care, such as, "Patient is past due for an eye exam," or "Patient should receive pneumovax [a vaccine against infection] this season."[20] The systems don't replace decision-making by doctors and nurses, but they do help to ensure that key issues are on a provider's radar.

More efficiencies and error checks show up when prescribing drugs. Docs are presented with a list of medications covered by that patient's insurance, allowing them to choose quality options while controlling costs. Safety issues, guidelines, and best practices are also displayed. When correct, safe medication in the right dose is selected, the electronic prescription is routed to the patient's pharmacy of choice. As Halamka puts it, going from "doctor's brain to patient's vein" without any of that messy physician handwriting, all while squeezing out layers where errors from human interpretation or data entry might occur.

Nearly every major technology company now has a health solutions group. And with the rise of efforts such as Apple's HealthKit and ResearchKit, expect even more solutions to allow consumers to gather data on their own health, with organizations offering insights on data-driven lifestyle improvements. At the introduction of ResearchKit, five apps were launched in conjunction with leading US health care institutions, including Dana-Farber, Massachusetts General Hospital, Stanford Medicine, Weill Cornell Medical College, and the Mayo Clinic. Apps focused on studying Parkinson's disease, diabetes, breast cancer, and heart health. Users opt-in to share data with research institutions, which can come from user input, quizzes, smartphone monitoring, the Apple Watch, or other external devices. Apple doesn't hold the data, it is encrypted, and names are not associated with results. Initial results suggest an influx of valuable data at a lower cost from these sorts of efforts. The asthma study app received more than 3,500 people within 72 hours, whereas it had previously taken about two years to recruit 500 to 1,000 participants in comparable efforts.[21] If systems like Halamka's, Apple's platform, and others realize their promise, big benefits may be just around the corner.

External Sources

Sometimes it makes sense to combine a firm's data with bits brought in from the outside. Many firms, for example, don't sell directly to consumers (this includes most drug companies and packaged goods firms). If your firm has partners that sell products for you, then you'll likely rely heavily on data collected by others.

Data bought from sources available to all might not yield competitive advantage on its own, but it can provide key operational insight for increased efficiency and cost savings. And when combined with a firm's unique data assets, it may give firms a high-impact edge.

Consider restaurant chain Brinker, a firm that runs seventeen hundred eateries in twenty-seven countries under the Chili's, On The Border, and Maggiano's brands. Brinker (whose ticker symbol is EAT), supplements its own data with external feeds on weather, employment statistics, gas prices, and other factors, and uses this in predictive models that help the firm in everything from determining staffing levels to switching around menu items.[22]

In another example, Carnival Cruise Lines combines its own customer data with third-party information tracking household income and other key measures. This data helps the firm target limited marketing dollars on those past customers that are more likely to be able to afford to go on a cruise. So far it's been a winning approach. For three years in a row, the firm has experienced double-digit increases in bookings by repeat customers.[23]

data aggregators

Firms that collect and resell data.

Who's Collecting Data about You?

There's a thriving industry collecting data about you. Buy from a catalog, fill out a warranty card, or have a baby, and there's a very good chance that this event will be recorded in a database somewhere, added to a growing digital dossier that's made available for sale to others. If you've ever gotten catalogs, coupons, or special offers from firms you've never dealt with before, this was almost certainly a direct result of a behind-the-scenes trafficking in the "digital you."

Firms that trawl for data and package them up for resale are known as **data aggregators**. These are companies that you've likely never heard of but that are thought to "have more data on you than Facebook or Google"[24]—information they are willing to make available to others, for a price. A report by the US Federal Trade Commission[25] highlighted Acxiom, CoreLogic, Datalogix, eBureau, ID Analytics, Intelius, PeekYou, Rapleaf, and Recorded Future. The report lists categories of information collected, including a lot of what you'd expect—name, address, Social Security number, and a category labeled "ability to afford products," but also all sorts of granular categorization. Quartz highlighted some of the more noteworthy ones, including: thrifty elders, new age/organic lifestyle adherents, bikers/Hell's Angels, people who do a lot of medical Googling (an "ailment and prescription online search propensity"), and even purchasers of "Novelty Elvis" products.[26]

The Internet also allows for easy access to data that had been public but is otherwise difficult to access. For one example, consider home sale prices and home value assessments. While technically in the public record, someone wanting this information previously had to traipse down to their Town Hall and speak to a clerk, who would hand over a printed log book. Not exactly a Google-speed query. Contrast this with a visit to Zillow.com. The free site lets you pull up a map of your town and instantly peek at how much your neighbors paid for their homes. And it lets them see how much you paid for yours, too.

Computerworld's Robert Mitchell uncovered a more disturbing issue when public record information is made available online. His New Hampshire municipality had digitized and made available some of his old public documents without obscuring that holy grail for identity thieves, his Social Security number.[27]

Then there are accuracy concerns. A record incorrectly identifying you as a cat lover is one thing, but being incorrectly named to the terrorist watch list is quite another. During a five-week period airline agents tried to block a particularly high-profile US citizen from boarding airplanes on five separate occasions because his name resembled an alias used by a suspected terrorist. That citizen? The late Ted Kennedy, who at the time was the senior US senator from Massachusetts.[28]

For the data trade to continue, firms will have to treat customer data as the sacred asset it is. Step over that "creep-out" line, and customers will push back, increasingly pressing for tighter privacy laws. Data aggregator Intelius used to track cell phone customers, but backed off in the face of customer outrage and threatened legislation.

Another concern—sometimes data aggregators are just plain sloppy, committing errors that can be costly for the firm and potentially devastating for victimized users. This was the case in the massive breach of credit reporting agency Equifax (for details, see Chapter 17—Barbarians at the Gateway). The firm has records on nearly everyone living in the US who has a bank account or credit card, yet Equifax's flawed policies and vulnerable software allowed hackers to steal names, addresses, Social Security numbers, driver's license information, and more, something that has the potential to plague victims with fraud and identity theft for years to come. Nearly every American adult and hundreds of thousands outside the country were victims. Equifax is estimated to have spent a quarter billion dollars in the months following the breach, with eventual costs expected to run into the billions.[29] Just because you can gather data and traffic in bits doesn't mean that you should. Any data-centric effort should involve input not only from business and technical staff, but from the firm's legal team as well (for more, see the box "Privacy Regulation: A Moving Target").

Privacy Regulation: A Moving Target

New methods for tracking and gathering user information appear daily, testing user comfort levels. For example, the firm Umbria uses software to analyze millions of blog and forum posts every day, using sentence structure, word choice, and quirks in punctuation to determine a blogger's gender, age, interests, and opinions. While Google refused to include facial recognition as an image search product ("too creepy," said its chairman),[30] Facebook, with great controversy, turned on facial recognition by default.[31] It's quite possible that in the future, someone will be able to upload a photo to a service and direct it to find all the accessible photos and video on the Internet that match that person's features. And while targeting is getting easier, a Carnegie Mellon study showed that it doesn't take much to find someone with a minimum of data. Simply by knowing gender, birth date, and postal zip code, 87 percent of people in the United States could be pinpointed by name.[32] Another study showed that publicly available data on state and date of birth could be used to predict US Social Security numbers—a potential gateway to identity theft.[33]

Some feel that Moore's Law, the falling cost of storage, and the increasing reach of the Internet have us on the cusp of a privacy train wreck. And that may inevitably lead to more legislation that restricts data-use possibilities. Noting this, strategists and technologists need to be fully aware of the legal environment their systems face and consider how such environments may change in the future. Unregulated firms seen as violating the public trust through poor policies or lax enforcement will be called to task, as is evidenced by Mark Zuckerberg's multi-hour grilling by US legislators following revelations that one-time partner firm Cambridge Analytica gathered data without consumer consent by using seemingly innocuous online quizzes to harvest data not only from test-takers, but also from their friends. The data was used in targeted political advertising, but also came to light when 13 Russians were indicted by the US special counsel, saying they'd used Facebook to perpetrate "information warfare" against the US. Many industries have strict guidelines on what kind of information can be collected and shared.[34]

While many large-scale data collection efforts remain unregulated, strict rules do apply to certain organizations and circumstances. For example, HIPAA (the US Health Insurance Portability and Accountability Act) includes provisions governing data use and privacy among health care providers, insurers, and employers. The financial industry has strict requirements for recording and sharing communications between firm and client (among many other restrictions). There are laws limiting the kinds of information that can be gathered on younger Web surfers. And there are several laws operating at the state level as well.

International laws also differ from those in the United States. Europe, in particular, has a strict European Privacy Directive. The directive includes governing provisions that limit data collection, require notice and approval of many types of data collection, and require firms to make data available to customers with mechanisms for stopping collection efforts and correcting inaccuracies at customer request. Australia is among the nations that mimic much of what it finds in European laws.[35] Data-dependent efforts plotted for one region may not fully translate to another effort if the law limits key components of technology use. The constantly changing legal landscape also means that what works today might not be allowed in the future.

Firms beware—the public will almost certainly demand tighter controls if the industry is perceived as behaving recklessly or inappropriately with customer data.

Key Takeaways

- For organizations that sell directly to their customers, transaction processing systems (TPS) represent a source of potentially useful data.
- Grocers and retailers can link you to cash transactions if they can convince you to use a loyalty card which, in turn, requires you to give up information about yourself in exchange for some kind of financial incentive such as points or discounts.
- Enterprise software (CRM, SCM, and ERP) is a source for customer, supply chain, and enterprise data.
- Survey data can be used to supplement a firm's operational data.
- Data obtained from outside sources, when combined with a firm's internal data assets, can give the firm a competitive edge.
- Data aggregators are part of a multibillion-dollar industry that provides genuinely helpful data to a wide variety of organizations.
- Data that can be purchased from aggregators may not in and of itself yield sustainable competitive advantage since others may have access to this data, too. However, when combined with a firm's proprietary data or integrated with a firm's proprietary procedures or other assets, third-party data can be a key tool for enhancing organizational performance.
- Data aggregators can also be quite controversial. Among other things, they represent a big target for identity thieves, are a method for spreading potentially incorrect data, and raise privacy concerns.
- Firms that mismanage their customer data assets risk lawsuits, brand damage, lower sales and fleeing customers, and can prompt more restrictive legislation.
- Further raising privacy issues and identity theft concerns, recent studies have shown that in many cases it is possible to pinpoint users through allegedly anonymous data, and to guess Social Security numbers from public data.
- New methods for tracking and gathering user information are raising privacy issues, which possibly will be addressed through legislation that restricts data use.

Questions and Exercises

1. Why would a firm use a loyalty card? What is the incentive for the firm? What is the incentive for consumers to opt in and use loyalty cards? What kinds of strategic assets can these systems create?
2. Make a list of the kind of data you might give up when using a cash register, a website, or a loyalty card, or when calling a firm's customer support line. How might firms leverage this data to better serve you and improve their performance?
3. Are you concerned by any of the data-use possibilities that you outlined in prior questions, discussed in this chapter, or that you've otherwise read about or encountered? If you are concerned, why? If not, why not? What might firms, governments, and consumers do to better protect consumers?
4. What are some of the sources data aggregators tap to collect information?
5. Privacy laws are in a near constant state of flux. Conduct research to identify the current state of privacy law. Has major legislation recently been proposed or approved? What are the implications for firms operating in effected industries? What are the potential benefits to consumers? Do consumers lose anything from this legislation?
6. Self-regulation is often proposed as an alternative to legislative efforts. What kinds of efforts would provide "teeth" to self-regulation? Are there steps firms could take to make you believe in their ability to self-regulate? Why or why not?
7. What is HIPAA? What industry does it impact?

8. How do international privacy laws differ from US privacy laws?
9. Many firms, including Google and Facebook, allow you to access the data they collect on you, or see how they've classified your Internet use. Search online to see what data these or other firms have on you. Come to class prepared to discuss your findings. Were you surprised at what you found? Do you feel these efforts should be regulated? Why or why not?

8.4 Data Rich, Information Poor

Learning Objectives

1. Know and be able to list the reasons why many organizations have data that can't be converted to actionable information.
2. Understand why transactional databases can't always be queried and what needs to be done to facilitate effective data use for analytics and business intelligence.
3. Recognize key issues surrounding data and privacy legislation.

Despite being awash in data, many organizations are data rich but information poor. A survey by consulting firm Accenture found 57 percent of companies reporting that they didn't have a beneficial, consistently updated, companywide analytical capability. Among major decisions, only 60 percent were backed by analytics—40 percent were made by intuition and gut instinct.[36] The big culprit limiting BI initiatives is getting data into a form where it can be used, analyzed, and turned into information. Here's a look at some factors holding back information advantages.

Incompatible Systems

legacy system

Older information systems that are often incompatible with other systems, technologies, and ways of conducting business. Incompatible legacy systems can be a major roadblock to turning data into information, and they can inhibit firm agility, holding back operational and strategic initiatives.

Just because data is collected doesn't mean it can be used. This limit is a big problem for large firms that have **legacy systems**, outdated information systems that were not designed to share data, aren't compatible with newer technologies, and aren't aligned with the firm's current business needs. The problem can be made worse by mergers and acquisitions, especially if a firm depends on operational systems that are incompatible with its partner. And the elimination of incompatible systems isn't just a technical issue. Firms might be under extended agreement with different vendors or outsourcers, and breaking a contract or invoking an escape clause may be costly. Folks working in M&A (the area of investment banking focused on valuing and facilitating mergers and acquisitions) beware—it's critical to uncover these hidden costs of technology integration before deciding if a deal makes financial sense.

Legacy Systems: A Prison for Strategic Assets

The experience of one *Fortune* 100 firm that your author has worked with illustrates how incompatible information systems can actually hold back strategy. This firm was the largest in its category, and sold identical commodity products sourced from its many plants worldwide. Being the biggest should have given the firm scale advantages. But many of the firm's manufacturing facilities and international locations developed or purchased separate, incompatible systems. Still more plants were acquired through acquisition, each coming with its own legacy systems.

The plants with different information systems used *different* part numbers and naming conventions even though they sold *identical* products. As a result, the firm had no timely information on how much of a particular item was sold to which worldwide customers. The company was essentially operating as a collection of smaller, regional businesses, rather than as the worldwide behemoth that it was.

After the firm developed an information system that standardized data across these plants, it was, for the first time, able to get a single view of worldwide sales. The firm then used this data to approach their biggest customers, negotiating lower prices in exchange for increased commitments in worldwide purchasing. This trade let the firm take share from regional rivals. It also gave the firm the ability to shift manufacturing capacity globally, as currency prices, labor conditions, disasters, and other factors impacted sourcing. The new information system in effect liberated the latent strategic asset of scale, increasing sales by well over a billion and a half dollars in the four years following implementation.

Operational Data Can't Always Be Queried

Another problem when turning data into information is that most transactional databases aren't set up to be simultaneously accessed for reporting and analysis. When a customer buys something from a cash register, that action may post a sales record and deduct an item from the firm's inventory. In most TPS systems, requests made to the database can usually be performed pretty quickly—the system adds or modifies the few records involved and it's done—in and out in a flash.

But if a manager asks a database to analyze historic sales trends showing the most and least profitable products over time, they may be asking a computer to look at thousands of transaction records, comparing results, and neatly ordering findings. That's not a quick in-and-out task, and it may very well require significant processing to come up with the request. Do this against the very databases you're using to record your transactions, and you might grind your computers to a halt.

Getting data into systems that can support analytics is where data warehouses and data marts come in, the topic of our next section.

Airbnb: Better Pricing Through Data

Airbnb might not own any of the properties that it rents, but the firm invests some serious coin in its analytics infrastructure. The firm's 150-plus data scientists crunch 15 petabytes of data daily. Over 3.5 million listings across nearly 200 countries generate upwards of 15 billion logged events that help maximize satisfaction from both property hosts and and their renting customers.[37]

Unique offerings, with different amenities, locations, and varying demand over time, make pricing a challenge, especially for new property listers. But Airbnb's data models allow little-guy property hosts to have the same sort of dynamic pricing that hotels might use. Airbnb's "smart pricing" feature uses machine learning to constantly tweak the accuracy of models that suggest the perfect rate.[38] While the data and the resulting, constantly updated model are proprietary to Airbnb, the firm uses, and heavily contributes to, an open source machine learning tool available to all—a product known as Aerosolve. All sorts of data can influence a price. Is there an event happening in the city that puts a property in demand? Is the property close to public transportation? The beach? Local attractions? What about amenities? A hair dryer adds around $10 per night. A hot tub? $26. Wi-Fi? $8. Cable TV? $16. Don't have many reviews? Data will advise you to cut your price. Properties with 10 or more reviews get booked 10 times as often.[39] While hosts can override smart pricing suggestions, most hosts use the firm's pricing dashboard to set a minimum and maximum price, then allow Airbnb to automatically adjust the prices for them.[40] Hosts ranked higher in likelihood of accepting accommodation request will rank higher in search result, so data smarts help renters have a better experience, as well. Impact is significant, boosting rentals by 13 percent on average.

Having numerate employees capable of crunching numbers and interpreting results prompted Airbnb to create an internal "data university" where employees can learn skills like SQL, R programming, how to use the firm's proprietary tools and dashboards, and learn best practices.[41] For Silicon Valley's second most-valuable startup, this constantly refined big data asset yields big results that keep rental properties full and owner wallets fat, and cements renter loyalty.

Key Takeaways

- A major factor limiting business intelligence initiatives is getting data into a form where it can be used (i.e., analyzed and turned into information).
- Legacy systems often limit data utilization because they were not designed to share data, aren't compatible with newer technologies, and aren't aligned with the firm's current business needs.
- Most transactional databases aren't set up to be simultaneously accessed for reporting and analysis. In order to run analytics the data must first be ported to a data warehouse or data mart.

Questions and Exercises

1. How might information systems impact mergers and acquisitions? What are the key issues to consider?
2. Discuss the possible consequences of a company having multiple plants, each with a different information system using different part numbers and naming conventions for identical products.
3. Why does it take longer, and require more processing power, to analyze sales trends by region and product, as opposed to posting a sales transaction?

8.5 Data Warehouses, Data Marts, and Technology behind "Big Data"

Learning Objectives

1. Understand what data warehouses and data marts are and the purpose they serve.
2. Know the issues that need to be addressed in order to design, develop, deploy, and maintain data warehouses and data marts.
3. Recognize and understand technologies behind "Big Data," how they differ from conventional data management approaches, and how they are currently being used for organizational benefit.

Since running analytics against transactional data can bog down a system, and since most organizations need to combine and reformat data from multiple sources, firms typically need to create separate data repositories for their reporting and analytics work. Such data repositories act as a kind of staging area from which to turn that data into information.

FIGURE 8.3 Information Systems for Operations and Analysis

Information systems supporting operations (such as TPS) are typically separate, and "feed" information systems used for analytics (such as data warehouses and data marts).

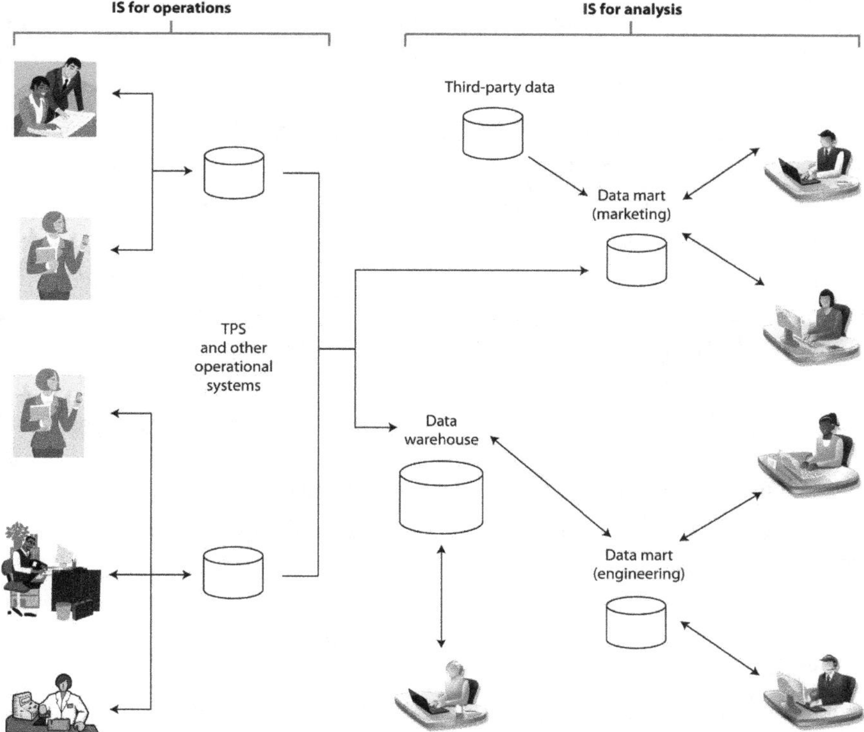

Two terms you'll hear for these kinds of repositories are **data warehouse** and **data mart**. A data warehouse is a set of databases designed to support decision-making in an organization. It is structured for fast online queries and exploration. Data warehouses may aggregate enormous amounts of data from many different operational systems.

A data mart is a database focused on addressing the concerns of a specific problem (e.g., increasing customer retention, improving product quality) or business unit (e.g., marketing, engineering).

data warehouse

A set of databases designed to support decision-making in an organization.

data mart

A database or databases focused on addressing the concerns of a specific problem (e.g., increasing customer retention, improving product quality) or business unit (e.g., marketing, engineering).

Marts and warehouses may contain huge volumes of data. For example, a firm may not need to keep large amounts of historical point-of-sale or transaction data in its operational systems, but it might want past data in its data mart so that managers can hunt for patterns and trends that occur over time.

It's easy for firms to get seduced by a software vendor's demonstration showing data at your fingertips, presented in pretty graphs. But as mentioned earlier, getting data in a format that can be used for analytics is hard, complex, and challenging work. Large data warehouses can cost millions and take years to build. Every dollar spent on technology may lead to five to seven more dollars on consulting and other services.[42]

Most firms will face a trade-off—do we attempt a large-scale integration of the whole firm, or more targeted efforts with quicker payoffs? Firms in fast-moving industries or with particularly complex businesses may struggle to get sweeping projects completed in enough time to reap benefits before business conditions change. Most consultants now advise smaller projects with narrow scope driven by specific business goals.[43]

Firms can eventually get to a unified data warehouse, but it may take time. Even analytics king Walmart has spent years getting to that point. The retail giant once reported having over seven hundred different data marts and hired Hewlett-Packard for help in bringing the systems together to form a more integrated data warehouse.[44]

The old saying from the movie *Field of Dreams*, "If you build it, they will come," doesn't hold up well for large-scale data analytics projects. This work should start with a clear vision with business-focused objectives. When senior executives can see objectives illustrated in potential payoff, they'll be able to champion the effort and, experts agree, having an executive champion is a key success factor. Focusing on business issues will also drive technology choice, with the firm better able to focus on products that best fit its needs.

Once a firm has business goals and hoped-for payoffs clearly defined, it can address the broader issues needed to design, develop, deploy, and maintain its system:[45]

- *Data relevance.* What data do we need in order to compete on analytics? What data do we need to meet our current and future goals?
- *Data sourcing.* Can we obtain all the data we'll need? From where? Can we get it through our internal systems or from third-party data aggregators, suppliers, or sales partners? Do we need to set up new collection efforts, surveys, or systems to obtain the data we need?
- *Data quantity.* How much data do we need?
- *Data quality.* Can this data be trusted; is it accurate, clean, complete, and reasonably free of errors? How can our data be made more accurate and valuable for analysis? Will we need to "scrub," calculate, and consolidate data so that it can be used?
- *Data hosting.* Where will the data systems be housed? What are the hardware and networking requirements for that effort?
- *Data governance.* What rules and processes are needed to manage this data, from creation through retirement? Are there operational (backup, disaster recovery), legal or privacy concerns? How should the company handle access and security ?

For some perspective on how difficult this can be, consider that an executive from one of the largest US banks once lamented how difficult it was to get his systems to do something as simple as properly distinguishing between men and women. The company's customer-focused data warehouse drew data from thirty-six separate operational systems—bank teller systems, ATMs, student loan reporting systems, car loan systems, mortgage loan systems, and more. Collectively these legacy systems expressed gender in *seventeen* different ways: "M" or "F"; "m" or "f"; "Male" or "Female"; "MALE" or "FEMALE"; "1" for man, "0" for woman; "0" for man, "1" for woman and more, plus various codes for "unknown." The best math in the world is of no help if the values used aren't any good. There's a saying in the industry, "Garbage in, garbage out."

Hadoop: Big Insights from Unstructured "Big Data"

Having neatly structured data warehouses and data marts are great—the tools are reliable and can often be turned over to end-users or specialists who can rapidly produce reports and other analyses. But roughly 80 percent of corporate data is messy and unstructured, and it is not stored in conventional, relational formats—think of data stored in office productivity documents, e-mail, call center conversations, and social media.[46] It's the three Vs of "Big Data"—volume, velocity, and variety—that distinguish it from conventional data analysis problems and require a new breed of technology. Big data is forcing companies to rethink both the technology infrastructure and the necessary skills needed to successfully interpret and act on the information.[47] Conventional tools often choke when trying to sift through the massive amounts of data collected by many of today's firms. The open source project known as Hadoop was created to analyze massive amounts of raw information better than traditional, highly structured databases. While there are other technologies that can be leveraged for big data projects, Hadoop is the clear leader, growing alongside big data trends to analyze massive amounts of unstructured data, so it merits distinct mention in this discussion.

Hadoop is made up of some half-dozen separate software pieces and requires the integration of these pieces to work. Hadoop-related projects have names such as Hive, Pig, and Zookeeper. Several commercial firms provide support, add-on products, or proprietary technology for big data implementations leveraging these technologies, including fast-growing Hadoop specialists such as Cloudera (which, after Red Hat, is only the second open source firm in history to crack $100 million in revenues), Hortonworks (which went public in 2014), and MapR. Amazon, IBM, and Pivotal (which is a venture by EMC and its VMware subsidiary) are among established tech giants that provide Hadoop products and services. Hadoop use is catching on like wildfire, with some expecting that within five years, more than half of the world's data will be stored in Hadoop environments.[48]

There are four primary advantages to Hadoop, although these advantages may also apply to competing big data technologies:[49]

- *Flexibility*: Hadoop can absorb any type of data, structured or not, from any type of source (geeks would say such a system is *schema-less*). But this disparate data can still be aggregated and analyzed.
- *Scalability*: Hadoop systems can start on a single PC, but thousands of machines can eventually be combined to work together for storage and analysis.
- *Cost effectiveness*: Since the system is open source and can be started with low-end hardware, the technology is cheap by data-warehousing standards. Many vendors also offer Hadoop as a cloud service, allowing firms to avoid hardware costs altogether.
- *Fault tolerance*: One of the servers running your Hadoop cluster just crashed? No big deal. Hadoop is designed in such a way so that there will be no single point of failure. The system will continue to work, relying on the remaining hardware.

Financial giant Morgan Stanley is a big believer in Hadoop. One senior technology manager at the firm contrasts Hadoop with highly structured systems, saying that in the past, "IT asked the business what they want, creates a data structure and writes structured query language, sources the data, conforms it to the table and writes a structured query. Then you give it to them and they often say that is not what they wanted." But with Hadoop overseeing a big pile of unstructured (or less structured) data, technical staff can now work with users to carve up and combine data in lots of different ways, or even set systems loose in the data to hunt for unexpected patterns (see the discussion of data mining later in this chapter). Morgan Stanley's initial Hadoop experiments started with a handful of old servers that were about to be retired, but the company has steadily ramped up its efforts. Now by using Hadoop, the firm sees that it is able to analyze data on a far larger scale ("petabytes of data, which is unheard of in the traditional database world") with potentially higher-impact results. The bank is looking at customers' financial objectives and trying to come up with investment insights to help them invest appropriately, and it is seeking "Big Data" insights to help the firm more effectively manage risk.[50]

Other big-name firms using Hadoop for "Big Data" insights include Bank of America, Disney, GE, LinkedIn, Nokia, Twitter, and Walmart. Hadoop is an open source project overseen by the Apache Software Foundation. It has an Internet pedigree and is based on ideas by Google and lots of software contributed by Yahoo! (two firms that regularly need to dive into massive and growing amounts of unstructured data—Web pages, videos, images, social media, user account information, and more). IBM used Hadoop as the engine that helped power Watson to defeat human opponents on *Jeopardy*, further demonstrating the technology's ability to analyze wildly different data for accurate insight. Other tech firms embracing Hadoop and offering some degree of support for the technology include HP, EMC, and Microsoft.

FIGURE 8.4 The Hadoop Logo

The project was named after a toy elephant belonging to the son of Hadoop Developer Doug Cutting.

Source: By Apache Software Foundation [Apache License 2.0 (http://www.apache.org/licenses/LICENSE-2.0)], via Wikimedia Commons.

Over 91 percent of *Fortune* 1000 senior executives surveyed said big data initiatives were planned or under way, with half of these execs expecting efforts to cost $10 million or more.[51] Yet while success stories for big data abound, many organizations lack the skills required to exploit big data.[52] McKinsey estimates a US talent shortfall of 140,000 to 190,000 data scientists and a further need for 1.5 million more managers and analysts who will have to be savvy consumers of big data analytics.[53] Time to double-down on studying big data and analytics.

Spotify: Your DJ in the Cloud

In 2014, the top music streaming service in the world, Stockholm-based Spotify, plunked down undisclosed millions for The Echo Nest, a Somerville, Massachusetts-based firm that had essentially created an automated music geek. While Apple's Beats 1 radio station uses a handful of charismatic human DJs to line up tracks,[54] Echo Nest is building a better hipster. According to Jim Lucchese, Echo Nest CEO at the time of acquisition, the firm systems do "what a great deejay does, or the friend that you rely on musically: to better understand who you are as a fan, understand all the music that's out there and make that connection."[55]

The Echo Nest was founded by the musically and technically talented team of Brian Whitman and Tristan Jehan, researchers who honed their craft at MIT's Media Lab. The duo built systems that could do two things: The first was to "listen" to music—analyze it to break down its characteristics: pitch, key, tempo, vocals or instrumental, live or studio, energy level, mood, and more.[56] While Pandora has human beings rating music, the idea struggles to scale and be consistent.[57] The Echo Nest, by contrast, created precision and speed. Over 30 million songs in that great musical catalog in the cloud[58] have been devoured and detailed, and 20,000 new ones are added each day.[59] And, with machine learning, the service only gets better the more data it's fed.[60]

The second big Echo Nest trick is to pay attention to what the world is saying about music. The firm's software constantly scours the Web, "reading" music blogs, news reports, and more—as many as 10 million documents each day. The firm's homegrown technology analyzes descriptions of artists, albums, tracks, and developing insight into trends and genres. In this, The Echo Nest has essentially built a cool hunting machine that listens to the world's music reviewers, music mavens, and rabid fans, constantly and planet-wide.[61]

Using The Echo Nest, Spotify is helping to curate the cloud according to your taste. Spotify's "Discover Weekly" is essentially a custom-built "station for you" created by examining your playlists, your listening habits, and what it learns about its millions of other users.[62] New services hint at where this can go. If you run, Spotify's smartphone app can pay attention to your running tempo, examine your song preferences, and build a playlist cued up based on how fast you move. Using The Echo Nest, Spotify is helping to curate the cloud according to your taste.[63] The future could be even more extraordinarily predictive. Does your phone tell Spotify you're at work? Queue up some non-distracting instrumental music to listen to in the background. Home cooking dinner? You'll get something smooth and relaxing. Gym patterns kicking in? Power mix. Big data, droppin' beats.[64]

Spotify has also launched tools to bring big data insights to its artists. The Spotify for Artists app gives all sorts of analytics, including overall streams and what playlists are creating new fans. The firm's Fans First program allows musicians to target their most rabid fans with special offers.

And the firm hasn't stopped with Echo Nest. Four acquisitions in 2017 alone fuel the firm's skill in APIs, machine learning, audio detection, and television recommendation. The firm even bought a blockchain company to help artists and labels with licensing and copyright issues.[65]

FIGURE 8.5 Spotify App

With over 70 million paying subscribers and an additional 90 million using the free service, Spotify is by far the world's most popular streaming music service. Big data leveraged by the firm's subsidiary, The Echo Nest, promises to leverage everything the firm knows about music, and about you, to queue up the best listening experience at exactly the right time.

Source: Spotify's public archive for media use at: https://press.spotify.com/no/pictures/application/.

e-discovery: Supporting Legal Inquiries

Data archiving isn't just for analytics. Sometimes the law requires organizations to dive into their electronic records. **e-discovery** refers to identifying and retrieving relevant electronic information to support litigation efforts. e-discovery is something a firm should account for in its archiving and data storage plans. Unlike analytics that promise a boost to the bottom line, there's no profit in complying with a judge's order—it's just a sunk cost. But organizations can be compelled by court order to scavenge their bits, and the cost to uncover difficult-to-access data can be significant, if not planned for in advance.

e-discovery

The process of identifying and retrieving relevant electronic information to support litigation efforts.

In one recent example, the Office of Federal Housing Enterprise Oversight (OFHEO) was subpoenaed for documents in litigation involving mortgage firms Fannie Mae and Freddie Mac. Even though the OFHEO wasn't a party in the lawsuit, the agency had to comply with the search—an effort that cost $6 million, a full 9 percent of its total yearly budget.[66]

Key Takeaways

- Data warehouses and data marts are repositories for large amounts of transactional data awaiting analytics and reporting.
- Large data warehouses are complex, can cost millions, and take years to build.
- The open source Hadoop effort provides a collection of technologies for manipulating massive amounts of unstructured data. The system is flexible, scalable, cost-effective, and fault-tolerant. Hadoop grew from large Internet firms but is now being used across industries.

Questions and Exercises

1. List the issues that need to be addressed in order to design, develop, deploy, and maintain data warehouses and data marts.
2. What is meant by "data relevance"?
3. What is meant by "data governance"?
4. What is the difference between a data mart and a data warehouse?
5. Why are data marts and data warehouses necessary? Why can't an organization simply query its transactional database?
6. How can something as simple as customer gender be difficult for a large organization to establish in a data warehouse?
7. What is Hadoop? Why would a firm use Hadoop instead of conventional data warehousing and data mart technologies?
8. Research the current state of "Big Data" analysis. Identify major firms leveraging Hadoop or similar technologies and share high-impact examples with your classmates and professor.
9. Think about examples where "Big Data" seems to have been used to target you or improve your experience with a firm or organization. Research the effort online to see if you can uncover any details. How does this make you feel on the spectrum spanning from "great service" to "creeped out"?

8.6 The Business Intelligence Toolkit

Learning Objectives

1. Know the tools that are available to turn data into information.
2. Identify the key areas where businesses leverage data mining.
3. Understand some of the conditions under which analytical models can fail.

So far we've discussed where data can come from, and how we can get data into a form where we can use it. But how, exactly, do firms turn that data into information? That's where the various software tools of business intelligence (BI) and analytics come in. Potential products in the business intelligence toolkit range from simple spreadsheets to ultrasophisticated data mining packages leveraged by teams employing "rocket-science" mathematics.

Query and Reporting Tools

The idea behind query and reporting tools is to present users with a subset of requested data, selected, sorted, ordered, calculated, and compared, as needed. Managers use these tools to see and explore what's happening inside their organizations.

Canned reports provide regular summaries of information in a predetermined format. They're often developed by information systems staff, and formats can be difficult to alter. By contrast, **ad hoc reporting tools** allow users to dive in and create their own reports, selecting fields, ranges, and other parameters to build their own reports on the fly. **Dashboards** provide a sort of heads-up display of critical indicators, letting managers get a graphical glance at key performance metrics. Some tools may allow data to be exported into spreadsheets. Yes, even the lowly spreadsheet can be a powerful tool for modeling "what if" scenarios and creating additional reports (of course, be careful: if data can be easily exported, then it can potentially leave the firm dangerously exposed, raising privacy, security, legal, and competitive concerns).

canned reports

Reports that provide regular summaries of information in a predetermined format.

ad hoc reporting tools

Tools that put users in control so that they can create custom reports on an as-needed basis by selecting fields, ranges, summary conditions, and other parameters.

dashboards

A heads-up display of critical indicators that allow managers to get a graphical glance at key performance metrics.

FIGURE 8.6 The Federal IT Dashboard

The Federal IT Dashboard offers federal agencies, and the general public, information about the government's IT investments.

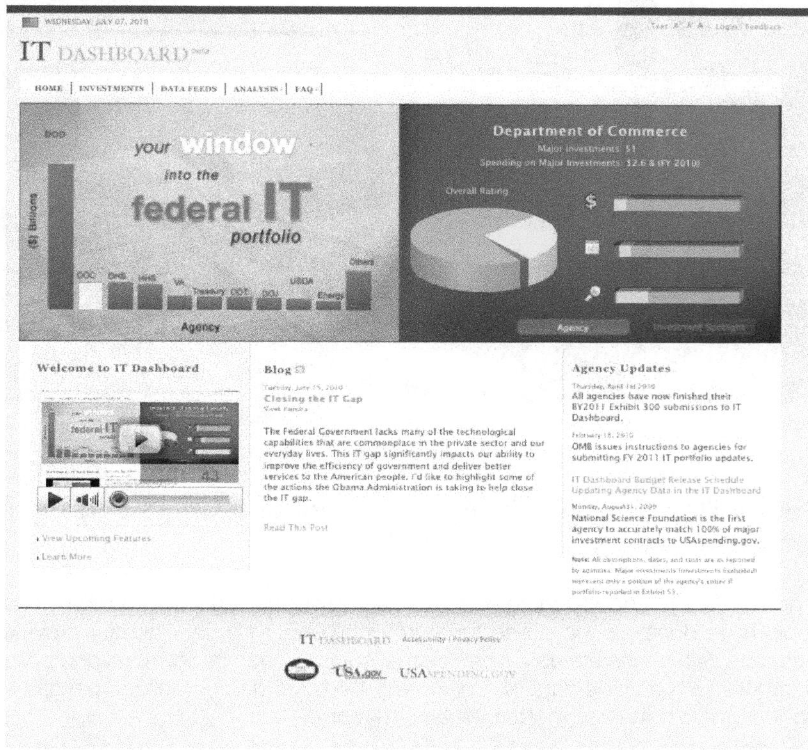

Source: USASpending.gov

A subcategory of reporting tools is referred to as **online analytical processing (OLAP)** (pronounced "oh-lap"). Data used in OLAP reporting is usually sourced from standard relational databases, but it's calculated and summarized in advance, across multiple dimensions, with the data stored in a special database called a **data cube**. This extra setup step makes OLAP fast (sometimes one thousand times faster than performing comparable queries against conventional relational databases). Given this kind of speed boost, it's not surprising that data cubes for OLAP access are often part of a firm's data mart and data warehouse efforts.

A manager using an OLAP tool can quickly explore and compare data across multiple factors such as time, geography, product lines, and so on. In fact, OLAP users often talk about how they can "slice and dice" their data, "drilling down" inside the data to uncover new insights. And while conventional reports are usually presented as a summarized list of information, OLAP results look more like a spreadsheet, with the various dimensions of analysis in rows and columns, with summary values at the intersection.

online analytical processing (OLAP)

A method of querying and reporting that takes data from standard relational databases, calculates and summarizes the data, and then stores the data in a special database called a data cube.

data cube

A special database used to store data in OLAP reporting.

FIGURE 8.7 Tableau

Business Intelligence tools such as Tableau (shown here) can gather data from multiple resources, and allow users to explore relationships and create powerful, consolidated reports and charts. For those interested, the questions at the end of the chapter include an exercise where you can download and try Tableau for free.

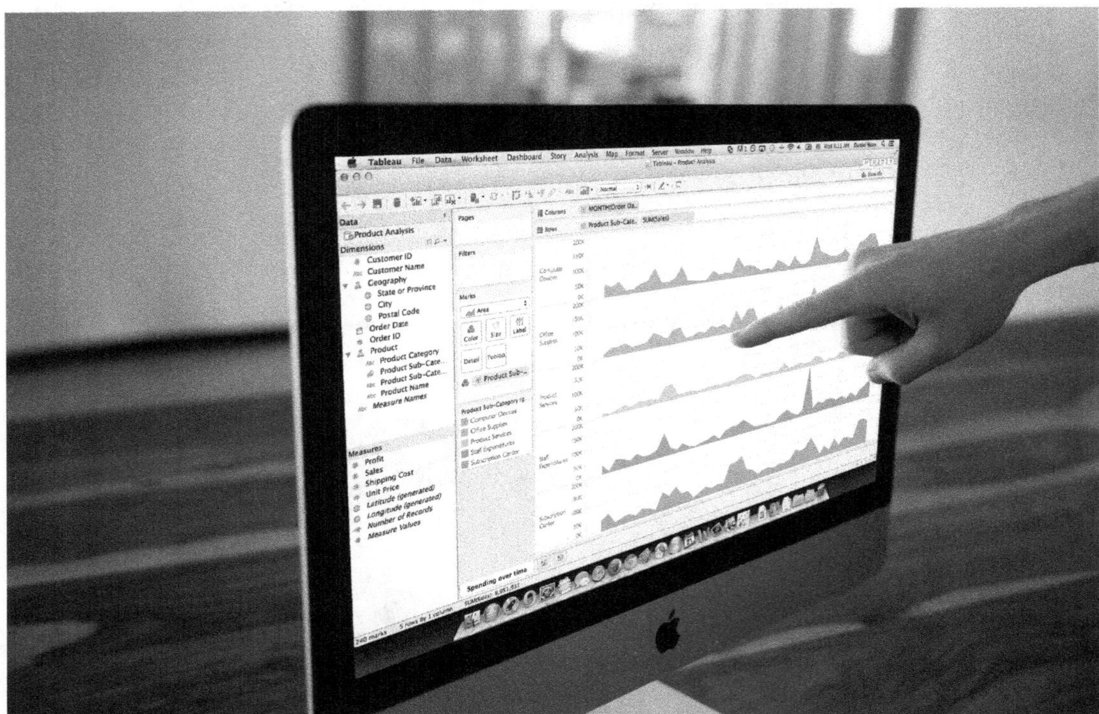

Source: Copyright SAS Institute, Inc, at https://www.tableau.com/about/media-download-center.

Public Sector Reporting Tools in Action: Fighting Crime and Fighting Waste

Access to ad hoc query and reporting tools can empower all sorts of workers. Consider what analytics tools have done for the police force in Richmond, Virginia. The city provides department investigators with access to data from internal sources such as 911 logs and police reports, and combines this with outside data including neighborhood demographics, payday schedules, weather reports, traffic patterns, sports events, and more.

Experienced officers dive into this data, exploring when and where crimes occur. These insights help the department decide how to allocate its limited policing assets to achieve the biggest impact. While IT staffers put the system together, the tools are actually used by officers with expertise in fighting street crime—the kinds of users with the knowledge to hunt down trends and interpret the causes behind the data. And it seems this data helps make smart cops even smarter—the system is credited with delivering a single-year crime-rate reduction of 20 percent.[67]

As it turns out, what works for cops also works for bureaucrats. When administrators for Albuquerque were given access to ad hoc reporting systems, they uncovered all sorts of anomalies, prompting excess spending cuts on everything from cell phone usage to unnecessarily scheduled overtime. And once again, BI performed for the public sector. The Albuquerque system delivered the equivalent of $2 million in savings in just the first three weeks it was used.[68]

L.L. Bean: Data Master

For a look at data-driven prowess, head to Maine and visit the over 100-year-old clothing and equipment retailer L.L. Bean. Bean's world has changed dramatically since the 1990s, when it had a highly structured, mostly relational information system to support a single marketing channel (catalog sales). Today Bean has retail stores, an adventure travel business, websites, apps, buying through Google Shopping and affiliates, social media, loyalty programs, and more—engaging customers through roughly 30 different channels overall. All of this inflates data collection—website traffic, app stats, A/B testing, purchases, items viewed but not purchased, returns, repairs, ad impressions, online marketing response, to name just a few.

Structured data didn't cut it any more. The business was changing too fast and data was flooding in like water from a firehose. So the firm began shifting from structured SQL to massive stores of unstructured data harnessed with Hadoop technology. Outside consultants were brought in to help develop a new systems architecture with new technologies.[69] The firm's classic 10TB enterprise data warehouse, stored onsite, was augmented with a 100TB cloud-based system. The conversation changed from the cost-focused "what data can we afford to keep" to the value-focused "what data can we afford to throw away." IT staff learned new skills, with the firm "turning its SQL developers into Hive and Impala NoSQL experts."[70] Marketing managers and new analytics team members were schooled in "Big Data Boot Camps" to show them how to dive deep into unstructured data to hunt down valuable insights. OLAP cubes and easy-to-use reporting tools were also made available to non-technical team members. One goal was to empower Bean staff for better insight and decision-making, increasing the users of firm data by at least ten times those who had prior reporting access.

Automated tools were also developed to leverage this data in real-time (making it not just "big data" but also "fast data"), allowing Bean to serve customers online, on the phone or in stores based on what the firm knows about them. This kind of integrated shopping experience and unified customer view across channels is sometimes referred to as **omnichannel**. Bean's web and app stores leverage these insights for on-the-fly personalization with a sharpshooter aim at what the customer wants. Additionally, iPad-wielding store staff and info-armed phone reps now have access to a deeply detailed real-time view of each customer, and these profiles are served up to create more relevant offers and better-received recommendations, and to deliver overall customer delight.[71] Need proof that customers see the benefit? Bean tied with Amazon as best in online retail customer satisfaction.[72]

Sources include: C. Wilson and D. Bryan, "Talk: Transitioning from Original Big Data to the New Big Data: L.L. Bean's Journey," at Strata+Hadoop World, Oct. 15-17, 2014, New York, NY (stream available at https://www.safaribooksonline.com/library/view/strata-conference-new/9781491900352/part110.html). And V. Heffernan, "Big Moose is Watching You," *Medium*, Oct. 31, 2014.

omnichannel

Providing customers with a unified experience across customer channels, which may include online, mobile, catalog, phone, and retail. Pricing, recommendations, and incentives should reflect a data-driven, accurate, single view of the customer.

Data Mining

While reporting tools can help users explore data, modern datasets can be so large that it might be impossible for humans to spot underlying trends. That's where data mining can help. **Data mining** is the process of using computers to identify hidden patterns and to build models from large datasets.

data mining

The process of using computers to identify hidden patterns in, and to build models from, large datasets.

Some of the key areas where businesses are leveraging data mining include the following:

- *Customer segmentation*—figuring out which customers are likely to be the most valuable to a firm.
- *Marketing and promotion targeting*—identifying which customers will respond to which offers at which price at what time.
- *Market basket analysis*—determining which products customers buy together, and how an organization can use this information to cross-sell more products or services.

- *Collaborative filtering*—personalizing an individual customer's experience based on the trends and preferences identified across similar customers.
- *Customer churn*—determining which customers are likely to leave, and what tactics can help the firm avoid unwanted defections.
- *Fraud detection*—uncovering patterns consistent with criminal activity.
- *Financial modeling*—building trading systems to capitalize on historical trends.
- *Hiring and promotion*—identifying characteristics consistent with employee success in the firm's various roles.

For data mining to work, two critical conditions need to be present: (1) the organization must have clean, consistent data, and (2) the events in that data should reflect current and future trends. The recent financial crisis provides lessons on what can happen when either of these conditions isn't met.

First let's look at problems with using bad data. A report in the *New York Times* has suggested that in the period leading up to the 2008 financial crisis, some banking executives deliberately deceived risk management systems in order to skew capital-on-hand requirements. This deception let firms load up on risky debt while carrying less cash for covering losses.[73] Deceive your systems with bad data and your models are worthless. In this case, wrong estimates from bad data left firms grossly overexposed to risk. When debt defaults occurred, several banks failed, and we entered the worst financial crisis since the Great Depression.

Now consider the problem of historical consistency: Computer-driven investment models can be very effective when the market behaves as it has in the past. But models are blind when faced with the equivalent of the "hundred-year flood" (sometimes called *black swans*); events so extreme and unusual that they never showed up in the data used to build the model.

We saw this in the late 1990s with the collapse of the investment firm Long-Term Capital Management. LTCM was started by Nobel Prize–winning economists, but when an unexpected Russian debt crisis caused the markets to move in ways not anticipated by its models, the firm lost 90 percent of its value in less than two months. The problem was so bad that the Fed had to step in to supervise the firm's multibillion-dollar bailout. Fast forward a decade to the banking collapse of 2008, and we again see computer-driven trading funds plummet in the face of another unexpected event—the burst of the housing bubble.[74]

over-engineer

Build a model with so many variables that the solution arrived at might only work on the subset of data you've used to create it.

Data mining presents a host of other perils, as well. It's possible to **over-engineer** a model, building it with so many variables that the solution arrived at might only work on the subset of data you've used to create it. You might also be looking at a random but meaningless statistical fluke. In demonstrating how flukes occur, Tyler Vigen, a geospatial intelligence analyst for the US Army, has put together a hilarious website demonstrating high correlations among impossibly linked data, most trending in near lockstep over a ten-year period. One graph shows a ten-year trend in per-capita US sour cream consumption and motorcycle riders killed in noncollision transport accidents. An unskilled person drawing inferences from what appears to be a very consistent trend between the two might erroneously conclude that sour cream kills bikers. The number of people who drowned by falling into a swimming pool is also highly correlated with the number of films Nicolas Cage has appeared in. Someone stop the actor before his reign of swimming pool tragedy continues![75]

One way to test to see if you're looking at a random occurrence in the numbers is to divide your data, building your model with one portion of the data, and using another portion to verify your results. This is the approach Netflix has used to test results achieved by teams in the Netflix Prize, the firm's million-dollar contest for improving the predictive accuracy of its movie recommendation engine (see [Content Removed: #fwk-38086-ch03]).

Analyst beware, it's also important to understand the source and consistency of data over time. Just because data may be expressed in a consistent format doesn't mean it was collected consistently or without distortive outside influence. Consider Google's initial success, then failure in identifying influenza trends from search data. Initial press trumpted the fact that Google queries could identify the spread of the flu more quickly and at least as accurately as the Centers for Disease Control. Two years later, Google was making more bad predictions than accurate ones. Researchers hunting for the breakdown point to the fact that Google regularly changes its search engine. For example, one update began recommending related search terms. Another began suggesting diagnoses. Suddenly Google was vastly overestimating CDC predictions, likely because its own tools accelerated the number of queries using flu-related terms.[76]

Finally, sometimes a pattern is uncovered, but determining the best choice for a response is less clear. Data-mining wizards at European retailer Tesco uncovered that product sales data showed several money-losing products, including a type of bread known as "milk loaf." Drop those products, right? Not so fast. Further analysis showed milk loaf was a "destination product" for a loyal group of high-value customers, and that these customers would shop elsewhere if milk loaf disappeared from Tesco shelves. The firm kept the bread as a loss-leader and retained those valuable milk loaf fans.[77] Data miner, beware—first findings don't always reveal an optimal course of action.

This last example underscores the importance of recruiting a data mining and business analytics team that possesses three critical skills: information technology (for understanding how to pull together data, and for selecting analysis tools), statistics (for building models and interpreting the strength and validity of results), and business knowledge (for helping set system goals and requirements, and offering deeper insight into what the data really says about the firm's operating environment). Miss one of these key functions and your team could make some major mistakes.

While we've focused on tools in our discussion above, many experts suggest that business intelligence is really an organizational process as much as it is a set of technologies. Having the right team is critical in moving the firm from goal setting through execution and results.

Key Takeaways

- Canned and ad hoc reports, digital dashboards, and OLAP are all used to transform data into information.
- OLAP reporting leverages data cubes, which take data from standard relational databases, calculating and summarizing data for superfast reporting access. OLAP tools can present results through multidimensional graphs, or via spreadsheet-style cross-tab reports.
- Modern datasets can be so large that it might be impossible for humans to spot underlying trends without the use of data mining tools.
- Businesses are using data mining to address issues in several key areas including customer segmentation, marketing and promotion targeting, collaborative filtering, and so on.
- Models influenced by bad data, missing or incomplete historical data, and over-engineering are prone to yield bad results.
- One way to test to see if you're looking at a random occurrence in your data is to divide your data, building your model with one portion of the data, and using another portion to verify your results.
- Analytics may not always provide the total solution for a problem. Sometimes a pattern is uncovered, but determining the best choice for a response is less clear.
- A competent business analytics team should possess three critical skills: information technology, statistics, and business knowledge.

Questions and Exercises

1. What are some of the tools used to convert data into information?
2. What is the difference between a canned report and ad hoc reporting?
3. How do reports created by OLAP differ from most conventional reports?
4. List the key areas where businesses are leveraging data mining.

5. What is market basket analysis?
6. What is customer churn?
7. For data mining to work, what two critical data-related conditions must be present?
8. Discuss occurrences of model failure caused by missing or incomplete historical data.
9. Why do researchers think Google's flu predictions became less accurate over time? How does this inform managerial caution on business intelligence projects? How can one avoid making similar errors?
10. Discuss Tesco's response to their discovery that "milk loaf" was a money-losing product.
11. List the three critical skills a competent business analytics team should possess.
12. One of the most popular analytics tools is a product called Tableau. Fortunately, the folks at Tableau allow college students to download a free version. A small exercise has been prepared for any students with access to a Mac or PC that they can install software on. Visit http://gallaugher.com/tableau to find this exercise and instruction video.

8.7 Artificial Intelligence, Big Data and Machine Learning: It's Now Everywhere!

Learning Objectives

1. Understand terms such as artificial intelligence, machine learning, and deep learning.
2. Name, recognize, and give examples of popular types of AI used in modern organizations.
3. Understand the rise of AI and machine learning, as well as the challenges associated with leveraging this technology in an organization, and its broader social implications.

artificial intelligence

Computer software that can mimic or improve upon functions that would otherwise require human intelligence.

The Data Mining topics discussed in the prior section have roots in a branch of computer science known as **artificial intelligence** (or AI). The goal of AI is to create computer programs that are able to mimic or improve upon functions that would otherwise require human intelligence. An explosion of tools is fueling the current spread of AI. These include a new generation of hardware chips that fuel AI through designs tailored to find patterns faster, cloud resources that any developer with a credit card can tap into, open source algorithms that can be applied to creating custom insights, software development kits that create standards for building AI into apps and other products, and data-capture tools that include sensors, cameras, and microphones.

Google CEO Sundar Pichai says that AI will have a "more profound" impact than electricity or fire.[78] With AI becoming more accessible and ubiquitous, the market is exploding. *The Economist* reports that the total market size for AI hardware and software was $12 billion in 2017 and will grow to $58 billion by 2021.[79] Public companies mentioned AI and machine learning in their earnings reports more than 700 times in Q4 2017—that's seven times more than the period just two years earlier. Mergers and acquisitions activity related to AI increased 26-fold in the same period.[80] Part of the acquisition frenzy in AI is a so-called aqui-hire play to bring in hard-to-lure talent. Startups without revenue are being priced at $5 million to $10 million for each AI expert that comes along with the deal. Yet despite interest, firms are struggling to capitalize on trends and technologies. As a report by MIT's *Sloan Management Review* and the Boston Consulting Group points out: some 85 percent of companies think AI will offer a competitive advantage, but only one in 20 is extensively employing it today.[81]

Understanding Popular Types of AI

The Data Mining topics discussed in the prior section have roots in a branch of computer science known as artificial intelligence (or AI). The goal of AI is to create computer programs that are able to mimic or improve upon functions that would otherwise require human intelligence. The definition of AI and some of its associated technologies don't have hard parameters, and the interpretation is often muddied by marketers trying to catch a trend, or hype-infused media reports. But the discussion below should provide a managerial understanding of key terms and how they are influencing organizations, decision-making, and products.

Machine learning is a type of AI often broadly defined as software with the ability to learn or improve without being explicitly programmed.[82] Many of the data mining techniques described in the prior section use machine learning.

Deep learning is a subcategory of machine learning. The "deep" in deep learning typically refers to the layers of interconnections and analysis that are examined to arrive at results. Some technologists refer to "deep" as having more than one "hidden" layer between input and output. That might not mean much to most managers, but just as "Big Data" is "a lot," "Deep Learning" has more analytical complexity.

There are also many subcategories of machine learning and other types of AI training, including *supervised learning* (where algorithms are trained by providing explicit examples of results sought, like defective vs. error-free, or stock price), *unsupervised learning* (where data are not explicitly labeled and don't have a predetermined result. Clustering customers into previously unknown groupings machine be one example), and semi-supervised learning (where data used to build models that determine an end result may contain data that has outputs explicitly labeled as well as unlabeled, e.g., "hey software, take a look at my categorizations and see if they are valid or you can come up with better or missing ones").

machine learning

A type of artificial intelligence that leverages massive amounts of data so that computers can improve the accuracy of actions and predictions on their own without additional programming.

deep learning

A type of machine learning that uses multiple layers of interconnections among data to identify patterns and improve predicted results. Deep learning most often uses a set of techniques known as neural networks and is popularly applied in tasks like speech recognition, image recognition, and computer vision.

FIGURE 8.8 Artificial Intelligence, Machine Learning, and deep learning

Deep learning is a subset of machine learning, which is a subset of artificial intelligence. These techniques involve some form of pattern recognition and are used in many applications, including those depicted above. ML automates discovery, which can improve as more data is added, while Deep Learning provides several layers of analysis and comparison to uncover results.

Artificial Intelligence
Software that automates and mimics or improves upon tasks that would otherwise require human intelligence.
Machine Learning
Subset of AI. Results improved without explicit programming
Deep Learning
Type of ML. Includes several layers of analysis between input data and output result.
AI can be found in:

Pattern Recognition

Medical diagnosis

Speech Recognition

Computer Vision

Self-driving Automobiles

Natural Language Processing

Source: John Gallaugher.

How Smart Is Today's AI

This video provides an animated, lay-person's explanation of how machine learning works from CGP Grey.

View the video online at: http://www.youtube.com/embed/R9OHn5ZF4Uo?rel=0

Own an Apple Product? You're Already Using a Whole Lot of AI

Here are just a few examples of how AI permeates Apple products: Data collected and constantly analyzed by Siri helps the voice assistant continually improve with better understanding of voices and accents worldwide, develop a greater understanding of context, and parse how devices are used so it can better service requests. Use ApplePay? AI fights fraud by improving analysis with each transaction. Maps? AI helps plot the best route by analyzing all sorts of traffic input. HealthKit? Machine learning can help keep cheats from climbing the leaderboard by identifying legitimate activity and filtering out bogus movement. Like your photos? AI recognizes faces and builds photo collages on what are determined to be your "best" pictures. Used FaceID or chatted with friends as a talking poop animoji? AI identifies the contours of your face to know you are you, and how to turn you into a cartoon. AI is behind extending device battery life, auto-switching between cellular and Wi-Fi networks, choosing news stories, apps, music, and video content you might enjoy. The iPad relies on AI to tell the difference between movements from the Apple Pencil and accidental swipes and taps from the pencil holder's hand. And the HomePod speaker combines sensor data with AI to optimize sound to suit the acoustics of the room.[83]

Expect even more since third parties have access to many of these tools, too. Apple's custom processors and the firm's Core ML software developer framework allow coders to tap into Apple and third-party machine learning algorithms so that apps can take advantage of image recognition, natural language processing, computer vision, and more.[84] Tools like these create standards and prevent developers from having to create things from scratch, enabling even small-time programmers to cheaply, easily, and quickly incorporate AI in their products.

Some of the more popular categories of software used in AI include:

neural networks

A statistical techniques used in AI, and particularly in machine learning. Neural networks hunt down and expose patterns, building multilayered relationships that humans can't detect on their own.

Neural networks, which are statistical techniques used to hunt down and expose patterns. Neural networks identify patterns by testing multilayered relationships that humans can't detect on their own. Many refer to the multilayered interconnections among data as mimicking the neurons of the brain (hence the name). If a set of interrelationships is strong, they go into the pattern-matching scheme. If a better set of relationships is found, old ones are tweaked or discarded. Neural networks are often referred to as a "black box," meaning that the weights and relationships of data that identify patterns approximate a mathematical function, but are difficult to break out as you would in a traditional mathematical formula. Massive amounts of data play a role here. Google leverages data it collects when users talk to and type into its search engine to improve its speech recognition algorithms, cutting errors by 25 percent in a single rollout.[85]

Expert systems are AI systems that leverage rules or examples to perform a task in a way that mimics applied human expertise. Expert systems are used in tasks ranging from medical diagnoses to product configuration. They may be programmed with explicit rules (think a big "if this, then do that" decision tree), or rules may be automatically built by analyzing specific cases against outcomes (e.g., make less product if the weather is below 40 degrees and rainy, since there will be less foot traffic).

Genetic algorithms are model-building techniques where computers examine many potential solutions to a problem, iteratively modifying (mutating) various mathematical models, and comparing the mutated models to search for a best alternative function. Many computer scientists would say that neural networks approximate functions, while genetic algorithms refine functions to optimize solutions. For most managers it's useful just to know the term as a type of automated model development that's another arrow in the AI quiver. Genetic algorithms have been used for everything from building financial trading models to handling complex airport scheduling to designing parts for the international space station.[86]

While AI is not a single technology—terms and categorizations may overlap or have debated definitions—various forms of AI can show up as part of analytics products, CRM tools, transaction processing systems, and other information systems. Many of these techniques that crunch massive amounts of data leverage the special AI-powering graphics chips and FPGAs mentioned in the Moore's Law and More chapter.

Examples of AI in Action

While the current uses of artificial intelligence and machine learning are varied, and the reach of technologies is expanding, it may be useful to look at some current examples to gain an appreciation of AI's expanding reach, and to help you brainstorm about how AI might be used in organizations where you work, or in products that you use.

Computer vision is everywhere: Uber uses Microsoft-provided computer vision to scan driver faces and confirm their identity when they are starting a shift. The congressional television network C-SPAN uses Amazon's image recognition tools to identify on-screen lawmakers so they can quickly place a name below their image.[87]

Helping delivery drivers optimize pickup and dropoff schedules is a particularly thorny problem helped by AI. United Parcel Service estimates that for every mile that its drivers reduce their daily route, the firm saves $50 million a year.[88]

AI is giving us better customer service and delivering many from "phone tree hell." China Merchants Bank, uses an AI-based messaging bot in WeChat, China's most popular mobile platform, to handle 1.5 million to 2 million queries a day, a volume that would otherwise require a staff of 7,000 human staff. Casino giant Caesars uses its Ivy virtual concierge to answer questions received via text, reducing calls to the human concierge desk by 30%. Airliner KLM has used customer service text bots to double the number of weekly customer inquiries to 120,000 while increasing the number of agents by only 6%. Insurers Humana and MetLife are using voice analysis software from the firm Cogito to identify if customer service reps have experienced "compassion fatigue." Identify an agent who shows signs an interaction may not be going well (speech speed, keywords, voice level), and the system can prompt service people with strategies to improve. This sort of advising-when-needed is especially useful in phone support, where employee turnover can easily exceed 40 percent a year.[89] And British grocer Ocado uses AI to scan 10,000 customer e-mails a day to escalate and prioritize response as well as identify sentiment (good vs. bad experiences) around keywords.[90] Applications like this don't get rid of humans, but they make existing staff more efficient and productive.

AI is increasingly embedding itself into the soft-skills discipline of human resources. Software from the SaaS vendor Workday provides software to improve employee retention by uncovering patterns of those most likely to leave. The firm's software examines some 60 factors, including salary, time between holidays taken, and turnover of the employee's manager. Another firm, Arena, provides technology to hospitals and home-care companies to use application and third-party data to screen job applicants for traits that indicate they may stay at their job longer. The firm claims median turnover has been reduced by nearly 40 percent in firms using their software.[91]

AI might also help make the workplace fairer, analyzing employee promotion and pay data for anomalies that suggest managers have hired staff that looks "more like them" rather than those who exhibit the characteristics and track record for success. For a look at AI for better hiring decisions, consider systems from the startup Pymetrics, used by firms as wide ranging as Unilever in packaged goods and Nielsen in ratings research. Pymetrics tests candidates on roughly 80 traits, including memory and attitude to risk, using machine learning to measure applicant scores against a firm's top performers and predict suitability and success.[92]

There's also a good chance you've been reading news items and other copy written by robo-journalists. The Associated Press uses software called Wordsmith by the firm Automated Insights to craft more than 3,000 financial reports per quarter, posting summaries online within minutes of their release. The *Los Angeles Times* uses "Quakebot" to analyze geological data, in one case breaking the story of a 4.7 magnitude earthquake in Southern California.[93] The Big Ten Network uses software from Narrative Science for updates of football and basketball games and for short recaps of collegiate baseball and softball. Box scores and other play-by-play data are all the inputs these systems need.[94]

A system developed by IBM and the Baylor College of Medicine "read" 100,000 research papers in two hours and "found completely new biology hidden in the data"—undiscovered, needle-like insights buried in the existing massive haystacks of human-generated knowledge, which no single researcher could digest and map. These specific insights "could provide routes to new cancer drugs."[95] Some hear about machine learning and have nightmares of Skynet from the *Terminator* movies (Elon Musk, Bill Gates, and Stephen Hawking are among well-known tech-forward crowds who have cautioned about AI's future),[96] but big brain insights from AI just might save your life one day.

Many sites have ranked AI skills as among the most sought-after in today's job market. Want to geek up with machine learning? Google is one of many firms that offers several free online course in how to use its AI technologies, including a free 15-hour crash course in machine learning.

It's Not as Easy as the Press Might State: Technical, Organizational, Legal, and Societal Challenges of AI and Machine Learning

AI starts with what are sometimes referred to as "naked algorithms" that need to be trained. These are starting point algorithms, and many are in the public domain or accessible from cloud provider services (e.g., Google TensorFlow) or through vendor APIs and inside software development kits (e.g., Apple Core ML). However, training implies access to a large quantity of consistent, reliable historical data. Since most data mining is a subset of AI, many of the challenges mentioned in the prior section also apply to machine learning. Issues that managers, as well as concerned citizens, might want to be aware of include:

- Data quality, inconsistent data, or the inability to integrate data sources into a single dataset capable of input into machine learning systems can all stifle efforts.[97]
- Not enough data. A firm might want to get into machine learning, but may lack underlying databases to begin this effort. It might, for example, be impossible to use machine learning to develop a system to predict failure when there are very few cases of failure that occur, and hence not enough examples to learn from.[98] This also applies to the inability to predict rare "black swan" events since, by definition, they are either exceedingly rare or have never previously occurred.
- Technical staff may require training in developing and maintaining such systems, and such skills are rare. In situations where AI makes a recommendation, but a human makes the final call, managers using such systems may need coaching on when to accept and when to question results (see the Tesco "milk loaf" example in the prior section).
- AI systems also involve a discipline known as "change management" that goes hand-in-hand with many IS projects. Change management seeks to identify how workflows and processes are to be altered, and how to manage the worker and organizational transition from one system to another. This can be key because many users of corporate AI will see their jobs significantly altered. They might have to do more, take on more responsibility, or remove instinct from some decisions and rely on recommendations made by a machine.[99]
- Some types of machine learning may be legally prohibited because of the data used or the inability to identify how a model works and whether or not it might be discriminatory. For example, while gender and religion could be used to predict some risks, they are unacceptable to regulators in some applications and jurisdictions. Redlining laws in the lending industry prevent geography from being used in calculating credit worthiness, since geography is often tightly correlated with race. In other industries, regulators won't accept the "black box" solutions offered by neural networks. And some areas such as the EU may have higher privacy protection that prohibits the gathering or use of certain data or techniques.[100]
- The negative unintended consequences of data misuse might also lead to regulation that limits techniques currently used. Some believe this helps give China an edge in some systems, since the government keeps a vast database of faces that can help train facial-recognition algorithms, and privacy is less of a concern than in the West. Jaywalkers in Shanghai can already be fined (or shamed) from facial recognition that identifies scofflaw citizens.[101] In another example, The Chinese financial firm Ping An uses app-based video interviews to spot shifty behavior worthy of further screening. Prospective borrowers answer a series of questions related to income and ability to replay a loan, while machine learning systems monitor and identify some fifty distinct facial expressions related to truthfulness.[102] The camera and the cloud are becoming a sort of real-time lie detector.
- Many workers are startled to find that in the United States, just about anything done on organizational networks or using a firm's computer hardware can be monitored.[103] While examining worker communications can help ensure employees don't break the law or commit crimes against the firm, and can offer help on how to do one's job better, the acceleration of these practices will undoubtedly raise additional privacy issues and have the potential to alienate workers, especially in a tight labor market.
- And as we think of how data relates to competitive advantage, firms that gain an early lead and benefit from scale may be in a position to collect more data than competitors, fueling a virtuous cycle where early winners generate more data, have stronger predictive capabilities, and can have an edge in entering new markets, offering new services, attracting customers, and cutting prices. Good for the winners and possibly good for consumers in the short run, but this may also fuel the kind of winner-take-all / winner-take-most dominance we see when network effects are present, something that might stifle innovation if it discourages competition and feeds near-monopolies. Indeed, many have referred to data as "the new oil," in that it is has the ability to create cash-gushing opportunities.[104]

How Smart Is Today's Artificial Intelligence?

A brief intro to AI and machine learning, with examples, expert commentary, promise, and current limitations.

View the video online at: http://www.youtube.com/embed/lJKjMlU55pE?rel=0

Catching the Golden State Killer: The Promise and Peril of Big Data's Reach

The fugitive known as the Golden State Killer is one of the most heinous criminals in US history. Police linked him to at least twelve murders, fifty rapes, and over 100 burglaries from 1976 to 1986. The criminal's sadism included extended torture of victims and family members, stealing victim's personal items and taunting them with messages following attacks. Yet despite pouring more resources into the investigation than any other in California history, the killer had eluded capture for four decades.[105] Despite the many attacks and the killer's grisly rituals, all leads reached a dead-end. That is, until, a community of online genealogists unwittingly led detectives to identify the alleged killer: one Joseph James DeAngelo, age 72 at the time of his 2018 apprehension.[106]

Using a well-preserved piece of biological evidence collected before the era of DNA testing, officers sequenced the killer's DNA, then uploaded it to the GEDmatch website. GEDmatch isn't one of the big consumer-oriented DNA analysis products, such as 23andMe or AncestryDNA. It's a modest side-project created by two volunteers in 2011, but it does act as a sort of open-source clearinghouse, providing matching among anyone interested in publicly sharing their DNA data. To be clear, the big names in consumer DNA analysis do not, under any circumstances, share identifying DNA information with others. A 23andMe spokesperson states that despite requests: no data has ever been "given out in any circumstance."[107] However, consumers can download their own DNA data from these sites to use as they'd like. Users who upload data to GEDmatch can be linked to and connect with genetic relatives, and the site has been used by hundreds of thousands of users, including amateur genealogists and those looking for clues regarding family diseases. While the suspect's DNA failed to match anything in criminal databases and he left no fingerprints, GEDmatch linked the police sample to several distant relatives—the equivalent of third cousins. Investigators then scoured census data, obituaries, death records, and modern databases to painstakingly piece together some 25 different family trees (the trees were built using a tool from Ancestry.com). The result was a lineage trail leading up to the killer's great-great-great grandparents, and eventually back down to DeAngelo—evidence gathered without a warrant and with no court order required.

Fast/cheap computing has enabled modern genetic analysis. The first human genome took nearly fifteen years to sequence and cost \$2.5 billion to complete,[108] but genotyping services like 23andMe and AncestryDNA provide services for less than \$100. True, consumer firms provide only a fraction of the analysis of full genome sequencing (one expert says it's like getting access to select words on a page instead of the entire page),[109] but the ability to use sub-\$100 tests to identify one's link to gene-related traits, disease susceptibility, and lineage, demonstrates the astonishing advances in data gathering and analysis. The suspect was employed as a police officer at the time of many of the crimes, a reason that may have offered him the training and access to a police radio that helped him hide any record of his crimes. But he couldn't predict a future with genetic profiling nor the roughly one million sharing their data in the GEDmatch database.

Catching a murder suspect is clearly a net benefit to society. No one would dispute that bringing the killer to justice would be a good thing. However, the case brought to light additional issues of privacy and ethical data use. Revealing one's own DNA on a site like GEDmatch is not a decision impacting only the poster. It potentially exposes all existing and future relatives to anyone who can match the posted DNA to their family tree. While Facebook users were shocked that friends could unwittingly reveal their personal data to Cambridge Analytica without their consent, the implications of having a genetic relative share DNA data could be far more severe. Would employers, insurance companies, or the unscrupulous be able to use a link to family member DNA? Is it possible that a person could be denied coverage or a job based on a link to a kin's genes? Could merged databases influence dating decisions if someone's relative had a genetic flaw? What are the implications if one distant family member's sharing suggests others are susceptible to addiction, mental illness, violence, or some characteristic seen as negative? And even if laws are passed in one country, this doesn't protect relatives around the globe who may live under more oppressive governments. At the time that the Golden State Killer suspect was caught, 23andMe had more than five million customers, and Ancestry.com had ten million.[110] Loose attitudes by one relative could potentially compromise a family for generations. Managers, consumers, and lawmakers will have to think with breadth and depth regarding unintended consequences. We are in the midst of navigating a world where big data and machine learning can keep us safe and deliver social good as well as expose others to discrimination, extortion, or the public release of sensitive information that they had not sought or even been aware of.[111]

Key Takeaways

- **Artificial intelligence** refers to software that can mimic or improve upon functions that would otherwise require human intelligence.
- **Machine learning** is a type of AI often broadly defined as software with the ability to learn or improve without being explicitly programmed.
- **Deep learning** is a subcategory of machine learning. The "deep" in deep learning refers to the layers of interconnections and analysis that are examined to arrive at results.
- **Neural networks** are a category of AI used to identify patterns by testing multilayered relationships that humans can't detect on their own. Neural network techniques are often used in machine learning and are popular in data mining.
- **Expert systems** are AI systems that leverage rules or examples to perform a task in a way that mimics applied human expertise.
- **Genetic algorithms** are model-building techniques where computers examine many potential solutions to a problem, iteratively modifying (mutating) various mathematical models, and comparing the mutated models to search for a best alternative function.
- The explosion of machine learning is due to several factors, including open source tools; cloud computing for low-cost, high-volume data crunching; tools accessible via API or as part of software development kits; and new chips specifically designed for the simultaneous pattern hunting and relationship testing used in neural networks and other types of AI. AI can now be found in all sorts of consumer products—it is enabling the first generation of autonomous vehicles; it's influencing soft-skill disciplines like human resources; it improves the efficiency of modern, complex operations; it's is a key component in many customer service initiatives; and it's even being used in medical diagnosis and research.
- Incorporating AI and machine learning remains challenging. Organizations require technical skills and must reeducate the workforce impacted by AI decision-making tools. Firms need a clean, deep, and accurate dataset. Predictions require a tight relationship between historical data and new data used for prediction. Legal issues may prohibit the use of machine learning and "black box" algorithms in industries requiring exposure of the decision-making process.

Varying international laws may allow techniques in one region of the globe that are prohibited in others.

- AI and machine learning have exposed the possibility of unintended consequences, including the possibility of introducing unintended bias, discrimination, and violations of privacy.

Questions and Exercises

1. How are the terms artificial intelligence, machine learning, and deep learning related?
2. What factors are leading to the new explosion in machine learning now used by organizations and making its way into consumer products? Research firms that provide low-cost access to machine learning tools and give examples of products and services developed using these technologies.
3. Do any of the products that you use leverage artificial intelligence? What kinds of AI might be used in Netflix's movie recommendation system, Apple's iTunes Genius playlist builder, or Amazon's website personalization? What kind of AI might help a physician make a diagnosis or help an engineer configure a complicated product in the field?
4. Research business applications of machine learning and come to class prepared to discuss new developments, organizations using this technology, and their current plus potential long-term impact.
5. Are you excited about the future of machine learning? Frightened? Why? How might these technologies create social change and spawn new business opportunities?
6. What ethical issues are created through public data-sharing sites like GEDmatch? List the positives and negatives. Do you feel sharing your personal data should be regulated? Why or why not? Could loopholes be plugged by preventing this data from being used in hiring, insurance, or other contexts? Why or why not?

8.8 Data Asset in Action: Technology and the Rise of Walmart

Learning Objectives

1. Understand how Walmart has leveraged information technology to become the world's largest retailer.
2. Be aware of the challenges that face Walmart in the years ahead.

Walmart demonstrates how a physical product retailer can create and leverage a data asset to achieve world-class supply chain efficiencies targeted primarily at driving down costs.

Walmart isn't just the largest retailer in the world; over the past several years it has popped in and out of the top spot on the *Fortune* 500 list—meaning that the firm has had revenues greater than *any* firm in the United States. Walmart is so big that in three months it sells more than a whole year's worth of sales at number two US retailer Home Depot.[112]

At that size, it's clear that Walmart's key source of competitive advantage is scale. But firms don't turn into giants overnight. Walmart grew in large part by leveraging information systems to an extent never before seen in the retail industry. Technology tightly coordinates the Walmart value chain from tip to tail, while these systems also deliver a minable data asset that's unmatched in US retail. To get a sense of the firm's overall efficiencies, at the end of the prior decade a McKinsey study found that Walmart was responsible for some 12 percent of the productivity gains in the *entire* US economy.[113] The firm's capacity as a systems innovator is so respected that many senior Walmart IT executives have been snatched up for top roles at Dell, HP, Amazon, and Microsoft. And lest one think that innovation is the province of only those located in the technology hubs of Silicon Valley, Boston, and Seattle, remember that Walmart is headquartered in Bentonville, Arkansas.

A Data-Driven Value Chain

The Walmart efficiency dance starts with a proprietary system called Retail Link, a system originally developed in 1991 and continually refined ever since. Each time an item is scanned by a Walmart cash register, Retail Link not only records the sale, it automatically triggers inventory reordering, scheduling, and delivery. This process keeps shelves stocked while keeping inventories at a minimum. An AMR report ranked Walmart as having the seventh best supply chain in the country.[114] The firm's annual **inventory turnover ratio** of 11.11 means that Walmart sells the equivalent of its entire inventory roughly every four to five weeks (by comparison, Target's turnover ratio is 5.7, Sears' is 3.6, and the average for US retail is less than 2).[115]

inventory turnover ratio

The ratio of a company's annual sales to its inventory.

Back-office scanners keep track of inventory as supplier shipments come in. Suppliers are rated based on timeliness of deliveries, and you've got to be quick to work with Walmart. In order to avoid a tractor-trailer traffic jam in store parking lots, deliveries are choreographed to arrive at intervals less than ten minutes apart. When Levi's joined Walmart, the firm had to guarantee it could replenish shelves every two days—no prior retailer had required a shorter-than-five-day window from Levi's.[116]

Walmart has been a catalyst for technology adoption among its suppliers. The firm is currently leading an adoption effort that requires partners to leverage RFID technology to track and coordinate inventories. While the rollout has been slow, a recent P&G trial showed RFID boosted sales nearly 20 percent by ensuring that inventory was on shelves and located where it should be.[117]

Keeping product stocked is one part of the streamlined value chain equation; prompting customers to return often and buy efficiently is another key element. The firm's Scan & Go app lets customers use their smartphones to scan bar codes of items they put in their cart. At checkout time, customers flash a total purchase barcode at a cash register kiosk screen and pay. Customers can keep an on-app shopping list that's checked off with each item scanned, and the app offers a shopping budget feature, too. App-delivered coupons and specials will help entice buyers to stick with Walmart instead of rivals.[118] If Walmart can cut the number of cashiers, labor savings could be significant, too. Walmart spends about $12 million every second on cashier wages across its US stores.[119] As for paying by app, Walmart's ready to play nice with competitors, too. Not every effort is a success. The firm partnered with over a dozen firms, including BestBuy, Target, Sears, and 7-Eleven, to plot a new pay-with-your-phone standard called MCX that also offered coupons, and loyalty programs.[120] Despite big name retail backing, the effort foundered and the technology was eventually purchased by JP Morgan Chase. While that was a grim outcome, the firm doubled down with its own Walmart Pay app, announcing that it was neck-and-neck with Apple Pay in terms of its acceptance by store shoppers.[121]

Data Mining Prowess

Walmart also mines its mother lode of data to get its product mix right under all sorts of varying environmental conditions, protecting the firm from "a retailer's twin nightmares: too much inventory, or not enough."[122] For example, the firm's data mining efforts informed buyers that customers stock up on certain products in the days leading up to predicted hurricanes. Bumping up prestorm supplies of batteries and bottled water was a no-brainer, but the firm also learned that Pop-Tarts sales spike sevenfold before storms hit, and that beer is the top prestorm seller. This insight has led to truckloads full of six packs and toaster pastries streaming into gulf states whenever word of a big storm surfaces.[123]

Data mining also helps the firm tighten operational forecasts, helping to predict things like how many cashiers are needed at a given store at various times of day throughout the year. Data drives the organization, with mined reports forming the basis of weekly sales meetings, as well as executive strategy sessions. The firm has developed what it calls its Data Café, a state-of-the-art analytics center at headquarters that leverages an industry-leading data trove that tops 40 petabytes. The system provides managers with a central clearinghouse where they can seek help on data-driven problem solving, and the system provides managers with alerts, prompting them to reach out to the Data Café for help in identifying and solving the problem.[124]

Walmart leverages its huge Hadoop-based data trove to support some of its data mining efforts, sifting through massive amounts of social media—Twitter posts, Facebook updates, and other so-called unstructured data—to gain insights on product offerings, sales leads, pricing, and more. The firm purchased social startup Kosmix for $300 million to deepen social and big data expertise in the company's @WalmartLabs.[125] Says Kosmix founder Anand Rajaraman (who previously sold a firm to Amazon and was an early investor in Facebook), "The first generation of e-commerce was about bringing the store to the Web. The next generation will be about building integrated experiences that leverage the store, the Web and mobile, with social identity being the glue that binds the experience."[126] The firm continues to hone tech chops and has aggressively established outposts in Silicon Valley. The firm's Global eCommerce unit is a 1,500-person operation headquartered across the street from Google's YouTube offices,[127] and Valley-based @WalmartLabs has grown from a slew of acquisitions, including social ad firm OneRiot, social commerce firm Tasty Labs, predictive analytics firm Inkiru, and the cloud startup OneOps.[128] The Arkansas giant's Valley offices host "hack days" in the best tradition of Facebook and other tech leaders, allowing developers to blue-sky new ideas that may eventually be put into practice.

Sharing Data, Keeping Secrets

While Walmart is demanding of its suppliers, it also shares data with them. Data can help firms become more efficient so that Walmart can keep dropping prices, and data can help firms uncover patterns that help suppliers sell more. P&G's Gillette unit, for example, claims to have mined Walmart data to develop promotions that increased sales as much as 19 percent. More than seventeen thousand suppliers are given access to their products' Walmart performance across metrics that include daily sales, shipments, returns, purchase orders, invoices, claims, and forecasts. And these suppliers collectively interrogate Walmart data warehouses to the tune of twenty-one million queries a year.[129]

While Walmart shares sales data with relevant suppliers, the firm otherwise fiercely guards this asset. Many retailers pool their data by sharing it with information brokers like Information Resources and ACNielsen. This sharing allows smaller firms to pool their data to provide more comprehensive insight on market behavior. But Walmart stopped sharing data with these agencies years ago. The firm's scale is so big, the additional data provided by brokers wasn't adding much value, and it no longer made sense to allow competitors access to what was happening in its own huge chunk of retail sales.

Other aspects of the firm's technology remain under wraps, too. Walmart custom builds large portions of its information systems to keep competitors off its trail. As for infrastructure secrets, the Walmart Data Center in McDonald County, Missouri, was considered so off limits that the county assessor was required to sign a nondisclosure statement before being allowed on-site to estimate property value.[130]

Betting Big on e-Commerce: Acquiring Jet.com, Bonobos, Flipkart and More

Walmart has also opened its wallet in eyebrow-raising ways to gain e-commerce expertise. The firm's 2016 purchase of Jet.com carried a $3.3 billion price tag for a relatively new, still unprofitable Amazon competitor. The founders of Jet.com had previously founded Quidsi, the firm behind Diapers.com and other brands, which Walmart sought and lost when outbid by Amazon. In the year after acquiring Jet.com, Walmart US e-commerce sales increased 63 percent year over year. In the same period, Walmart pumped up the number of products sold on its website, from 10 million to over 67 million items. The firm also slashed its free shipping threshold and offered additional discounts for customers who pick up products in its stores, even installing pickup towers in some locations to streamline this process. And the firm's acquisition of trendier brands, including Bonobos, ModCloth, ShoeBuy, and Moosejaw, are helping Walmart fight its dowdy, low-budget image when compared to rival Target.[131]

Walmart Flipkart Deal

Walmart also outbid Amazon, paying $16 billion for a 77 percent stake in India's e-commerce and payments leader, Flipkart. This was the largest foreign direct investment in an Indian firm, involves prior investors Softbank (Japan) and Tencent (China) among others, and gives Walmart a strong presence in a market where it has previously struggled, plus a leadership role for challenging Amazon, which has also invested heavily in India.

View the video online at: //www.youtube.com/embed/_Z5ch8aHJrE?rel=0

Challenges Abound

But despite success, challenges continue. While Walmart grew dramatically throughout the 1990s, the firm's US business has largely matured. And as a mature business, it faces a problem not unlike the example of Microsoft discussed at the end of Chapter 6; Walmart needs to find huge markets or dramatic cost savings in order to boost profits and continue to move its stock price higher.

The firm's aggressiveness and sheer size also increasingly make Walmart a target for criticism. Those low prices come at a price, and the firm has faced accusations of subpar wages and remains a magnet for union activists. Others have identified poor labor conditions at some of the firm's contract manufacturers. Suppliers that compete for Walmart's business are often faced with a catch-22. If they bypass Walmart they miss out on the largest single chunk of world retail sales. But if they sell to Walmart, the firm may demand prices so aggressively low that suppliers end up cannibalizing their own sales at other retailers. Still more criticism comes from local citizen groups that have accused Walmart of ruining the market for mom-and-pop stores.[132]

While some might see Walmart as invincibly standing at the summit of world retail, it's important to note that other megaretailers have fallen from grace. In the 1920s and 1930s, the A&P grocery chain controlled 80 percent of US grocery sales, at its peak operating five times the number of stores that Walmart has today. But market conditions changed, and the government stepped in to draft antipredatory pricing laws when it felt A&P's parent was too aggressive.

For all of Walmart's data brilliance, historical data offers little insight on how to adapt to more radical changes in the retail landscape. The firm's data warehouse wasn't able to foretell the rise of Target and other up-market discounters. Savvy managers recognize that data use is a vital tool, but not the only tool in management's strategic arsenal.

Key Takeaways

- Walmart demonstrates how a physical product retailer can create and leverage a data asset to achieve world-class value chain efficiencies.
- Walmart uses data mining in numerous ways, from demand forecasting to predicting the number of cashiers needed at a store at a particular time.
- To help suppliers become more efficient, and as a result lower prices, Walmart shares data with them.
- Despite its success, Walmart is a mature business that needs to find huge markets or dramatic cost savings in order to boost profits and continue to move its stock price higher. The firm's success also makes it a high-impact target for criticism and activism. And the firm's data assets could not predict impactful industry trends such as the rise of Target and other upscale discounters.

Questions and Exercises

1. List the functions performed by Retail Link. What is its benefit to Walmart?
2. Which supplier metrics does Retail Link gather and report? How is this valuable to Walmart and suppliers?
3. Name the technology that Walmart requires partners to use to track and coordinate inventory. Do you know of other uses for this technology?
4. What steps has Walmart taken to protect its data from competitors?
5. Research Walmart's current e-commerce efforts as compared to Amazon and other rivals. Do you think Walmart will catch Amazon? Does it need to? What advantages does Walmart enjoy by blending retail stores with e-commerce efforts?
6. List the criticisms leveled at Walmart. Do you think these critiques are valid or not? What can Walmart do to counteract this criticism? Should it take these steps? Why or why not?

Endnotes

1. Editorial Team, "The Exponential Growth of Data," *InsideBigData*, Feb. 16, 2017.
2. L. Mearian, "Digital Universe and Its Impact Bigger than We Thought," *Computerworld*, March 18, 2008.
3. B. Marr, "The Little Black Book of Billionaire Secrets Really Big Data At Walmart: Real-Time Insights From Their 40+ Petabyte Data Cloud," *Forbes*, Jan. 23, 2017.
4. B. Marr, "The Little Black Book of Billionaire Secrets Really Big Data At Walmart: Real-Time Insights From Their 40+ Petabyte Data Cloud," *Forbes*, Jan. 23, 2017.
5. A. McAfee and E. Brynjolfsson, "Big Data: The Management Revolution" *Harvard Business Review*, October 2012.
6. T. Davenport and J. Harris, *Competing on Analytics: The New Science of Winning* (Boston: Harvard Business School Press, 2007).
7. C. Gayomali, "How Google's Robots Can Learn Like Humans," *Fast Company*, Feb. 11, 2014.

8. A. Lampitt, "The real story of how big data analytics helped Obama win," *InfoWorld*, Feb. 14, 2013.
9. S. Baker, "Math Will Rock Your World," *BusinessWeek*, January 23, 2006, http://www.businessweek.com/magazine/content/06_04/b3968001.htm.
10. J. Soat, "P&G's CIO Puts IT at Users' Service," *InformationWeek*, December 15, 2007.
11. Patrick Rishe, "Dynamic Pricing: The Future of Ticket Pricing in Sports," *Forbes*, January 6, 2012.
12. L. Gomes, "Data Analysis Is Creating New Business Opportunities," *MIT Technology Review*, May 2, 2011.
13. M. Gorman, "San Francisco Giants (and Most of MLB) Adopt Apple's iBeacon for an Enhanced Ballpark Experience," *Engadget*, March 28, 2014.
14. M. Gorman, "San Francisco Giants (and Most of MLB) Adopt Apple's iBeacon for an Enhanced Ballpark Experience," *Engadget*, March 28, 2014.
15. M. Harvey, "Probe into How Google Mix-Up Caused $1 Billion Run on United," *Times Online*, September 12, 2008, http://technology.timesonline.co.uk/tol/news/tech_and_web/article4742147.ece.
16. R. Braddock, "Lessons of Internet Marketing from FreshDirect," *Wall Street Journal*, May 11, 2009.
17. J. Zhang, "Recession Likely to Boost Government Outlays on Health Care," *Wall Street Journal*, February 24, 2009.
18. S. Milligan, "Business Warms to Democratic Leaders," *Boston Globe*, May 28, 2009.
19. A. Cha, "Researchers: Medical Errors Now the Third Leading Cause of Death in the United States," *The Washington Post*, May 3, 2016.
20. J. Halamka, "IT Spending: When Less Is More," *BusinessWeek*, March 2, 2009.
21. C. Boehret, "ResearchKit, Apple's Medical Data Experiment, Explained," *Re/code*, May 20, 2015.
22. R. King, "Intelligence Software for Business," *BusinessWeek* podcast, February 27, 2009.
23. R. King, "Intelligence Software for Business," *BusinessWeek* podcast, February 27, 2009.
24. L. Mirani, N. Nisen, "The nine companies that know more about you than Google or Facebook," *Quartz*, May 27, 2014.
25. "FTC Recommends Congress Require the Data Broker Industry to be More Transparent and Give Consumers Greater Control Over Their Personal Information," *U.S. Federal Trade Comission*, May 27, 2014.
26. L. Mirani, N. Nisen, "The nine companies that know more about you than Google or Facebook," *Quartz*, May 27, 2014.
27. R. Mithchell, "Why You Should Be Worried about Your Privacy on the Web," *Computerworld*, May 11, 2009.
28. R. Swarns, "Senator? Terrorist? A Watch List Stops Kennedy at Airport," *New York Times*, August 20, 2004.
29. L. Dignan, "Equifax has spent $242.7 million on its data breach so far," *ZDNet*, April 26, 2017.
30. M. Warman, "Google Warns against Facial Recognition Database," *Telegraph*, May 16, 2011.
31. N. Bilton, "Facebook Changes Privacy Settings to Enable Facial Recognition," *New York Times*, June 7, 2011.
32. A. Gefter and T. Simonite, "What the Data Miners Are Digging Up about You," *CNET*, December 1, 2008.
33. E. Mills, "Report: Social Security Numbers Can Be Predicted," *CNET*, July 6, 2009, http://news.cnet.com/8301-1009_3-10280614-83.html.
34. C. Cadwalladr and E. Graham-Harrison, "Revealed: 50 million Facebook profiles harvested for Cambridge Analytica in major data breach," *The Guardian*, March 17, 2018.
35. L. Spencer, "Australian data laws to mirror the UK, Germany: Fieldfisher," *ZDNet*, June 6, 2014.
36. R. King, "Business Intelligence Software's Time Is Now," *BusinessWeek*, March 2, 2009.
37. N. Ho, "Airbnb uses big data and machine learning to enhance user experience," *ComputerWorld*, June 1, 2017.
38. Unattributed, "Using Data to Help Set Your Price," *Airbnb Blog*, June 4, 2015.
39. H. Taylor, "Airbnb Gives Pricing Tips to Users, Expects Revenue Boost," *CNBC*, May 9, 2016.
40. N. Ho, "Airbnb uses big data and machine learning to enhance user experience," *ComputerWorld*, June 1, 2017.
41. N. Ho, "Airbnb uses big data and machine learning to enhance user experience," *ComputerWorld*, June 1, 2017.
42. R. King, "Intelligence Software for Business," *BusinessWeek* podcast, February 27, 2009.
43. D. Rigby and D. Ledingham, "CRM Done Right," *Harvard Business Review*, November 2004; and R. King, "Intelligence Software for Business," *BusinessWeek* podcast, February 27, 2009.
44. H. Havenstein, "HP Nabs Walmart as Data Warehousing Customer," *Computerworld*, August 1, 2007.
45. Key points adapted from T. Davenport and J. Harris, *Competing on Analytics: The New Science of Winning* (Boston: Harvard Business School Press, 2007).
46. R. King, "Getting a Handle on Big Data with Hadoop," *BusinessWeek*, September 7, 2011.
47. A. McAfee and E. Brynjolfsson, "Big Data: The Management Revolution" *Harvard Business Review*, October 2012.
48. R. King, "Getting a Handle on Big Data with Hadoop," *BusinessWeek*, September 7, 2011.
49. IBM Big Data, "What Is Hadoop?" YouTube video, May 22, 2012, http://www.youtube.com/watch?v=RQr0qd8gxW8.
50. T. Groenfeldt, "Morgan Stanley Takes on Big Data with Hadoop," *Forbes*, May 30, 2012.
51. R. Boucher. "How Big Data Is Influencing Big Companies." *Sloan Management Review*, November 25, 2013.
52. N. Heudecker, "Gartner: Hype Cycle for Big Data, 2013," *Gartner*, July 31, 2103
53. J. Bughin, M. Chui, and J. Manyika, "Ten IT- Enabled Business Trends for the Decade Ahead," *McKinsey Quarterly*, May 2013.
54. S. Buhr, "Apple Launches Beats1, A 24/7 Worldwide Radio Station," *TechCrunch*, June 8, 2015.
55. S. Ransbotham, "Analytics in E Major," *Sloan Management Review*, Feb. 24, 2015.
56. S. Ransbotham, "Analytics in E Major," *Sloan Management Review*, Feb. 24, 2015.
57. C. Wilkinson, "How Pandora's Music Genome Could Fail Against the Likes of Apple," *TheStreet.com,* Oct. 7, 2013.
58. Spotify Information accessed on June 22, 2015 at: https://press.spotify.com/no/information/.
59. J. Constine, "Inside The Spotify—Echo Nest Skunkworks," *TechCrunch*, Oct. 19, 2014.
60. S. Ransbotham, "Analytics in E Major," *Sloan Management Review*, Feb. 24, 2015.
61. S. Ransbotham, "Analytics in E Major," *Sloan Management Review*, Feb. 24, 2015.
62. B. Marr, "The Amazing Ways Spotify Uses Big Data, AI And Machine Learning to Drive Business Success," *Forbes*, Oct. 10, 2017
63. T. Ricker, "First Click: Spotify Running is a surprisingly great music discovery tool," *The Verge*, June 1, 2015.
64. Current stats from: C. Borrington, "Why the Free Version of Spotify Is About to Get a Lot Better," *Slate*, April 24, 2018.
65. B. Marr, "The Amazing Ways Spotify Uses Big Data, AI and Machine Learning to Drive Business Success," *Forbes*, Oct. 10, 2017
66. A. Conry-Murray, "The Pain of E-discovery," *InformationWeek*, June 1, 2009.
67. S. Lohr, "Reaping Results: Data-Mining Goes Mainstream," *New York Times*, May 20, 2007.
68. R. Mulcahy, "ABC: An Introduction to Business Intelligence," *CIO*, March 6, 2007.
69. V. Heffernan, "Big Moose is Watching You," *Medium*, Oct. 31, 2014.
70. C. Wilson and D. Bryan, "Talk: Transitioning from Original Big Data to the New Big Data: L.L.Bean's Journey," at Strata+Hadoop World, Oct. 15–17, 2014, New York, NY.
71. V. Heffernan, "Big Moose is Watching You," *Medium*, Oct. 31, 2014.
72. M. Wilson, "Survey: LLBean.com tops in customer satisfaction among online apparel retailers," ChainStorage (citing J.D. Power and Associates 2012 Online Apparel Retailer Satisfaction Report), Nov. 21, 2012.
73. S. Hansell, "How Wall Street Lied to Its Computers," *New York Times*, September 18, 2008.
74. P. Wahba, "Buffeted 'Quants' Are Still in Demand," *Reuters*, December 22, 2008.
75. Sourced from the Spurious Correlations website, http://www.tylervigen.com, accessed June 4, 2014.
76. J. Stromberg, "Why Google Flu Trends Can't Track the Flu (Yet)," *Smithsonian Magazine*, March 13, 2014. Read more: http://www.smithsonianmag.com/science-nature/why-google-flu-trends-cant-track-flu-yet-180950076/#S0Jo2ITpGsegKVch.99 Give the gift of Smithsonian magazine for only $12! http://bit.ly/1cGUiGv Follow us: @SmithsonianMag on Twitter.
77. B. Helm, "Getting Inside the Customer's Mind," *BusinessWeek*, September 11, 2008.
78. T. Schleifer, "Google CEO Sundar Pichai says AI is more profound than electricity and fire," *Recode*, Jan. 19, 2018.
79. Unattributed, "AI providers will increasingly compete with management consultancies," *The Economist*, March 21, 2018.
80. Unattributed, "Non-tech businesses are beginning to use artificial intelligence at scale," *The Economist*, May 31, 2018.
81. S. Ransbotham, D. Kiron, P. Gerbert, and M. Reeves, "Reshaping Business through AI," *Sloan Management Review*, Sept. 6, 2017.
82. The term "machine learning" is thought to have first been coined by Arthur Samuelin 1959, who referred to it as "the ability to learn without being explicitly programmed." S. Choudhury, "Machines will soon be able to learn without being programmed," *CNBC*, April 27, 2018
83. Fast Company Staff, "How Apple, Facebook, Amazon, and Google Use AI To Best Each Other," *Fast Company*, Oct. 11, 2017. And S. Levy, "The iBrain is Here and It's Already Inside Your Phone," *Wired*, Aug. 24, 2016.
84. For details see Apple's Machine Learning page: https://developer.apple.com/machine-learning/

85. R. Hof, "Meet the Guy Who Helped Google Beat Apple's Siri," *Forbes*, May 1, 2013.

86. Adapted from J. Kahn, "It's Alive," *Wired*, March 2002; O. Port, "Thinking Machines," *BusinessWeek*, August 7, 2000; and L. McKay, "Decisions, Decisions," *CRM Magazine*, May 1, 2009.

87. Unattributed, "AI providers will increasingly compete with management consultancies," *The Economist*, March 31, 2018.

88. Unattributed, "How AI is spreading throughout the supply chain," *The Economist*, March 31, 2018.

89. Unattributed, "Customer service could start living up to its name," *The Economist*, March 31, 2018.

90. A. Voica, "How Ocado uses machine learning to improve customer service," *Ocado Technology Blog*, Oct. 13, 2016.

91. Unattributed, "Managing human resources is about to become easier," *The Economist*, March 31, 2018.

92. Unattributed, "Managing human resources is about to become easier," *The Economist*, March 31, 2018.

93. S. Lohr, "In Case You Wondered, a Real Human Wrote This Column," *The New York Times*, Sept. 10, 2011.

94. S. Podolny, "If an Algorithm Wrote This, How Would You Even Know?" *The New York Times*, March 7, 2015.

95. H. Hodson, "Supercomputers make discoveries that scientists can't," *New Scientist*, Aug. 27, 2014.

96. S. Kohli, "Bill Gates joins Elon Musk and Stephen Hawking in saying artificial intelligence is scary," *Quartz*, Jan. 29, 2015.

97. J. Vincent, "These are three of the biggest problems facing today's AI," *The Verge*, Oct. 10, 2016.

98. S. Ransbotham, D. Kiron, P. Gerbert, and M. Reeves, "Reshaping Business through AI," *MIT Sloan Management Review*, Sept. 6, 2017.

99. U. Kerzel and S. Neubauer, "A Cultural Change—How AI Drives Change Management," *Blue Yonder*, April 27, 2017.

100. C. Miller, "When Algorithms Discriminate," *The New York Times*, July 8, 2015. and B. Goodman and S. Flaxman, "European Union Regulations on Algorithmic Decision Making and a 'Right to Explanation,'" *Oxford Internet Institute*, Aug. 31, 2016.

101. J. Chin and L. Lin, "China's All-Seeing Surveillance State Is Reading Its Citizens' Faces," *The Wall Street Journal*, June 26, 2017.

102. Unattributed, "Non-tech businesses are beginning to use artificial intelligence at scale," *The Economist*, May 31, 2018.

103. Unattributed, "There will be little privacy in the workplace of the future," *The Economist*, March 31, 2018.

104. Unattributed, "The world's most valuable resource is no longer oil, but data," *The Economist*, May 6, 2017.

105. J. Jouvenal, "To find alleged Golden State Killer, investigators first found his great-great-great-grandparents," *The Washington Post*, April 30, 2018.

106. G. Kolata and H. Murphy, "The Golden State Killer Is Tracked Through a Thicket of DNA, and Experts Shudder," *The New York Times*, April 27, 2018.

107. G. Kolata and H. Murphy, "The Golden State Killer Is Tracked Through a Thicket of DNA, and Experts Shudder," *The New York Times*, April 27, 2018.

108. Z. Elinson and E. Schwartzel, "So-Called Golden State Killer Captured, Authorities Say" *The Wall Street Journal*, April 27, 2018.

109. E. Levin, "DNA Technologies 101: Genotyping vs. Sequencing, and What They Mean For You," *Helix*, Aug. 4, 2017.

110. G. Kolata and H. Murphy, "The Golden State Killer Is Tracked Through a Thicket of DNA, and Experts Shudder," *The New York Times*, April 27, 2018.

111. T. Zwilich, "Genealogy Service Helps Catch Golden State Killer," *The Takeaway*, April 30, 2018.

112. From 2006 through 2009, Walmart has appeared as either number one or number two in the *Fortune* 100 rankings.

113. C. Fishman, "The Walmart You Don't Know," *Fast Company*, December 19, 2007.

114. T. Friscia, K. O'Marah, D. Hofman, and J. Souza, "The AMR Research Supply Chain Top 25 for 2009," *AMR Research*, May 28, 2009, http://www.amrresearch.com/Content/View.aspx?compURI=tcm:7-43469.

115. Accessed from CSIMarkets.com, June 20, 2016.

116. C. Fishman, "The Walmart You Don't Know," *Fast Company*, December 19, 2007.

117. D. Joseph, "Supermarket Strategies: What's New at the Grocer," *BusinessWeek*, June 8, 2009.

118. M. Isaac, "Taking Cues from Silicon Valley, Walmart Brings the Shotgun Approach to E-Commerce," *AllThingsD*, March 27, 2013.

119. D. Dorf, "Walmart's Mobile Self-Checking," *Oracle Corporation Insight-Driven Retailing Blog*, September 11, 2012.

120. R. Kim, "Target, Walmart, and Co.: Why Leave Mobile Payments to Others?" *GigaOM*, August 15, 2012.

121. P. Malinowska, "Walmart Bounces Back from MCX Failure," *Shopper Marketing*, Nov. 17, 2017.

122. C. Hays, "What Walmart Knows about Customer Habits," *New York Times*, November 14, 2004.

123. C. Hays, "What Walmart Knows about Customer Habits," *New York Times*, November 14, 2004.

124. B. Marr, "Really Big Data At Walmart: Real-Time Insights From Their 40+ Petabyte Data Cloud," Forbes, Jan. 23, 2017.

125. R. King, "Getting a Handle on Big Data with Hadoop," *BusinessWeek*, September 7, 2011.

126. C. Nicholson, "Walmart Buys Social Media Firm Kosmix," *New York Times*, April 19, 2011.

127. M. Isaac, "Taking Cues from Silicon Valley, Walmart Brings the Shotgun Approach to E-Commerce," *AllThingsD*, March 27, 2013.

128. D. Harris, "Walmart Keeps Getting Smarter with Inkiru Acquisition," *GigaOM*, June 10, 2013.

129. K. Evans-Correia, "Dillman Replaced as Walmart CIO," *SearchCIO*, April 6, 2006.

130. M. McCoy, "Walmart's Data Center Remains Mystery," *Joplin Globe*, May 28, 2006.

131. J. Bowman, "1 Year Later, Wal-Mart's Jet.com Acquisition Is an Undeniable Success," *The Motley Fool*, Oct. 3, 2017.

132. C. Fishman, "The Walmart You Don't Know," *Fast Company*, December 19, 2007.

CHAPTER 9

Dirty Data, Analytical Design, and Data Visualization

9.1 What Is Dirty Data and Why Should You Avoid It?

What is Dirty Data?

Dirty data is data that contains some sort of error. The problem with dirty data is that when you analyze it, it may give you incorrect results, which can lead to poor decision making. Good decision making from data analysis begins with good, clean data.

Dirty data can come from several different sources. Some data is obviously incorrect. Data can be typed incorrectly, misspelled, or otherwise entered incorrectly. Dirty data can also come from incomplete data where a record doesn't include all of the necessary data or is outdated. On the other end of the spectrum, data can be perfectly correct but still dirty if it is needlessly duplicated, such as having the same customer entered twice or having an app registered in a store more than once.

It is often impractical and nearly impossible to get perfect data, especially in very large sets of data. Fortunately, there are ways to protect against dirty data and ways to scrub the data clean before you analyze it to help make more informed decisions.

Sources of Dirty Data

View the video online at: http://www.youtube.com/embed/h12MQ3d1Z1Y?rel=0

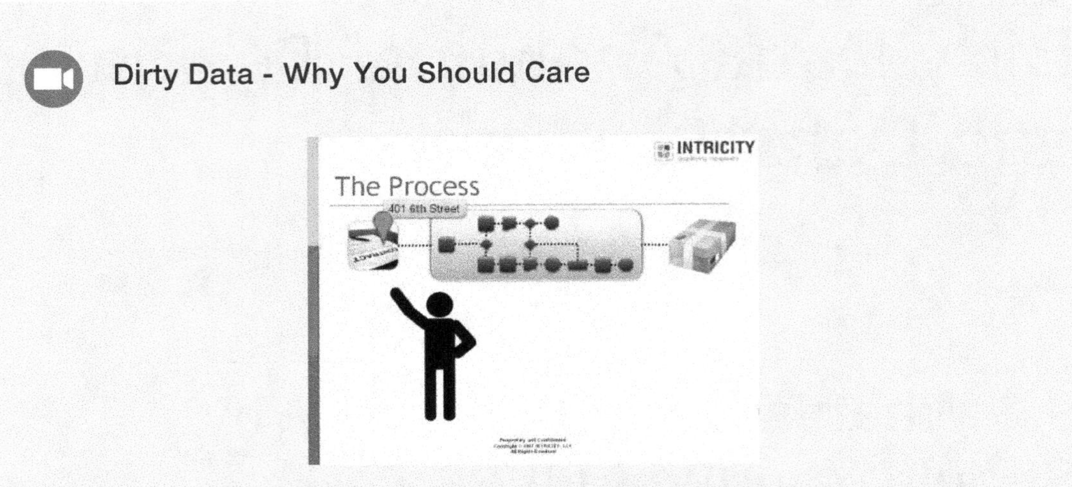

View the video online at: http://www.youtube.com/embed/yVXYfXylFKg?rel=0

Don't Use Dirty Data

View the video online at: http://www.youtube.com/embed/GfTJFjYi5eQ?rel=0

Preventing Dirty Data in Excel

The best time to clean data is at the time it is entered. It is easier to fix errors before they get into your data than after the fact. Six database management controls help:

1. Data validation
2. Menu-based questions
3. Primary keys
4. Referential integrity
5. Domains
6. Logic rules

Of these controls, only data validation and menu-based questions are typically built into spreadsheets. Why? Because spreadsheets are not true database products. Database products are more difficult to learn, less visual, and less intuitive in their interface. Therefore, the more familiar, visual, and intuitive spreadsheet is often used to manage data. As a result, it is important to learn how to clean up the errors that make their way into the data. Below we describe ways to protect your data on input and the consequences of not having those protections. After, we will describe how to clean up the errors that make it through the gate.

Data Validation - Supported

Data validation on input forms provide pattern- or range-based constraints on the values that can be entered. The email and URL fields on the store input forms both contain data validation to test for well-formed patterns:

- An email must be of the form **something@something.something**
- A URL must begin with **https://**
- A field can not be left blank

These constraints help but are not perfect. For example, the user could still enter their information in any combination of upper/lower case. The email address and URL could still point to nonexistent accounts and pages, respectively.

Menu-Based Questions - Supported

Menu-based questions such as multiple choice, radio buttons, or drop-down menus constrain what the user can enter from a predefined list. Our catalog form contained many multiple choice questions. For example, "Where do you live?" with on campus and off campus as the choices. Menu-based questions form very robust data controls, though they might be somewhat limiting in not accounting for all possible options.

Primary Keys - NOT Supported

Primary keys are unique identifiers for each record in a table. This means that defining a field as the primary key guarantees that you will not have duplicate records because, at a minimum, the primary key values would NOT be the same.

The absence of primary keys allows duplicate or nearly duplicate records to creep into our data and we will need to eliminate them. In general, we will assume that the latest record is the most valid and remove the older duplicates.

Referential Integrity - NOT Supported

Referential integrity specifies that there be no unmatched foreign key values. Every child record must have a parent. Catalog is the parent table and Sales is the child. We should not allow a sale unless the app is listed in the catalog.

Because our customers are also our app designers, we should not allow a sale unless the customer is in the catalog. Again, Catalog is the parent table and Sales is the child.

We do not enforce referential integrity in our database design, so referential integrity violations will need to be cleaned up. There will be sales for apps that don't exist; there will be sales made by customers that don't exist. If we can figure out which parent record should have been referenced, then we will edit and fix the child record, otherwise we need to eliminate the child record.

Domains - NOT Supported

Domains specify a set of allowable values for any field. For example, email addresses must come from the set of email addresses for students registered in the class.

We need to remove/convert email addresses that are not proper university email addresses. If a student uses their Gmail or other address by mistake, then those records must be edited or eliminated.

Logic Rules - NOT Supported

To some extent all the constraints listed above are logic rules. However, here we are talking about rules to address errors that could pass through the other filters. For example, each user should be allowed to buy only one copy of a given app. Each user should be allowed to register their app only once. Technically, these situations do not represent duplicates because the time stamps are different.

We need to remove near duplicates when logic tells us that the duplicate records do not belong.

Cleaning Dirty Data

Note that the violations described above require action to clean the data. It is a good idea to wait until the data is completely collected to take these actions. Otherwise, we will have to repeat the process as new data is entered. When you consider these data management issues, you begin to see why large company databases should be stored in a database management system. Nevertheless, data entry errors are common and we should know how to clean them up.

Download to Excel

The data is in Google Sheets format. Data manipulation is easier in Excel. The first step is to download the sheet and then open it in Excel. Click on the download link in the store to begin.

Remove Duplicates

Duplicate or nearly duplicate records (for example, records that differ in the timestamp only) materially represent the same data. To remove duplicates, we need to:

1. Sort the records by date
2. Determine which set of fields should not be repeated
3. [Optional] Conditional Formatting > Highlight Cell Rules > Duplicate values
4. Remove the earlier duplicate records using Data > Remove Duplicates

We remove the earlier duplicate records under the assumption that the user would have made a new entry because they perceive a problem with the prior entry.

Referential Integrity

Use the match function in order to find referential integrity violations. A record in the child table without a matching parent needs to either be assigned a parent or removed from the table.

Group Application 11.1: Data Cleaning

	A	B	C	D
1	Timestamp	App	App URL	Your OU Email
2	4/7/2015 0:22:30	Inveigle	http://sites.google.com/site/inveigleal	jw389513@ohio.edu
3	4/7/2015 0:23:09	Kickback	http://sites.google.com/site/grouphangout12	jw389513@ohio.edu
4	4/7/2015 0:24:48	CampusCrowControl	http://sites.google.com/Campuscrowdcontrol/test	jw389513@ohio.edu
5	4/7/2015 0:25:20	EmergenSee	https://sites.google.com/site/emergenseetyler	jw389513@hio.edu
6	4/7/2015 0:26:39	The Land	http://sites.google.com/siteclevelandtheland216440/	jw389513@ohio.edu
7	4/7/2015 0:27:31	SnapKing	http://sites.google.com/site/snapkingofficial	jw389513@ohio.edu
8	4/7/2015 0:28:19	The Cal	https://sites.google.com/site/martysappssite/	jw389513@ohio.edu
9	4/7/2015 0:29:05	Grocery Pro	http://sites.google.com/site/GroceryProSlavik	jw389513@ohio.edu
10	4/7/2015 0:29:26	Fashion Finder	https://sites.google.com/site/fashionfindergrozenski/	jw389513@ohio.edu
11	4/7/2015 0:30:32	wardrobifier	https://sites.google.com/site/wardrobifier/	jw389513@ohio.edu
12	4/7/2015 0:34:44	ApolloMusic	http://sites.google.com/site/Apolloonline	sp043913@ohio.edu
13	4/7/2015 0:40:20	ApolloMusic	http://sites.google.com/site/Apolloonline	jw389513@ohio.edu
14	4/7/2015 0:43:51	College Bizznus	https://sites.google.com/site/collegebizznus/	jw389513@ohio.edu
15	4/7/2015 0:52:44	wardrobifier	https://sites.google.com/site/wardrobifier/	jw389513@ohio.edu

1. On the Data tab, Excel has a built in button to eliminate duplicates in a table. Which fields or fields together should be chosen to eliminate duplicates in the Sales table?
   A. Timestamp
   B. App & App URL
   C. App, App URL, and Your OU Email

Excel has many text filter options:

- Equals
- Does Not Equal
- Begins With
- Does Not Begin With
- Ends With
- Does Not End With
- Contains
- Does Not Contain
- Custom Filter

You can combine two filters with AND or OR.

Use ? to represent any single character.

Use * to represent any series of characters.

2. Which filter would best show invalid OU email addresses?
   A. Does Not Contain @ohio.edu
   B. Does Not Contain @*.edu
   C. Does Not End With @ohio.edu
   D. Does Not End With @*.edu
3. Which filter would best show invalid URLs?
   A. Does Not Begin With http://sites.google.com/site/
   B. Does Not Begin With https://sites.google.com/site/
   C. Does Not Begin With http://sites.google.com/site/ AND Does Not Begin With https://sites.google.com/site/
   D. Does Not Begin With http://sites.google.com/site/ OR Does Not Begin With https://sites.google.com/site/
4. It would be better to avoid these data issues than to have to fix them later. Looking at the Sales table and entry form, what could we ask a software developer to do to ***prevent*** these problems in the future?

Exercise 11.1: Cleaning Dirty Data

As you learned in this unit you need good data to support good decision-making. Although you can prevent a significant amount of dirty data through the use of carefully designed form-based questions, data validation, and specific database features, it is very difficult to prevent all dirty data. Even in our simple class store we run into multiple kinds of dirty data, and this dirty data must be scrubbed clean before it is analyzed.

In this exercise you will identify errors in the catalog and sales data collected from our class store. Before you even started buying apps, your professor had to scrub some dirty data from in the Catalog table because a number of apps had been registered in the Catalog section more than once. You are responsible for finding the dirty data issues listed under the Sales table and issues between the Catalog and Sales tables – where the data between them might not sync up correctly.

To begin, go to your class store for this semester. Click the 'Download App Catalog Data to Excel' link and Click **File** > **Download As** > **Microsoft Excel.** Now download the sales data from the 'Download Sales Data to Excel' link in the same manner**.** Once both files have been opened in Excel, combine the sheets into the same workbook. Convert each sheet of data into a table. Save it as Semester Year YourLastName (e.g. Fall 2015 Kenyo).

Catalog Table (Identified and Fixed By Your Professor)

Even though we tried to protect against dirty data by using a form for App registration into the Catalog, there were still errors. Some came from the open-ended entry boxes (incorrect URLs, Last name and First name switched, spaces in the App Name, etc.), and some apps were registered with correct data, but they were registered more than once. We know that duplicated data is dangerous because one of the records may be different than the other, which can create many problems. In our Catalog table, these were the most duplication issues found (and fixed).

- Duplicated URL (meaning the app site was registered more than once)
- Combination of App Name AND email repeated (meaning an app creator registered more than one app or one app under two different URLs) *Caution: App Name alone wasn't compared because two developers might have used the same name
- Near duplicate: App Name doesn't match because of word spacing

Sales Table Duplicates (To Be Identified By You)

In the sales table, some apps were purchased more than once by the same customer. (Usually the 'culprit' is the creator testing to make sure that the buy button works correctly.) Use the 'Remove Duplicates' button to identify how many records are duplicated by comparing the URL and the email address of the buyer. Delete the duplicated records.

Catalog and Sales Tables Lack Referential Integrity

As you read in this unit, referential integrity in a relational database essentially means that a field in one table should match a field in a related table. For example, the URL you use to register the app should be the same URL recorded for each purchase of the app. (This, by the way, is why it was so important to make sure those matched when you registered your app and created your Buy button.) There are several dirty data issues prevalent in our class store data. You will use the Match function to identify this type of dirty data.

Create a column in your spreadsheet for each of the 4 scenarios below. Use the Match function to find matching records. N/A results indicate mismatched, e.g. dirty data.

1. Do all apps names in the sales records match the app names in the Catalog
2. Does the developer email match the purchaser email? (This could also indicate a developer not purchasing any apps)
3. Do the Sales and Catalog registration URLs match?
4. Are the sales for each app recorded under the same category with which it was registered?

Create another column and count the number of dirty data issues in each sales record.

Now in a last column (leave at least one blank column between this cell and the table), count the total records with no issues and compare that to the total number of records in the table by calculating the percentage of records that had no issues. The rest of the records have dirty data issues that would need to be fixed or thrown out before completing any analysis.

Submitting your Exercise

Please submit your Excel file in the submission area.

Follow this link to the Excel file and video tutorial: http://tinyurl.com/zm59sa9

9.2 Tufte Principles of Analytical Design

What Are the Principles?

There are sound principles for the display of quantitative information. Perhaps the greatest theorist in the quantitative arena is Edward Tufte. He has written a number of books and articles on the subject and draws huge audiences worldwide when he speaks.

Tufte virtually founded the field of analytical design—the field that studies how best to represent information—especially quantitative information. He has developed a number of principles over the years. However, in *Beautiful Evidence*[1] he organized the principles under six major headings:

1. **Comparisons**: Show comparisons, contrasts, differences. Comparison is the fundamental act in statistics. Always ask the question, "Compared to what?" The comparison often is in time, such as a trend over the last five years. A comparison of multiple trends would be even better. Comparisons inform and invite reflection by the reader. For example, showing the growth rate of platforms using the Mac iOS vs. other smartphone operating systems helps show whose market share is growing or shrinking.

2. **Causality**: Show Causality, Mechanism, Systematic Structure, Explanation. If one variable causes another, then show both on the same graph. Sometimes the data clearly suggest a cause or lack of a cause. For example, many predicted a drop in iPhone 4 sales after news that the antenna dropped calls when the phone was held in a certain way. However, the predicted sales drop during "antennagate" was not borne out by the data, and the product launch was wildly successful.

3. **Multivariate Analysis**: Show more than one or two variables. It is a complex world, the more variables you show, the better chance that you have of offering an explanation. For example, it is better to show sales of paid apps *and* sales of free apps across all platforms on the same graph.

4. **Integration of Evidence**: Completely integrate words, numbers, images, diagrams. Annotate key data points on the graph. As a courtesy to the reader, include explanations right on the graph rather than burying them in the text. For example, on a time series label key events.

5. **Documentation**: Thoroughly describe the evidence. Provide a detailed title, indicate the authors and sponsors, document the data sources, show complete measurement scales, point out relevant issues. Documentation establishes the credibility of the evidence. Are these numbers something that we should believe? For example, always show your data sources, and list your name as an author. If the data only holds under certain conditions, then state what those are.

6. **Content Counts Most of All**: Analytical presentations ultimately stand or fall depending on the quality, relevance, and integrity of their content. The only reason to have data is to help further an explanation. Any data that does not help clarify the relevant issues should be omitted. If your data is no good, then get better data!

The following table repeats the six principles and can be used as a way to critique information displays. For each principle, if the display exhibits the principle then indicate how; if not then put N/A.

This is a graph of...	
Analytical Design Principle	Example From This Graphic
Comparisons: Show comparisons, contrasts, differences.	
Causality: Show Causality, Mechanism, Structure, Explanation.	
Multivariate Analysis: Show more than one or two variables.	
Integration of Evidence: Completely integrate words, numbers, images, diagrams.	
Documentation: Thoroughly describe the evidence and sources.	
Content: Quality, relevance, and integrity of content.	

It is much easier to understand the principles by looking at an example. Minard's map of Napoleon's March on Moscow, available at https://www.edwardtufte.com/tufte/minard, embodies all six principles.

Napoleon's March on Moscow

Tufte at the Metropolitan Museum of Art explaining his Grand Principles

View the video online at: http://www.youtube.com/embed/HfXSltIDfDw?rel=0

Graph Design Principles

Notice the graphs on the following page. The "after" graph has six design improvements over the first. They deal specifically with formatting the graph to maximize information transfer to the reader. Most of the graph design guidelines come from Edward Tufte's principles of analytical design. These principles require refining the graph after Excel has applied its default settings.

Though the design of a graph is important, the content is even more crucial to the delivery of information. Graphs can have good design, but if the data or content is flawed, the graph has no purpose. The data on the X and Y axis of a graph should always have some correlation, or some relationship that can be demonstrated.

Before: While this graph looks cool, there is no scale. What quantities do the bars represent?

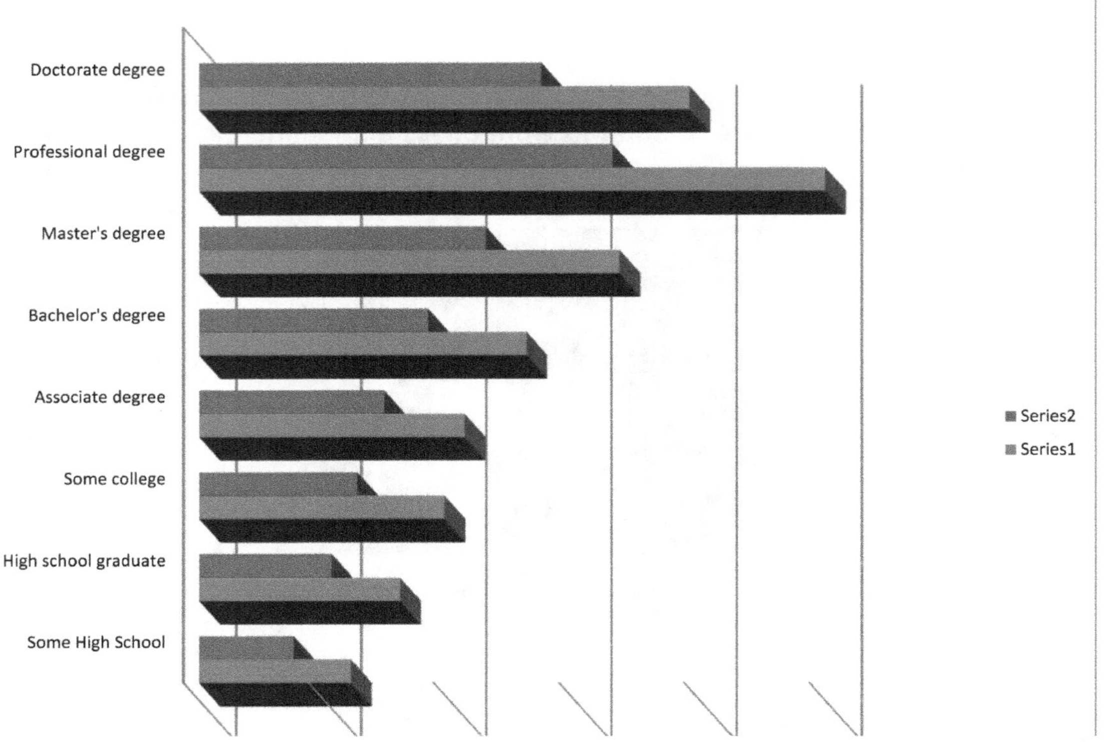

After: Even though this graph is somewhat dull, it conveys information far more effectively.

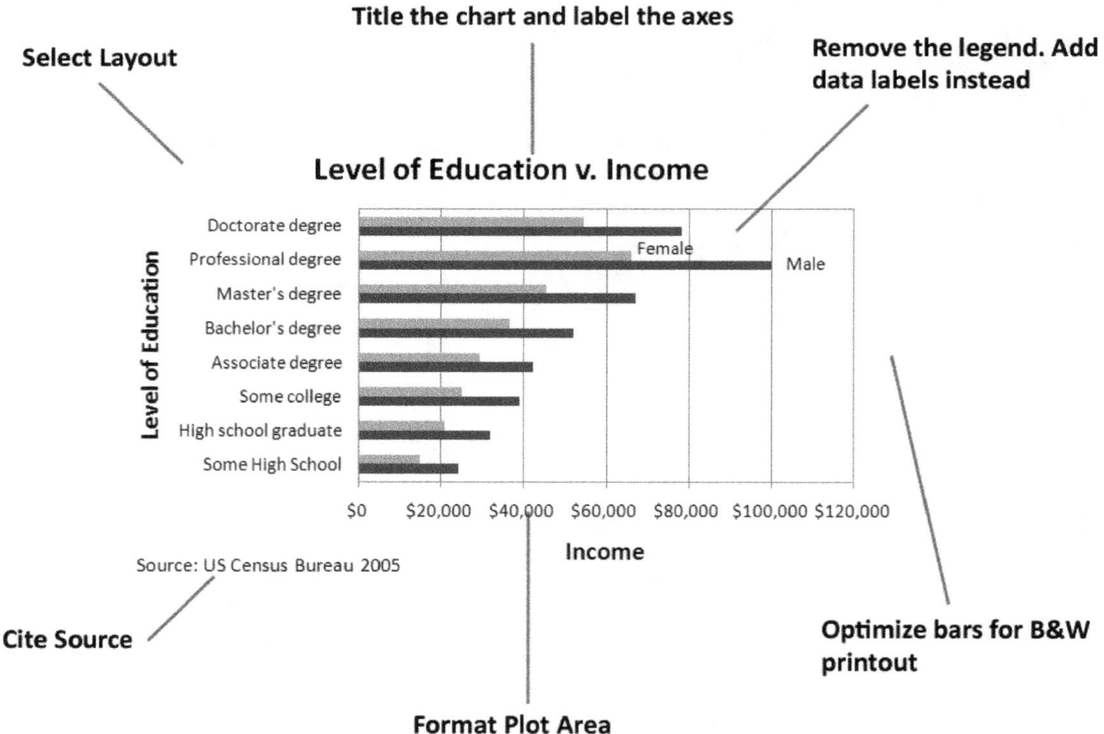

Matching Graph to Data Type

After you establish the integrity and relevance of the content, you will next need to focus on the type of graph you will use to display the information. Most business graphs (bar graphs, line graphs, and pie charts) compare categories on a quantitative dimension. For example, comparing salaries for persons of different education levels.

Bar graph. Bar graphs are used to compare discrete categories on a common measure. In other words, the measure is quantitative and the categories are qualitative. For example, compare sales figures (quantitative) in different geographic regions (qualitative).

Line graph. Line graphs compare continuous categories on a common measure. They are often seen in business, especially to show trends over time. The time appears on the X axis, and the quantitative data to be measured appears on the Y axis. Examples are sales, stock market trends, or mortgage rates over time. A text box is often placed near these graphs to explain the reasoning behind changes in trends.

Pie chart. Much like a bar graph, a pie chart compares discrete categories on a common measure. Unlike a bar graph, a pie chart can only show one series of data. Although pie charts are commonly used in the media, a bar graph is a better way to convey the same information in a way that allows for much easier comparisons between categories. The relative height of bars is easier to compare than pie slices that must be mentally rotated and aligned for comparison. Bar graphs also allow for multiple data series to be compared on the same graph, but pie charts are limited to one data series. Overall, pie charts should be avoided.

Scatterplots. Scatterplots do the best job of adhering to Tufte's principles of showing multivariate data and causal relationships. In a scatterplot, both sets of data are quantitative. The cause (independent variable) appears on the X axis, and the effect (dependent variable) appears on the Y axis. For example, in economics, scatterplots can be used to show trends in price versus demand. Greater demand for a product or service (independent variable) leads to higher price (dependent variable). In spite of their explanatory power, scatterplots are rarely found in business.

Bar graph

Compares discrete (distinct) categories on a common measure.

Line graph

Compares continuous categories such as time on a common measure.

Pie chart

Compares discrete categories on a common measure.

Scatterplots

Suggests causality by plotting independent and dependent variables on the same graph.

Bar Graph - Compares categories

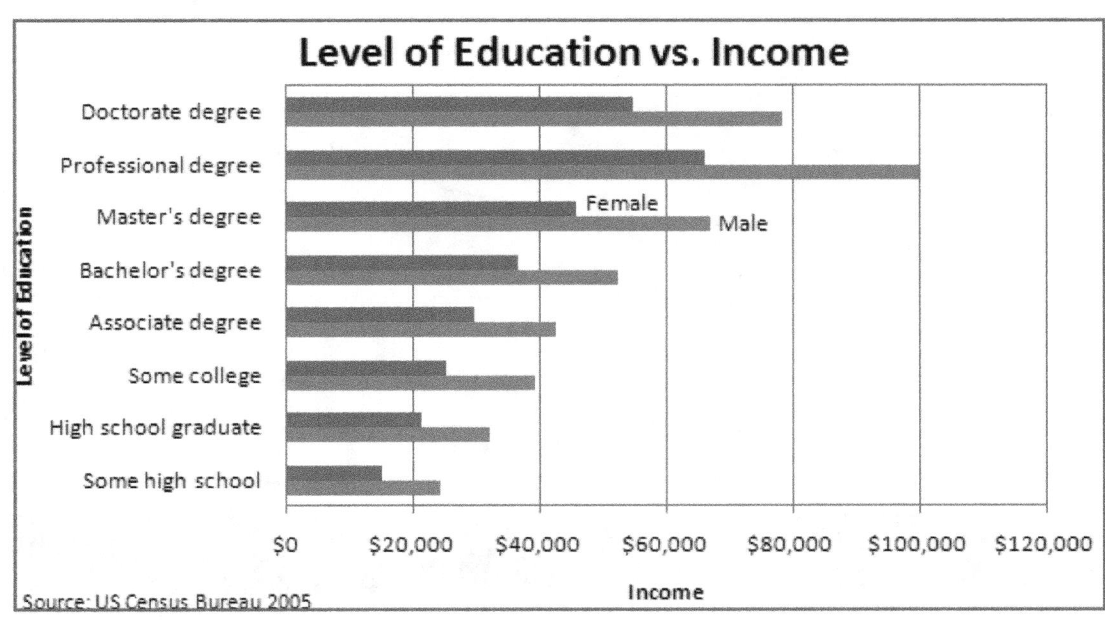

Line Graph - Shows trends

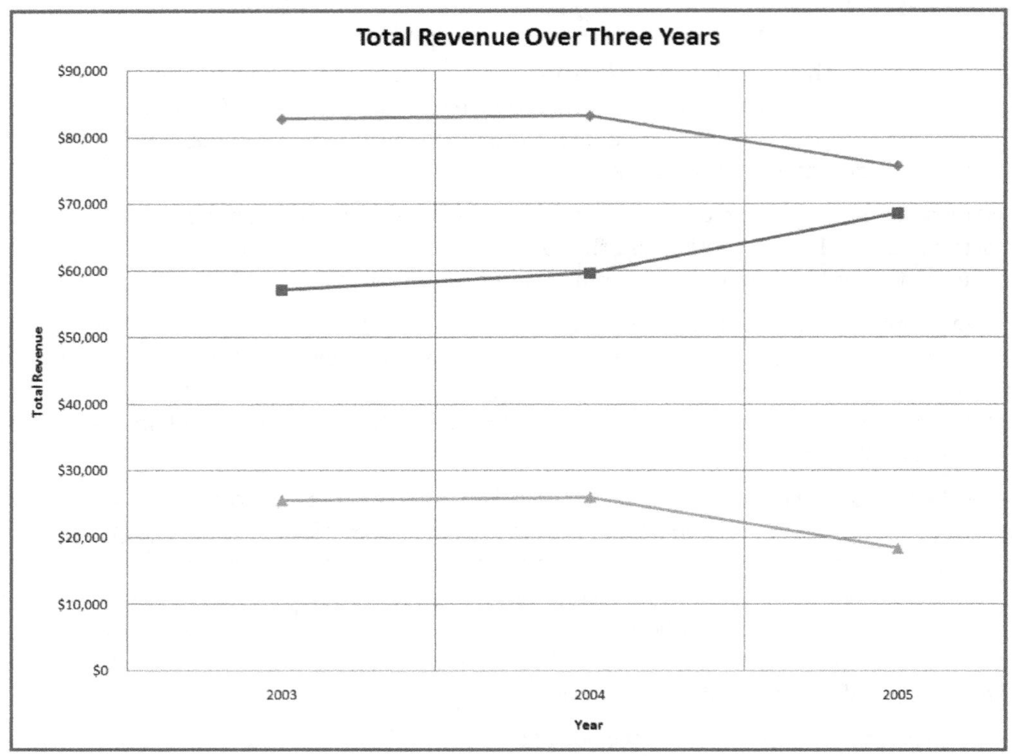

Scatterplot - Shows causal relationships

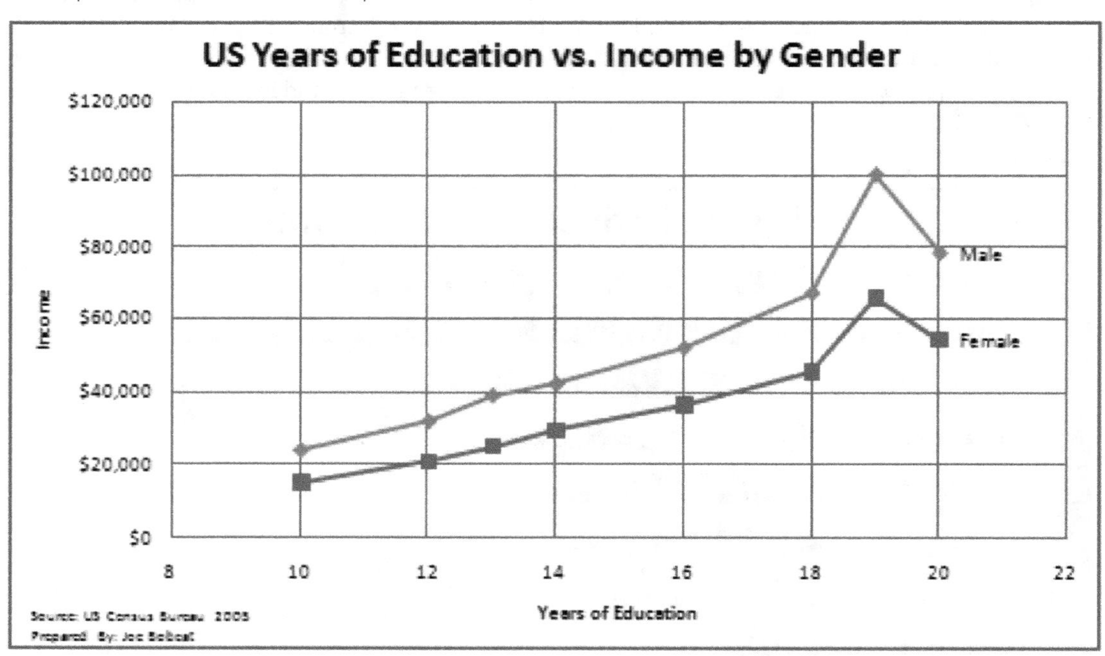

Group Application 13.1a: Analytical Design

Evaluate the graphic at Information is Beautiful (http://www.informationisbeautiful.net/visualizations/when-sea-levels-attack-2/) using the Tufte Principles.

This is a graph of...	
Analytical Design Principle	Example From This Graphic
Comparisons: Show comparisons, contrasts, differences.	
Causality: Show Causality, Mechanism, Structure, Explanation.	
Multivariate Analysis: Show more than one or two variables.	
Integration of Evidence: Completely integrate words, numbers, images, diagrams.	
Documentation: Thoroughly describe the evidence and sources.	
Content: Quality, relevance, and integrity of content.	

Group Application 13.1b: Choose The Best Graph

Choose the best graph—provide a reason for each choice. (Examples adapted from *The Wall Street Journal Guide to Information Graphics*)

1) Choice/Reason:

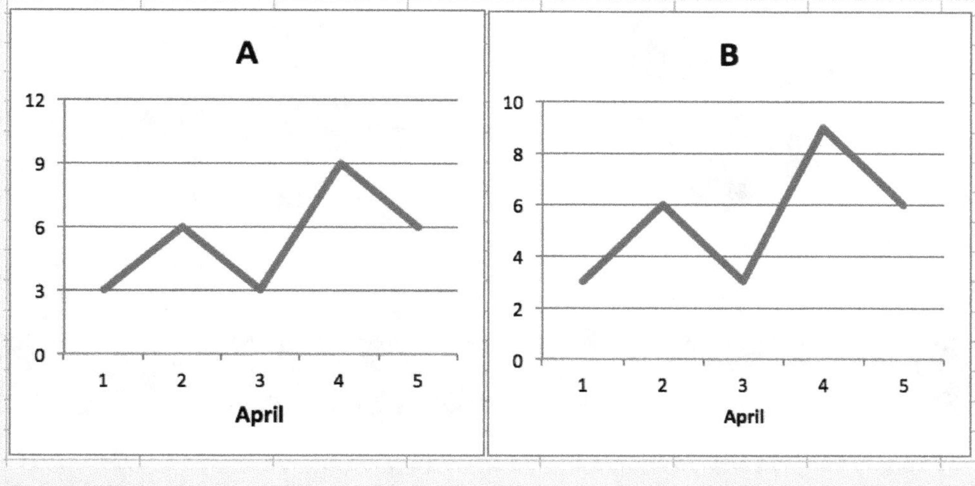

2) Choice/Reason:

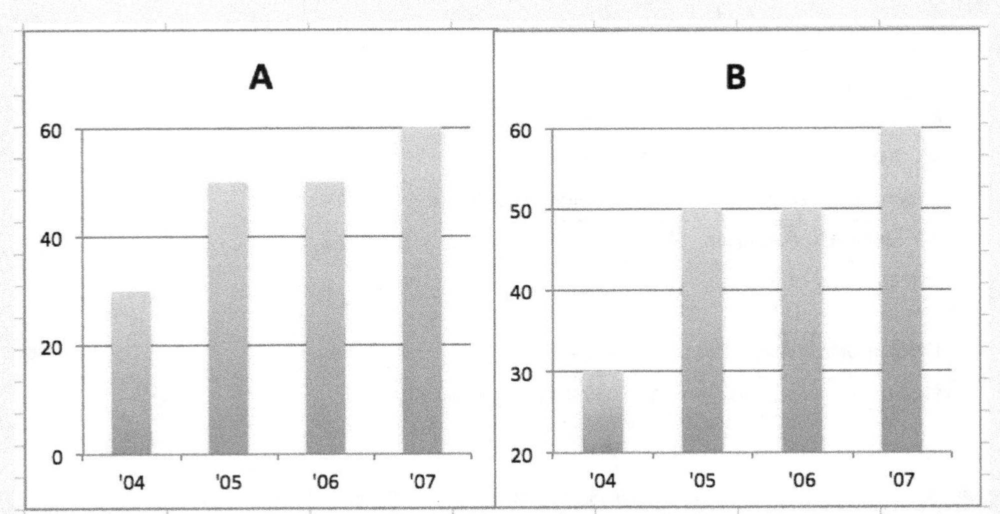

3) Choice/Reason:

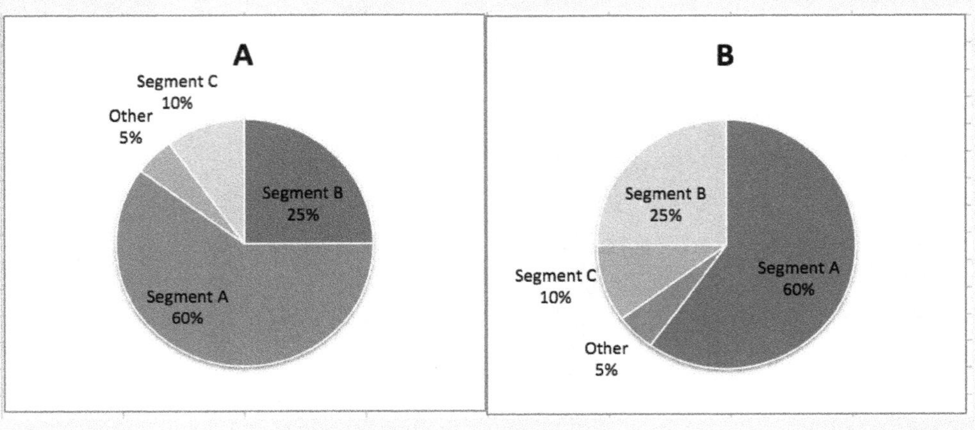

Exercise 13.1: Evaluate Graphics

We are bombarded by data every day. In magazines, newspapers and online. Social media sites, for example, flood us with us with all sorts of data every time we sign in. To make sense of large amount of data, it is often displayed in a chart or graph. When created carefully and specifically, graphics transfer a huge amount of data to readers, enabling them to learn and retain much more than if the data was all written out as text.

However, not all graphics are created with care. They may be put together hastily. Unknowingly, bad data could be used. Even worse, data can be cherry picked to deliberately skew the results. These graphics may then misrepresent the data and disseminate bad information.

So how can you avoid the above pitfalls and create truthful, clear and information-dense graphics? Follow Tufte's Principles of Analytical Design. As you read in Tufte's principles of analytical design, there are particular components and features of analytical design, such as showing comparison, causality and documentation that should be used when creating graphics. In this exercise you will apply those 6 analytical design principles to critically evaluate information displays.

To begin, visit either or both of these websites:

www.edwardtufte.com

http://www.informationisbeautiful.net

Choose and copy three graphics. Then evaluate each graphic according to Tufte's principles using the template introduced in this chapter. If the graphic does not exhibit a principle, then you should put n/a in that row. Ideally, each graphic and evaluation table would be on a single page in your document. See the following three student examples as a guide, and please do not choose the same graphics used in these examples.

When you have completed 3 evaluations, make sure your name is included in the footer (bottom section) of the page and submit your Word document into the submission area online.

Student Example: See the graphic at http://www.informationisbeautiful.net/visualizations/best-in-show-whats-the-top-data-dog/ and consider these questions.

Tufte Principles	Yes/No? Why
Comparisons	Yes, the graph is comparing which types of dogs are publicly popular and some that are overlooked.
Causality	N/A. No variable causes another. It is a scatter of information.
Multivariate Analysis	Yes, it shows multiple variables such as a Saint Bernard and a Basset Hound.
Integration of Evidence	Yes, instead of just using the type of dog it has a silhouette of the dog and it shows the information in a graph form. Also, it has an index on the top to show for example if the dog is a working dog or a hound.
Documentation	Yes, David McCandless made the graph and the sources are provided by the American Kennel Club.
Content Counts Most of All	Yes, the data shown does help further the explanation that shows which dogs are best in show. Only the data that is necessary is included in the graph.

9.3 The Beauty of Data Visualization

David McCandless: The Billion-Dollar-O-Gram

David McCandless is a British data-journalist and information designer based in London. He is the founder of the visual blog *Information Is Beautiful.* His interactive graphs are good examples of Tufte's principles of analytical design. Through comparisons, McCandless shows the most relevant information.

Review The Billion-Dollar-O-Gram at http://www.informationisbeautiful.net/visualizations/the-billion-dollar-o-gram-2009/.

The Beauty of Data Visualization by David McCandless

View the video online at: http://www.youtube.com/embed/5Zg-C8AAIGg?rel=0

Group Application 13.2: Choose the Best Graph

Choose the Best Graph—Provide a Reason for Each Choice

1. **Reason:**

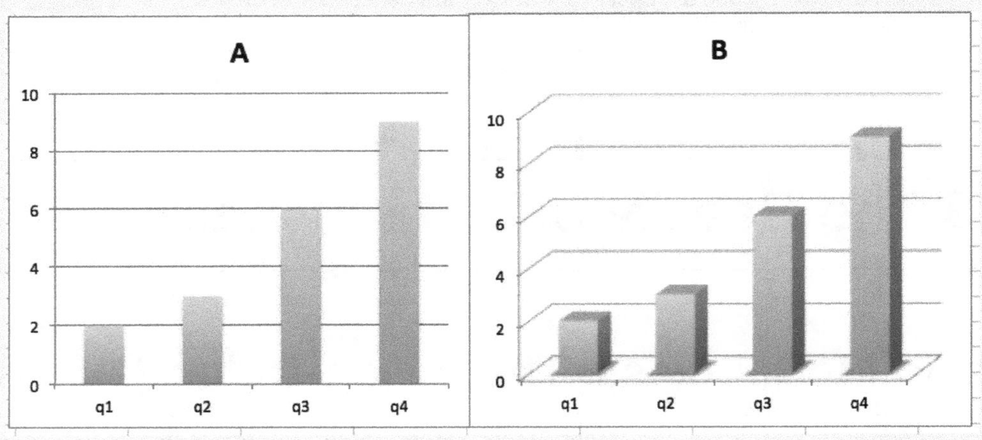

2. **Reason:**

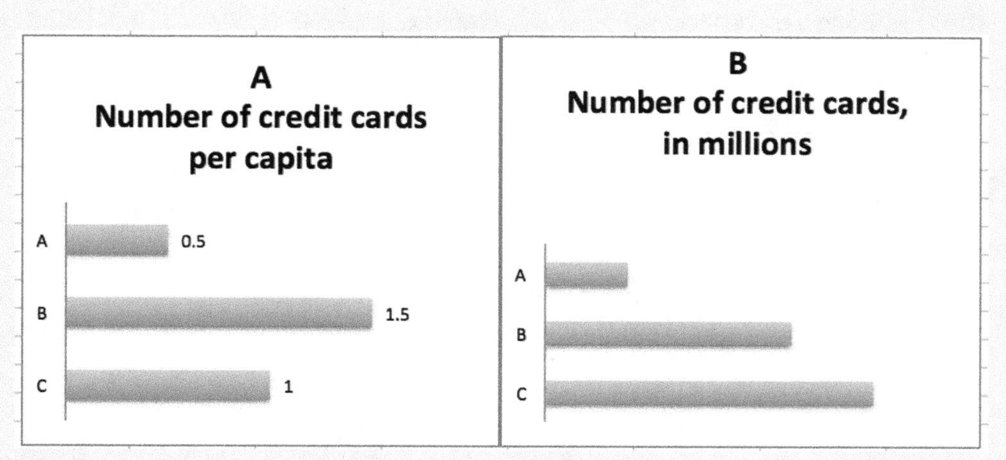

3. **Reason:**

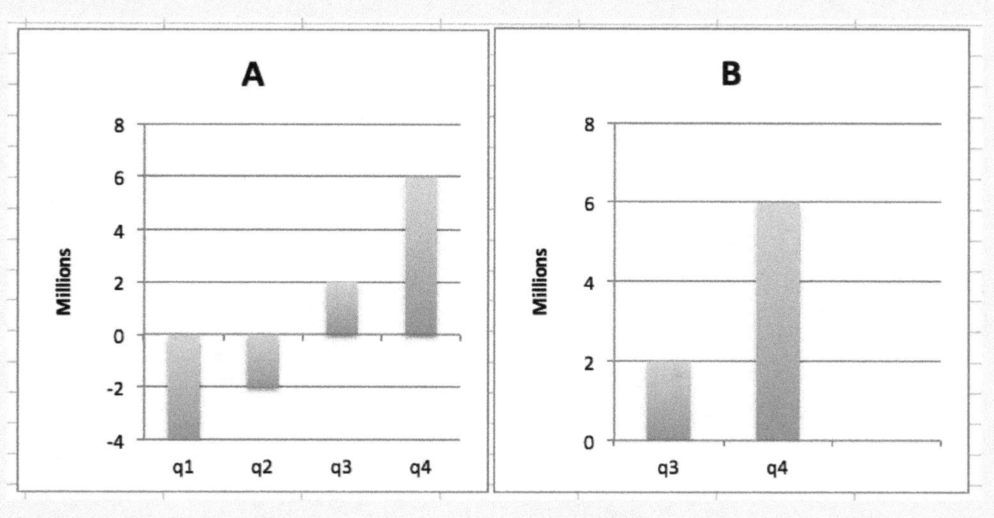

Exercise 13.2: Infographic

You have analyzed the sales from your class store in several exercises. Now you want to focus on your app, where you stand in your category and the store, and what you could do to improve your current competitive position. (If your app has no sales data, please choose another app from your category and note that in your write-up.)

In Excel Please create a 1-2 tab analysis of your app's competitive position. Though it is in Excel, the analysis should include lots of write up in text boxes.

First determine your competitors. For most apps competitors come from your own category, but not always. You might also get a hint by examining your cross sell data from a previous exercise. You will then have to visit sites and make a determination if they really are a competitor.

We are interested in documenting comparisons between you and the competition. We collected demographic data on each sale and want to see whether there are any interesting differences among each of the competitors with the different demographics. For example:

- Sales with men/with women
- Sales off/on campus
- and so forth...

For any area that you find a significant difference you should produce a chart as well.

Then write up your findings in text boxes.

Follow this link to the video tutorial: http://tinyurl.com/zm59sa9

Endnotes

1. Tufte, Edward R. Beautiful Evidence. Cheshire, CT: Graphics Press, 2006.

EDITED

CHAPTER 10

Understanding Software: A Primer for Managers

10.1 Introduction

Learning Objectives

1. Recognize the importance of software and its implications for the firm and strategic decision making.
2. Understand that software is everywhere; not just in computers, but also cell phones, cars, cameras, and many other technologies.
3. Know what software is and be able to differentiate it from hardware.
4. List the major classifications of software and give examples of each.

We know **computing hardware** is getting faster and cheaper, creating all sorts of exciting and disruptive opportunities for the savvy manager. But what's really going on inside the box? It's **software** that makes the magic of computing happen. Without software, your PC would be a heap of silicon wrapped in wires encased in plastic and metal. But it's the instructions—the software code—that enable a computer to do something wonderful, driving the limitless possibilities of information technology.

computer hardware

The physical components of information technology, which can include the computer itself plus peripherals such as storage devices, input devices like the mouse and keyboard, output devices like monitors and printers, networking equipment, and so on.

software

A computer program or a collection of programs. It is a precise set of instructions that tells hardware what to do.

Software is everywhere. An inexpensive "dumb" cell phone has about 1 million lines of code.[1] Ford automobiles actually have more lines of code than Twitter and Facebook combined.[2] Software might even be in grandpa. The average pacemaker has between 80,000 and 100,000 lines of code.[3] In this chapter we'll take a peek inside the chips to understand what software is. A lot of terms are associated with software: operating systems, applications, enterprise software, distributed systems, and more. We'll define these terms up front, and put them in a managerial context. A follow-up chapter, [Content Removed: #fwk-38086-ch10], will focus on changes impacting the software business, including open source software, software as a service (SaaS), cloud computing, virtualization, and the rise of apps. These changes are creating an environment radically different from the software industry that existed in previous decades—confronting managers with a whole new set of opportunities and challenges.

Managers who understand software can better understand the possibilities and impact of technology. They can make better decisions regarding the strategic value of IT and the potential for technology-driven savings. They can appreciate the challenges, costs, security vulnerabilities, legal and compliance issues, and limitations involved in developing and deploying technology solutions. And since firms that cannot communicate will struggle to work in tandem, managers who understand software can appreciate the key role that technology plays in partnerships, merger and acquisitions, and firm valuation. Given the pervasiveness of tech in all managerial disciplines, a firm without technologists in the boardroom is setting itself up for failure. In the next two chapters we will closely examine the software industry and discuss trends, developments and economics—all of which influence decisions managers make about products to select, firms to partner with, and firms to invest in.

What Is Software?

When we refer to computer hardware (sometimes just hardware), we're talking about the physical components of information technology—the equipment that you can physically touch, including computers, storage devices, networking equipment, and other peripherals.

Software refers to a computer program or collection of programs—sets of instructions that tell the hardware what to do. Software gets your computer to behave like a Web browser or word processor, lets your smartphone play music and video, and enables your bank's ATM to spit out cash.

It's when we start to talk about the categories of software that most people's eyes glaze over. To most folks, software is a big, incomprehensible alphabet soup of acronyms and geeky phrases: API, ERP, OS, SQL, to name just a few.

operating system

The software that controls the computer hardware and establishes standards for developing and executing applications.

applications

Includes desktop applications, enterprise software, utilities, and other programs that perform specific tasks for users and organizations.

Don't be intimidated. The basics are actually pretty easy to understand. But it's not soup; it's more of a layer cake. Think about computer hardware as being at the bottom of the layer cake. The next layer is the **operating system**, the collection of programs that control the hardware. Windows, Mac OS X, iOS, and Linux are operating systems. On top of that layer are **applications**—a range of which include end-user programs like those in Office, apps that run on smartphones, and the complex set of programs that manage a business's inventory, payroll, and accounting. At the top of the cake are users.

FIGURE 10.1 The Hardware/Software Layer Cake

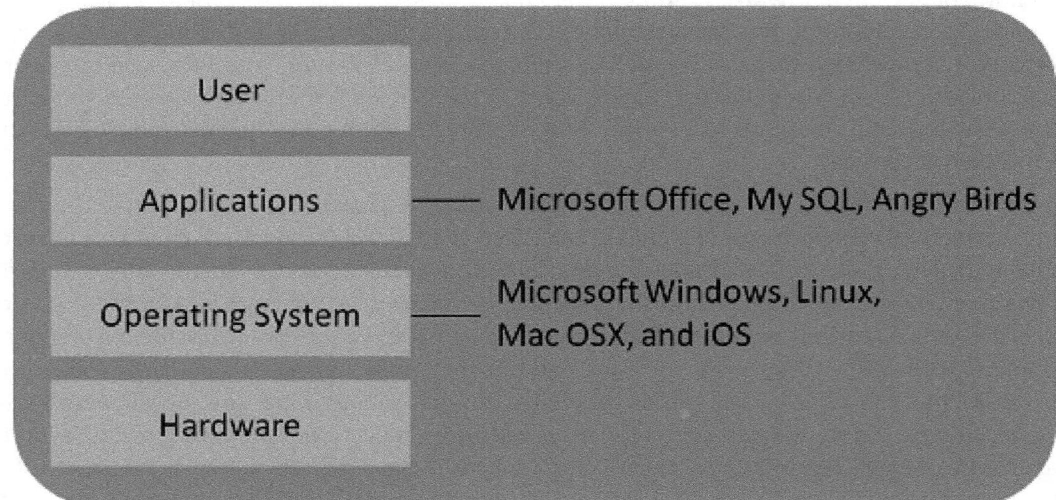

The flexibility of these layers gives computers the customization options that managers and businesses demand. Understanding how the layers relate to each other helps you make better decisions on what options are important to your unique business needs, can influence what you buy, and may have implications for everything from competitiveness to cost overruns to security breaches. What follows is a manager's guide to the main software categories with an emphasis on why each is important.

Key Takeaways

- Software refers to a computer program or collection of programs. It enables computing devices to perform tasks.
- You can think of software as being part of a layer cake, with hardware at the bottom; the operating system controlling the hardware and establishing standards; the applications executing one layer up, and the users at the top.
- How these layers relate to one another has managerial implications in many areas, including the flexibility in meeting business demand, costs, legal issues, and security.
- Software is everywhere—not just in computers, but also in cell phones, cars, cameras, and many other technologies.

Questions and Exercises

1. Explain the difference between hardware and software.
2. Why should a manager care about software and how software works? What critical organizational and competitive factors can software influence?
3. What role has software played in your decision to select certain products? Has this influenced why you favored one product or service over another?
4. Find the *Fortune* 500 list online. Which firm is the highest ranked software firm? While the *Fortune* 500 ranks firms according to revenue, what's this firm's profitability rank? What does this discrepancy tell you about the economics of software development? Why is the software business so attractive to entrepreneurs?
5. Refer to earlier chapters (and particularly to [Content Removed: #fwk-38086-ch02]): Which resources for competitive advantage might top software firms be able to leverage to ensure their continued dominance? Give examples of firms that have leveraged these assets, and why they are so strong.

10.2 Operating Systems

Learning Objectives

1. Understand what an operating system is and why computing devices require operating systems.
2. Appreciate how embedded systems extend Moore's Law, allowing firms to create "smarter" products and services.

Computing hardware needs to be controlled, and that's the role of the operating system. The operating system (sometimes called the "OS") provides a common set of controls for managing computer hardware, making it easier for users to interact with computers and for programmers to write application software. Just about every computing device has an operating system—desktops and laptops, enterprise-class server computers, your mobile phone. Even specialty devices like video game consoles, television set-top boxes, Kindles, and smart applicances run some form of OS.

Some firms, like Apple and Nintendo, develop their own proprietary OS for their own hardware. Microsoft sells operating systems to everyone from Dell to the ATM manufacturer Diebold (listen for the familiar Windows error beep on some cash machines). And there are a host of specialty firms, such as Wind River (purchased by Intel), that help firms develop operating systems for all sorts of devices that don't necessarily look like a PC, including cars, video editing systems, and fighter jet control panels.

Anyone who has used both a PC and a Mac and has noticed differences across these platforms can get a sense of the breadth of what an operating system does. Even for programs that are otherwise identical for these two systems (like the Firefox browser), subtle differences are visible. Screen elements like menus, scroll bars, and window borders look different on the Mac than they do in Windows. So do the dialogue boxes that show up when you print or save.

user interface (UI)

The mechanism through which users interact with a computing device. The UI includes elements of the graphical user interface (or GUI, pronounced *"gooey"*), such as windows, scroll bars, buttons, menus, and dialogue boxes; and can also include other forms of interaction, such as touch screens, motion sensing controllers, or tactile devices used by the visually impaired.

These items look and behave differently because each of these functions touches the hardware, and the team that developed Microsoft Windows created a system distinctly different from their Macintosh counterparts at Apple. Graphical **user interface (UI)** items like scroll bars and menus are displayed on the hardware of the computer display. Files are saved to the hardware of a hard drive or other storage device. Most operating systems also include control panels, desktop file management, and other support programs to work directly with hardware elements like storage devices, displays, printers, and networking equipment. The Macintosh Finder and the Windows Explorer are examples of components of these operating systems. The consistent look, feel, and functionality that operating systems enforce across various programs help make it easier for users to learn new software, which reduces training costs and operator error.

Operating systems are also designed to give programmers a common set of commands to consistently interact with the hardware. These commands make a programmer's job easier by reducing program complexity and making it faster to write software while minimizing the possibility of errors in code. Consider what an OS does for the game developer writing for the Nintendo Switch. Nintendo's Switch OS provides programmers with a set of common standards to use to access the controllers, play sounds, draw graphics, save files, and more. Without this, games would be a lot more difficult to write, they'd likely look different, be less reliable, would cost more, and there would be fewer titles available.

Similarly, when Apple provided developers with a common set of robust, easy-to-use standards for the iPhone and (via the App Store) an easy way for users to install these applications on top of the iPhone/iPod touch/iPad's operating system (iOS), software development boomed, and Apple became hands-down the most versatile mobile computing device available.[4] In Apple's case, some fifty thousand apps became available through the App Store in less than one year, and well over two million apps in total are available today. A good OS and software development platform can catalyze network effects (see Chapter 5). While the OS seems geeky, its effective design has very strategic business implications!

FIGURE 10.2 Smartphone OS Market Share

Operating system market share is notoriously difficult to calculate, and a search online will reveal widely varying numbers. That said, this interactive graphic will give you a sense of the variance in major mobile operating systems worldwide. A slider will allow you to compare how share has changed.

Source: Kanta World Panel website; http://www.kantarworldpanel.com/global/smartphone-os-market-share/.

Firmware and Embedded Systems

Most personal computers have an operating system installed on their hard drives. This system allows the OS to be replaced or upgraded easily. But many smaller, special-purpose computing devices have their operating systems installed on nonvolatile memory, often on read-only memory (ROM) chips. Control programs stored on chips are sometimes referred to as **firmware**. The OS in an iPad, automobile, your TV's set-top box, and in the hardware that controls Philips Hue lightbulbs is most likely stored as firmware. Your PC also has a tiny bit of firmware that allows it to do very basic functions like start-up (boot) and begin loading its operating system from disc.

Another term you might hear is **embedded systems**. As computing gets cheaper, special-purpose technology is increasingly becoming embedded into all sorts of devices like cars, picture frames, aircraft engines, photocopiers, and heating and air conditioning systems. The software programs that make up embedded systems are often stored as firmware too. Using microprocessors and embedded software to enable commonly encountered devices to communicate with one another (think of the Nest thermostat or app-controlled lighting and door locks) is sometimes referred to as the Internet of Things. Embedded systems are now found in everything from herd-tracking cow collars[5] to pipeline monitoring sensors, eliminating the need for workers to trek out and monitor operations.[6]

Moore's Law (see Chapter 3) enables embedded systems, and these systems can create real strategic value. The Otis Elevator Company, a division of United Technologies, uses embedded systems in its products to warn its service centers when the firm's elevators, escalators, and moving walkways need maintenance or repair. This warning provides Otis with several key benefits:

1. Since products automatically contact Otis when they need attention, these systems generate a lucrative service business for the firm and make it more difficult for third parties to offer a competing business servicing Otis products.
2. Products contact service technicians to perform maintenance based on exact needs (e.g., lubricant is low, or a part has been used enough to be replaced) rather than guessed schedules, which makes service more cost-effective, products less likely to break down, and customers happier.

firmware

Software stored on nonvolatile memory chips (as opposed to being stored on devices such as hard drives or removable discs). Despite the seemingly permanent nature of firmware, many products allow for firmware to be upgraded online or by connecting to another device.

embedded systems

Special-purpose software designed and included inside physical products (often on firmware). Embedded systems help make devices "smarter," sharing usage information, helping diagnose problems, indicating maintenance schedules, providing alerts, or enabling devices to take orders from other systems.

3. Any product failures are immediately detected, with embedded systems typically dispatching technicians before a client's phone call.
4. The data is fed back to Otis's R&D group, providing information on reliability and failure so that engineers can use this info to design better products.

Collectively, software embedded on tiny chips yields very big benefits, for years helping Otis remain at the top of its industry.

Key Takeaways

- The operating system (OS) controls a computer's hardware and provides a common set of commands for writing programs.
- Most computing devices (enterprise-class server computers, PCs, phones, set-top boxes, video games, cars, the Mars Rover) have an operating system.
- Some products use operating systems provided by commercial firms, while others develop their own operating system. Others may leverage open source alternatives (see [Content Removed: #fwk-38086-ch10] "Software in Flux: Partly Cloudy and Sometimes Free").
- Embedded systems are special-purpose computer systems designed to perform one or a few dedicated functions, and are frequently built into conventional products like thermostats, door locks, cars, air conditioners, industrial equipment, and elevators.
- Embedded systems can make products and services more efficient, more reliable, and more functional, and can enable entire new businesses and create or reinforce resources for competitive advantage.

Questions and Exercises

1. What does an operating system do? Why do you need an operating system? How do operating systems make a programmer's job easier? How do operating systems make life easier for end users?
2. What kinds of operating systems are used in the devices that you own? On your personal computer? Your mobile phone? The set-top box on top of your television? Are there other operating systems that you come into contact with? If you can't tell which operating system is in each of these devices, see if you can search the Internet to find out.
3. For your list in the prior question (and to the extent that you can), diagram the hardware/software "layer cake" for these devices.
4. For this same list, do you think each device's manufacturer wrote all of the software that you use on these devices? Can you add or modify software to all of these devices? Why or why not? What would the implications be for cost, security, complexity, reliability, updates and upgrades, and the appeal of each device?
5. Operating system market share is notoriously difficult to calculate. Do some research on major OS markets (PCs, tablets, smartphones, or other products). Gather data and share with your class. Is your data inconsistent with classmates' data? Why do you suppose there are such discrepancies? Even if data are precisely inaccurate, are there rough trends that you can trust, and if so, what sorts of managerial decisions might these influence?
6. Which mobile OS has a larger global market share: Android or iOS? Which has returned more money to developers through its app store? Is this data what you'd expect? Why or why not?
7. Some ATM machines use Windows. Why would an ATM manufacturer choose to build its systems using Windows? Why might it want to avoid this? Are there other non-PC devices you've encountered that were running some form of Windows?
8. What are embedded systems? When might firms want to install software on chips instead of on a hard drive? Why are embedded systems important for the Internet of Things?

9. It's important to understand how technology impacts a firm's strategy and competitive environment. Consider the description of Otis elevator's use of embedded systems. Which parts of the value chain does this impact? How? Consider the "five forces": How does the system impact the firm's competitive environment? Are these systems a source of competitive advantage? If not, explain why not. If they are, what kinds of resources for competitive advantage can these kinds of embedded systems create?
10. Can you think of other firms that can or do leverage embedded systems? Provide examples and list the kinds of benefits these might offer firms and consumers.
11. Research the Americans with Disabilities Act of 1990 (or investigate if your nation has a similar law), and the implications of this legislation for software developers and website operators. Have firms been successfully sued when their software or websites could not be accessed by users with physical challenges? What sorts of issues should developers consider when making their products more accessible? What practices might they avoid?

10.3 Application Software: Apps, Desktop Products, and Enterprise Systems

Learning Objectives

1. Appreciate the difference between desktop and enterprise software.
2. List the categories of enterprise software.
3. Understand what an ERP (enterprise resource planning) software package is.
4. Recognize the relationship of the DBMS (database system) to the other enterprise software systems.
5. Recognize both the risks and rewards of installing packaged enterprise systems.

Operating systems are designed to create a **platform** so that programmers can write additional applications, allowing the computer to do even more useful things. While operating systems control the hardware, *application software* (sometimes referred to as *software applications*, *applications*, or even just *apps*) performs the work that users and firms are directly interested in accomplishing. Think of applications as the place where the user's or organization's real work gets done. As we learned in Chapter 5, the more application software that is available for a platform (the more games for a video game console, the more apps for your phone), the more valuable it potentially becomes.

platforms

Products and services that allow for the development and integration of software products and other complementary goods. Windows, iOS, Android, and the standards that allow users to create Facebook apps are all platforms.

desktop software

Applications installed on a personal computer, typically supporting tasks performed by a single user.

enterprise software

Applications that address the needs of multiple users throughout an organization or work group.

software package

A software product offered commercially by a third party.

enterprise resource planning (ERP)

A software package that integrates the many functions (accounting, finance, inventory management, human resources, etc.) of a business.

Desktop software refers to applications installed on a personal computer—your browser, your Office suite (e.g., word processor, spreadsheet, presentation software), photo editors, and computer games are all desktop software. **Enterprise software** refers to applications that address the needs of multiple, simultaneous users in an organization or work group. Most companies run various forms of enterprise software programs to keep track of their inventory, record sales, manage payments to suppliers, cut employee paychecks, and handle other functions. Another term you might hear is *apps*. While the definition of *apps* is somewhat fluid, most folks use the term *app* to refer to smaller pieces of software that are designed for a specific platform, such as the programs that are executed on a smartphone, tablet, television, or specialized platform like the Apple Watch or Oculus Rift.

Some firms write their own enterprise software from scratch, but this can be time consuming and costly. Since many firms have similar procedures for accounting, finance, inventory management, and human resource functions, it often makes sense to buy a **software package** (a software product offered commercially by a third party) to support some of these functions. So-called **enterprise resource planning (ERP)** software packages serve precisely this purpose. In the way that Microsoft can sell you a suite of desktop software programs that work together, many companies sell ERP software that coordinates and integrates many of the functions of a business. The leading ERP vendors include the firms SAP and Oracle, although there are many firms that sell ERP software, and there are ERP and other enterprise products delivered "through the cloud" to browsers or apps, requiring no back-end software to be run on-site.

A company also doesn't have to install all of the modules of an ERP suite, but it might add functions over time—for example, to plug in an accounting program that is able to read data from the firm's previously installed inventory management system. And although a bit more of a challenge to integrate, a firm can also mix and match components, linking software the firm has written with modules purchased from different enterprise software vendors.

FIGURE 10.3 ERP in Action[7]

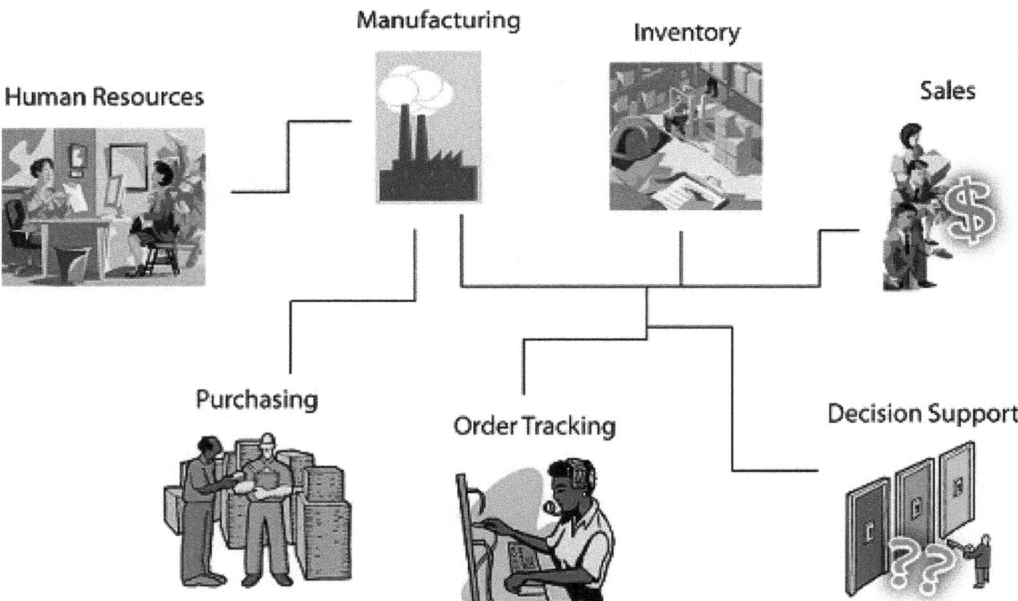

An ERP system with multiple modules installed can touch many functions of the business:

- *Sales*—A sales rep from Vermont-based SnowboardCo. takes an order for five thousand boards from a French sporting goods chain. The system can verify credit history, apply discounts, calculate price (in euros), and print the order in French.

- *Inventory*—While the sales rep is on the phone with his French customer, the system immediately checks product availability, signaling that one thousand boards are ready to be shipped from the firm's Burlington warehouse, the other four thousand need to be manufactured and can be delivered in two weeks from the firm's manufacturing facility in Guangzhou.
- *Manufacturing*—When the customer confirms the order, the system notifies the Guangzhou factory to ramp up production for the model ordered.
- *Human Resources*—High demand across this week's orders triggers a notice to the Guangzhou hiring manager, notifying her that the firm's products are a hit and that the flood of orders coming in globally mean her factory will have to hire more workers to keep up.
- *Purchasing*—The system keeps track of raw material inventories, too. New orders trigger an automatic order with SnowboardCo.'s suppliers, so that raw materials are on hand to meet demand.
- *Order Tracking*—The French customer can log in to track her SnowboardCo. order. The system shows her other products that are available, using this as an opportunity to cross-sell additional products.
- *Decision Support*—Management sees the firm's European business is booming and plans a marketing blitz for the continent, targeting board models and styles that seem to sell better for the Alps crowd than in the US market.

Other categories of enterprise software that managers are likely to encounter include the following:

- **customer relationship management (CRM)** systems used to support customer-related sales and marketing activities
- **supply chain management (SCM)** systems that can help a firm manage aspects of its value chain, from the flow of raw materials into the firm through delivery of finished products and services at the point-of-consumption
- **business intelligence (BI) systems**, which use data created by other systems to provide reporting and analysis for organizational decision-making

Major ERP vendors are now providing products that extend into these and other categories of enterprise application software, as well.

Most enterprise software works in conjunction with a **database management system (DBMS)**, sometimes referred to as a "database system." The database system stores and retrieves the data that an application creates and uses. Think of this as an additional layer in our cake analogy. Although the DBMS is itself considered an application, it's often useful to think of a firm's database systems as sitting above the operating system, but under the enterprise applications. Many ERP systems and enterprise software programs are configured to share the same database system so that an organization's different programs can use a common, shared set of data. This system can be hugely valuable for a company's efficiency. For example, this could allow a separate set of programs that manage an inventory and point-of-sale system to update a single set of data that tells how many products a firm has to sell and how many it has already sold—information that would also be used by the firm's accounting and finance systems to create reports showing the firm's sales and profits.

Firms that don't have common database systems with consistent formats across their enterprise often struggle to efficiently manage their value chain. Common procedures and data formats created by packaged ERP systems and other categories of enterprise software also make it easier for firms to use software to coordinate programs between organizations. This coordination can lead to even more value chain efficiencies. Sell a product? Deduct it from your inventory. When inventory levels get too low, have your computer systems send a message to your supplier's systems so that they can automatically build and ship replacement product to your firm. In many cases these messages are sent without any human interaction, reducing time and errors. And common database systems also facilitate the use of BI systems that provide critical operational and competitive

customer relationship management (CRM)

Systems used to support customer-related sales and marketing activities.

supply chain management (SCM)

Systems that can help a firm manage aspects of its value chain, from the flow of raw materials into the firm, through delivery of finished products and services at the point-of-consumption.

business intelligence (BI) systems

Systems that use data created by other systems to provide reporting and analysis for organizational decision making.

database management system (DBMS)

Sometimes referred to as database software; software for creating, maintaining, and manipulating data.

knowledge and empower decision making. For more on CRM and BI systems, and the empowering role of data, see Chapter 8.

FIGURE 10.4 Database Management System

An organization's database management system can be set up to work with several applications both within and outside the firm.

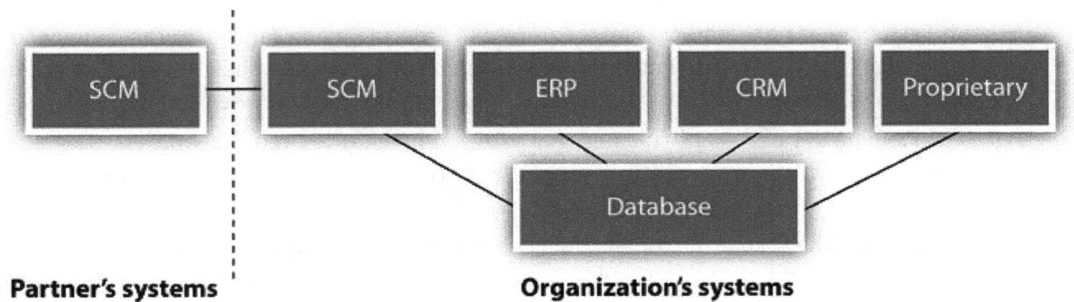

And That's Just the Start

Be prepared for even more discussions on software categories and the changing nature of software. Future chapters will discuss additional topics, such as cloud computing—where software and other computing functions are delivered as a service through an Internet connection rather than being installed on a user or firm's computer hardware. Many products, from hefty ERP systems (NetSuite is one leader, which Oracle has acquired) to end-user application suites (think Google Docs, Sheets, and Presentation) are being delivered "via the cloud."

You'll also learn about additional classifications of software, including artificial intelligence and machine learning systems. These systems mimic or improve upon functions that would otherwise require human intelligence. As you continue through this book, be sure to see the connections with earlier topics, as well. The spread of software from your tiny doorbell to the massive data crunched to target advertising, is all being powered by the fast/cheap computing trends we learned about in earlier chapters.

The Rewards and Risks of Packaged Enterprise Systems

When set up properly, enterprise systems can save millions of dollars and turbocharge organizations. For example, the CIO of office equipment maker Steelcase credited the firm's ERP with an $80 million reduction in operating expenses saved from eliminating redundant processes and making data more usable. The CIO of Colgate Palmolive also praised their ERP, saying, "The day we turned the switch on, we dropped two days out of our order-to-delivery cycle."[8] Packaged enterprise systems can streamline processes, make data more usable, and ease the linking of systems with software across the firm and with key business partners. Plus, the software that makes up these systems is often debugged, tested, and documented with an industrial rigor that may be difficult to match with proprietary software developed in-house.

But for all the promise of packaged solutions for standard business functions, enterprise software installations have proven difficult. Standardizing business processes in software that others can buy means that those functions are easy for competitors to match, and the vision of a single monolithic system that delivers up wondrous efficiencies has been difficult for many to achieve. The average large company spends roughly $15 million on ERP software, with some installations running into the hundreds of millions of dollars.[9] And many of these efforts have failed disastrously.

FoxMeyer was once a six-billion-dollar drug distributor, but a failed ERP installation led to a series of losses that bankrupted the firm. The collapse was so rapid and so complete that just a year after launching the system, the carcass of what remained of the firm was sold to a rival for less than $80 million. Hershey Foods blamed a $466 million revenue shortfall on glitches in the firm's ERP rollout. Among the problems, the botched implementation prevented the candy maker from getting product to stores during the critical period before Halloween. Nike's first SCM and ERP implementation was labeled a "disaster"; their systems were blamed for over $100 million in lost sales.[10] Even tech firms aren't immune to software implementation blunders. HP once blamed a $160 million loss on problems with its ERP systems.[11] Manager beware—there are no silver bullets. For insight on the causes of massive software failures, and methods to improve the likelihood of success, see Section 4 of this chapter.

Companies that have efficient, flexible information systems don't just see value through operations efficiency and cost savings. Technology can also influence a firm's options with respect to inter-firm partnerships, as well as merging with, acquiring, or getting acquired by other firms (M&A, or mergers and acquisitions). Firms that have systems that work smoothly internally may find it easier to partner with others. Consulting firm McKinsey suggests that many mergers don't live up to expectations because firms struggle when trying to combine complex and incompatible information systems. Efficient and integrated enterprise systems may also make firms more attractive acquisition targets or make it easier for a firm to acquire other firms and realize the benefit from acquisition. McKinsey suggests acquired firms may be more valuable and acquirers may be justified in bidding more for acquisition targets since efficient tech may allow firms to capture the 10 to 15 percent cost savings that successful mergers can usually realize by combining IT systems. McKinsey points to Oracle as an example of a firm whose efficiency has helped it win at M&A (mergers and acquisition). Oracle, which sells ERP systems, consolidated seventy of its own information systems into a single ERP for the entire firm, saving an estimated $1 billion annually. Serious coin, but from a strategic perspective, it also created internal systems that were streamlined and simplified, making it easier to integrate acquired firms. Oracle bought over fifty firms in a four-year period and can now integrate most acquisitions in six months or less.[12]

Key Takeaways

- Application software focuses on the work of a user or an organization.
- Desktop applications are typically designed for a single user. Enterprise software supports multiple users in an organization or work group.
- Popular categories of enterprise software include ERP (enterprise resource planning), SCM (supply chain management), CRM (customer relationship management), and BI (business intelligence) software, among many others.
- These systems are used in conjunction with database management systems, programs that help firms organize, store, retrieve, and maintain data.
- ERP and other packaged enterprise systems can be challenging and costly to implement, but can help firms create a standard set of procedures and data that can ultimately lower costs and streamline operations.
- The more application software that is available for a platform, the more valuable that platform becomes.
- The DBMS stores and retrieves the data used by the other enterprise applications. Different enterprise systems can be configured to share the same database system in order to share common data.
- Firms that don't have common database systems with consistent formats across their enterprise often struggle to efficiently manage their value chains, and often lack the flexibility to introduce new ways of doing business. Firms with common database systems and standards often benefit from increased organizational insight and decision-making capabilities.
- Enterprise systems can cost millions of dollars in software, hardware, development, and consulting fees, and many firms have failed when attempting large-scale enterprise system integration. Simply buying a system does not guarantee its effective deployment and use.

- When set up properly, enterprise systems can save millions of dollars and turbocharge organizations by streamlining processes, making data more usable, and easing the linking of systems with software across the firm and with key business partners.
- Efficient enterprise systems may also make it easier for firms to partner with other organizations, and can give it advantages when considering mergers and acquisitions.

Questions and Exercises

1. What is the difference between desktop and enterprise software?
2. Who are the two leading ERP vendors?
3. List the functions of a business that might be impacted by an ERP.
4. What do the acronyms ERP, CRM, SCM, and BI stand for? Briefly describe what each of these enterprise systems does.
5. Where in the "layer cake" analogy does the DBMS lie?
6. Name two companies that have realized multimillion-dollar benefits as a result of installing enterprise systems.
7. Name two companies that have suffered multimillion-dollar disasters as a result of failed enterprise system installations.
8. How much does the average large company spend annually on ERP software?
9. How do efficient enterprise systems help firms with respect to partnering with other organizations, as well as decisions around M&A?

10.4 Software Development Methodologies: From Waning Waterfall to Ascending Agile, plus a Sprint through Scrum

Learning Objectives

1. Understand why firms use software methodologies.
2. Know the benefits and weaknesses of waterfall and agile methodologies.
3. Understand scrum and its various components.

A Brief Introduction to Popular Approaches to Developing Software

Firms are also well served to leverage established project planning and software development methodologies that outline critical business processes and stages when executing large-scale software development projects. The idea behind these methodologies is straightforward—why reinvent the wheel when there is an opportunity to learn from and follow blueprints used by those who have executed successful efforts? When methodologies are applied to projects that are framed with clear business goals and business metrics, and that engage committed executive leadership, success rates can improve dramatically.[13]

Software development methodologies (*sometimes referred to as the software development lifecycle, or SDLC*) are methods to divide tasks related to software creation and deployment up into tasks targeted at building better products with stronger product management guidelines and techniques. While software development methodologies are the topic of more advanced technology and project management courses, the savvy manager knows enough to inquire about the development methodologies and quality programs used to support large-scale development projects, and can use these investigations as further input when evaluating whether those overseeing large-scale efforts have what it takes to get the job done. There are many different software development methodologies, but it helps to know key terms and some key strengths and weaknesses to be better prepared for the inevitability of being involved in a software development project.

software development methodologies

Sometimes also referred to as the SDLC or software development life cycle—methods to divide tasks related to software creation and deployment up into tasks targeted at building better products with stronger product management guidelines and techniques.

The waterfall method (*the classic, but increasingly out-of-favor approach*) is a relatively linear sequential approach to software development (and other projects). There are several variants of waterfall, but most see project progress flowing in largely one direction (downwards, from one step to another, like a waterfall) through the phases often listed as: requirements identification (documenting what it will take and showing use cases), design (what technologies should be used, who are the stakeholders impacted), implementation (building the product), verification (installation, testing, debugging), and maintenance (improving quality, fixing bugs). The goal of using these steps is to clarify what needs to be done and unearth problems early, before the project is built and deployed (which, as discussed, should reduce costs). The use of upfront documentation can help prevent "**feature creep**," or expansion of the scope of a project. And the plan helps provide strong documentation that can be helpful in future maintenance of the product.

waterfall

A relatively linear sequential approach to software development (and other projects). Benefits include surfacing requirements up front and creating a blueprint to follow throughout a project. Often criticized for being too rigid, slow, and demanding project forethought that's tough to completely identify early on.

The most significant criticism of the waterfall approach is that it is very rigid, can take a long time to implement, and requires precise forethought on all requirements needed at the end of the project. Waterfall has largely fallen out of favor, as many firms have found it restricts ongoing interaction and can take too much time, with needs in fast-changing industries shifting before a lengthy product can be completed.[14] Waterfall has even fallen out of favor in the US military, an organization often thought to use rigid planning and documentation.[15]

feature creep

An expansion of the scope of a project.

Agile development: While waterfall is on the way out in most organizations, the agile development approach (and variants) has become a dominant software development methodology.[16] Agile targets the weaknesses of waterfall, tackling work continually and iteratively, with a goal of more frequent product rollouts and constant improvement across smaller components of the larger project. Agile focuses on customer needs and organizational goals. Teams tackle smaller, targeted tasks with the hope of building products more quickly, with greater user input. Goals can evolve as needs unfold and new priorities come to the fore. Agile is popular due to its speed and flexibility. While some criticize the approach as one that might force products to develop too quickly and with less quality or documentation than classic approaches, there are several additional techniques often used in agile that target specific weaknesses, including test-driven design, behavior-driven development, pair programming, extreme programming, and refactoring. You may also hear other terms used with agile, including lean software (which provides additional methods for improved efficiency while cutting waste and excess), and scrum (which is a popular way to implement agile development).

agile development

Developing work continually and iteratively, with a goal of more frequent product rollouts and constant improvement across smaller components of the larger project.

scrum

An approach to organizing and managing agile projects that breaks deliverables into "sprints" delivered in one to six week increments by teams of less than ten. Scrum defines functions (roles) for management and development, meetings (ceremonies), and how the process is documented and tracked (artifacts).

Scrum is an approach to organizing and managing agile projects and is worth mentioning due to its popularity. Scrum breaks projects up into tasks called sprints that are meant to be completed in one to six weeks. Scrum teams are self-organizing and work cross-functionally, with managers, developers, designers, and users in regular contact. You'll often hear scrum described as having roles, artifacts, and ceremonies:

Roles (job functions):

- **Product owner**—represents the "voice of the customer," advocates for the needs of the organization, helps in setting requirements, and is ultimately held accountable for deliverables.
- **Scrum master**—serves the team by running meetings, keeping teams on process, and acting as a buffer to external team distractions. The scrum master may also coach the team, work with stakeholders, and partner with the product owner to manage task priority.
- **Team**—often held to a small number of task-focused workers (three to nine is common). The team provides analysis, design, development, testing, documentation, and more.

Artifacts (a way of documenting work and its current state):

1. *Product vision*—a business case for the task and value to be delivered.
2. *Product backlog*—a collection of user stories (product features described in natural language from the user's perspective). These describe a feature set. "As a user I need <something> so that <reason>." These are defined by the product owner in conjunction with other stakeholders.
3. *Sprint backlog*—the stories that are incorporated into the next sprint—e.g., what needs to be done in the next one to three weeks.
4. Many firms implementing scrum will have a *task board* with Post-it notes that should move between columns "stories" (task requirements), "to do" (prioritized tasks, not yet started), "in-progress," "testing," and "done." Others may include a *burndown chart* or some other variant showing products completed until reaching zero. The goal is to keep everyone on task to move "stories" from "to do" to "done" within a one-to-six-week timeline.

Ceremonies (meetings):

1. *Sprint planning*—a team planning meeting where stories (requirements defined from user perspective) are fleshed out, and the goal and scope of the sprint is determined.
2. *Daily scrum*—a daily stand-up team meeting (standing keeps things quick—often limited to, or "time boxed" to no more than 15 minutes), to discuss what was completed since the previous meeting, what individuals are working on, and raising things that are blocked and need help. This meeting is meant to keep people in sync and on track, and surface insights and expertise to help.
3. *Sprint demo* and *review and retrospective* (sometimes separated)—team demonstrates completed work to product owner and discusses what worked and what can be improved for the next sprint.

Scrum in Two Minutes

A brief introduction to scrum concepts

View the video online at: http://www.youtube.com/embed/Qoa5CS9JJPQ?rel=0

Key Takeaways

- Software development methodologies seek to bring planning and structure to software development projects. When methodologies are applied to projects that are framed with clear business goals and business metrics, and that engage committed executive leadership, success rates can improve dramatically.
- The waterfall methodology is a relatively linear sequential approach to software development (and other projects). Benefits include surfacing requirements up front and creating a blueprint to follow throughout a project. Waterfall is often criticized for being too rigid, slow, and demanding project forethought that's tough to completely identify early on.
- The agile development approach (and variants) tackles work continually and iteratively, with a goal of more frequent product rollouts and constant improvement across smaller components of the larger project. Teams tackle smaller, targeted tasks with the hope of building products more quickly, with greater user input.
- Scrum is an approach to organizing and managing agile projects and is worth mentioning due to its popularity. Scrum breaks projects up into tasks called sprints that are meant to be completed in one to six weeks. Scrum teams are self-organizing and work cross-functionally, with managers, developers, designers, and users in regular contact.

Questions and Exercises

1. Interview a systems development person at your university or at another organization. Does the firm use software development methodologies? If so, do they use one approach for all projects? What factors went into their decision? What do they see as the pros and cons of each approach?
2. Investigate scrum. Is it possible to get scrum training online? What alternatives have you discovered? Does this seem like something you would want to pursue? Why or why not?

3. Scrum isn't limited to technology projects. Would scrum work for projects that you are working on—including school group projects or more complex tasks in other organizations? If so, try using scrum and report back to your class with results, if you have them before semester's end.
4. Investigate some of the other approaches that are sometimes combined with agile development, such as paired programming and team programming. Would you prefer to use these approaches? Why or why not?

10.5 Beyond the Price Tag: Total Cost of Ownership and the Cost of Tech Failure

Learning Objectives

1. List the different cost categories that comprise total cost of ownership.
2. Understand that once a system is implemented, the costs of maintaining and supporting the system continue.
3. List the reasons why technology development projects fail and the measures that can be taken to increase the probability of success.
4. Examine the failed launch and eventual fix associated with HealthCare.gov, understanding the factors associated with the system's botched rollout and techniques used to recover the effort.

Managers should recognize that there are a whole host of costs that are associated with creating and supporting an organization's information systems. Of course, there are programming costs for custom software as well as purchase, configuration, and licensing costs for packaged software, but there's much, much more.

There are costs associated with design and documentation (both for programmers and for users). There are also testing costs. New programs should be tested thoroughly across the various types of hardware the firm uses, and in conjunction with existing software and systems, *before* being deployed throughout the organization. Any errors that aren't caught can slow down a business or lead to costly mistakes that could ripple throughout an organization and its partners. Studies have shown that errors not caught before deployment could be one hundred times more costly to correct than if they were detected and corrected beforehand.[17]

Once a system is "turned on," the work doesn't end there. Firms need to constantly engage in a host of activities to support the system, which may also include:

compliance

Ensuring that an organization's systems operate within required legal constraints, and industry and organizational obligations.

- providing training and end user support;
- collecting and relaying comments for system improvements;
- auditing systems to ensure **compliance** (i.e., that the system operates within the firm's legal constraints and industry obligations);
- providing regular backup of critical data;
- planning for redundancy and disaster recovery in case of an outage; and
- vigilantly managing the moving target of computer security issues.

With so much to do, it's no wonder that firms spend 70 to 80 percent of their information systems (IS) budgets just to keep their systems running.[18] The price tag and complexity of these tasks can push some managers to think of technology as being a cost sink rather than a strategic resource. These tasks are often collectively referred to as the **total cost of ownership** (TCO) of an information system. Understanding TCO is critical when making technology investment decisions. TCO is also a major driving force behind the massive tech industry changes discussed in [Content Removed: #fwk-38086-ch10].

total cost of ownership

An economic measure of the full cost of owning a product (typically computing hardware and/or software). TCO includes direct costs such as purchase price, plus indirect costs such as training, support, and maintenance.

Why Do Technology Projects Fail?

Even though information systems represent the largest portion of capital spending at most firms, an astonishing one in three technology development projects fails to be successfully deployed.[19] Imagine if a firm lost its investment in one out of every three land purchases, or when building one in three factories. These statistics are dismal! Writing in *IEEE Spectrum*, risk consultant Robert Charette provides a sobering assessment of the cost of software failures, stating, "The yearly tab for failed and troubled software conservatively runs somewhere from $60 to $70 billion in the United States alone. For that money, you could launch the space shuttle one hundred times, build and deploy the entire twenty-four-satellite Global Positioning System, and develop the Boeing 777 from scratch—and still have a few billion left over."[20]

Why such a bad track record? Sometimes technology itself is to blame, other times it's a failure to test systems adequately, and sometimes it's a breakdown of process and procedures used to set specifications and manage projects. In one example, a multimillion-dollar loss on the NASA Mars Observer was traced back to a laughably simple oversight: Lockheed Martin contractors using English measurements, while the folks at NASA used the metric system.[21] Yes, a $125 million taxpayer investment was lost because a bunch of rocket scientists failed to pay attention to third grade math. When it comes to the success or failure of technical projects, the devil really is in the details.

Projects rarely fail for just one reason. Project postmortems often point to a combination of technical, project management, and business decision blunders. The most common factors include the following:[22]

- Unrealistic or unclear project goals
- Poor project leadership and weak executive commitment
- Inaccurate estimates of needed resources
- Badly defined system requirements and allowing "feature creep" during development
- Poor reporting of the project's status
- Poor communication among customers, developers, and users
- Use of immature technology
- Unmanaged risks
- Inability to handle the project's complexity
- Sloppy development and testing practices
- Poor project management
- Stakeholder politics
- Commercial pressures (e.g., leaving inadequate time or encouraging corner-cutting)

Managers need to understand the complexity involved in their technology investments, and that achieving success rarely lies with the strength of the technology alone.

capability maturity model integration (CMMI)

A process-improvement approach (useful for but not limited to software engineering projects) that can assist in assessing the maturity, quality, and development of certain organizational business processes, and suggest steps for their improvement.

But there is hope. Information systems organizations can work to implement procedures to improve the overall quality of their development practices. Mechanisms for quality improvement include **capability maturity model integration (CMMI)**, which gauge an organization's process maturity and capability in areas critical to developing and deploying technology projects, and provides a carefully chosen set of best practices and guidelines to assist quality and process improvement.[23]

Firms are also well served to leverage established project planning and software development methodologies that outline critical business processes and stages when executing large-scale software development projects. The idea behind these methodologies is straightforward—why reinvent the wheel when there is an opportunity to learn from and follow blueprints used by those who have executed successful efforts.? When methodologies are applied to projects that are framed with clear business goals and business metrics, and that engage committed executive leadership, success rates can improve dramatically.[24]

Lessons Learned from the Failure and Rescue of HealthCare.gov

To say the Affordable Care Act was controversial is an understatement. What many regard as the signature legislation of President Obama's domestic agenda had barely passed the US Senate, squeaking by with just one vote. The US House of Representatives has voted at least fifty times to repeal or roll back parts of the law.[25] But politics aside, for the law to be successful, technology needed to work, and at rollout, it didn't.

The Affordable Care Act (a.k.a. Obamacare) called for a website, HealthCare.gov, that served as a national health care exchange where citizens could shop for, compare, and enroll in health care plans. The site would also offer subsidies for low-income enrollees and assist those eligible to sign up for Medicaid. Interest surged the first day the site went live.[26] Over 250,000 users were said to have visited HealthCare.gov on day one. What is the total enrollment after the first day? Eight.[27] That's not a typo. The system implementing HealthCare.gov was so full of bugs and design flaws that it had enrolled very few people, the number of which is enough to count using your two hands. And this is for a system where the government had agreed to pay the lead contractor $292 million.[28]

FIGURE 10.5 Healthcare.gov Website
The HealthCare.gov website.

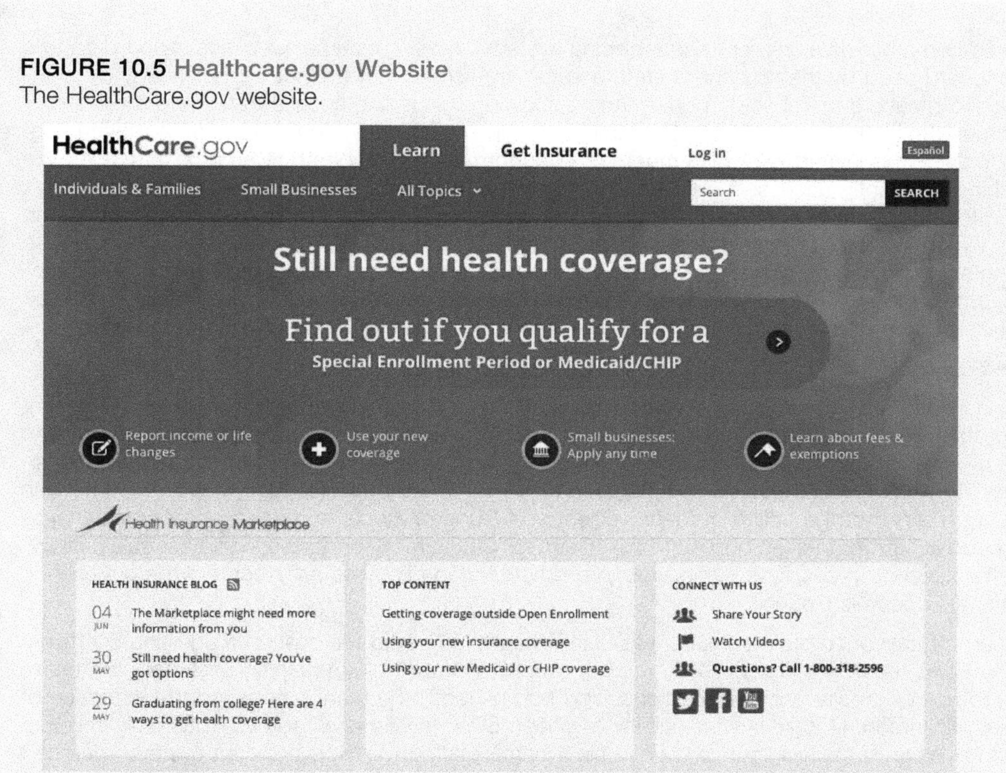

Source: https://www.healthcare.gov/.

The Problems

Problems with the website could have been predicted by anyone who read the previous section. The most critical issue was a lack of clear authority. Consultants brought in to fix the problem claimed they couldn't figure out who was in charge of the HealthCare.gov launch. What was seen after the launch were "multiple contractors bickering with one another and no one taking ownership for anything."[29] Technologists were also not involved in top-level planning. The president regularly ended meetings on the Affordable Care Act by saying, "I want to remind the team that this only works if the technology works." However, no one in the meetings had any idea whether the technology worked.[30] In fact, in the months leading up to the site's launch, the White House health-reform director kept the White House CTO (an executive who had previously launched two commercial health care firms), "off the invitation list for the planning meetings."

Most large-scale systems will have clear stages: requirements definition, design, development, and testing phases, but consultants brought in to survey HealthCare.gov pointed out that these phases were started on top of one another, where design and development began before requirements definition was even complete.[31]

While so-called "agile software development" methodologies allow for iterative development, they also rely on regular testing of modules developed along the way, but there were no such precautions taken with HealthCare.gov. Predeployment testing was minimal or nonexistent,[32] and the system was implemented in a single big bang rollout. One of the executives brought in to help diagnose problems and consult on fixes was former Twitter CTO Mike Abbott. Abbott knows how to fix websites in crisis. He's credited with getting Twitter past incessant "fail whale" site-down messages. Abbott said, "You never open a service like this to everyone at once. You open it in small concentric circles and expand"—such as one state first, then a few more—"so you can watch it, fix it and scale it."[33] The lack of testing also led to no credible verification on project status. The administration was so clueless to potential problems that even thirty-six hours beforehand, White House Chief of Staff Denis McDonough told a friend that "when we turn it on we're going to knock your socks off."[34]

There were also several technical and design problems with the implementation of the site. It was immediately obvious that HealthCare.gov could not scale to handle national demands. At best, the site could tolerate 1,100 simultaneous users at launch, nowhere near the 50,000–60,000 that was expected, or the 250,000 that had been reported as visiting the first day.[35] The site also lacked common measurement and reporting systems. Most consumer websites report data to a dashboard used by their technical staff, a summary screen that provides a quick way for engineers to measure a website's performance, showing things like access traffic and the number of times the page was loaded, and helping to pinpoint where system problems are occurring. HealthCare.gov lacked even the most basic performance dashboard. Common practices like caching frequently accessed data (storing high-demand items in memory so databases don't need to be repeatedly accessed) also weren't implemented. Also, from a design perspective, the user experience was horrible. For example, consumers were required to create an account before being able to compare plans, and the registration process created a bottleneck that further exacerbated issues, increasing wait times. Using the browser's "Back" button frequently broke the site, and users who were kicked off mid-enrollment often had to restart efforts from scratch.

The Fix

Fixing HealthCare.gov in a few weeks' time was a daunting challenge. No one knew the extent of problems or even if the system could be saved or needed to be scrapped entirely. Fixing the site required bringing in experienced management with clear leadership authority and responsibility. The White House tapped Jeff Zients, a highly regarded businessman, who at the time was deputy director of the Office of Management and Budget. Zients had experience running large bureaucratic programs (among them the "Cash for Clunkers" effort that spurred car sales following the 2008 US recession). Zients was also scheduled to take over as director of the president's National Economic Council.

A team of seasoned technologists was also brought in to lead the system triage and site fixes. Todd Park, the White House CTO, took a front-and-center role in helping assemble the team. In addition to on-site and remote consulting from Abbott, the team harnessed the expertise of Mikey Dickerson, Google's site reliability engineer. Dickerson was an administration ally and had taken a leave from Google in 2012 to help Obama staffers develop big data systems deemed responsible for getting out the winning vote.[36] Also part of the effort was Gabriel Burt, CTO at Chicago-based Civis Analytics, the firm founded by many of the analytics specialists involved in the 2012 campaign. Both men showed up in October and stayed into December.

The team needed more than leadership, they needed developer commitment. Abbott said, "The first red flag you look for is whether there is a willingness by the people there to have outside help. If not, then I'd say it's simpler to write it new than to understand the code base as it is, if the people who wrote it are not cooperating. But they were eager to cooperate."[37]

At times, it seemed that bureaucracy was conspiring to halt goodwill. Government regulations don't allow for volunteers to work on government projects for sustained periods of time. So new leadership actually had to be put on the payroll of contractor QSSI as hourly workers, earning Dickerson what he reported was "a fraction" of his Google pay.[38]

Clear priority setting, results reporting, and coordination were implemented through stand-up meetings, which is common among practitioners of agile development and popular inside the development groups of many leading tech firms and startups. In a stand-up meeting, technologists stand up (no sitting, be quick and to the point), identify a problem or a set of problems they're facing, identify obstacles to gaining a solution, gain quick feedback from the group, then disperse to solve presented problems, reporting back at the end of the day at a recap stand-up. An open phone line would connect people working on the website at other locations. The stand-ups helped everyone feel progress toward common goals and offered coordination that early project management lacked.

The Result

The nonpartisan Congressional Budget Office (CBO) originally projected seven million enrollees and revised that figure down to six million after persistent website glitches plagued HealthCare.gov. Despite what was likely the most disastrous and embarrassing rollout of a consumer-facing government technology initiative, HealthCare.gov had actually signed up over eight million insurance users by mid-April (roughly two weeks after the original deadline, which was extended due to rollout problems).

While the system's failure was large and public, it was by no means an anomaly. Research firm the Standish Group estimates that in the past ten years, some 94 percent of large federal information technology projects were unsuccessful: "More than half were delayed, over budget, or didn't meet user expectations, and 41.4 percent failed completely." The United States isn't alone in government technology failures. The United Kingdom's National Health Service wasted almost $20 billion to computerize medical records before eventually abandoning the project. Wise managers will learn from the lessons of HealthCare.gov.[39]

Key Takeaways

- The care and feeding of information systems can be complex and expensive. The total cost of ownership of systems can include software development and documentation, or the purchase price and ongoing license and support fees, plus configuration, testing, deployment, maintenance, support, training, compliance auditing, security, backup, and provisions for disaster recovery. These costs are collectively referred to as TCO, or a system's total cost of ownership.
- Information systems development projects fail at a startlingly high rate. Failure reasons can stem from any combination of technical, process, and managerial decisions.
- System errors that aren't caught before deployment can slow down a business or lead to costly mistakes that could ripple throughout an organization. Studies have shown that errors not caught before deployment could be 100 times more costly to correct than if they were detected and corrected beforehand.
- Firms spend 70 percent to 80 percent of their IS budgets just to keep their systems running.
- IS organizations can employ project planning and software development methodologies to implement procedures and to improve the overall quality of their development practices.
- IS organizations can leverage software development methodologies to improve their systems development procedures, and firms can strive to improve the overall level of procedures used in the organization through models like CMMI. However, it's also critical to engage committed executive leadership in projects, and to frame projects using business metrics and outcomes to improve the chance of success.
- A combination of managerial and technical issues conspired to undermine the rollout of HealthCare.gov. While the website was effectively unusable at launch, a systematic effort of management authority, communication, coordination, and expertise rescued the effort, allowing the site to exceed enrollment projections.

Questions and Exercises

1. Search online for examples of failed information systems development efforts. Come to class prepared to describe the failure, give its size and scope, the perceived reasons for the failure, and what managers could have done to prevent this failure. As a class, see if any key takeaways emerge. Are there any examples highlighting issues not mentioned in this chapter? If so, tweet links to any articles to #BizTechBook.
2. Healthcare.gov was clearly botched at the start. Some have claimed this suggests private enterprise is better suited to lead such projects than the government, but are there examples of corporations that have failed, as well? Are there any additional takeaways that would help both government planners as well as corporate managers?

EDITED

10.6 Introduction to Open Source Software

Learning Objectives

1. Understand how low marginal costs, network effects, and switching costs have combined to help create a huge and important industry.
2. Recognize that the software industry is undergoing significant and broadly impactful change brought about by several increasingly adopted technologies including open source software, cloud computing, and software as a service.

marginal costs

The costs associated with each additional unit produced.

For many, software has been a magnificent business. It is the $400 billion-per-year juggernaut[40] that placed Microsoft's Bill Gates and Oracle's Larry Ellison among the wealthiest people in the world. Increasingly, even defining the software industry is difficult. It powers everything from media consumption (Netflix, Spotify) to appliances (Nest, Apple Homekit). It drives modern farming, scientific discovery, and even the most mundane task such as driving (self-parking features have become commonplace, and software drives functions ranging from airbags to GPS). Once a successful software product has been written, the economics for a category-leading offering are among the best you'll find in any industry.[41] Unlike physical products assembled from raw materials, the **marginal cost** to produce an additional copy of a software product is effectively zero. Just duplicate, no additional input required. That quality leads to businesses that can gush cash. Microsoft generates one and a half billion dollars a month from Windows and Office alone.[42] Network effects and switching cost can also offer a leading software firm a degree of customer preference and lockin that can establish a firm as a standard and, in many cases, creates winner-take-all (or at least winner-take-most) markets.

But as great as the business has been, the fundamental model powering the software industry is under assault. **Open source software (OSS)** offerings—free alternatives where anyone can look at and potentially modify a program's code—pose a direct challenge to the assets and advantages cultivated by market leaders. Giants shudder—"How can we compete with free?"—while others wonder, "How can we make money and fuel innovation on free?" And if free software wasn't enough of a shock, the way firms and users think about software is also changing. A set of services referred to as **cloud computing** is making it more common for a firm to move software out of its own IS shop so that it is run on someone else's hardware. In one variant of this approach known as **software as a service (SaaS)**, users access a *vendor's software* over the Internet, usually by simply starting up a Web browser. With SaaS, you don't need to own the program or install it on your own computer. Hardware clouds can let firms take *their software* and run it on someone else's hardware—freeing them from the burden of buying, managing, and maintaining the physical computing that programs need. Another software technology called **virtualization** can make a single computer behave like many separate machines. This function helps consolidate computing resources and creates additional savings and efficiencies.

Perhaps equally remarkable are the firms that are pioneering these efforts. A few years back you might have expected giants like IBM, HP, Microsoft, and Sun to drive the future of computing. But if you look at the leading contributors to many of the most widely used open source efforts or providers of widely used cloud infrastructure, you will see that major players include (as *BusinessWeek* put it) a retailer (Amazon), an entertainment company (Netflix), an advertiser (Google), a résumé site (LinkedIn), and a social network (Facebook).[43] And our notion of packaged software is also challenged by instant access to a cornucopia of offerings through device app stores, covering smartphones, tablets, televisions, smart speakers, and more. App offerings further change the underlying economics and possibilities of the software industry and have been a catalyst for the birth of several innovative, billion-dollar-plus businesses.

These transitions are important. They mean that smaller firms have access to the kinds of burly, sophisticated computing power that only giants had access to in the past. Startups can scale quickly and get up and running with less investment capital. Existing firms can leverage these technologies to reduce costs. Got tech firms in your investment portfolio? Understanding what's at work here can inform decisions you make on which stocks to buy or sell. If you make tech decisions for your firm or make recommendations for others, these trends may point to which firms have strong growth and sustainability ahead, or which may be facing troubled times.

open source software (OSS)
Software that is free and where anyone can look at and potentially modify the code.

cloud computing
Replacing computing resources—either an organization's or individual's hardware or software—with services provided over the Internet.

software as a service (SaaS)
A form of cloud computing where a firm subscribes to a third-party software and receives a service that is delivered online.

virtualization
A type of software that allows a single computer (or cluster of connected computers) to function as if it were several different computers, each running its own operating system and software. Virtualization software underpins most cloud computing efforts, and can make computing more efficient, cost-effective, and scalable.

Key Takeaways

- The software business is attractive due to near-zero marginal costs and an opportunity to establish a standard—creating the competitive advantages of network effects and switching costs.
- New trends in the software industry, including open source software (OSS), cloud computing, software as a service (SaaS), and virtualization are creating challenges and opportunities across tech markets. Understanding the impact of these developments can help a manager make better technology choices and investment decisions.

Questions and Exercises

1. What major trends, outlined in this section, are reshaping how we think about software? What industries and firms are potentially impacted by these changes? Why do managers, investors, and technology buyers care about these changes?
2. Which organizations might benefit from these trends? Which might be threatened? Why?

3. What are marginal costs? Are there other industries that have cost economics similar to the software industry?
4. Investigate the revenues and net income of major software players: Microsoft, Google, Oracle, Red Hat, and Salesforce.com. Which firms have higher revenues? Net income? Which have better margins? What do the trends in OSS, SaaS, and cloud computing suggest for these and similar firms?
5. How might the rise of OSS, SaaS, and cloud computing impact hardware sales? How might it impact entrepreneurship and smaller businesses?

10.7 Open Source

Learning Objectives

1. Define open source software and understand how it differs from conventional offerings.
2. Provide examples of open source software and how firms might leverage this technology.

Linux

An open source software operating system.

Who would have thought a twenty-one-year-old from Finland could start a revolution that continues to threaten the Microsoft Windows empire? But Linus Torvalds did just that. During a marathon six-month coding session, Torvalds created the first version of Linux[44] marshaling open source revolutionaries like no one before him. Instead of selling his operating system, Torvalds gave it away. Now morphed and modified into scores of versions by hundreds of programmers, **Linux** can be found just about everywhere, and most folks credit Linux as being the most significant product in the OSS arsenal. Today Linux powers everything from cell phones to stock exchanges, set-top boxes to supercomputers. You'll find the OS on the majority of smartphones, tablets,[45] and supercomputers,[46] and supporting most Web servers (including those at Google, Amazon, and Facebook). Linux makes up roughly 92 percent of servers in Amazon's AWS cloud business,[47] while even Microsoft's Azure cloud is over 40 percent Linux.[48] Linux forms the core of the TiVo operating system, it underpins Google's Android and Chrome OS offerings, and it has even gone interplanetary. Linux has been used to power the Phoenix Lander and to control the Spirit and Opportunity Mars rovers.[49] Yes, Linux is even on Mars!

n00b

Written with two zeros, pronounced "newb." Geek-slang (leet speak), derogatory term for an uninformed or unskilled person.

How Do You Pronounce Linux?

Most English speakers in the know pronounce Linux in a way that rhymes with "*cynics*." You can easily search online to hear video and audio clips of Linus (whose name is actually pronounced "Lean-us" in Finnish) pronouncing the name of his OS. In deference to Linux, some geeks prefer something that sounds more like "*lean-ooks*" (for example, see http://suseroot.com/about-suse-linux/how-do-you-pronounce-linux.php). Just don't call it "*line-ucks*," or the tech-savvy will think you're an open source **n00b**! Oh yeah, and while we're on the topic of operating system pronunciation, the Macintosh operating system OS X is pronounced "oh es ten."

FIGURE 10.6 Tux, the Linux Mascot

Source: lewing@isc.tamu.edu Larry Ewing and The GIMP [Attribution], via Wikimedia Commons.

Open source software (OSS) is often described as free. While most OSS can be downloaded for free over the Internet, it's also "free" as in liberated (you may even see the acronym FLOSS for free/libre/open source software). The source code for OSS products is openly shared. Anyone can look at the source code, change it, and even redistribute it, provided the modified software continues to remain open and free.[50] This openness is in stark contrast to the practice of conventional software firms, who treat their intellectual property as closely guarded secrets and who almost never provide the source code for their commercial software products. As the movement began to pick up steam, many software industry execs became downright hostile toward OSS. The former president of SAP once referred to the open source movement as "socialism," while a former Microsoft CEO has called Linux a "cancer."[51]

But while execs at some firms saw OSS as a threat undermining the lifeblood of their economic model, other big-name technology companies are now solidly behind the open source movement. The old notion of open source being fueled on the contributions of loners tooling away for the glory of contributing to better code is now largely inaccurate. The vast majority of people who work on efforts like Linux are now paid to do so by commercially motivated employers.[52] Nearly every major hardware firm and a list of tech giants (e.g., Apple, Box, Facebook, Google, IBM, LinkedIn, Netflix, and Twitter) have paid staff contributing to open source projects[53]—an open source workforce collectively numbers in the thousands.[54] Most firms also work together to fund foundations that set standards and coordinate the release of product revisions and improvements. Such coordination is critical—helping, for example, to ensure that various versions of products can work alike and operate together.

LAMP

An acronym standing for **L**inux, the **A**pache Web server software, the **M**ySQL database, and any of several programming languages that start with **P** (e.g., Perl, Python, or PHP).

Turn on the LAMP—It's Free!

FIGURE 10.7 The Lamp Stack

Open source is big on the Web. In fact, you'll often hear Web programmers and open source advocates refer to the LAMP stack. **LAMP** is an acronym that stands for the Linux operating system, the Apache Web server software, the MySQL database, and any of several programming languages that start with the letter "P"—Python, Perl, and PHP. From Facebook to YouTube, you'll find LAMP software powering many of the sites you visit each day.

Key Takeaways

- OSS is not only available for free, but also makes source code available for review and modification (for the Open Source Initiatives list of the criteria that define an open source software product, see http://opensource.org/docs/osd).
- While open source alternatives are threatening to conventional software firms, some of the largest technology companies now support OSS initiatives and work to coordinate standards, product improvements, and official releases.
- The flagship OSS product is the Linux operating system, now available on all scales of computing devices from cell phones to supercomputers.
- The LAMP stack of open source products is used to power many of the Internet's most popular websites. Linux can be found on a large percentage of corporate servers; supports most Web servers, smartphones, tablets, and supercomputers; and is integral to TiVo and Android-based products.
- The majority of people who work on open source projects are paid by commercially motivated employers.

Questions and Exercises

1. Who developed Linux?
2. Who develops it today?
3. List the components of the LAMP stack. Which commercial products do these components compete with (investigate online, if necessary)?
4. Why do commercial firms contribute to open source consortia and foundations?
5. Free doesn't always win. Why might a firm turn down free software in favor of a commercial alternative?

10.8 Background - Open Source

Learning Objectives

1. Understand the concept of cloud computing.
2. Identify the major categories of cloud computing, including SaaS, PaaS, and IaaS.

When folks talk about cloud computing they're really talking about replacing computing resources—either an organization's or an individual's hardware or software—with *services* provided over the Internet. The name actually comes from the popular industry convention of drawing the Internet or other computer network as a big cloud. The various businesses that fall under the rubric of cloud computing are predicted to continue to grow tremendously from an estimated $260 billion in 2017 to over $411 billion by 2020.[55]

Cloud computing encompasses a bunch of different efforts. We'll concentrate on describing, providing examples of, and analyzing the managerial implications of two separate categories of cloud computing: (1) *software as a service (SaaS)*, where a firm subscribes to a third-party software-replacing service that is delivered online, and (2) models often referred to as **utility computing**, which can include variants such as *platform as a service* (PaaS) and *infrastructure as a service* (IaaS). Think of SaaS as delivering end-user software to a firm over the Internet instead of on the organization's own computing resources. PaaS delivers tools (a.k.a., a platform) so an organization can develop, test, and deploy software in the cloud. These could include programming languages, database software, product testing and deployment software, and an operating system. IaaS offers an organization a more bare-bones set of services that are an alternative to buying its own physical hardware—that is, computing, storage, and networking resources are instead allocated and made available over the Internet and are paid for based on the amount of resources used. With IaaS firms get the most basic offerings but can also do the most customization, putting their own tools (operating systems, databases, programming languages) on top. Typically, the further down this stack you go, the more support and maintenance services your own organization needs to perform (less for SaaS, the most for IaaS since that's where a firm heavily customizes and runs its own tech). A later section on virtualization will discuss how some organizations are developing their own private clouds, pools of computing resources that reside inside an organization and that can be served up for specific tasks as need arrives.

utility computing

A form of cloud computing where a firm develops its own software, and then runs it over the Internet on a service provider's computers.

The benefits and risks of SaaS and the utility computing-style efforts are very similar, but understanding the nuances of each effort can help you figure out if and when the cloud makes sense for your organization. The evolution of cloud computing also has huge implications across the industry: from the financial future of hardware and software firms, to cost structure and innovativeness of adopting organizations, to the skill sets likely to be most valued by employers.

Key Takeaways

- Cloud computing refers to replacing computing resources—of either an organization or individual's hardware or software—with services provided over the Internet.
- Software as a service (SaaS) refers to a third-party software-replacing service that is delivered online.
- Platform as a service (PaaS) delivers tools (a.k.a., a platform) so an organization can develop, test, and deploy software in the cloud. These could include programming languages, database software, and product testing and deployment software.

- Infrastructure as a service (IaaS) offers an organization an alternative to buying its own physical hardware. Computing, storage, and networking resources are instead allocated and made available over the Internet and are paid for based on the amount of resources used. IaaS offers the most customization, with firms making their own choices on what products to install, develop, and maintain (e.g., operating systems, programming languages, databases) on the infrastructure they license.
- SaaS typically requires the least amount of support and maintenance; IaaS requires the most, since firms choose the tech they want to install, craft their own solution, and run it on what is largely a "blank canvas" of cloud-provided hardware.
- Cloud computing is reshaping software, hardware, and service markets and is impacting competitive dynamics across industries.

Questions and Exercises

1. Define cloud computing.
2. Identify and contrast the categories of cloud computing. Which typically requires the most support and maintenance, and why? Why would firms choose a platform that requires more support and maintenance?

10.9 Why Open Source?

Learning Objectives

1. Know the primary reasons firms choose to use OSS.
2. Understand how OSS can beneficially impact industry and government.

There are many reasons why firms choose open source products over commercial alternatives:

Cost—Free alternatives to costly commercial code can be a tremendous motivator, particularly since conventional software often requires customers to pay for every copy used and to pay more for software that runs on increasingly powerful hardware. Banking giant Barclays has been able to reduce software costs by 90 percent by switching to open source products.[56] Online broker E*TRADE estimates that its switch to open source helped save over $13 million a year.[57] And Amazon claimed in SEC filings that the switch to open source was a key contributor to nearly $20 million in tech savings.[58] Firms like TiVo, which use OSS in their own products, eliminate a cost spent either developing their own operating system or licensing similar software from a vendor like Microsoft.

Reliability—There's a saying in the open source community, "Given enough eyeballs, all bugs are shallow."[59] What this means is that the more people who look at a program's code, the greater the likelihood that an error will be caught and corrected. The open source community harnesses the power of legions of geeks who are constantly trawling OSS products, looking to squash bugs and improve product quality. And studies have shown that the quality of popular OSS products outperforms proprietary commercial competitors.[60] In one study, Carnegie Mellon University's Cylab estimated the quality of Linux code to be less buggy than commercial alternatives by a factor of two hundred![61]

Security—OSS advocates also argue that by allowing "many eyes" to examine the code, the security vulnerabilities of open source products come to light more quickly and can be addressed with greater speed and reliability.[62] High-profile hacking contests have frequently demonstrated the strength of OSS products. In one event, laptops running Windows and the Mac OS were both hacked (the latter in just two minutes), while a laptop running Linux remained uncompromised.[63] Government agencies and the military often appreciate the opportunity to scrutinize open source efforts to verify system integrity (a particularly sensitive issue among foreign governments leery of legislation like the USA PATRIOT Act of 2001).[64] Many OSS vendors offer **security-focused** (sometimes called *hardened*) versions of their products. These can include systems that monitor the integrity of an OSS distribution, checking file size and other indicators to be sure that code has not been modified and redistributed by bad guys who've added a back door, malicious routines, or other vulnerabilities.

security-focused

Also known as "hardened." Term used to describe technology products that contain particularly strong security features.

Scalability—Many major OSS efforts can run on everything from cheap commodity hardware to high-end supercomputing. **Scalability** allows a firm to grow from startup to blue chip without having to significantly rewrite their code, potentially saving big on software development costs. Not only can many forms of OSS be migrated to more powerful hardware, software like Linux has also been optimized to balance a server's workload among a large number of machines working in tandem. Brokerage firm E*TRADE claims that usage spikes following sweeping US Federal Reserve moves flooded the firm's systems, creating the highest utilization levels in five years. But E*TRADE credits its scalable open source systems for maintaining performance while competitors' systems struggled.[65]

scalability

Ability to either handle increasing workloads or to be easily expanded to manage workload increases. In a software context, systems that aren't scalable often require significant rewrites or the purchase or development of entirely new systems.

Agility and Time to Market—Vendors who use OSS as part of product offerings may be able to skip whole segments of the software development process, allowing new products to reach the market faster than if the entire software system had to be developed from scratch, in-house. Motorola has claimed that customizing products built on OSS has helped speed time-to-market for the firm's mobile phones, while the team behind the Zimbra e-mail and calendar effort built their first product in just a few months by using some forty blocks of free code.[66]

When the Open Source Army Doesn't Show Up: Lessons from Heartbleed

Many open source projects are very well maintained, with tightly coordinated contribution armies overseen by well-funded, paid professionals. For example, Red Hat is one of many private firms helping maintain and improve Linux, the firm EnterpriseDB is heavily involved in supporting the PostgreSQL database product, and Google's many open source efforts include stewardship of the Python programming language. But some widely used open source products have been woefully neglected, and this became abundantly clear with the exposure of the Heartbleed bug in spring 2014.

Heartbleed was an error in the OpenSSL security toolkit, a product used by some two-thirds of Internet websites, and underpinning security related to the little padlock many Web browsers show when sending secure information over the Internet.[67] But for a product that handles a significant chunk of the thirty billion annual e-commerce transactions, OpenSSL was maintained by a pitifully undersourced effort. Most of the work was done by "two guys named Steve" who had never met and didn't have much of a budget to speak of. A routine coding error in the widely distributed software opened a hole that could potentially have been used to allow hackers to gather passwords, encryption keys, and other sensitive information, triggering "the largest security breach in the history of the human race."[68]

In order to help funnel money and resources to underserved and high-value open source projects, the Linux Foundation developed a multimillion-dollar project called the Core Infrastructure Initiative, designed "to fund open source projects that are in the critical path for core computing functions." Big name and deep-pocketed backers include Google, IBM, Facebook, and Microsoft. An initial earmark of $3.9 million was committed for the first three years of the effort, with larger firms committed to pay at least $100,000 into the annual funding pot. It shouldn't be surprising that OpenSSL is first up on the initiative's support list.

Heartbleed provides a cautionary tale to managers: Just because a tool is used by many doesn't mean one shouldn't audit its software products to understand the strength of support and potential risks associated with use.

Key Takeaways

- The most widely cited benefits of using OSS include low cost; increased reliability; improved security and auditing; system scalability; and helping a firm improve its time to market.
- Free OSS has resulted in cost savings for many large companies in several industries.
- OSS often has fewer bugs than its commercial counterparts due to the large number of software developers who have looked at the code.
- The huge exposure to scrutiny by developers and other people helps to strengthen the security of OSS.
- "Hardened" versions of OSS products often include systems that monitor the integrity of an OSS distribution, checking file size and other indicators to be sure that code has not been modified and redistributed by bad guys who have added a back door, malicious routines, or other vulnerabilities.
- OSS can be easily migrated to more powerful computers as circumstances dictate, and also can balance workload by distributing work over a number of machines.
- Vendors who use OSS as part of product offerings may be able to skip whole segments of the software development process, allowing new products to reach the market faster.

Questions and Exercises

1. What advantages does OSS offer TiVo? What alternatives to OSS might the firm consider, and why do you suppose the firm decided on OSS?
2. What's meant by the phrase, "Given enough eyeballs, all bugs are shallow"? Provide evidence that the insight behind this phrase is an accurate one. How does this phrase relate to the Heartbleed bug?
3. How has OSS benefited E*TRADE? Amazon? Motorola? Zimbra? What benefits were achieved in each of these examples?
4. Describe how OSS provides a firm with scalability. What does this mean, and why does this appeal to a firm? What issues might a firm face if chosen systems aren't scalable?
5. The website NetCraft (http://www.netcraft.com) is one of many that provide a tool to see the kind of operating system and Web server software that a given site is running. Visit NetCraft or a similar site and enter the address of some of your favorite websites. How many run open source products (e.g., the Linux OS or Apache Web server)? Do some sites show their software as "unknown"? Why might a site be reluctant to broadcast the kind of software that it uses?

10.10 Software in the Cloud: Why Buy When You Can Rent?

Learning Objectives

1. Know how firms using SaaS products can dramatically lower several costs associated with their information systems.
2. Know how SaaS vendors earn their money.
3. Be able to list the benefits to users that accrue from using SaaS.
4. Be able to list the benefits to vendors from deploying SaaS.

If open source isn't enough of a threat to firms that sell packaged software, a new generation of products, collectively known as SaaS, can deliver your computing through your Web browser or app. Don't install software—let someone else run it for you and deliver the results over the Internet.

Software as a service (SaaS) refers to software that is made available by a third party online. You might also see the terms ASP (application service provider) or HSV (hosted software vendor) used to identify this type of offering, but those are now used less frequently. SaaS is potentially a very big deal. Firms using SaaS products can dramatically lower several costs associated with the care and feeding of their information systems, including software licenses, server hardware, system maintenance, and IT staff. Most SaaS firms earn money via a usage-based pricing model akin to a monthly subscription. Others offer free services that are supported by advertising, while others promote the sale of upgraded or premium versions for additional fees.

Make no mistake, SaaS is yet another direct assault on traditional software firms. The most iconic SaaS firm is Salesforce.com, an enterprise customer relationship management (CRM) provider. This "un-software" company even sports a logo featuring the word "software" crossed out, *Ghostbusters*-style.[69]

Other enterprise-focused SaaS firms compete directly with the biggest names in software. Some of these upstarts are even backed by leading enterprise software executives. Examples include NetSuite (funded in part by Oracle's Larry Ellison, and which Oracle eventually bought for over $9 billion), which offers a comprehensive SaaS ERP suite; Workday (launched by founders of PeopleSoft), which has SaaS offerings for managing human resources; HubSpot, which provides marketing software; ServiceNow, which monitors and manages a firm's IT infrastructure via a SaaS model; and Splunk, which provides SaaS-based analytics tools. Several traditional software firms have countered startups by offering SaaS efforts of their own. IBM offers an SaaS version of its Cognos business intelligence products, Oracle offers CRM On Demand and also purchased NetSuite, and SAP's Business ByDesign includes a full suite of enterprise SaaS offerings. Even Microsoft has gone SaaS, with a variety of Web-based services that include CRM, Web meeting tools, collaboration, e-mail, and calendaring.

FIGURE 10.8 Salesforce.com Origina Logo

The antisoftware message is evident in the original logo of SaaS leader Salesforce.com.

Source: Used with permission from Salesforce.com.

SaaS is also taking on desktop applications. Intuit has online versions of its QuickBooks and TurboTax software, while the firm's cloud-based Mint is used by many instead of Intuit's Quicken desktop product. Adobe has moved the bulk of its business from desktop software to products delivered as SaaS subscription, and the move has been lauded as an overwhelming success.[70] Google, Apple, and Zoho offer office suites that compete with desktop alternatives, prompting Microsoft's own introduction of an online version of Office.

The Benefits of SaaS

Firms can potentially save big using SaaS. Organizations that adopt SaaS forgo the large upfront costs of buying and installing software packages. For large enterprises, the cost to license, install, and configure products like ERP and CRM systems can easily run into the hundreds of thousands or even millions of dollars. And these costs are rarely a one-time fee, with many products requiring an annual maintenance contract.[71]

Firms that adopt SaaS don't just save on software and hardware, either. There's also the added cost for the IT staff needed to run these systems. Forrester Research estimates that SaaS can bring cost savings of 25 to 60 percent if all these costs are factored in.[72]

There are also accounting and corporate finance implications for SaaS. Firms that adopt software as a service never actually buy a system's software and hardware, so these systems become a variable operating expense. This flexibility helps mitigate the financial risks associated with making a large capital investment in information systems. For example, if a firm pays Salesforce.com seventy-five dollars per month per user for its CRM software, it can reduce payments during a slow season with a smaller staff, or pay more during heavy months when a firm might employ temporary workers. At these rates, SaaS not only looks good to large firms, it makes very sophisticated technology available to smaller firms that otherwise wouldn't be able to afford expensive systems, let alone the IT staff and hardware required to run them.

service level agreement (SLA)

A negotiated agreement between the customer and the vendor. The SLA may specify the levels of availability, serviceability, performance, operation, or other commitment requirements.

In addition to cost benefits, SaaS offerings also provide the advantage of being highly scalable. This feature is important because many organizations operate in environments prone to wide variance in usage. Some firms might expect systems to be particularly busy during tax time or the period around quarterly financial reporting deadlines, while others might have their heaviest system loads around a holiday season. A music label might see spikes when an artist drops a new album. Using conventional software, an organization would have to buy enough computing capacity to ensure that it could handle its heaviest anticipated workload. But sometimes these loads are difficult to predict, and if the difference between high workloads and average use is great, a lot of that expensive computer hardware will spend most of its time doing nothing. In SaaS, however, the vendor is responsible for ensuring that systems meet demand fluctuation. Vendors frequently sign a **service level agreement (SLA)** with their customers to ensure a guaranteed uptime and define their ability to meet demand spikes.

When looking at the benefits of SaaS, also consider the potential for higher quality and service levels. SaaS firms benefit from economies of scale that not only lower software and hardware costs, but also potentially boost quality. The volume of customers and the diversity of their experiences mean that an established SaaS vendor is most likely an expert in dealing with all sorts of critical computing issues. SaaS firms handle backups, instantly deploy upgrades and bug fixes, and deal with the continual burden of security maintenance—all costly tasks that must be performed regularly and with care, although each offers little strategic value to firms that perform these functions themselves in-house. The breadth of an SaaS vendor's customer base typically pushes the firm to evaluate and address new technologies as they emerge, like quickly offering accessibility from smartphones and tablets. And many contend that cloud computing can actually be greener. SaaS and other cloud firms often have data centers that are better designed to pool and efficiently manage computing resources, and they are often located in warehouse-style buildings designed for computers, not people. Contrast that with corporate data centers that may have wasteful excess capacity to account for service spikes and may be crammed inside inefficiently cooled downtown high-rises. For all but the savviest of IT shops, an established SaaS vendor can likely leverage its scale and experience to provide better, cheaper, more reliable standard information systems than individual companies typically can.

Software developers who choose to operate as SaaS providers also realize benefits. While a packaged software company like SAP must support multiple versions of its software to accommodate operating systems like Windows, Linux, and various flavors of Unix, a SaaS provider develops, tests, deploys, and supports just one version of the software executing on its own servers.

Since SaaS firms run a customer's systems on the SaaS firm's own hardware, these firms have a tighter feedback loop in understanding how products are used (and why products may fail)—potentially accelerating their ability to enhance their offerings. And once made, enhancements or fixes are immediately available to customers the next time they log in.

SaaS applications also impact distribution costs and capacity. As much as 30 percent of the price of traditional desktop software is tied to the cost of distribution—pressing CD-ROMs, packaging them in boxes, and shipping them to retail outlets.[73] Going direct to consumers can cut out the middleman, so vendors can charge less or capture profits that they might otherwise share with a store or other distributor. Going direct also means that SaaS applications are available anywhere someone has an Internet connection, making them truly global applications. This feature has allowed many SaaS firms to address highly specialized markets (sometimes called **vertical niches**). For example, the Internet allows a company writing specialized legal software, or a custom package for the pharmaceutical industry, to have a national deployment footprint from day one. Vendors of desktop applications that go SaaS benefit from this kind of distribution, too.

vertical niches

Sometimes referred to as vertical markets. Products and services designed to target a specific industry (e.g., pharmaceutical, legal, apparel retail).

Finally, SaaS allows a vendor to counter the vexing and costly problem of software piracy. It's just about impossible to make an executable, illegal copy of a subscription service that runs on an SaaS provider's hardware.

Key Takeaways

- SaaS firms may offer their clients several benefits including the following:
  - *lower costs* by eliminating or reducing software, hardware, maintenance, and staff expenses
  - *financial risk mitigation* since startup costs are so low
  - potentially *faster deployment times* compared with installed packaged software or systems developed in-house
  - costs that are a *variable operating expense* rather than a large, fixed capital expense
  - *scalable systems* that make it easier for firms to ramp up during periods of unexpectedly high system use
  - *higher quality and service levels* through instantly available upgrades, vendor scale economies, and expertise gained across its entire client base
  - *remote access and availability*—most SaaS offerings are accessed through any Web browser, and often even by phone or other mobile device
- Vendors of SaaS products benefit from the following:
  - *limiting development to a single platform*, instead of having to create versions for different operating systems
  - *tighter feedback loop* with clients, helping fuel innovation and responsiveness
  - ability to *instantly deploy bug fixes and product enhancements* to all users
  - *lower distribution costs*
  - *accessibility* to anyone with an Internet connection
  - greatly *reduced risk of software piracy*
- SaaS (and the other forms of cloud computing) are also thought to be better for the environment, since cloud firms more efficiently pool resources and often host their technologies in warehouses designed for cooling and energy efficiency.

Questions and Exercises

1. Firms that buy conventional enterprise software spend money buying software and hardware. What additional and ongoing expenses are required as part of the "care and feeding" of enterprise applications?
2. In what ways can firms using SaaS products dramatically lower costs associated with their information systems?
3. How do SaaS vendors earn their money?
4. Give examples of enterprise-focused SaaS vendors and their products. Visit the websites of the firms that offer these services. Which firms are listed as clients? Does there appear to be a particular type of firm that uses its services, or are client firms broadly represented?
5. Give examples of desktop-focused SaaS vendors and their products. If some of these are free, try them out and compare them to desktop alternatives you may have used. Be prepared to share your experiences with your class.
6. List the cost-related benefits to users that accrue from using SaaS.
7. List the benefits other than cost-related that accrue to users from using SaaS.
8. List the benefits realized by vendors that offer SaaS services instead of conventional software.
9. Why might cloud computing be greener than conventional computing alternatives? Research online and share examples suggesting that cloud firms could be less environmentally taxing than if a firm built and ran its own corporate data center.

10.11 SaaS: Not without Risks

Learning Objective

1. Be able to list and appreciate the risks associated with SaaS.

Like any technology, we also recognize there is rarely a silver bullet that solves all problems. A successful manager is able to see through industry hype and weigh the benefits of a technology against its weaknesses and limitations. And there are still several major concerns surrounding SaaS.

The largest concerns involve the tremendous dependence a firm develops with its SaaS vendor. While some claim that the subscription-based SaaS model means that you can simply walk away from a vendor if you become dissatisfied, in fact there is quite a bit of lockin with SaaS vendors, too. Having all of your eggs in one basket can leave a firm particularly vulnerable. If a traditional software company goes out of business, in most cases its customers can still go on using its products. But if your SaaS vendor goes under, you're hosed. They've got all your data, and even if firms could get their data out, most organizations don't have the hardware, software, staff, or expertise to quickly absorb an abandoned function.

Beware with whom you partner. Any hot technology is likely to attract a lot of startups, and most of these startups are unlikely to survive. In just a single year, the leading trade association found the number of SaaS vendors dropped from seven hundred members to four hundred fifty.[74] One of the early efforts to collapse was Pandesic, a joint venture between SAP and Intel—two large firms that might have otherwise instilled confidence among prospective customers. In another example, Danish SaaS firm "IT Factory" was declared "Denmark's Best IT Company" by *Computerworld*, only to follow the award one week later with a bankruptcy declaration.[75] Indeed, despite the benefits, the costs of operating as an SaaS vendor can be daunting. NetSuite's founder claimed it "takes ten years and $100 million to do right"[76]—maybe that's why the firm still wasn't profitable, even three and a half years after going public.

Firms that buy and install packaged software usually have the option of sticking with the old stuff as long as it works, but organizations adopting SaaS may find they are forced into adopting new versions. This fact is important because any radical changes in an SaaS system's user interface or system functionality might result in unforeseen training costs, or increase the chance that a user might make an error.

Keep in mind that SaaS systems are also reliant on a network connection. If a firm's link to the Internet goes down, its link to its SaaS vendor is also severed. Relying on an Internet connection also means that data is transferred to and from an SaaS firm at Internet speeds, rather than the potentially higher speeds of a firm's internal network. Solutions to many of these issues are evolving as Internet speeds become faster and Internet service providers become more reliable. Many SaaS offerings also allow for offline use of data that is typically stored in SaaS systems. With these products a user can download a subset of data to be offline (say, on a plane flight or other inaccessible location) and then sync the data when the connection is restored. Ultimately, though, SaaS users have a much higher level of dependence on their Internet connections.

And although a SaaS firm may have more security expertise than your organization, that doesn't mean that security issues can be ignored. Any time a firm allows employees to access a corporation's systems and data assets from a remote location, a firm is potentially vulnerable to abuse and infiltration. Some firms may simply be unacceptably uncomfortable with critical data assets existing outside their own network. There may also be contractual or legal issues preventing data from being housed remotely, especially if an SaaS vendor's systems are in another country operating under different laws and regulations. "We're very bound by regulators in terms of client data and country-of-origin issues, so it's very difficult to use the cloud," says Rupert Brown, a chief architect at Merrill Lynch.[77]

SaaS systems are often accused of being less flexible than their installed software counterparts—mostly due to the more robust configuration and programming options available in traditional software packages. It is true that many SaaS vendors have improved system customization options and integration with standard software packages. And at times a lack of complexity can be a blessing—fewer choices can mean less training, faster startup time, and lower costs associated with system use. But firms with unique needs may find SaaS restrictive.

Here's another challenge for a firm and its IT staff: SaaS means a greater *consumerization* of technology. Employees, at their own initiative, can go to firms such as Atlassian or PBworks and set up a wiki, WordPress to start blogging, and subscribe to an SaaS offering like Salesforce.com and start storing potentially sensitive corporate files in Dropbox, all without corporate oversight and approval. This work can result in employees operating outside established firm guidelines and procedures, potentially introducing operational inconsistencies or even legal and security concerns.

The consumerization of corporate technology isn't all bad. Employee creativity can blossom with increased access to new technologies, costs might be lower than home-grown solutions, and staff could introduce the firm to new tools that might not otherwise be on the radar of the firm's IS department. But all this creates an environment that requires a level of engagement between a firm's technical staff and the groups that it serves that is deeper than that employed by any prior generation of technology workers. Those working in an organization's information systems group must be sure to conduct regular meetings with representative groups of employees across the firm to understand their pain points and assess their changing technology needs. Non-IT managers should regularly reach out to IT to ensure that their needs are on the tech staff's agenda. Organizations with internal IT staff R&D functions that scan new technologies and critically examine their relevance and potential impact on the firm can help guide an organization through the promise and peril of new technologies. Now more than ever, IT managers must be deeply knowledgeable about business areas, broadly aware of new technologies, and able to bridge the tech and business worlds. Similarly, any manager looking to advance his or her organization has to regularly consider the impact of new technologies.

Key Takeaways

The risks associated with SaaS include the following:

- *dependence on a single vendor*
- concern about the long-term *viability of partner firms*
- users *may be forced to migrate to new versions*—possibly incurring unforeseen training costs and shifts in operating procedures
- *reliance on a network connection*—which may be slower, less stable, and less secure
- *data asset stored off-site*—with the potential for security and legal concerns
- *limited configuration, customization, and system integration options* compared to packaged software or alternatives developed in-house
- *The user interface of Web-based software is often less sophisticated and lacks the richness of most desktop alternatives.*
- Ease of adoption *may lead to pockets of unauthorized IT* being used throughout an organization.

Questions and Exercises

1. Consider the following two firms: a consulting startup and a defense contractor. Leverage what you know about SaaS and advise whether each might consider SaaS efforts for CRM or other enterprise functions? Why or why not?
2. Think of firms you've worked for, or firms you would like to work for. Do SaaS offerings make sense for these firms? Make a case for or against using certain categories of SaaS.
3. What factors would you consider when evaluating an SaaS vendor? Which firms are more appealing to you and why?
4. Discuss problems that may arise because SaaS solutions rely on Internet connections. Discuss the advantages of through-the-browser access.
5. Evaluate trial versions of desktop SaaS offerings (offered by Adobe, Apple, Google, Microsoft, or others). Do you agree that the interfaces of Web-based versions are not as robust as desktop rivals? Are they good enough for you? For most users?

10.12 Make, Buy, or Rent

Learning Objectives

1. Know the options managers have when determining how to satisfy the software needs of their companies.
2. Know the factors that must be considered when making the make, buy, or rent decision.

So now you realize managers have a whole host of options when seeking to fulfill the software needs of their firms. An organization can purchase packaged software from a vendor, use open source offerings, leverage SaaS or other types of cloud computing, outsource development or other

IT functions to another firm either domestically or abroad, or a firm can develop all or part of the effort themselves. When presented with all of these options, making decisions about technologies and systems can seem pretty daunting.

First, realize that that for most firms, technology decisions are not binary options for the whole organization in all situations. Few businesses will opt for an IT configuration that is 100 percent in-house, packaged, or SaaS. Being aware of the parameters to consider can help a firm make better, more informed decisions. It's also important to keep in mind that these decisions need to be continuously reevaluated as markets and business needs change. What follows is a summary of some of the key variables to consider.

Competitive Advantage—*Do we rely on unique processes, procedures, or technologies that create vital, differentiating competitive advantage?* If so, then these functions aren't good candidates to outsource or replace with a packaged software offering. Amazon had originally used recommendation software provided by a third party, and Netflix and Dell both considered third-party software to manage inventory fulfillment. But in all three cases, these firms felt that mastery of these functions was too critical to competitive advantage, so each firm developed proprietary systems unique to the circumstances of each firm.

Security—*Are there unacceptable risks associated with using the packaged software, OSS, cloud solution, or an outsourcing vendor? Are we convinced that the prospective solution is sufficiently secure and reliable? Can we trust the prospective vendor with our code, our data, our procedures and our way of doing business? Are there noncompete provisions for vendor staff that may be privy to our secrets? For off-site work, are there sufficient policies in place for on-site auditing?* If the answers to any of these questions is no, outsourcing might not be a viable option.

Legal and Compliance—*Is our firm prohibited outright from using technologies? Are there specific legal and compliance requirements related to deploying our products or services?* Even a technology as innocuous as instant messaging may need to be deployed in such a way that it complies with laws requiring firms to record and reproduce the electronic equivalent of a paper trail. For example, SEC Rule 17a-4 requires broker dealers to retain client communications for a minimum of three years. HIPAA laws governing health care providers state that electronic communications must also be captured and stored.[78] While tech has gained a seat in the board room, legal also deserves a seat in systems planning meetings.

Skill, Expertise, and Available Labor—*Can we build it?* The firm may have skilled technologists, but they may not be sufficiently experienced with a new technology. Even if they are skilled, managers must consider the costs of allocating staff away from existing projects for this effort.

Cost—*Is this a cost-effective choice for our firm?* A host of factors must be considered when evaluating the cost of an IT decision. The costs to build, host, maintain, and support an ongoing effort involve labor (software development, quality assurance, ongoing support, training, and maintenance), consulting, security, operations, licensing, energy, and real estate. Any analysis of costs should consider not only the aggregate spending required over the lifetime of the effort but also whether these factors might vary over time.

Time—*Do we have time to build, test, and deploy the system?*

Vendor Issues—*Is the vendor reputable and in a sound financial position? Can the vendor guarantee the service levels and reliability we need? What provisions are in place in case the vendor fails or is acquired? Is the vendor certified via the Carnegie Mellon Software Institute or other standards organizations in a way that conveys quality, trust, and reliability?*

The list above is a starter. It should also be clear that these metrics are sometimes quite tough to estimate. Welcome to the challenges of being a manager! At times an environment in flux can make an executive feel like he or she is working on a surfboard, constantly being buffeted about by unexpected currents and waves. Hopefully the issues outlined in this chapter will give you the surfing skills you need for a safe ride that avoids the organizational equivalent of a wipeout.

Key Takeaways

- The make, buy, or rent decision may apply on a case-by-case basis that might be evaluated by firm, division, project, or project component. Firm and industry dynamics may change in a way that causes firms to reassess earlier decisions, or to alter the direction of new initiatives.
- Factors that managers should consider when making a make, buy, or rent decision include the following: competitive advantage, security, legal and compliance issues, the organization's skill and available labor, cost, time, and vendor issues.
- Factors must be evaluated over the lifetime of a project, not at a single point in time.
- Managers have numerous options available when determining how to satisfy the software needs of their companies: purchase packaged software from a vendor, use OSS, use SaaS or utility computing, outsource development, or develop all or part of the effort themselves.
- If a company relies on unique processes, procedures, or technologies that create vital, differentiating, competitive advantages, the functions probably aren't a good candidate to outsource.

Questions and Exercises

1. What are the options available to managers when seeking to meet the software needs of their companies?
2. What are the factors that must be considered when making the make, buy, or rent decision?
3. What are some security-related questions that must be asked when making the make, buy, or rent decision?
4. What are some vendor-related questions that must be asked when making the make, buy, or rent decision?
5. What are some of the factors that must be considered when evaluating the cost of an IT decision?
6. Why must factors be evaluated over the lifetime of a project, not at a single point in time?

Endnotes

1. R. Charette, "Why Software Fails," *IEEE Spectrum*, September 2005.
2. S. Lacy, "Is Atlassian the Next Big Enterprise Software IPO?" *Pando Daily*, February 22, 2012.
3. Z. Jiang and R. Mangharam, "University of Pennsylvania Develops Electrophysiological Heart Model for Real-Time Closed-Loop Testing of Pacemakers," *Mathworks Newsletter*, 2013 Edition.
4. The iPhone and iPod touch OS is derived from Apple's Mac OS X operating system.
5. C. Scott, "Why Farmers Are Connecting Their Cows to the Internet," *SingularityHub*, April 3, 2014.
6. M. Overfelt, "A $15 trillion dream of GE-Silicon Valley hybrid," *CNBC*, April 22, 2014.
7. Adapted from G. Edmondson, "Silicon Valley on the Rhine," *BusinessWeek International*, November 3, 1997.
8. A. Robinson and D. Dilts, "OR and ERP," *ORMS Today*, June 1999.
9. C. Rettig, "The Trouble with Enterprise Software," *MIT Sloan Management Review* 49, no. 1 (2007): 21–27.
10. C. Koch, "Nike Rebounds: How (and Why) Nike Recovered from Its Supply Chain Disaster," *CIO*, June 15, 2004.
11. R. Charette, "Why Software Fails," *IEEE Spectrum*, September 2005.
12. H. Sarrazin and A. West, "Understanding the strategic value of IT in M&A," *McKinsey Quarterly*, January 2011.
13. A. Shenhar and D. Dvir, *Reinventing Project Management: The Diamond Approach to Successful Growth and Innovation* (Boston: Harvard Business School Press, 2007).
14. J. Fair, "Agile versus Waterfall (Presented at the 2012 Global Congress of the PMI," *Project Management Institute*, Oct. 2012.
15. S. Pahuja, "US Department of Defense (DoD) is Going Agile," *InfoQ*, May 31, 2014.
16. S. Denning, "Agile: The World's Most Popular Innovation Engine," *Forbes*, July 23, 2015.
17. R. Charette, "Why Software Fails," *IEEE Spectrum*, September 2005.
18. C. Rettig, "The Trouble with Enterprise Software," *MIT Sloan Management Review* 49, no. 1 (2007): 21–27.
19. L. Dignan, "Survey: One in 3 IT Projects Fail; Management OK with It," *ZDNet*, December 11, 2007.
20. R. Charette, "Why Software Fails," *IEEE Spectrum*, September 2005.
21. R. Lloyd, "Metric Mishap Caused Loss of NASA Orbiter," *CNN*, September 20, 1999.
22. List largely based on R. Charette, "Why Software Fails," *IEEE Spectrum*, September 2005.
23. R. Kay, "QuickStudy: Capability Maturity Model Integration (CMMI)," *Computerworld*, January 24, 2005; and Carnegie Mellon Software Engineering Institute, *Welcome to CMMI*, 2009, http://www.sei.cmu.edu/cmmi.
24. A. Shenhar and D. Dvir, *Reinventing Project Management: The Diamond Approach to Successful Growth and Innovation* (Boston: Harvard Business School Press, 2007).
25. E. O'Keefe, "The House Has Voted 54 Times in Four Years on Obamacare: Here's the Full List," *Washington Post*, March 21, 2014.
26. K. Pallarito, "Design and Software Problems Plague Health Exchanges: Report," *HealthDay*, October 7, 2013.
27. S. Brill, "'Code Red': Steve Brill on HealthCare.gov, Video Excerpt from the Charlie Rose Show," *BloombergTV*, March 4, 2014.
28. G. Kessler, "How Much Did HealthCare.gov Cost?" *Washington Post*, October 24, 2013.
29. S. Brill, "Obama's Trauma Team," *Time*, February 27, 2014.
30. S. Brill, "Obama's Trauma Team," *Time*, February 27, 2014.

31. E. Hu, "This Slide Shows Why HealthCare.gov Wouldn't Work at Launch," *NPR*, November 19, 2013.
32. M. Kelley, "Why the Obamacare Website Failed in One Slide," *Business Insider*, November 19, 2013.
33. S. Brill, "Obama's Trauma Team," *Time*, February 27, 2014.
34. S. Brill, "'Code Red': Steve Brill on HealthCare.gov, Video Excerpt from the Charlie Rose Show," *BloombergTV*, March 4, 2014.
35. F. Thorp, "'Stress Tests' Show HealthCare.gov Was Overloaded," *NBC News*, November 6, 2013.
36. B. Hughes, "Michael Dickerson: The Invisible Man behind Obamacare's Tech Surge," *Washington Examiner*, December 6, 2013.
37. S. Brill, "Obama's Trauma Team," *Time*, February 27, 2014.
38. S. Brill, "Obama's Trauma Team," *Time*, February 27, 2014.
39. L. Woodhill, "The Obamacare Website Failed for the Same Reason the Soviet Union Did," *Forbes*, November 13, 2013.
40. R. Kelly, "DC: Worldwide IT Spending Growth to Slow in 2014," *Campus Technology*, February 5, 2014.
41. G. Winfrey, "The 5 Most Profitable Industries in the U.S.," *Inc.*, March 9, 2015.
42. F. Vogelstein, "Rebuilding Microsoft," *Wired*, October 2006.
43. A. Vance, "Netflix Announces $100,000 in Prizes for Coders," *Business-Week*, March 14, 2013.
44. D. Diamond, "The Good-Hearted Wizard—Linus Torvalds," *Virtual Finland*, January 2008.
45. S. Vaughan-Nichols, "The Five Most Popular End-User Linux Distributions," *ZDNet*, May 30, 2014.
46. K. Noyes, "94 Percent of the World's Top 500 Supercomputers Run Linux," *Linux*, November 14, 2012.
47. D. Price, "The True Market Shares of Windows vs. Linux Compared," *Make Use Of*, March 27, 2018.
48. M. Foley, "Microsoft says 40 percent of all VMs in Azure now are running Linux," *ZDNet*, Oct. 31, 2017.
49. J. Brockmeier, "NASA Using Linux," *Unix Review*, March 2004; and S. Barrett, "Linux on Mars," *Science News, Space News, Technology News*, June 6, 2008.
50. A list of criteria defining open source software can be found at the Open Source Initiative at http://opensource.org/osr.
51. J. Fortt, "Why Larry Loves Linux (and He's Not Alone)," *Fortune*, December 19, 2007.
52. D. Woods, "The Commercial Bear Hug of Open Source," *Forbes*, August 18, 2008.
53. M. Hinkle, "No Longer Why Open Source, but How to Do Open Source," *BlackDuck Software Blog*, May 7, 2014.
54. C. Preimesberger, "Sun's 'Open'-Door Policy," *eWeek*, April 21, 2008.
55. L. Columbus, "Cloud Computing Market Projected To Reach $411B By 2020," *Forbes*, Oct. 18, 2017.
56. C. Stokel-Walker, "The Internet Is Being Protected by Two Guys Named Steve," *BuzzFeed*, April 25, 2014.
57. R. King, "Cost-Conscious Companies Turn to Open-Source Software," *BusinessWeek*, December 1, 2008.
58. S. Shankland, M. Kane, and R. Lemos, "How Linux Saved Amazon Millions," *CNET*, October 30, 2001.
59. E. Raymond, *The Cathedral and the Bazaar: Musings on Linux and Open Source by an Accidental Revolutionary* (Sebastopol, CA: O'Reilly, 1999).
60. J. Ljungberg, "Open Source Movements as a Model for Organizing," *European Journal of Information Systems* 9, no. 4 (December 2000): 208–16.
61. M. Castelluccio, "Enterprise Open Source Adoption," *Strategic Finance*, November 2008.
62. D. Wheeler, *Secure Programming for Linux and Unix*, 2003, http://www.dwheeler.com/secure-programs/Secure-Programs-HOWTO/index.html.
63. R. McMillan, "Gone in Two Minutes," *InfoWorld*, March 27, 2008.
64. S. Lohr, "Microsoft to Give Governments Access to Code," *New York Times*, January 15, 2003.
65. R. King, "Cost-Conscious Companies Turn to Open-Source Software," *BusinessWeek*, December 1, 2008.
66. R. Guth, "Virtual Piecework: Trolling the Web for Free Labor, Software Upstarts Are a New Force," *Wall Street Journal*, November 13, 2006.
67. D. Goodin, "Critical Crypto Bug in OpenSSL Opens Two-Thirds of the Web to Eavesdropping," *ArsTechnica*, April 7, 2014.
68. C. Stokel-Walker, "The Internet Is Being Protected by Two Guys Named Steve," *BuzzFeed*, April 25, 2014.
69. J. Hempel, "Salesforce Hits Its Stride," *Fortune*, March 2, 2009.
70. E. Shelley, "Adobe's $4.2B ARR pivot to SaaS: The strategy behind the numbers," *ChartMogul*, April 13, 2017.
71. S. Lacy, "On-Demand Computing: A Brutal Slog," *BusinessWeek*, July 18, 2008.
72. J. Quittner, "How SaaS Helps Cut Small Business Costs," *BusinessWeek*, December 5, 2008.
73. M. Drummond, "The End of Software as We Know It," *Fortune*, November 19, 2001.
74. M. Drummond, "The End of Software as We Know It," *Fortune*, November 19, 2001.
75. R. Wauters, "The Extraordinary Rise and Fall of Denmark's IT Factory," *TechCrunch*, December 2, 2008.
76. S. Lacy, "On-Demand Computing: A Brutal Slog," *BusinessWeek*, July 18, 2008.
77. G. Gruman, "Early Experiments in Cloud Computing," *InfoWorld*, April 7, 2008.
78. D. Shapiro, "Instant Messaging and Compliance Issues: What You Need to Know," *SearchCIO*, May 17, 2004.

CHAPTER 11

Protecting the Assets: Information Security

11.1 Introduction

Learning Objectives

1. Recognize that information security breaches are on the rise.
2. Understand the potentially damaging impact of security breaches.
3. Recognize that information security must be made a top organizational priority.

"There are two kinds of companies: those who have been breached and those who don't know they've been breached"—former Cisco CEO John Chambers

Let's set the stage for our discussion of security issues, vulnerabilities, and organizational failure by examining two of the best known and most widely impactful breaches in US business history—the hack at Equifax, and the hack at Target.

Got a Bank Account or Credit Card? You've Been Hacked!

You've been hacked; or rather, an organization that has your personal data has almost certainly been hacked. One of the largest breaches ever occurred in Summer 2017 against Equifax, one of three leading firms whose business it is to monitor the creditworthiness of adults in the US and abroad. Hackers exploiting a known vulnerability grabbed data on 143 million consumers. Pretty much everyone in the US with a bank account or credit card was compromised. The stolen information included addresses, Social Security numbers, tax IDs, driver's license numbers, hundreds of thousands of credit card numbers, and more. The hack impacted those beyond US borders, with some 400,000 hit in the UK, and over 100,000 Canadians.[1] The exploit targeted a vulnerability in the widely used open source Apache Struts product. Equifax had two months to patch the vulnerability, but the firm failed at basic maintenance, leaving the door open for an easily preventable intrusion.

There was clearly something wrong with procedures and follow-through at Equifax. Even the site that Equifax set up to answer consumer questions and offer free credit monitoring was riddled with vulnerabilities.[2] Executive negligence looks even shadier considering leaders sold roughly $2 million in stock before the hack was publicly exposed.[3] The CEO promptly "retired" but was still dragged before a Congress demanding answers. The *Wall Street Journal* estimates the eventual total cost of the breach, already the most expensive in corporate history, will run into the billions.[4] Those wishing to learn more and who have a tolerance for not-suitable-for-work humor might don headphones and explore the informative, albeit curse-laden, summary of the Equifax breach and its aftermath by John Oliver on *Last Week Tonight*.

A Look at the Target Hack

After being victimized in one of the worst consumer-targeted hacking incidents in US history, the Target logo was plastered across media reports, depicted as a bull's-eye that lured cyber criminals. In the days prior to Thanksgiving 2013, a perfect time to take advantage of what would soon be a peak retail shopping season, hackers managed to install malware in Target's security and payments system. This code was designed to steal every credit card used in the company's 1,797 US stores. The bad guys' data-snarfing malware went operational on November 27. The hack shouldn't have been as damaging as it eventually became. Target had previously paid roughly $1.6 million for software from the security firm FireEye to detect breaches in real time, and the software worked. A FireEye notification went off shortly after unauthorized software began collecting data inside Target's network, but Target ignored the warning. Another alert went up within the week and Target's team ignored that warning as well. At this point, the malware hadn't begun transmitting the captured data out of Target's network, so had Target heeded the warnings, the firm could have prevented the data theft. Even worse, the firm's security software has an option to automatically delete malware as it's detected, but Target's security team had turned that function off. As a result, hackers operating out of Odessa and Moscow vacuumed up records on roughly one-third of US consumers for more than two weeks. Target's investigation didn't start until federal law enforcement contacted the firm in mid-December to report suspicious activities on cards used in its stores.[5]

The malware used to breach Target was described by one security expert as "absolutely unsophisticated and uninteresting." The code was likely snuck into Target's system using the security credentials of one of Target's partners, a heating and ventilation firm. While the area where credit card transactions are processed is supposed to be walled off from other areas of the Target network (e.g., the air conditioning guys should never be able to touch systems that read credit cards) hackers, found holes and eventually nestled their code in a sweet spot for grabbing customer data, disguising the code with the label "BladeLogic" the name of a legitimate data center management product.[6]

The damage Target suffered should lead to sleepless nights among managers in any organization that accepts sensitive customer data. Reports say 40 million cards used at Target were stolen and additional personal information on 70 million customers was exposed. The firm's CEO was booted within months. And Target isn't alone in having been caught with their guard down. Neiman Marcus Group, the crafts chain Michael's, and several other merchants were also hacked at about the same time.[7] According to one study, only 5 percent of retailers discover breaches through their own monitoring. Analysts estimate the cost of the Target breach will run into the billions: ninety lawsuits had been filed within ninety days of the attack's public disclosure; on top of that, Target's holiday quarter profits fell 46 percent from the prior year, and the retailer reported its biggest ever decline in transactions.[8] The massive impact of the Target breach should make it clear that security must be a top organizational priority. According to Accenture, the average cost of a data breach is up 23 percent in a single year, to $11.7 million.[9] IBM claims the average time to identify a breach in the study was 201 days, and the average time to contain a breach was 70 days.[10] Annual worldwide cybercrime costs a jaw-dropping $600 billion per year.[11] Health insurer Anthem and the US Government Office of Personnel Management are among the organizations that have since suffered high-profile and deeply damaging hacks that have released personal information on tens of millions of people.[12] While the examples and scenarios presented here are shocking, the good news is that the vast majority of security breaches can be prevented. Let's be clear from the start: no text can provide an approach that will guarantee that you'll be 100 percent secure. And that's not the goal of this chapter. The issues raised in this brief introduction can, however, help make you aware of vulnerabilities; improve your critical thinking regarding current and future security issues; and help you consider whether a firm has technologies, training, policies, and procedures in place to assess risks, lessen the likelihood of damage, and respond in the event of a breach. A constant vigilance regarding security needs to be part of your individual skill set and a key component in your organization's culture. An awareness of the threats and approaches discussed in this chapter should help reduce your chance of becoming a victim.

As we examine security issues, we'll first need to understand what's happening, who's doing it, and what their motivation is. We'll then examine how these breaches are happening, with a focus on technologies and procedures. Finally, we'll sum up with what can be done to minimize the risks of being victimized and quell potential damage of a breach for both the individual and the organization.

Key Takeaways

- Information security is everyone's business and needs to be made a top organizational priority.
- Firms suffering a security breach can experience direct financial loss, exposed proprietary information, fines, legal payouts, court costs, damaged reputations, plummeting stock prices, and more.
- Information security isn't just a technology problem; a host of personnel, operational, and procedural factors can create and amplify a firm's vulnerability.

Questions and Exercises

1. The data breaches at Equifax and Target Corporation are among the largest ever in US history. Were you impacted by this breach (or any other)? How did you find out about the breach? Did you take action as a result? Research and report the estimated costs associated with this breach. Has the theft resulted in additional security issues for the individuals who had their data stolen?
2. What factors were responsible for the Target and Equifax breaches? Who should have been responsible for these breaches? How do you think the firms could have prevented the attacks, and what should they do in the future to heighten security and win back customer trust?
3. As individuals or in groups assigned by your instructor, search online for recent reports on information security breaches. Come to class prepared to discuss a breach you've researched, its potential impact, and how it might have been avoided. What should the key takeaways be for managers studying your example?
4. Think of firms that you've done business with online. Search to see if these firms have experienced security breaches in the past. What have you found out? Does this change your attitude about dealing with the firm? Why or why not?

11.2 Why Is This Happening? Who Is Doing It? And What's Their Motivation?

Learning Objectives

1. Understand the source and motivation of those initiating information security attacks.
2. Relate examples of various infiltrations in a way that helps raise organizational awareness of threats.

Thieves, vandals, and other bad guys have always existed, but the environment has changed. Today, nearly every organization is online, making any Internet-connected network a potential entry point for the growing worldwide community of computer criminals, state-sponsored infiltrators, corporate spies, and other malfeasants. Software and hardware solutions are also more complex than ever. Different vendors, each with its own potential weaknesses, provide technology components that may be compromised by misuse, misconfiguration, or mismanagement. With the rise of "big data," corporations have become data pack rats, hoarding information in hopes of turning bits into bucks by licensing databases, targeting advertisements, or cross-selling products. And flatter organizations also mean that lower-level employees may be able to use technology to reach deep into corporate assets—amplifying threats from operator error, a renegade employee, or one compromised by external forces.

There are a lot of bad guys out there, and motivations vary widely, including the following:

- Account theft and illegal funds transfer
- Stealing personal or financial data
- Compromising computing assets for use in other crimes
- Extortion
- Intellectual property theft
- Espionage
- Cyberwarfare
- Terrorism
- Pranksters
- Protest hacking (hacktivism)
- Revenge (disgruntled employees)

British insurance company Lloyd's estimates that cybercrime and cyber espionage will cost the US economy $2 trillion by 2019.[13] Nearly all of this is done "without drawing a gun or passing a note to a teller."[14] While some steal cash for their own use, others resell their hacking take to others. There is a thriving cybercrime underworld market in which **data harvesters** sell to **cash-out fraudsters**: criminals who might purchase data from the harvesters in order to buy (then resell) goods using stolen credit cards or create false accounts via identity theft. These collection and resale operations are efficient and sophisticated. Law enforcement has taken down sites like DarkMarket and ShadowCrew, in which card thieves and hacking tool peddlers received eBay-style seller ratings vouching for the "quality" of their wares.[15]

data harvesters

Cybercriminals who infiltrate systems and collect data for illegal resale.

cash-out fraudsters

Criminals who purchase assets from data harvesters to be used for illegal financial gain. Actions may include using stolen credit card numbers to purchase goods, creating fake accounts via identity fraud, and more.

Hackers might also infiltrate computer systems to enlist hardware for subsequent illegal acts. A cybercrook might deliberately hop through several systems to make his path difficult to follow, slowing cross-border legal pursuit or even thwarting prosecution if launched from nations without extradition agreements.

In fact, your computer may be up for rent by cyber thieves right now. **Botnets** (or zombie networks) of zombie computers (networks of infiltrated and compromised machines controlled by a central command) are used for all sorts of nefarious activity. This includes sending spam from thousands of difficult-to-shut-down accounts, launching tough-to-track click fraud efforts or staging what's known as **distributed denial of service (DDoS)** attacks (effectively shutting down websites by overwhelming them with a crushing load of seemingly legitimate requests sent simultaneously by thousands of machines). Botnets have been discovered that are capable of sending out 100 billion spam messages a day,[16] and botnets as large as 10 million zombies have been identified. Such systems theoretically control more computing power than the world's fastest supercomputers.[17]

botnets

Hordes of surreptitiously infiltrated computers, linked and controlled remotely, also known as zombie networks.

distributed denial of service (DDoS)

An attack where a firm's computer systems are flooded with thousands of seemingly legitimate requests, the sheer volume of which will slow or shut down the site's use. DDoS attacks are often performed via botnets.

Extortionists might leverage botnets or hacked data to demand payment to avoid retribution. Three eastern European gangsters used a botnet and threatened DDoS to extort $4 million from UK sports bookmakers,[18] while an extortion plot against the state of Virginia threatened to reveal names, Social Security numbers, and prescription information stolen from a medical records database.[19] Competition has also lowered the price to inflict such pain. *BusinessWeek* reports that the cost of renting out ten thousand machines, which at the time was enough to cripple a site like Twitter, had tumbled to just $200 a day.[20]

Ransomware allow, criminals to move beyond extortion to take data assets hostage. Ransomware will lock and encrypt infected computers, rendering them unusable and irrecoverable unless instructions are followed—often involving payment in untraceable bitcoin. IBM pins total losses at more than $8 billion.[21]

In Spring 2018, the city of Atlanta fell victim to a well-known, but crippling ransomware exploit known as SamSam. The attack disrupted five government departments, hobbling the city's court system, blocking the payment of residential water bills, making it impossible for the city to collect parking fines, and causing the police department to shift to inefficient paper instead of electronic reports.[22] SamSam attacks on governments, hospitals, and non-profits have extorted roughly $850,000 in bitcoin payments from victims.[23]

Corporate espionage might be performed by insiders, rivals, or even foreign governments. Gary Min, a scientist working for DuPont, was busted when he tried to sell information valued at some $400 million, including R&D documents and secret data on proprietary products.[24] Spies also breached the $300 billion US Joint Strike Fighter project, siphoning off terabytes of data on navigation and other electronics systems.[25] Hackers infiltrated security firm RSA, stealing data keys used in the firm's commercial authentication devices. The hackers then apparently leveraged the heist to enter the systems of RSA customers, US Defense contractors L3, Lockheed Martin, and Northrop Grumman.[26] Google has identified China as the nation of origin for a series of hacks targeting the Google accounts of diplomats and activists.[27] The US government has indicted Chinese military officials, even printing up "Most Wanted" posters, claiming those named were behind terabytes of theft from organizations including Alcoa, US Steel, the US Steelworkers Union, electricity and nuclear energy firm Westinghouse, Allegheny Technologies Inc., and SolarWorld.[28] US federal authorities blamed the embarrassing hacking and exposure of internal documents and e-mail from Sony Entertainment on operatives for the government of North Korea, angry about the release of the Kim Jong-un–ridiculing comedy *The Interview*, while researchers suggested the Sony hack was actually perpetrated by insiders.[29] And the government of Tunisia even attempted a whole-scale hacking of local users' Facebook accounts during protests that eventually led to the ouster of the regime. The so-called man-in-the-middle style attack intercepted Facebook traffic at the state-affiliated ISP as it traveled between Tunisian Web surfers and Facebook's servers, enabling the government to steal passwords and delete posts and photos that criticized the regime (Facebook has since made these efforts more difficult to perpetrate).[30]

FIGURE 11.1 Chinese Military Officials Charged with Cyber Espionage Against the US

FBI posted images of indicted Chinese military officials charged with cyber espionage against the United States.

Source: FBI.gov website, accessed May 26, 2013, http://www.fbi.gov/news/news_blog/five-chinese-military-hackers-charged-with-cyber-espionage-against-u.s.

Cyberwarfare has also become a legitimate threat, with several attacks demonstrating how devastating technology disruptions by terrorists or a foreign power might be (see sidebar on Stuxnet). Brazil has seen hacks that cut off power to millions; attacks in Spring 2018 cut off communications of at least seven US pipeline firms;[31] and the *60 Minutes* news program showed a demonstration by "white hat" hackers that could compromise a key component in an oil refinery, force it to overheat, and cause an explosion. Taking out key components of the vulnerable US power grid may be particularly devastating, as the equipment is expensive, much of it is no longer made in the United States, and some components may take three to four months to replace.[32]

Stuxnet: A New Era of Cyberwarfare

Stuxnet may be the most notorious known act of cyberwarfare effort to date (one expert called it "the most sophisticated worm ever created").[33] Suspected to have been launched by either US or Israeli intelligence (or both), Stuxnet infiltrated Iranian nuclear facilities and reprogrammed the industrial control software operating hundreds of uranium-enriching centrifuges. The worm made the devices spin so fast that the centrifuges effectively destroyed themselves, in the process setting back any Iranian nuclear ambitions. The attack was so sophisticated that it even altered equipment readings to report normal activity so that operators didn't even know something was wrong until it was too late.

Some might fear Stuxnet in the wild—what happens if the code spread to systems operated by peaceful nations or systems controlling critical infrastructure that could threaten lives if infected? In Stuxnet's case the worm appears to have been designed to target very specific systems. If it got onto a nontarget machine, it would become inert. Propagation was also limited, with each copy designed to infect only three additional machines. And the virus was also designed to self-destruct at a future date.[34] Despite these precautions, other malicious code that appears to have a common heritage with Stuxnet has been spotted on systems outside of Iran.[35] Spy code has been leaked to the public. This includes the 2017 release by the hacker group Shadow Brokers of a suite of tools believed developed by the US National Security Agency. Related documents in Wikileaks claim one of the tools in this suite allowed the CIA to spy on users using Samsung TVs that were set in a "fake off" mode.[36]

Stuxnet showed that with computers at the heart of so many systems, it's now possible to destroy critical infrastructure without firing a shot.[37] What does the rise of cyberwarfare mean for future combat and for citizen vulnerability, and what might this mean for businesses whose products, services, or organizations may become targets?

How Bots and Trolls Targeted US Elections

This video explains how bots and trolls targeted US elections.

View the video online at: http://www.youtube.com/embed/sZmrlkRDMsU?rel=0

Espionage efforts have also expanded beyond threats against infrastructure and into attempts to influence democracy and create political chaos. A 2018 indictment filed by the US Special Counsel alleged a Russian government-linked conspiracy aimed at *"impairing, obstructing and defeating the lawful governmental functions of the United States."* The indictment claims a multi-year effort backed by tens of millions of dollars aimed at influencing American opinion.[38] Alleged efforts were specifically designed to benefit campaigns of Bernie Sanders and underdog-turned-president Donald Trump. Russian-linked efforts allegedly included an army of false-fact-spewing fake social media personas, as well as social media groups posing as initiatives led by US citizen activists. It is believed some of these groups accrued over 100,000 followers. Similar attempts to influence European democracies were also alleged.[39] The US news program *60 Minutes* further alleges a Russian-conducted "sweeping assault" on American voting systems. While systems had been penetrated, at the time of writing there was no evidence that voting records or votes were altered (in fact, the largely aging voting systems themselves are not connected to the Internet). However, agencies worldwide have alleged the goal was not direct altering of data, but rather psychological influence fanning the flames of division and casting doubt on the integrity of leading democracies.[40]

Other threats come from malicious pranksters (sometimes called *griefers* or *trolls*), like the group that posted seizure-inducing images on websites frequented by epilepsy sufferers.[41] Others are **hacktivists**, targeting firms, websites, or even users as a protest measure. Twitter was once brought down and Facebook and LiveJournal were hobbled as Russian-sympathizing hacktivists targeted the social networking and blog accounts of the Georgian blogger known as Cyxymu. The silencing of millions of accounts was simply collateral damage in a massive DDoS attack meant to mute this single critic of the Russian government.[42]

hacktivists

A protester seeking to make a political point by leveraging technology tools, often through system infiltration, defacement, or damage.

And as power and responsibility are concentrated in the hands of a few, revenge-seeking employees can do great damage. The San Francisco city government lost control of a large portion of its own computer network over a ten-day period when a single disgruntled employee refused to divulge critical passwords.[43]

Is Your Government Spying on You?

While sinister and invasive government espionage tools have long been a plot vehicle in Hollywood films, the extent of government surveillance came under scrutiny when a former CIA employee and NSA contractor, Edward Snowden, gathered over 1.7 million digital documents from US, British, and Australian agencies and began leaking them to the press.

FIGURE 11.2 Edward Snowden

Source: Laura Poitras / Praxis Films [CC BY 3.0 (https://creativecommons.org/licenses/by/3.0)], via Wikimedia Commons.

The Snowden disclosures revealed that several US government agencies, including the NSA and FBI, had data-monitoring efforts far more pervasive than many realized. These included mechanisms for the "direct access to audio, video, photographs, e-mails, documents and connection logs" at nine major US Internet companies, including Google, Facebook, Yahoo!, Microsoft, and Apple,[44] and *unlimited* access to phone records from Verizon's US customers.[45] Another tool, XKeyscore, has been described as allowing the collection of data on "nearly everything a user does on the Internet" and enabling "analysts to search with no prior authorization through vast databases containing emails, online chats and the browsing histories of millions of individuals."[46] A program tapping undersea cables has allowed US and British intelligence authorities to sift through some 21 million GB of data each day.[47] The British intelligence agency GCHQ, using a system code-named "Optic Nerve," allegedly collected Web cam images "from millions of Yahoo users, regardless of whether they were suspected of illegal activity," and up to 11 percent of secretly collected images were thought to have been sexually explicit.[48] Snowden also revealed monitoring programs targeting US allies, including one that eavesdropped on the private phone conversations of German Chancellor Angela Merkel.[49]

Whether Snowden was a whistle-blower or traitor is hotly debated. After the revelations, Snowden fled to Russia via Hong Kong (where he had previously been living during the document disclosure), and the Putin government has granted him temporary asylum. The US government has charged Snowden with espionage and revoked his passport, but during this time, Snowden has spoken via remote link at the South by Southwest Conference, appeared via video conference at a TED event, and has been elected rector of the University of Glasgow. Regardless of whether you feel that Edward Snowden is a hero, a villain, or something in between, the Snowden case underscores the sensitivity of data collection and the peril that governments and organizations face when technology without adequate safeguards is used along the frontier where privacy and national security meet.

The US government contends that hundreds of terrorists have been captured using techniques revealed by Snowden, implying that this surveillance makes the world more secure.[50] The US government claims that safeguards are in place to prevent widespread abuse. For example, under US law, the NSA is required to obtain a warrant from the Foreign Intelligence Surveillance Court (or FISA) when specifically targeting surveillance in the United States.[51] However, no such warrants are required for intercepting communication between US-based persons and "foreign targets,"[52] and FISA has rejected only eleven of the more than 33,900 requests (less than 0.03 percent) made in over three decades since the act was established.[53] Even if such surveillance programs are well intentioned, risks include having the data fall into the hands of foreign spies, rogue employees, criminals, or unscrupulous government employees. US technology firms have also complained that the actions of surveillance agencies have put them at a disadvantage, with customers looking for alternatives free of the tarnished perception of having (complicitly or unwittingly) provided private information to authorities.[54] European firms, in particular, have noticed an uptick in business, and one estimate pins projected collective losses to US firms at $35 billion through 2016.[55]

The bad guys are legion, and the good guys often seem outmatched and underresourced. Law enforcement agencies dealing with computer crime are increasingly outnumbered, outskilled, and underfunded. Many agencies are staffed with technically weak personnel who were trained in a prior era's crime-fighting techniques. Governments can rarely match the pay scale and stock bonuses offered by private industry. Organized crime networks now have their own R&D labs and are engaged in sophisticated development efforts to piece together methods to thwart current security measures.

"Hacker": Good or Bad?

The terms **hacker** and **hack** are widely used, but their meaning is often based on context. When referring to security issues, the media often refers to hackers as bad guys who try to break into (hack) computer systems. Some geezer geeks object to this use, as the term *hack* in computer circles originally referred to a clever (often technical) solution and the term *hacker* referred to a particularly skilled programmer. Expect to see the terms used both positively and negatively.

You might also encounter the terms **white hat hackers** and **black hat hackers**. The white hats are the good guys who probe for weaknesses, but don't exploit them. Instead, they share their knowledge in hopes that the holes they've found will be plugged and security will be improved. Many firms hire consultants to conduct "white hat" hacking expeditions on their own assets as part of their auditing and security process. "Black hats" are the bad guys. Some call them "crackers." There's even a well-known series of hacker conventions known as the Black Hat conference.

hacker

A term that, depending on the context, may be applied to either 1) someone who breaks into computer systems, or 2) to a particularly clever programmer.

hack

A term that may, depending on the context, refer to either 1) breaking into a computer system, or 2) a particularly clever solution.

white hat hackers

Someone who uncovers computer weaknesses without exploiting them. The goal of the white hat hacker is to improve system security.

black hat hackers

A computer criminal.

Key Takeaways

- Computer security threats have moved beyond the curious teen with a PC and are now sourced from a number of motivations, including theft, leveraging compromised computing assets, extortion, espionage, warfare, terrorism, national security, pranks, protest, and revenge.
- Threats can come from both within the firm as well as from the outside.
- Cybercriminals operate in an increasingly sophisticated ecosystem where data harvesters and tool peddlers leverage robust online markets to sell to cash-out fraudsters and other crooks.
- Technical and legal complexity make pursuit and prosecution difficult.
- Government surveillance efforts can put citizens and corporations at risk if poorly executed and ineffectively managed.
- Many law enforcement agencies are underfunded, underresourced, and underskilled to deal with the growing hacker threat.

Questions and Exercises

1. What is a botnet? What sorts of exploits would use a botnet? Why would a botnet be useful to cybercriminals?
2. Why are threats to the power grid potentially so concerning? What are the implications of power grid failure and of property damage? Who might execute these kinds of attacks? What are the implications for firms and governments planning for the possibility of cyberwarfare and cyberterror?
3. Scan the trade press for examples of hacking that apply to the various motivations mentioned in this chapter. What happened to the hacker? Were they caught? What penalties do they face?
4. Why do cybercriminals execute attacks across national borders? What are the implications for pursuit, prosecution, and law enforcement?
5. Why do law enforcement agencies struggle to cope with computer crime?
6. A single rogue employee effectively held the city of San Francisco's network hostage for ten days. What processes or controls might the city have created that could have prevented this kind of situation from taking place?
7. Research recent revelations on the extent of government data surveillance. What concerns do government surveillance raise for the computer security of individuals and corporations? Do you believe that there are adequate safeguards to prevent abuse? As a citizen and manager, what changes (if any) would you lobby for and why?
8. The Geneva Conventions are a set of international treaties that in part set standards for protecting citizens in and around a war zone. Should we have similar rules that set the limits of cyberwarfare? Would such limits even be effective? Why or why not?
9. What does the rise of cyberwarfare suggest for businesses and organizations? What sorts of contingencies should firms consider and possibly prepare for? How might considerations also impact a firm's partners, customers, and suppliers?

11.3 Taking Action

Learning Objectives

1. Identify critical steps to improve your individual and organizational information security.
2. Be a tips, tricks, and techniques advocate, helping make your friends, family, colleagues, and organization more secure.
3. Recognize the major information security issues that organizations face, as well as the resources, methods, and approaches that can help make firms more secure.

Taking Action as a User

The weakest link in security is often a careless user, so don't make yourself an easy mark. Once you get a sense of threats, you understand the kinds of precautions you need to take. Security considerations then become more common sense than high tech. Here's a brief list of major issues to consider:

- *Surf smart.* Think before you click—question links, enclosures, download requests, and the integrity of websites that you visit. Avoid suspicious e-mail attachments and Internet downloads. Be on guard for phishing and other attempts to con you into letting in malware. Verify anything that looks suspicious before acting. Avoid using public machines (libraries, coffee shops) when accessing sites that contain your financial data or other confidential information.
- *Stay vigilant.* Social engineering con artists and rogue insiders are out there. An appropriate level of questioning applies not only to computer use, but also to personal interactions, be it in person, on the phone, or electronically.
- *Stay updated.* Turn on software update features for your operating system and any application you use (browsers, applications, plug-ins, and applets), and manually check for updates when needed. Malware toolkits specifically scan for older, vulnerable systems, so working with updated programs that address prior concerns lowers your vulnerable attack surface.
- *Stay armed.* Install a full suite of security software. Many vendors offer a combination of products that provide antivirus software that blocks infection, personal firewalls that repel unwanted intrusion, malware scanners that seek out bad code that might already be nesting on your PC, antiphishing software that identifies if you're visiting questionable websites, and more. Such tools are increasingly being built into operating systems, browsers, and are deployed at the ISP or service provider (e-mail firm, social network) level. But every consumer should make it a priority to understand the state of the art for personal protection. In the way that you regularly balance your investment portfolio to account for economic shifts, or take your car in for an oil change to keep it in top running condition, make it a priority to periodically scan the major trade press or end-user computing sites for reviews and commentary on the latest tools and techniques for protecting yourself (and your firm).
- *Be settings smart.* Don't turn on risky settings like unrestricted folder sharing that may act as an invitation for hackers to drop off malware payloads. Secure home networks with password protection and a firewall. Encrypt hard drives—especially on laptops or other devices that might be lost or stolen. Register mobile devices for location identification or remote wiping. Don't click the "Remember me" or "Save password" settings on public machines, or any device that might be shared or accessed by others. Similarly, if your machine might be used by others, turn off browser settings that auto-fill fields with prior entries—otherwise you make it easy for someone to use that machine to track your entries and impersonate you. And when using public hotspots, be sure to turn on your VPN software to encrypt transmission and hide from network eavesdroppers.
- *Be password savvy.* Change the default password on any new products that you install. Update your passwords regularly. Using guidelines outlined earlier, choose passwords that are tough to guess but easy for you (and only you) to remember. Generate your passwords so that you're not using the same access codes for your most secure sites. Never save passwords in nonsecured files, e-mail, or written down in easily accessed locations. Consider a secure password management tool such as 1Password or LastPass and be sure to use the software and manage the master password effectively.
- *Be disposal smart.* Shred personal documents. Wipe hard drives with an industrial strength software tool before recycling, donating, or throwing away—remember in many cases "deleted" files can still be recovered. Destroy media such as CDs and DVDs that may contain sensitive information. Erase USB drives when they are no longer needed.

- *Back up.* The most likely threat to your data doesn't come from hackers; it comes from hardware failure.[56] Yet most users still don't regularly back up their systems. This is another do-it-now priority. Cheap, plug-in hard drives work with most modern operating systems to provide continual backups, allowing for quick rollback to earlier versions if you've accidentally ruined some vital work. And services like Carbonite or Mozy provide regular backup over the Internet for a monthly fee that's likely less than what you spent on your last lunch (a fire, theft, or similar event could also result in the loss of any backups stored on-site, but Internet backup services can provide off-site storage and access if disaster strikes).
- *Check with your administrator.* All organizations that help you connect to the Internet—your ISP, firm, or school—should have security pages. Many provide free security software tools. Use them as resources. Remember—it's in their interest to keep you safe, too!

Taking Action as an Organization

Frameworks, Standards, and Compliance

Developing organizational security is a daunting task. You're in an arms race with adversaries that are tenacious and constantly on the lookout for new exploits. Fortunately, no firm is starting from scratch—others have gone before you and many have worked together to create published best practices.

There are several frameworks, but perhaps the best known of these efforts comes from the International Organization for Standards (ISO), and is broadly referred to as ISO27k or the ISO 27000 series. According to ISO.org, this evolving set of standards provides "a model for establishing, implementing, operating, monitoring, reviewing, maintaining, and improving an Information Security Management System."

Firms may also face compliance requirements—legal or professionally binding steps that must be taken. Failure to do so could result in fine, sanction, and other punitive measures. At the federal level, examples include HIPAA (the Health Insurance Portability and Accountability Act), which regulates health data; the Gramm-Leach-Bliley Act, which regulates financial data; and the Children's Online Privacy Protection Act, which regulates data collection on minors. US government agencies must also comply with FISMA (the Federal Information Security Management Act), and there are several initiatives at the other government levels. Some level of state data breach laws have been passed in most US states, while multinationals face a growing number of statues throughout the world. Your legal team and trade associations can help you understand your domestic and international obligations. Fortunately, there are often frameworks and guidelines to assist in compliance. For example, the ISO standards include subsets targeted at the telecommunications and health care industries, and major credit card firms have created the PCI (payment card industry) standards. And there are skilled consulting professionals who can help bring firms up to speed in these areas and help expand their organizational radar as new issues develop.

Here is a word of warning on frameworks and standards: compliance does not equal security. Outsourcing portions of security efforts without a complete, organizational commitment to being secure can also be dangerous. Some organizations simply approach compliance as a necessary evil, a sort of checklist that can reduce the likelihood of a lawsuit or other punitive measure.[57] While you want to make sure you're doing everything in your power not to get sued, this isn't the goal. The goal is taking all appropriate measures to ensure that your firm is secure for your customers, employees, shareholders, and others. Frameworks help shape your thinking and expose things you should do, but security doesn't stop there—this is a constant, evolving process that needs to pervade the organization from the CEO suite and board, down to front line workers and potentially out to customers and partners. And be aware of the security issues associated with any mergers and acquisitions. Bringing in new firms, employees, technologies, and procedures means reassessing the security environment for all players involved.

The Heartland Breach: Compliance ≠ Security

Credit card processor Heartland, at the time of the attack that would become one of the largest security breaches in history, was the nation's fifth largest payments processor. Its business was responsible for handling the transfer of funds and information between retailers and cardholders' financial institutions. That means infiltrating Heartland was like breaking into Fort Knox.

It's been estimated that as many as 100 million cards issued by more than 650 financial services companies may have been compromised during the Heartland breach. Said the firm's CEO, this was "the worst thing that can happen to a payments company and it happened to us."[58] Wall Street noticed. The firm's stock tanked—within a month, its market capitalization had plummeted over 75 percent, dropping over half a billion dollars in value.[59]

The Heartland case provides a cautionary warning against thinking that security ends with compliance. Heartland had in fact passed multiple audits, including one conducted the month before the infiltration began. Still, at least thirteen pieces of malware were uncovered on the firm's servers. Compliance does not equal security. Heartland was compliant, but a firm can be compliant and not be secure. Compliance is not the goal, security is.

Since the breach, the firm's executives have championed industry efforts to expand security practices, including encrypting card information at the point it is swiped and keeping it secure through settlement. Such "cradle-to-grave" encryption can help create an environment where even compromised networking equipment or intercepting relay systems wouldn't be able to grab codes.[60] Recognize that security is a continual process, it is never done, and firms need to pursue security with tenacity and commitment.

Education, Audit, and Enforcement

Security is as much about people, process, and policy, as it is about technology.

From a people perspective, the security function requires multiple levels of expertise. Operations employees are involved in the day-to-day monitoring of existing systems. A group's R&D function is involved in understanding emerging threats and reviewing, selecting, and implementing updated security techniques. A team must also work on broader governance issues. These efforts should include representatives from specialized security and broader technology and infrastructure functions. It should also include representatives from general counsel, audit, public relations, and human resources. What this means is that even if you're a nontechnical staffer, you may be brought in to help a firm deal with security issues.

Processes and policies will include education and awareness—this is also everyone's business. As the vice president of product development at security firm Symantec puts it, "We do products really well, but the next step is education. We can't keep the Internet safe with antivirus software alone."[61] Companies should approach information security as a part of their "collective corporate responsibility...regardless of whether regulation requires them to do so."[62]

For a lesson in how important education is, look no further than former head of the CIA and US Director of Intelligence John Deutch. Deutch engaged in shockingly loose behavior with digital secrets, including keeping a daily journal of classified information—some 1,000+ pages—on memory cards he'd transport in his shirt pocket. He also downloaded and stored Pentagon information, including details of covert operations, at home on computers that his family used for routine Internet access.[63]

Employees need to know a firm's policies, be regularly trained, and understand that they will face strict penalties if they fail to meet their obligations. Policies without eyes (audit) and teeth (enforcement) won't be taken seriously. Audits include real-time monitoring of usage (e.g., who's accessing what, from where, how, and why; sound the alarm if an anomaly is detected), announced audits, and surprise spot-checks. This function might also stage white hat demonstration attacks—attempts to hunt for and expose weaknesses, hopefully before hackers find them. Frameworks offer guidelines on auditing, but a recent survey found most organizations don't document enforcement procedures in their information security policies, that more than one-third do not audit or monitor user compliance with security policies, and that only 48 percent annually measure and review the effectiveness of security policies.[64]

A firm's technology development and deployment processes must also integrate with the security team to ensure that from the start, applications, databases, and other systems are implemented with security in mind. The team will have specialized skills and monitor the latest threats and are able to advise on precautions necessary to be sure systems aren't compromised during installation, development, testing, and deployment.

What Needs to Be Protected and How Much Is Enough?

A worldwide study by PricewaterhouseCoopers and *Chief Security Officer* magazine revealed that most firms don't even know what they need to protect. Only 33 percent of executives responded that their organizations kept accurate inventory of the locations and jurisdictions where data was stored, and only 24 percent kept inventory of all third parties using their customer data.[65] What this means is that most firms don't even have an accurate read on where their valuables are kept, let alone how to protect them.

So information security should start with an inventory-style auditing and risk assessment. Technologies map back to specific business risks. What do we need to protect? What are we afraid might happen? And how do we protect it? Security is an economic problem, involving attack likelihood, costs, and prevention benefits. These are complex trade-offs that must consider losses from theft or resources, systems damage, data loss, disclosure of proprietary information, recovery, downtime, stock price declines, legal fees, government and compliance penalties, and intangibles such as damaged firm reputation, loss of customer and partner confidence, industry damage, promotion of adversary, and encouragement of future attacks.

While many firms skimp on security, firms also don't want to misspend, targeting exploits that aren't likely while underinvesting in easily prevented methods to thwart common infiltration techniques. Hacker conventions like DefCon can show some really wild exploits. But it's up to the firm to assess how vulnerable it is to these various risks. The local donut shop has far different needs than a military installation, law enforcement agency, financial institution, or firm housing other high-value electronic assets. A skilled risk assessment team will consider these vulnerabilities and what sort of countermeasure investments should take place.

Economic decisions usually drive hacker behavior, too. While in some cases attacks are based on vendetta or personal reasons, in most cases exploit economics largely boils down to:

$$\text{Adversary ROI} = \text{Asset value to adversary} - \text{Adversary cost.}$$

An adversary's costs include not only the resources, knowledge, and technology required for the exploit, but also the risk of getting caught. Make things tough to get at, and lobbying for legislation that imposes severe penalties on crooks can help raise adversary costs and lower your likelihood of becoming a victim.

Technology's Role

Technical solutions often involve industrial strength variants of the previously discussed issues individuals can employ, so your awareness is already high. Additionally, an organization's approach will often leverage multiple layers of protection and incorporate a wide variety of protective measures.

Patch. Firms must be especially vigilant to pay attention to security bulletins and install software updates that plug existing holes, (often referred to as *patches*). Firms that don't plug known problems will be vulnerable to trivial and automated attacks. Unfortunately, many firms aren't updating all components of their systems with consistent attention. With operating systems automating security update installations, hackers have moved on to application targets. But a major study recently found that organizations took at least twice as long to patch application vulnerabilities as they take to patch operating system holes.[66] And remember, software isn't limited to conventional PCs and servers. Embedded systems abound, and connected, yet unpatched devices are vulnerable. Malware has infected everything from unprotected ATM machines[67] to restaurant point-of-sale systems[68] to fighter plane navigation systems.[69]

As an example of unpatched vulnerabilities, consider the DNS cache poisoning exploit described earlier in this chapter. The discovery of this weakness was one of the biggest security stories the year it was discovered, and security experts saw this as a major threat. Teams of programmers worldwide raced to provide fixes for the most widely used versions of DNS software. Yet several months after patches were available, roughly one-quarter of all DNS servers were still unpatched and exposed.[70]

To be fair, not all firms delay patches out of negligence. Some organizations have legitimate concerns about testing whether the patch will break their system or whether the new technology contains a change that will cause problems down the road.[71] And there have been cases where patches themselves have caused problems. Finally, many software updates require that systems be taken down. Firms may have uptime requirements that make immediate patching difficult. But ultimately, unpatched systems are an open door for infiltration.

Lock down hardware. Firms range widely in the security regimes used to govern purchase-through-disposal system use. While some large firms such as Kraft are allowing employees to select their own hardware (Mac or PC, desktop or notebook, iPhone or BlackBerry),[72] others issue standard systems that prevent all unapproved software installation and force file saving to hardened, backed-up, scanned, and monitored servers. Firms in especially sensitive industries such as financial services may regularly re-image the hard drive of end-user PCs, completely replacing all the bits on a user's hard drive with a pristine, current version—effectively wiping out malware that might have previously sneaked onto a user's PC. Other lock-down methods might disable the boot capability of removable media (a common method for spreading viruses via inserted discs or USBs), prevent Wi-Fi use or require VPN encryption before allowing any network transmissions, and more. The cloud helps here, too (see [Content Removed: #fwk-38086-ch10]). Employers can also require workers to run all of their corporate applications inside a remote desktop where the actual executing hardware and software is elsewhere (likely hosted as a virtual machine session on the organization's servers), and the user is simply served an image of what is executing remotely. This seals the virtual PC off in a way that can be thoroughly monitored, updated, backed up, and locked down by the firm.

In the case of Kraft, executives worried that the firm's previously restrictive technology policies prevented employees from staying in step with trends. Employees opting into the system must sign an agreement promising they'll follow mandated security procedures. Still, financial services firms, law offices, health care providers, and others may need to maintain stricter control, for legal and industry compliance reasons.

Lock down the network. Network monitoring is a critical part of security, and a host of technical tools can help.

Firms employ **firewalls** to examine traffic as it enters and leaves the network, potentially blocking certain types of access, while permitting approved communication. **Intrusion detection systems** specifically look for unauthorized behavior, sounding the alarm and potentially taking action if something seems amiss. Some firms deploy **honeypots**—bogus offerings meant to distract attackers. If attackers take honeypot bait, firms may gain an opportunity to recognize the hacker's exploits, identify the IP address of intrusion, and take action to block further attacks and alert authorities.

Many firms also deploy **blacklists**—denying the entry or exit of specific IP addresses, products, Internet domains, and other communication restrictions. While blacklists block known bad guys, **whitelists** are even more restrictive—permitting communication only with approved entities or in an approved manner.

These technologies can be applied to network technology, specific applications, screening for certain kinds of apps, malware signatures, and hunting for anomalous patterns. The latter is important, as recent malware has become polymorphic, meaning different versions are created and deployed in a way that their signature, a sort of electronic fingerprint often used to recognize malicious code, is slightly altered. This also helps with zero-day exploits, and in situations where whitelisted websites themselves become compromised.

Many technical solutions, ranging from network monitoring and response to e-mail screening, are migrating to "the cloud." This can be a good thing—if network monitoring software immediately shares news of a certain type of attack, defenses might be pushed out to all clients of a firm (the more users, the "smarter" the system can potentially become—again we see the power of network effects in action).

Lock down partners. Insist that partner firms be compliant, and audit them to ensure this is the case. This includes technology providers and contract firms, as well as value chain participants such as suppliers and distributors. Anyone who touches your network is a potential point of weakness. Many firms will build security expectations and commitments into performance guarantees known as service level agreements (SLAs).

Lock down systems. Audit for SQL injection and other application exploits. The security team must constantly scan exploits and then probe its systems to see if it's susceptible, advising and enforcing action if problems are uncovered. This kind of auditing should occur with all of a firm's partners.

Access controls can also compartmentalize data access on a need-to-know basis. Such tools can not only enforce access privileges, they can help create and monitor audit trails to help verify that systems are not being accessed by the unauthorized, or in suspicious ways.

Audit trails are used for deterring, identifying, and investigating these cases. Recording, monitoring, and auditing access allows firms to hunt for patterns of abuse. Logs can detail who, when, and from where assets are accessed. Giveaways of nefarious activity may include access from unfamiliar IP addresses, from nonstandard times, accesses that occur at higher than usual volumes, and so on. Automated alerts can put an account on hold or call in a response team for further observation of the anomaly.

Single-sign-on tools can help firms offer employees one very strong password that works across applications, is changed frequently (or managed via hardware cards or mobile phone log-in), and can be altered by password management staff.

Multiple administrators should jointly control key systems. Major configuration changes might require approval of multiple staffers, as well as the automatic notification of concerned personnel. And firms should employ a recovery mechanism to regain control in the event that key administrators are incapacitated or uncooperative. This balances security needs with an ability to respond in the event of a crisis. Such a system was not in place in the earlier described case of the rogue IT staffer who held the city of San Francisco's networks hostage by refusing to give up vital passwords.

firewalls

A system that acts as a control for network traffic, blocking unauthorized traffic while permitting acceptable use.

intrusion detection systems

A system that monitors network use for potential hacking attempts. Such a system may take preventative action to block, isolate, or identify attempted infiltration, and raise further alarms to warn security personnel.

honeypots

A seemingly tempting, but bogus target meant to draw hacking attempts. By monitoring infiltration attempts against a honeypot, organizations may gain insight into the identity of hackers and their techniques, and they can share this with partners and law enforcement.

blacklists

Programs that deny the entry or exit of specific IP addresses, products, Internet domains, and other communication restrictions.

whitelists

Highly restrictive programs that permit communication only with approved entities and/or in an approved manner.

Have failure and recovery plans. While firms work to prevent infiltration attempts, they should also have provisions in place that plan for the worst. If a compromise has taken place, what needs to be done? Do stolen assets need to be devalued (e.g., accounts terminated, new accounts issued)? What should be done to notify customers and partners, educate them, and advise them through any necessary responses? Who should work with law enforcement and with the media? Do off-site backups or redundant systems need to be activated? Can systems be reliably restored without risking further damage?

Best practices are beginning to emerge. While postevent triage is beyond the scope of our introduction, the good news is that firms are now sharing data on breaches. Given the potential negative consequences of a breach, organizations once rarely admitted they'd been compromised. But now many are obligated to do so. And the broad awareness of infiltration both reduces organizational stigma in coming forward, and allows firms and technology providers to share knowledge on the techniques used by cybercrooks.

Information security is a complex, continually changing, and vitally important domain. The exploits covered in this chapter seem daunting, and new exploits constantly emerge. But your thinking on key issues should now be broader. Hopefully you've now embedded security thinking in your managerial DNA, and you are better prepared to be a savvy system user and a proactive participant working for your firm's security. Stay safe!

Key Takeaways

- End users can engage in several steps to improve the information security of themselves and their organizations. These include surfing smart, staying vigilant, updating software and products, using a comprehensive security suite, managing settings and passwords responsibly, backing up, properly disposing of sensitive assets, and seeking education.
- Frameworks such as ISO27k can provide a road map to help organizations plan and implement an effective security regime.
- Many organizations are bound by security compliance commitments and will face fines and retribution if they fail to meet these commitments.
- The use of frameworks and being compliant is not equal to security. Security is a continued process that must be constantly addressed and deeply ingrained in an organization's culture.
- Security is about trade-offs—economic and intangible. Firms need to understand their assets and risks in order to best allocate resources and address needs.
- Information security is not simply a technical fix. Education, audit, and enforcement regarding firm policies are critical. The security team is broadly skilled and constantly working to identify and incorporate new technologies and methods into their organizations. Involvement and commitment is essential from the boardroom to frontline workers, and out to customers and partners.

Questions and Exercises

1. Visit the security page for your ISP, school, or employer. What techniques do they advocate that we've discussed here? Are there any additional techniques mentioned and discussed? What additional provisions do they offer (tools, services) to help keep you informed and secure?
2. What sorts of security regimes are in use at your university, and at firms you've worked or interned for? If you don't have experience with this, ask a friend or relative for their professional experiences. Do you consider these measures to be too restrictive, too lax, or about right?

3. While we've discussed the risks in having security that is too lax, what risk does a firm run if its security mechanisms are especially strict? What might a firm give up? What are the consequences of strict end-user security provisions?
4. What risks does a firm face by leaving software unpatched? What risks does it face if it deploys patches as soon as they emerge? How should a firm reconcile these risks?
5. What methods do firms use to ensure the integrity of their software, their hardware, their networks, and their partners?
6. An organization's password management system represents "the keys to the city." Describe personnel issues that a firm should be concerned with regarding password administration. How might it address these concerns?

Endnotes

1. Unattributed, "Equifax data breach snares 100,000 Canadians," *BBC News*, Sept. 20, 2017
2. L. Newman, "Equifax Officially Has No Excuse," *Wired*, Sept. 14, 2017.
3. A. Melin, "Three Equifax Managers Sold Stock Before Cyber Hack Revealed," *Bloomberg*, Sept. 8, 2017.
4. A. Janofsky, "Equifax Breach Could Cost Billions," *The Wall Street Journal*, Sept. 15, 2017.
5. M. Riley, B. Elgin, D. Lawrence, and C. Matlack, "Missed Alarms and 40 Million Stolen Credit Card Numbers: How Target Blew It," *BusinessWeek*, March 13, 2014.
6. M. Riley, B. Elgin, D. Lawrence, and C. Matlack, "Missed Alarms and 40 Million Stolen Credit Card Numbers: How Target Blew It," *BusinessWeek*, March 13, 2014.
7. "Why the Target Data Hack is Just the Beginning," *Bloomberg View*, January 16, 2014.
8. M. Riley, B. Elgin, D. Lawrence, and C. Matlack, "Missed Alarms and 40 Million Stolen Credit Card Numbers: How Target Blew It," *BusinessWeek*, March 13, 2014.
9. Report: "The Cost of Cybercrime," *Accenture*, 2017.
10. B. Lovelace, "Cost of Data Breaches Hits $4 Million on Average: IBM," *CNBC*, June 15, 2016.
11. G. Gross, "The Cost of Cybercrime," *Internet Society*, Feb. 23, 2018.
12. A. Shalal and M. Spetalnick, "Data hacked from U.S. government dates back to 1985: U.S. official," *Reuters*, June 5, 2015.
13. S. Morgan, "Cybercrime Costs Projected to Reach $2 Trillion by 2019," *Fortune*, June 17, 2016.
14. S. Kroft, "Cyberwar: Sabotaging the System," *60 Minutes*, November 8, 2009.
15. R. Singel, "Underground Crime Economy Health, Security Group Finds," *Wired*, November 24, 2008.
16. K. J. Higgins, "SecureWorks Unveils Research on Spamming Botnets," *DarkReading*, April 9, 2008.
17. B. Krebs, "Storm Worm Dwarfs World's Top Supercomputer," *Washington Post*, August 31, 2007.
18. *Trend Micro*, "Web Threats Whitepaper," March 2008.
19. S. Kroft, "Cyberwar: Sabotaging the System," *60 Minutes*, November 8, 2009.
20. J. Schectman, "Computer Hacking Made Easy," *BusinessWeek*, August 13, 2009.
21. K. Parish, "Hackers are now favoring ransomware over personal data theft," *Digital Trends*, April 5, 2018.
22. L. Newman, "The Ransomeware that Hobbled Atlanta Will Strike Again," *Wired*, March 30, 2018. and M. Wright, "A ransomware attack brought Atlanta to its knees—and no one seems to care," *The Hill*, April 4, 2018.
23. S. Rangan, "SamSam ransomware attacks have earned nearly $850,000," *CSO*, March 23, 2018.
24. J. Vijayan, "Software Consultant Who Stole Data on 110,000 People Gets Five-Year Sentence," *Computerworld*, July 10, 2007.
25. S. Gorman, A. Cole, and Y. Dreazen. "Computer Spies Breach Fighter-Jet Project," *Wall Street Journal*, April 21, 2009.
26. E. Mills, "China Linked to New Breaches Tied to RSA," *CNET*, June 6, 2011.
27. P. Eckert, "Analysis: Can Naming, Shaming Curb Cyber Attacks from China?" *Reuters*, June 3, 2011.
28. S. Ackerman and J. Kaiman, "Chinese Military Officials Charged with Stealing U.S. Data as Tensions Escalate," *Guardian*, May 20, 2014.
29. R. Faughnder and S. Hamedy, "Sony insider—not North Korea—likely involved in hack, experts say," *The Los Angeles Times*, Dec. 30, 2014.
30. A. Madrigal, "The Inside Story of How Facebook Responded to Tunisian Hacks," *Atlantic*, January 24, 2011.
31. R. Collins, "U.S. Offers $25 Million Cybersecurity Grant After Pipeline Attacks," *BusinessWeek*, April 16, 2018.
32. S. Kroft, "Cyberwar: Sabotaging the System," *60 Minutes*, November 8, 2009.
33. N. Firth, "Computer Super-Virus 'Targeted Iranian Nuclear Power Station' but Who Made It?" *Daily Mail*, September 24, 2010.
34. M. Gross, "A Declaration of Cyber-War," *Vanity Fair*, April 2011.
35. K. Zetter, "Son of Stuxnet Found in the Wild on Systems in Europe," *Wired*, October 18, 2011.
36. S. Larson, "The hacks that left us exposed in 2017," *CNN*, Dec. 20, 2017.
37. T. Butterworth, "The War against Iran Has Already Started," *Forbes*, September 21, 2010.
38. M. McKew, "Did Russia Influence the 2016 Election? It's Now Undeniable," *Wired*, Feb. 16, 2018.
39. Unattributed, "Russian disinformation distorts American and European democracy," *The Economist*, Feb. 22, 2018.
40. B. Whitiker, "When Russian Hackers Targeted the U.S. Election Infrastructure," 60 Minutes, April 8, 2018.
41. M. Schwartz, "The Trolls among Us," *New York Times*, August 3, 2008.
42. J. Schectman, "Computer Hacking Made Easy," *BusinessWeek*, August 13, 2009.
43. J. Vijayan, "After Verdict, Debate Rages in Terry Childs Case," *Computerworld*, April 28, 2010.
44. Domestic Surveillance Directorate website, "Surveillance Techniques: How Your Data Becomes Our Data," accessed April 14, 2014, http://nsa.gov1.info/surveillance.
45. G. Greenwald, "NSA Collecting Phone Records of Millions of Verizon Customers Daily," *Guardian*, June 5, 2013.
46. G. Greenwald, "XKeyscore: NSA Tool Collects 'Nearly Everything a User Does on the Internet'," *Guardian*, July 31, 2013.
47. O. Khazan, "The Creepy, Long-Standing Practice of Undersea Cable Tapping," *Atlantic*, July 16, 2013.
48. N. Perlroth and V. Goel, "British Spies Said to Intercept Yahoo Webcam Images," *New York Times*, February 27, 2014.
49. P. Lewis and P. Otterman, "Angela Merkel Denied Access to Her NSA File," *Guardian*, April 10, 2014.
50. G. Greenwald, "XKeyscore: NSA Tool Collects 'Nearly Everything a User Does on the Internet,'" *Guardian*, July 31, 2013.
51. N. Totenberg, "Why the FISA Court Is Not What It Used to Be," *NPR*, June 18, 2013.
52. G. Greenwald, "XKeyscore: NSA Tool Collects 'Nearly Everything a User Does on the Internet,'" *Guardian*, July 31, 2013.
53. E. Perez, "Secret Court's Oversight Gets Scrutiny," *Wall Street Journal*, June 9, 2013.
54. C. Cain Miler, "Revelations of N.S.A. Spying Cost U.S. Tech Companies," *New York Times*, March 21, 2014.
55. R. Cowan, "Exclusive: U.S. tech industry appeals to Obama to keep hands off encryption," *Reuters*, June 9, 2015.
56. C. Taylor, "The Tech Catastrophe You're Ignoring," *Fortune*, October 26, 2009.
57. M. Davis, "What Will It Take?" *InformationWeek*, November 23, 2009.
58. R. King, "Lessons from the Data Breach at Heartland," *BusinessWeek*, July 6, 2009.
59. T. Claburn, "Payment Card Industry Gets Encryption Religion," *InformationWeek*, November 13, 2009.
60. T. Claburn, "Payment Card Industry Gets Encryption Religion," *InformationWeek*, November 13, 2009; R. King, "Lessons from the Data Breach at Heartland," *BusinessWeek*, July 6, 2009.
61. D. Goldman, "Cybercrime: A Secret Underground Economy," *CNNMoney*, September 17, 2009.

62. Knowledge@Wharton, "Information Security: Why Cybercriminals Are Smiling," August 19, 2009.
63. N. Lewis, "Investigation of Ex-Chief of the C.I.A. Is Broadened," *New York Times*, September 17, 2000.
64. A. Matwyshyn, *Harboring Data: Information Security, Law, and the Corporation* (Palo Alto, CA: Stanford University Press, 2009).
65. A. Matwyshyn, *Harboring Data: Information Security, Law, and the Corporation* (Palo Alto, CA: Stanford University Press, 2009).
66. S. Wildstrom, "Massive Study of Net Vulnerabilities: They're Not Where You Think They Are," *BusinessWeek*, September 14, 2009.
67. P. Lilly, "Hackers Targeting Windows XP-Based ATM Machines," *Maximum PC*, June 4, 2009.
68. R. McMillan, "Restaurants Sue Vendors after Point-of-Sale Hack," *CIO*, December 1, 2009.
69. C. Matyszczyk, "French Planes Grounded by Windows Worm," *CNET*, February 8, 2009.
70. IBM, *X-Force Threat Report: 2008 Year in Review*, January 2009.
71. For example, the DNS security patch mentioned was incompatible with the firewall software deployed at some firms.
72. N. Wingfield, "It's a Free Country…So Why Can't I Pick the Technology I Use in the Office?" *Wall Street Journal*, November 15, 2009.

Index

Printed in the USA
CPSIA information can be obtained
at www.ICGtesting.com
LVHW051749101023
760522LV00016B/261